Meltdown in Haditha

Meltdown in Haditha

*The Killing of 24 Iraqi
Civilians by U.S. Marines and
the Failure of Military Justice*

KENNETH F. ENGLADE

McFarland & Company, Inc., Publishers
Jefferson, North Carolina

LIBRARY OF CONGRESS CATALOGUING-IN-PUBLICATION DATA

Englade, Ken, author.
 Meltdown in Haditha : the killing of 24 Iraqi civilians by U.S. Marines and the failure of military justice / Kenneth F. Englade.
   p.   cm.
 Includes bibliographical references and index.

 ISBN 978-0-7864-9734-8 (softcover : acid free paper) ∞
 ISBN 978-1-4766-1879-1 (ebook)

 1. Courts-martial and courts of inquiry—United States. 2. War crime trials—United States. 3. Marines—Legal status, laws, etc.—United States. 4. United States. Marine Corps. Marine Regiment, 3rd. Battalion, 1st—Trials, litigation, etc. 5. Wuterich, Frank, 1980- —Trials, litigation, etc. 6. Iraq War, 2003–2011—Atrocities—Iraq—Hadithah. I. Title.
 KF7654.3.E54 2015
 343.73'0143—dc23   2014045879

BRITISH LIBRARY CATALOGUING DATA ARE AVAILABLE

© 2015 Kenneth F. Englade. All rights reserved

No part of this book may be reproduced or transmitted in any form or by any means, electronic or mechanical, including photocopying or recording, or by any information storage and retrieval system, without permission in writing from the publisher.

On the cover: U.S. Marines © zabelin/iStock/Thinkstock; map of Iraq © Romanista/iStock/Thinkstock

Printed in the United States of America

*McFarland & Company, Inc., Publishers
 Box 611, Jefferson, North Carolina 28640
   www.mcfarlandpub.com*

For
H J E
... for everything

Table of Contents

Acknowledgments ix
Preface 1

Part I: Anbar Province
1. Haditha Prelude — 7
2. The Convoy — 15
3. Collateral Damage — 26
4. The Lid Comes Off — 37

Part II: Repercussions
5. Kicking the Ant Hill — 47
6. Charges — 60
7. Outflanking the Corps — 68
8. The Bargewell Report — 76

Part III: The Hearings
9. Captain Randy Stone — 87
10. Lieutenant Colonel Jeffrey Chessani — 99
11. Captain Lucas McConnell — 115
12. Lance Corporal Justin Sharratt — 118
13. Lance Corporal Stephen Tatum — 129
14. Staff Sergeant Frank Wuterich — 136
15. First Lieutenant Andrew Grayson — 148

Part IV: The Trials
16. The CBS Fiasco — 155
17. Unlawful Command Influence — 167

18. The Grayson Debacle	176
19. Chessani Resolution	180
20. Wuterich's Offensive	193
21. Court-Martial	200
Epilogue	210
Conclusions	216
Appendix A: USMC Iraq Command, Mid-November 2005	227
Appendix B: Abbreviations	228
Appendix C: Marine Corps Personnel Abbreviations	229
Appendix D: Significant Dates	230
Appendix E: Military and Legal Terms and Expressions	234
Chapter Notes	241
Bibliography	257
Index	261

Acknowledgments

Would that I were able to thank all those who came to my assistance during the eight years this book was in gestation. *Meltdown* took longer to research and write than all my other books combined, and was by far the most difficult.

Because of the specialized nature of the topic, few could offer concrete guidance or help me through the military law labyrinth. Corps spokespeople and the Haditha defense lawyers were unwilling to cooperate. The same was true for all the active-duty, retired or Reservist judge advocates I contacted even though they were not involved in the proceedings. Eventually, however, I found several who were interested in sharing their knowledge about the Uniform Code of Military Justice provided I did not use their names. I'm keeping that agreement, but I want them to know how much I appreciate their insight. I hope I accurately absorbed what they had to say.

I also got considerable much-needed help from old friend Mike Webb, a civilian lawyer in Decatur, Georgia. He was extremely generous with his time and advice, offering suggestions on content and keeping me honest when using legal terms. His aid was invaluable.

My wife, Heidi, was a blessing. She reined me in when I wandered off into military and legal jargon, forgetting that not everyone who might read this was as familiar with the dialect as I. "What are you thinking?" she'd say. "No one is going to know what you're talking about." Often, I was so frustrated I wanted to quit, but she wouldn't let me reminding me it was a story worth telling.

Some helped without even realizing it. A prime example was a federal lawyer I contacted very early in my research. He was a friend of a friend, recommended to me because he had been an Army judge advocate in Vietnam and had even written a book about his experiences. When I contacted him and asked if he would serve as a guide, he replied with a crisp "No." A little taken aback, I asked why not. "Because you're wasting your time," he said. "The fix is in. You're never going to get anything meaningful." Being a stubborn soul, that only encouraged me. It confirmed I was looking at a story worth chasing.

Special thanks go to those who devoted time and energy to reading and commenting on portions of *Meltdown*, offering pertinent suggestions that were always welcome. Among those are my sister-in-law, Regina Englade, Joe Cotruzzola, Frank Bush, Bonnie Remsberg, Paul and Amy Doak, Peter and Mickey Frazier-Koontz, Marilyn Abbey, Ed Mahr, and Larry Lorenz. One thing I have learned in my long career is that I am a lousy proofreader. Melissa Birks covered me on this, spending many hours sifting through copy riddled with typos, omissions, inconsistencies, and outright mistakes. Thanks, Melissa.

I'd also like to thank Sandy Bergo and the Fund for Investigative Journalism for helping finance my research.

Preface

At 0713 Hours on November 19, 2005, an insurgent triggered an improvised explosive device (IED) buried beneath a road often used by members of a Marine Corps battalion operating in Haditha, a city of about 100,000 restive Sunnis in Iraq's Anbar Province. The blast—aimed at the last of four vehicles traveling in a convoy returning from a routine resupply mission—tossed the 5,000-pound Humvee into the air in a dark cloud of smoke and pulverized paving, killing the driver, a well-liked 20-year-old lance corporal from El Paso, Texas, and wounding two others. Minutes later, the Marines gunned down five Iraqis who happened upon the site in a white Opel sedan. Four of them were students at a nearby technical school and the fifth was the man they had hired to drive them to classes. Thinking they were being shot at by insurgents hiding in a group of buildings to their south, the Marines assaulted two houses, killing 15 Iraqis. Among the dead were a 76-year-old man, his 66-year-old wife, and six children between the ages of 3 and 14. After several hours of tense calm, two of the Marines invaded a third house, killing four brothers they said threatened them with AK-47s. By the time the squad was relieved some eight hours after the IED attack, they left behind 24 dead and three wounded children, one of them a 13-year-old girl who survived by faking death.

The Corps' Iraq command—discounting the need to take a closer look at why so many civilians had died—validated the episode as a legitimate "troops in contact" reaction to an alleged post–IED small-arms attack by determined insurgents. Because of the command's decision to write off the incident as a normal occurrence, the world was unaware of the bloody event until March 19, 2006, four months after it took place, when *Time* published an article exposing a few bare details.[1] Subsequent media reports provided more information, feeding a mushrooming mood of public revulsion. Within weeks, anti-war sentiment across the country and abroad was as strong as it had been after the disclosures of abuses at Abu Ghraib three years earlier.

In mid–March 2006, only three days before publication of the *Time* article, the head of the Corps' Iraq command, Maj. Gen. Richard Zilmer, asked the Naval Criminal Investigative Service (NCIS) to conduct an in-depth examination. To the Corps' discredit, Zilmer did not act until after the number two commander in the country, Army Lt. Gen. Peter Chiarelli, twice sent investigators to Haditha to look into possible law-of-war violations.

A task force of more than 50 NCIS agents spent four months scrutinizing the available evidence. However, much of their work was in vain because the investigation began too late: the bodies had long ago been buried, the houses repaired, valuable material including the two rifles allegedly recovered from the third house could not be found, and memories had faded. Nevertheless, the NCIS reported that it had found enough evidence of criminal activity to warrant legal action. In late December 2006—13 months after the incident—the Corps announced that charges ranging from dereliction of duty to multiple counts of murder had been preferred against four officers and four enlisted men from the 3rd Battalion, 1st Marine Regiment, the unit that had been responsible for keeping the peace in northwestern Anbar Province. The former battalion commander and the non-commissioned officer (NCO) who led the assaults were among the accused.[2]

The perception was that the Corps was going to make up for its earlier mistake in not conducting a probe by moving forward in its usual aggressive manner to see that possible wrongdoing would be exposed, individual actions assessed, and personal accountability enforced. But that is not what occurred. Instead, the Corps—with help from willing civilian defense attorneys—cloaked the proceedings in secrecy, shut out the media, and prolonged the processes for an unprecedented five years. In the end, charges were dismissed against six of the accused, including the former battalion commander. One junior officer was tried and acquitted. The only conviction was that of the NCO who led the assaults. Originally accused of murdering 18 people, the sergeant was allowed to plead guilty to a misdemeanor and was given a general discharge under honorable conditions.[3] He never spent a day in the brig and was absolved of paying a fine that could have been assessed as a result of his plea.[4]

Meltdown is a narrative of the Haditha incident—a recounting of developments as they occurred from the morning the convoy was attacked through the sergeant's trial. Despite the numerous obstructions put into place by the Corps in its diverse efforts to suppress critical information, this book cuts through the obfuscations to present an accurate rendition of the causes and effects resulting from the worst episode of its kind in the nine-year-long Iraq

War. It is not the definitive work on Haditha, but it is the first about the episode with a detailed examination of the legal proceedings.

The incident and the immediate aftermath are covered in Parts I and II of the book. My primary focus, though, is on what occurred after charges were preferred. Those details are presented in Parts III and IV. In reality, there was no resolution; the proceedings raised more questions than they answered. No one is likely to ever know precisely what occurred in Haditha or what would have been revealed had the Corps allowed the legal proceedings to progress in the manner established during 60 years of adherence to the Uniform Code of Military Justice (UCMJ).

Meltdown does not attempt to determine *why* the Corps acted as it did once the evidence was turned over to the three-star general officer at Camp Pendleton, California, who was responsible for conducting the legal proceedings. It does, however, tell *how* the Corps achieved its apparent goal of burying forever (or at least for the foreseeable future) particulars that would have helped fill gaps in the history of this country's misguided attempts to bring an American solution to a Middle East problem.

The Corps resorted to a succession of techniques to camouflage developments in the cases and deny the public its right to know what was happening. Among them was refusing to provide copies of documents such as motions and petitions, which were vital to gaining a thorough knowledge of the issues. It effectively flouted the Freedom of Information Act (FOIA) by responding to requests slowly, incompletely, and with thinly veiled contempt. Interviews were prohibited; there were no attempts to explain delicate points of law in a system that is foreign to all but those who practice it. Answers were not forthcoming to questions about even the most basic facts. For example, the Corps denied requests to provide the names and ranks of the prosecutors or to divulge background information on the presiding officers, such as how long they had held their positions or whether they have experience in previous General Court-Martial cases.

Instead of treating the Haditha cases in open court, the Corps chose to hide its movements in a string of appeals, cross-appeals and still more appeals. The flow did not cease until the judges of the Navy-Marine Court of Criminal Appeals (NMCCA)—after hearing one case three times—finally declared enough was enough.[5]

Also damaging to comprehension were the protracted delays that marked the proceedings from beginning to end. For example, the trial of the NCO that led the assaults was postponed for five years—an incredible extension without precedent in U.S. military history.

In the face of the Corps' indisputable intransigence, I had to turn to more indirect sources for my information. I relied heavily on four sources:

- Reports submitted by presiding officers following pretrial hearings were particularly useful because they not only referred to testimony but also gave a degree of interpretation that the Corps' Public Affairs Office (PAO) was unwilling to provide. The reports composed by the officer who presided at the hearings for all of the accused were less than objective. I had to remind myself that it was his job to present his opinion in whatever form he chose. He was not a judge but there were no restraints on what he was allowed to say or how he said it.
- Official documents such as appeals court opinions played a huge role in my research. Because lawyers for both sides showed an uninhibited penchant for appeals, the stack of opinions grew incredibly high. A quick shuffle through my boxes of files shows 19 appeals court opinions, ranging in length from scant to enormous. Wading through the legalese was sometimes a daunting task. Without my experience in writing about legal issues in civilian courts, I would have been lost several times. I stumbled upon a real goldmine when I received a response to a request for a Chessani appeals court document. I got not only the document, but also a CD containing files that were part of the court record. The files were transcriptions of testimony presented at the more important of Chessani's hearings. One of the files was 378 pages long,[6] the other totaled 247.[7] Although the transcripts were redacted, they were of immense help.
- Probably the single most useful document in my files is the 100-page report compiled by Army Maj. Gen. Eldon Bargewell, the second and most thorough of the two investigators sent to Haditha by Lieutenant General Chiarelli.[8] It is comprehensive, well-presented without undue military jargon and covers issues on every level of command involved in the incident's immediate aftermath. Lieutenant General Mattis classified the document as soon as it was filed in June 2006, probably because it was critical, sometimes painfully so, of some of the top officers in the Corps' Iraq Command. Ten months after he classified it, Mattis lifted the prohibition. Unfortunately, the releasable version does not include the almost 200 attachments contained in the original. The NCIS report on the incident is still listed as classified; it is said be several thousand pages long.

- I also referenced more than 50 books dealing with previous courts-martial from the fifties through the Vietnam era, tomes on the Corps itself and others on military law. I dug through thousands of digital files, including media reports on the proceedings, editorials and op-ed page columns.

Regrettably missing from my research is information obtained in interviews. Any Marine connected with the case was strictly off limits. In an attempted end-run around this prohibition, I approached more than two dozen retired, reservist, active duty, or former Marines hoping they would talk to me about Corps polices and procedures rather than about Haditha. Not one agreed. I also e-mailed the civilian lawyers involved in each case, seeking to establish a connection. The majority did not respond; the others said no.

There are no "made up" quotes in *Meltdown*. Some passages unquestionably could have profited from improvised dialogue, but I made no attempt to fill those gaps by inserting what I thought a character might have said. The sources of every quotation is cited and the source is listed in the Notes section. In unusual situations such as what was said at the ambush site, the quotations are the words of the participants taken from their official statements.

Practitioners of military law will notice that I often switch between military and civilian legal terms. To make the story more understandable for those with no knowledge of military terminology, I chose to use "prosecutor" rather than "trial counsel"; "accused" rather than "defendant"; "judge" as opposed to "military judge," and "jury" in place of "panel." On the other hand, I retained "judge advocate," the military term for lawyer, and I say that charges were "preferred" rather than "filed."

Undoubtedly, I have made errors in describing some legal procedures. The mistakes are mine. Similarly, because I was never a Marine, I may have incorrectly interpreted certain aspects of the Corps culture. I accept all responsibility for any errors.

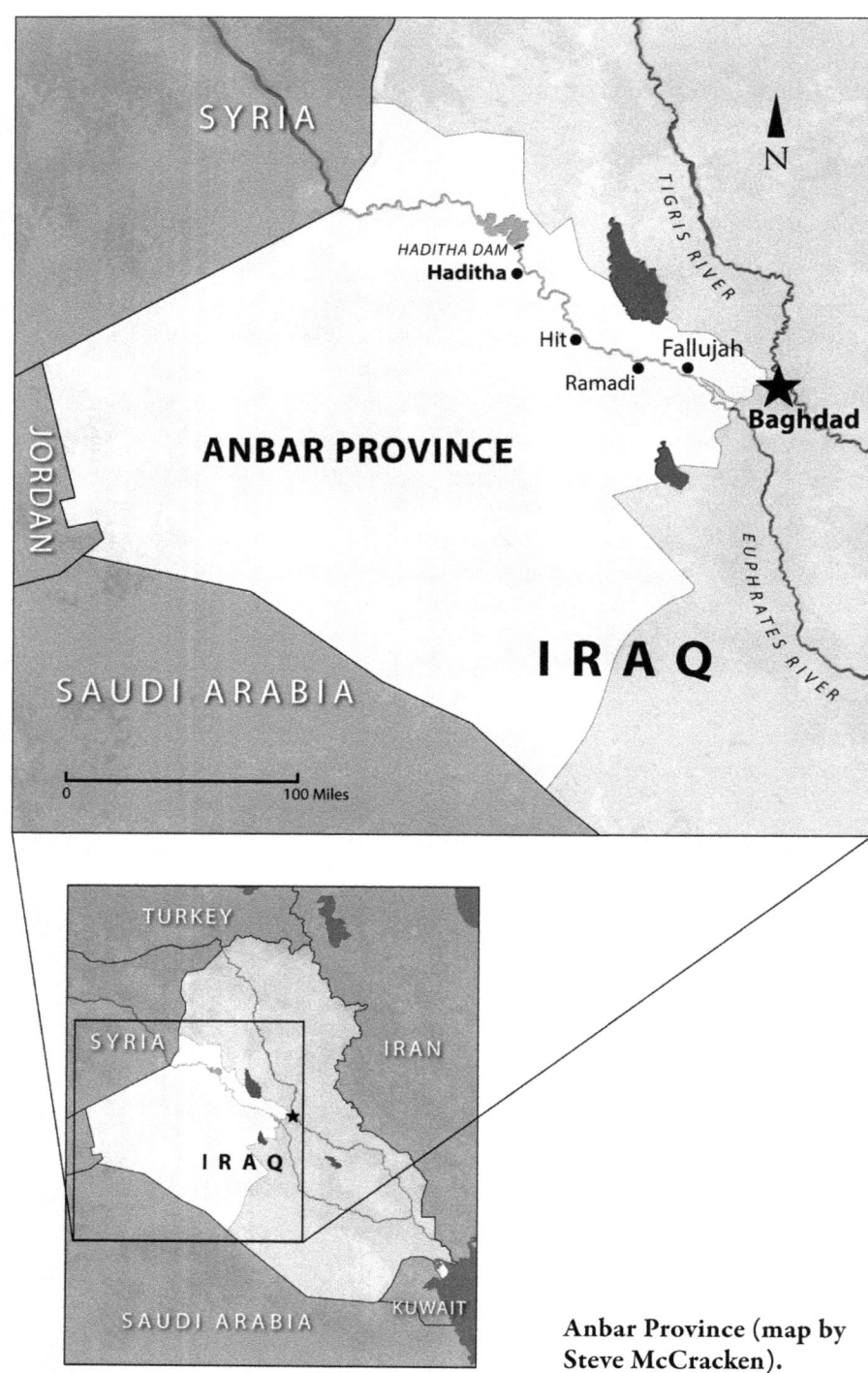

Anbar Province (map by Steve McCracken).

Part I: Anbar Province

1. Haditha Prelude

The 3rd Battalion 1st Marine Regiment deployed to Anbar Province for the first time in July 2004, joining its parent organization—the 24,000-member I Marine Expeditionary Force (MEF)—in its efforts to pacify the country's most restive governorate. By then, the I MEF had been in command in the province for four months and had experienced little more success than the Army units it replaced in subduing the diehard Islamists and foreign fighters violently opposing the 16-month-old occupation.

Anbar is Iraq's largest province in area and the least populated. Located in the southwestern part of the country, it borders on Syria, Jordan, and Saudi Arabia, although the latter two are accessible by road only by traversing long stretches of barrenness and virtual wasteland. Anbar is mostly desert; its saving grace is a fertile strip in the north watered by the Euphrates River as it flows southeast, toward Baghdad, until it merges with the Tigris River near Basra on the Persian Gulf. Part of what once was called Mesapotamia ("the land between the rivers"), the irrigated countryside produces dates, lentils, chickpeas, wheat, potatoes, barley, and maize: staples of the Iraqi diet. In contrast, its major cities—Ramadi, Fallujah, Haditha, and Hit—produce a disproportionate number of anti–Westerners and anti–Shia. Anbar's inhabitants are almost all Sunni Muslims, except for a sizable collection of Wahhabists in Fallujah—immigrants or descendants of immigrants from Saudi Arabia who brought with them their devotion to the teaching of Ibn Abd al-Wahhab, the founder of what arguably is Islam's most fundamentalist sect. To demonstrate their piety, Fallujahans erected more than 200 houses of worship within the 25-square-mile city (about the size of Cheyenne, Wyoming), roughly one for every 200 inhabitants. Before November 2004, Fallujah was known through the Middle East as the City of Mosques.

In addition to being famous for its houses of prayer, Fallujah also was renowned for its resistance to the coalition troops who became its wardens after the 2003 invasion. Successive Army units—from the 82nd Airborne to the 3rd Cavalry—were unable to soothe the unruly Fallujahans. One clash led to another, establishing a pattern of escalating violence. An apogee of sorts may have been reached in June 2003 when an explosion of unknown origin ripped through one of the city's mosques, killing the imam and eight others. Fallujahans said a coalition missile caused the blast, but the Army insisted it occurred when apprentice bomb makers made a slip while trying to build an IED. By late 2003, the Pentagon had made a decision to rotate the troops in Anbar, replacing soldiers who had been there since the invasion with Marines. The I MEF under Lt. Gen. James Conway (a future Corps commandant) formally took command on March 24, 2004. Conway and the commander of the I MEF's ground units—Maj. Gen. James Mattis of the 1st Marine Division (a future commander of the U.S. Central Command, or CENTCOM)—initially had expectations that a more amiable attitude toward the Iraqis would defuse the obviously hostile situation. While the I MEF was still at Camp Pendleton, word leaked of the changes the Corps would execute once it got to Anbar: a list of new guidelines ranging from a ban on mirrored sunglasses to a cessation of nighttime raids on Iraqi homes. Unfortunately, the Corps never got the chance to carry through on its plans. On April 1, only a week after the I MEF assumed responsibility for the pacification program, Fallujah jihadists attacked two SUVs belonging to the private security firm Blackwater USA. The vehicles' four occupants were killed, their bodies burned, and their severed limbs hung from a bridge over the Euphrates. President Bush was enraged, as were the secretary of defense, the head of the Coalition Provisional Authority (L. Paul Bremer), the commander of CENTCOM (Gen. John Abizaid), and the Iraqi prime minister (Nouri al-Malaki). As a result, the I MEF was ordered to go into Fallujah "and clobber people."[1]

The First Battle of Fallujah

The command conflicted with the wishes of the I MEF leaders, but orders are orders, so planning began for Operation Vigilant Resolve, an assault by more than 2,000 soldiers, sailors, and Marines. Facing the coalition troops were an estimated 600 hardcore insurgents (martyrs), plus another thousand men (jihadists) eager to participate in any attack as long as it gave them the chance to kill coalition troops. The fighting, which was heavier than expected, lasted for only four days—April 5–9—before the United States unilaterally declared a cease-fire, which evolved into an on-again, off-again truce. This continued through April, when negotiators agreed to form a theoretical peacekeeping unit known as the Fallujah Brigade. On April 28, President Bush—as overly optimistic as he had been in his "mission accomplished" speech from the USS *Abraham Lincoln* a year earlier—told reporters, "Most of Fallujah is returning to normal."[2]

Not true, said author Thomas Ricks:

> It was a stunningly inaccurate statement. Not one of the objectives of the Marine attack had been achieved.... When the fight ended, the murderers had not been apprehended and law and order had not been restored. What's worse, in the following weeks it would become painfully clear that it was the murderers of the contractors who enjoyed free rein in the city, not the Marines.[3]

Thirty-nine coalition troops were killed in Fallujah alone during Vigilant Resolve; insurgent deaths were estimated at 600.[4] Although a large number of civilians had fled the city in anticipation of the assault, as many as 600 may have died during the air, ground, and artillery attack. However, fighting was not confined to Fallujah. Attacks also erupted in nearby Ramadi, apparently in support of the Fallujah conflict. This resulted in more deaths. All told, in April, 48 Marines and a Navy corpsman were killed fighting insurgents and more than 400 Marines were wounded.[5]

While the coalition racked up a one-sided kill ratio in Fallujah, it was debatable whether it could be called a victory. The coalition tactics drew considerable criticism, including dismissive remarks from former Army lawyer Jonathan Keiler, which were published in the prestigious Naval Institute Press magazine *Proceedings*:

> Marines gained access to the urban area (in that case, outlying industrial neighborhoods), but did not penetrate to the heart of the city, much less take it. After a few days of active combat, Marines cordoned off the area and the matter was "resolved" politically. The bulk of the enemy force remained at large in the city and was reinforced. Fallujah became an insurgent stronghold and base for kidnappings, murders, and attacks that would cost the coalition dearly in the following months.[6]

The Fallujah Brigade—the unrealistic political creation once proclaimed to be the guardian of peace—was a failure. What had begun as a 500-man unit quickly grew to a force of more than 2,000. Composed of former members of Saddam's Iraqi Army and alleged previous insurgents, it was riven by struggles for control and internal disagreements. Although only about two-thirds of the size of a Marine regiment (which may be commanded by a one-star general), the Fallujah Brigade was home to a wildly disproportionate number of 23 generals and 375 other officers.[7] It was disbanded in September, and none too soon because the coalition could not sustain more of the brigade's peacekeeping. From April to November 2004, both the insurgents and the Marines girded for a second, more violent, showdown. "[They] busily prepared for a rematch," said Keiler. "Iraqi insurgents and foreign mujahadeen dug tunnels, emplaced mines and booby-traps, and improved their defenses."[8] While the I MEF was drawing up invasion plans and positioning troops and equipment, the insurgents were constructing elaborate fighting locations and caching weapons. By late fall, it was evident that a larger confrontation was unavoidable. By then, almost all civilians had fled the city, leaving Fallujah under the control of a significant number of anti-coalition forces spoiling for a fight.

The Second Battle of Fallujah

The I MEF launched its second offensive—called Operation Phantom Fury or, to the Iraqis, Operation Al-Fajr ("New Dawn")—on November 7, 2004, with ground troops, helicopters, fixed-wing aircraft, drones, tanks, mortars, and artillery. This time, the attack force was not the relatively puny contingent of Vigilant Resolve, but an augmented group composed of two regimental combat teams—RCT-1 (four Marine battalions and the 2nd Battalion of the Army's 7th Cavalry) and RCT-7 (three Marine battalions and the 2nd Battalion of the Army's 2nd Infantry Regiment)—the 3rd Marine Air Wing, various armored and artillery units, three battalions of Iraqi troops, and the British Black Watch Battalion to guard the city's perimeter.[9] Altogether, it was about 15,000 soldiers, sailors, Marines and airmen, 10,000 of whom would be in the attack force with the others serving in support roles. It was the largest gathering of coalition forces since the invasion. It also was the first and last time a major insurgent force—2,000 to 3,000 men—would participate in a set-piece battle.

Operation Phantom Fury began with air strikes and an artillery-and-mortar barrage, followed by the ground attack with RCT-7 coming in from the northeast and RCT-1 from the north. RCT-1 had the most crucial duty: seize the formidable Jolan District, the major mosques supporting the insurgents, and the government center.[10] The fighting was street by street, house by house, hand to hand. Old-timers said it was the most intense urban warfare experienced by the Corps since the battle to liberate the citadel in Hue after the 1968 Vietnamese Tet offensive.

Leading the charge was Battalion 3/1, whose first objective was to capture the train station on the city's north side. Its capture would create a hole in the insurgent's defenses, making an entryway for the rest of RCT-1. The battalion then would move into the heart of the Jolan. Although most of Fallujah was laid out on a grid system, the Jolan was a jumble of twisted streets, dark alleys, shuttered businesses, and even a sprawling amusement park, all of which created a dream environment for insurgents who had made the best of the seven months allotted them by the failed Fallujah Brigade to ready for the attack.[11]

On November 13—after seven days of arduous and bloody struggle—Battalion 3/1 ran into its biggest challenge of the campaign. At 1017 Hours —while on a mission to clear the southern and last enemy-controlled section of the city—K Company confidently approached what appeared to be an inconspicuous structure sitting directly in its path. Rather than being harmless, the dwelling would more than earn its epithet as the House from Hell, or Hell House. As described by one of the attackers, it was "a pretty small, nondescript, light yellow cement house, with a dome shaped roof and a small second story."[12] What was not apparent from the outside was that the interior featured a large rotunda with a catwalk—an architectural feature that created "an outstanding kill zone" because insurgents could shoot down on anyone who entered. "All the windows were bolted shut and there was only one way in or out. The enemy had chosen well," said one Marine.

Kilo Company first tried attacking in the conventional manner: fire teams through the only doorway; but the insurgents picked them off as they crossed the threshold.

> Several Marines fell wounded [while] six insurgents on the upper floor prevented four of them from being evacuated. First Sergeant Bradley A. Kasal ran forward ... providing cover for the endangered Marines and joined a squad making a fresh assault inside the house. Killing one insurgent at close quarters, he was struck down by rifle fire and fell with another Marine. He shielded the wounded Marine with his body from hand grenade fragments and then refused evacuation until all other Marines had been removed.... Inside the house, Cpl. Robert J. Mitchell, Jr. ... charged through rifle fire and grenades to reach a critically wounded Marine and begin first aid treatment. His covering fire permitted a corpsman to join him, and he was then hit while re-crossing the lower room to assist other casualties. At close quarters, he killed an insurgent with his combat knife and then turned to assist in the evacuation of the wounded.[13]

One Marine was killed and almost a dozen wounded, several seriously, before it was decided to blow up the house rather than try to capture it. Corporal Richard Gonzales, known as "the Mad Bomber," placed explosives on the house's outer wall and then pushed the detonator button. "The house exploded in a huge flash of red, followed by chunks of concrete thudding down as a vast cloud of dust," said author Bing West. "A pink mist mixed with the dust and gunpowder in the air."[14] Four days later, Kilo Company entered an area they had already cleared only to face more stiff resistance when they got to the next-to-the-last house on the street. One man was wounded before the squad decided to employ the lesson they had learned at Hell House. Instead of trying to roust the insurgents with small arms, they called for a bulldozer. As the demolition started, four insurgents ran to the roof and were quickly cut down by men from Company L.[15]

Fifty-four American troops were killed in Fallujah II, and insurgent losses were estimated at more than 1,000.[16] There were so many jihadists' bodies littering the landscape that the coalition was hard put to see that they were properly buried. According to one officer, "the remains were consecrated and buried according to Muslim religious tenets."[17]

The overriding question after the battle was who won. The kill ratio was indisputably on the side of the coalition, as it had been in Fallujah I, but was that enough to declare victory? "The Marine Corps' military operations in urban terrain doctrine recognizes that tactical success does not necessarily translate to strategic victory," intoned Jonathan Keiler. He continued,

> What would have happened had we met a tougher, more professional opponent in Fallujah? The insurgents were formidable because many were willing to fight to the death—but in the main, they were an indifferently armed rabble that could inflict casualties because of the nature of urban warfare and U.S. sensibilities. What if U.S. forces find themselves facing Syrian commandos or well-trained Hezbollah guerrillas?[18]

"Enter Every Room with a Boom"

Battalion 3/1 paid dearly for Fallujah. Although it was only one of seven infantry battalions taking part in Phantom Fury, 24 of its men were killed there, more than any other single unit and in excess of 44 percent of all the Marines who died. All the dead were enlisted men: fifteen lance corporals, four corporals, four sergeants, and one staff sergeant. Four of them were 19 years old; none was older than 28.[19] These ranks form the nucleus of the Corps' combat units and their absence would be felt. The battalion's battle losses—combined with vacancies resulting from men leaving the service, being reassigned, or becoming no longer physically fit for active duty—were registered at every level. Statistics are not available revealing precisely how many men were absent when 3/1 was restructured in March 2005, but estimates indicate the battalion's ranks were so thinned by replacements that a full one-third of the new unit had no battlefield experience.

The need for new bodies started at the top. Fallujah's 3/1 commander—

Lt. Col. Willard Buhl—was promoted and reassigned so he was replaced with a former regimental staff officer, Lt. Col. Jeffrey Chessani. Kilo Company—the Hell House veterans—also had a surfeit of fresh faces. The K Company commander in Fallujah—Capt. Timothy Jent—was replaced by Capt. Lucas McConnell, an Annapolis graduate who had never seen combat. It was not known if Jent was reassigned or if he left the service. One of the greater losses was that of 1st Lt. Jesse Grapes, who distinguished himself by his courage, leadership, and tenacity at the House from Hell. He resigned his commission after Fallujah, leaving the Corps to become a Roman Catholic lay missionary.[20] His replacement as commander of Kilo's 3rd Platoon was 2nd Lt. William Kallop, a recent graduate of the Officer Candidate School. These three men subsequently would play prominent roles in the battalion's next deployment, as would Sgt. Frank Wuterich, the new leader of 3rd Platoon's 1st Squad. Wuterich had not been in Fallujah and was another in the ill-fated battalion, which had never been shot at.

Just as the I MEF had to carry out orders to attack in Fallujah I over the objections of its top commanders, Battalion 3/1 had to prepare for its next operation even if it meant returning to Iraq sorely lacking in experienced personnel. After completing a rigorous, seven-month training period, the battalion departed for Haditha—its second appearance in Anbar Province in 14 months and its third trip to Iraq in the two and a half years since Operation Iraqi Freedom—in September 2005.

It is not known how the new command regarded the Haditha deployment, whether its leaders were expecting another Fallujah or had realized that Fallujah had been an anomaly and different tactics would be required. In retrospect, it is clear that Haditha was *not* Fallujah. When Battalion 3/1 arrived, it would not find a fortified city; there were no cleverly planned obstacles designed to channel troops into ambushes; there were no land mines or booby traps, and the insurgents were mainly transients—foreign fighters using Haditha as a stopping-off point while they headed for more active areas such as Ramadi and Mosul. Unlike Fallujah, Haditha was a civilian center, a place where the almost exclusively noncombatant population was focused on commerce rather than rebellion. Except for a handful of predominantly foreign radicals who persisted in launching sporadic attacks against coalition troops, Haditha was not the seething pit that had existed in Fallujah.

One positive facet of the Fallujah conflicts was that the Corps had been shaken out of its complacency about the need for more emphasis on innercity combat. After Fallujah, urban warfare training was given high priority. However, there was a danger of too much accentuation. As bitter a lesson as

Fallujah had been, the experience could not be used as a model for future encounters. Apparently, this concept was not clear even to the Corps' top officer. Shortly after Fallujah, Gen. Michael Hagee told officers at a celebratory gathering in Quantico that, as far as he was concerned, "Fallujah is an example of what we're going to fight in the future—and not a bad example of how to fight it. It is about individual Marines with small arms going from house-to-house killing. We may not want to say that, but that's what it is about."[21]

As far as is known, Hagee never tried to clarify this statement; even now, it is unknown precisely what he was trying to say. Nevertheless, the fact that he said it raises the question of how much consideration he gave to those words before speaking them, or if he wondered how they might be interpreted down the chain of command. In the Corps, a commandant speaks with pope-like authority, so it is not unreasonable to assume that lower-ranking Marines took him literally: "small arms ... house-to-house killing ... that's what it is about."

Troops in Fallujah had a dictum, a shorthand way of offering instruction on how to clear a house: "enter every room with a boom."[22] While this served in Fallujah, it was not a commandment. There were ways of clearing a house other than kicking in doors, tossing in grenades, and blasting away with small arms.

2. The Convoy

The location is immaterial, 0530 Hours is early. Needless to say, the 200 men of Company K, 3rd Battalion 1st Marines, were not delighted to be roused from their cots more than an hour before sunrise in temperatures brisk enough to require a light jacket. On the bright side, there was hot food waiting—a real treat for company-sized units who often were stuck with packaged MREs (meals ready to eat). Kilo Company had lucked out. When they had moved into the former school administration compound several weeks earlier, the accommodations had been much better than expected. There was plenty of room, and Firm Base Sparta was as well protected as any headquarters in Anbar Province. The buildings, which would never win an architectural award, were squat and ugly but sturdy enough to withstand a mortar or rocket-propelled grenade (RPG) attack. Just to make sure, Hesco bastions—collapsible wire mesh containers filled with sand and gravel to absorb explosions or small arms fire—were placed strategically around the courtyard. The men did not worry as long as they were inside Sparta; it was outside the walls where the danger lay.

After breakfast, Sgt. Frank Wuterich, the leader of the 3rd Platoon's 1st Squad, called his men together in the makeshift briefing room. It was their turn, he told them, to make the daily run to the traffic control point (TCP), which was located about five miles south of Sparta. In Kilo Company, the assignment rotated among the unit's nine squads. Each morning, a 12-man team boarded four Humvees to travel in convoy from Sparta to the TCP and back. The mission's primary purpose was to deliver the day's classified radio codes to the small group of Marines manning the outpost. Without the codes, there could be no secure communication between the TCP and Kilo's headquarters. The squad also brought hot food and provided transportation back to Sparta for Iraqi troops going off duty. The mission took about 45 minutes, and in the six weeks the program had been operating a convoy had never been attacked.

Wuterich cautioned the men to be alert, perhaps mindful of an intelligence briefing a few days earlier warning that a group of insurgents had infiltrated into Haditha from Syria. Rather than moving on to other areas as they usually did, the new arrivals were believed to be settling in while planning a series of attacks. The number of insurgents was vague, but reports from friendly Iraqis indicated that they were traveling in a white sedan. That bit of information was virtually useless because white sedans were ubiquitous in Anbar Province. In the eventuality that they were to be struck, Wuterich reminded them of the post-attack basics: clear the kill zone, set up a defensive perimeter, and look for an individual who appeared responsible for the assault.

As the convoy commander, it was Wuterich's job to decide which route the squad would take to and from the TCP. It was standard operating practice to vary the route as much as possible to avoid predictability. However, because there were only a small number of viable roads in Haditha, it was impossible to avoid a high degree of repetition. As a result, insurgents could be certain a convoy would eventually travel a particular thoroughfare, if not on one day, then the next or the next. Bomb detection teams swept the roads daily, but that was no guarantee that an IED had not been cleverly concealed and awaited only a radio signal to be detonated.

The section of the city frequented most often by K Company was an irregular square of roughly two by two miles. On the north was Haditha Road and on the south was Route Chestnut, the city's only boulevard. Although there were a number of dirt tracks running north and south off Route Chestnut, the paved roads—the only ones considered suitable for military traffic— were Route Leopard on the west and River Road on the east. The TCP was south of Route Chestnut but the only accessible paved thoroughfare to the outpost was River Road, which paralleled the Euphrates. The road was separated from the waterway by a large date plantation called the Palm Groves, which stretched from above Haditha Road to below the TCP.

Before a squad could leave FB Sparta for the TCP, the commander was required to plot the proposed route and give a hard copy to the watch officer so he could track the convoy's progress via periodic radio reports. While Wuterich was working on the route, the men checked the communication gear and their weapons, which were both powerful and abundant. Most of the men carried the standard-issue M-16A4 rifle fitted with a 30-round magazine. At least one squad member carried an M-203 40-mm grenade launcher, which fits under the barrel of an M-16, giving the weapon dual capability. At least one also was armed with an M-249 Squad Automatic Weapon, or SAW. The SAW can fire from a 30-round magazine like the M-16, but to take full advantage of its sustained fire capability it can be fitted with a 200-round box magazine. The SAW is almost twice as heavy as the M-16 but can pump out 85 rounds per minute. The insurgent's primary weapon, on the other hand, was the venerable AK-47. It fires a heavier round than the M-16 and SAW (7.62 × 39mm compared to 5.56 × 45mm) and can be fired at 100 rounds per minute on full automatic. Each 1st Squad member also carried multiple M-67 fragmentation grenades that had a kill radius of more than five yards.

Another of Wuterich's jobs was to assign men to the Humvees, a task that had to be done judiciously because of the uneven mix of experienced and inexperienced personnel. Like every other unit in the battalion, 1st Squad could have used more veterans. Of the dozen squad members, only five had seen combat: Lance Corporals Miguel Terrazas, Justin Sharratt, Stephen Tatum and James Crossan all had fought at Hell House in Fallujah, and Cpl. Sanick Dela Cruz was a veteran of the fighting in the cemetery outside Najaf in 2004 against the fanatical forces of the Islamist Mahdi Army led by the volatile cleric Muqtada al-Sadr. Interestingly, considering he was a senior non-commissioned officer, the 26-year-old Wuterich had never been in combat. A former honor student, band member, and drama club star at his Meriden, Connecticut, high school, Wuterich had seven years in the Corps, some of it spent in lush Hawaii and some of it as a rifle range instructor at Camp Pendleton, but none of it on a battlefield. He could have taken his discharge the previous spring, but instead he re-enlisted because he wanted a deployment to Iraq or Afghanistan.

Wuterich's solution was to scatter the experienced men among the vehicles. His Humvee—Vehicle Three—was the only one without a combat veteran. His also was the only one to have a non–Marine on board: Navy Hospitalman Brian Whitt, the unit corpsman. Wuterich waited until the squad members were in place before climbing into his Humvee. "Let's go, Marines," he yelled, slamming the door.[1]

Vehicle One eased out of Sparta's rear gate at precisely 0630 Hours, turning left onto Haditha Road, away from the Euphrates River. One by one, the other three Humvees fell into line, forming a 300-yard-long caravan of desert-camouflaged behemoths rumbling into the new day. Minutes later, the convoy again turned left onto Route Leopard, gathering speed for a sprint to the Command Operation Post (COP), where the occupants were anticipating their daily meals-on-wheels delivery.

Hostile Haditha

Conflicts between coalition and Iraqi forces had begun in Anbar Province in the spring of 2003 when men from B and C Companies, 3rd Battalion,

75th Ranger Regiment, seized Haditha's most valuable attribute, a 5.6-mile-long, 66-foot-wide, 187-foot-tall dam located about 11 miles north of the city.[2] The Haditha, or Qadisiya, Dam opened in 1987, following ten years of construction subsidized by the Soviet Union. As the country's second largest such facility, it manufactures electrical power and controls the Euphrates' flow on its journey to the Persian Gulf. It is the dam that makes the area fertile. Unlike the rest of Anbar Province, the Upper Euphrates River Valley is lavish; farms making use of its water produce a considerable share of Iraq's crops: wheat, potatoes, barley, maize, and vegetables. Recognizing the dam's military value, Iraqi soldiers, then still under Saddam Hussein's command, tried to recapture the facility using tanks, artillery, and companies of infantry. However, the Rangers repulsed them in occasionally heavy fighting. In 2004, a year into the occupation, a Corps battalion was detailed to Haditha to protect the dam, although there was little danger the insurgents could do any serious harm because they lacked the heavy weaponry needed to dislodge the defenders. Lieutenant Colonel Chessani set up his headquarters in the dam, moving his seven-man staff and the battalion's Headquarters Company into its safe environs. Besides Kilo Company at Haditha, Lima Company was headquartered at FB Raider at Barwana, and India Company at FB Horno at Haqlaniyah. Still, if the jihadists could not capture the dam, they had enough manpower and small arms to harass and inflict severe damage upon the occupying forces and local residents.

Before Battalion 3/1 arrived in September 2005, the jihadists' main target had been the newly activated 3rd Battalion, 25th Marines (3/25), a reservist unit from Ohio. The ill-fated unit suffered mightily during its time in Haditha, worse than any single Corps element throughout the long war. Not long after its arrival, the battalion lost four men in an assault designed to free hostages seized by jihadists occupying the Haditha General Hospital.[3] But that was only the beginning of the battalion's woes. On the last day of July 2005, fighters from the jihadist Ansar al-Sunna Army surrounded and overwhelmed a unit foot patrol outside Haditha, killing six members of a sniper-and-scout unit.[4] And three day later, only weeks before 3/1 was scheduled to arrive, an exceptionally robust IED exploded under an Amtrac personnel carrier, which was part of a convoy transporting men, fuel, and ammunition. Fourteen Marines and their Iraqi interpreter died in the blast; it was the most lethal IED attack of the war at that time.[5] During its seven-month deployment, Battalion 3/25 lost 41 men, almost twice as many as Battalion 3/1 lost in Fallujah. The dead included 16 men from one company alone, the one that pre–Haditha had been called "Lucky Lima."[6] The unit was deactivated a year later, four months after returning from Haditha.

"I'm Not Seeing 4"

Twilight was not an unpleasant time to be traveling through Haditha, an old, shabby city of 100,000 antagonistic Sunni Arabs who divided their hatred between coalition troops and Shia Muslims, who became more high-profile enemies after the January 2005 elections installed a Shia government, replacing the Sunnis who had ruled for more than three decades. As the convoy traveled down Route Leopard, there was no trouble on the horizon. In that golden pre-dawn period so loved by photographers and early risers, Haditha appeared tranquil. The city proper was on the squad's left: a haphazard collection of dun-colored houses erected in seemingly random fashion along undistinguished dirt and gravel roads. At that time of day, with much of the population still abed, nothing was stirring except the men of 1st Squad. The 15-minute drive to the TCP was uneventful: the squad encountered neither man nor vehicle.[7]

It took about 15 minutes to unload the food containers and settle three Iraqi soldiers seeking a ride back to Sparta in the rear of Wuterich's Humvee. At 0705 Hours, the convoy set off north on River Road, heading toward FB Sparta. A few minutes later, Vehicle One made a sharp left turn onto Route Chestnut. The return route was the flip side of the path the convoy had followed to the TCP. The vehicles were to travel west on Chestnut until it intersected with Route Leopard, and then turn right to Haditha Road. From there, it would be only a short jog back to FB Sparta.

Vehicles One and Two were headed toward Route Leopard when Wuterich's Vehicle Three made the turn. On impulse, Wuterich decided to jump the concrete divider in the center of Chestnut so his Humvee occupied the boulevard's eastbound lane, running parallel to Vehicles One and Two.[8] He had gone only a few score of yards when a powerful explosion broke the calm. Vehicle Four, which had been about a hundred yards behind Vehicle Three, had barely reached the spot where a dirt road called Route Viper emptied onto Chestnut from the north when a bomb detonated by remote control blew the Humvee several feet into the air, where it hung for several seconds before crashing to the ground, pointed in the same direction it had been traveling. Vehicles One and Two had passed over the spot minutes before and their occupants had not detected so much as a seam in the road's surface.

Lance Corporal Trent Graviss, who was in the passenger seat in Wuterich's Humvee, grabbed the vehicle's AN/PRC-148 handheld radio and screamed the news to the company Command Operations Center (COC): the convoy had been hit. "Send the QRF," he urged, referring to the Quick Reaction Force, which always was on standby when a convoy was in progress.[9]

Lance Corporal Sharratt, who had been riding in the gunner's turret in Vehicle One, craned his neck and screamed: "I'm not seeing [Vehicle] four!" he bellowed. "I'm not seeing four!"[10] Confirmation of Vehicle Four's fate came seconds later from Lance Cpl. Rene Rodriguez, Vehicle One's driver: "Fourth vehicle is hit; [Terrazas] is dead," he howled.[11] "Shit!" exclaimed Sharratt. Rodriguez acknowledged: "Fucking A, man."[12]

Corpsman Whitt, who had been in the rear of Wuterich's vehicle when the bomb went off, leaped to the road and raced toward Vehicle Four, a morphine syringe already in his hand.[13] "Help me, doc," mumbled Lance Cpl. James Crossan, who had been in the passenger seat—a position called "alternate driver"—in the stricken Humvee. The recipient of a Purple Heart for wounds suffered in Fallujah, Crossan had been ejected from the Humvee and was supine on Route Chestnut, pinned under the Humvee's armored door.[14] Lance Corporal Stephen Tatum, Vehicle Two's alternate driver, arrived at the blast site just in time to see Pfc. Salvador Guzman, who had been riding as gunner in the rear of Vehicle Four, crawl out of the smoke and drag himself to the side of the road.[15]

Vehicle Four's driver, Terrazas—a Hell House veteran and one of the most popular men in K Company—was blown in half by the explosion: his upper torso came to rest on Route Chestnut while the lower potion of his body was wedged beneath the Humvee's steering wheel.

As the Marines scrambled to form a defensive position, a white vehicle unexpectedly approached from the west, traveling down the lane that Wuterich had commandeered. Corporal Sanick Dela Cruz waved his arms and shouted at the driver in broken Arabic to stop. Looking as astonished as the Marines by the unanticipated encounter, the man at the Opel's wheel first appeared to be trying to back away, then shifted gears and inched forward, coming to a stop with the front half of the vehicle on Route Chestnut's southern shoulder. Slowly, the man and four obviously frightened occupants got out and stood next to the car. The driver was a man close to middle age but the passengers all were youths in their late teens or early twenties.

Wuterich leaped into action. Dropping to his right knee, he raised his M-16 and opened fire on the Iraqis with his rifle on burst mode, which meant it was operating in spurts of three rounds as long as his finger was on the trigger or until the magazine was empty.[16] The men, hit several times, fell to the ground, either dying or already dead. Dela Cruz, who had been standing on Wuterich's right and a few yards behind him, rushed forward, his M-16 at waist level. Without hesitation, he shot each of the Opel's occupants again, performing a routine procedure called a "dead check."[17] Satisfied the Iraqis no longer posed a threat, Dela Cruz unzipped his trousers and urinated into a cavernous wound in the head of one of the men.[18]

The Iraqi National Guardsmen who were being ferried back to FB Sparta watched Wuterich and Dela Cruz in terror. Eyes bulging, limbs shaking, they looked at each other and silently communicated their fear that the Marines might next turn on them.

Wuterich and Dela Cruz searched the sedan but found no weapons or any device that could have been used as a detonator. As Wuterich and Dela Cruz were replacing the magazines in their rifles, a Humvee barreled toward them from the east. Second Lieutenant William Kallop, leader of the 3rd Platoon, who had remained at Sparta as QRF commander, was driving. He was among those who had never seen combat and he seemed staggered by the sight of Terrazas' mangled body, the demolished Humvee, and the bodies of the white Opel Iraqis strewn along the road.

Corporal Hector Salinas yelled at Kallop to take cover because several men had reported incoming fire from the south, supposedly from one or more insurgents sheltering in the lee of a house about 200 yards away. Some of the Marines—including Vehicle Four's gunner, Guzman, who had escaped with only a broken ankle from the blast that killed Terrazas—were popping rounds at the house, which was located off a dirt road called Route Zebra.

Kallop, crouching behind the QRF Humvee, asked what was going on.

Salinas pointed toward the south, saying he had seen someone shooting at them from a corner of a house in their line of sight. If they had been fired upon, the contact was quickly broken and no Marines were hit.

At the urging of Wuterich and Salinas, Kallop decided that the areas on both sides of Route Chestnut needed to be secured to make sure that insurgents were not preparing a follow-up attack, a tactic that often followed an IED ambush. "Clear south!" he told Wuterich, who selected Salinas, Lance Cpl. Stephen Tatum and Pfc. Humberto Mendoza to join him. Kallop turned to Dela Cruz, ordering him to take three other men to check the houses on the north side of the boulevard.[19] While most orders issued in a combat situation are unequivocal, a command to "clear" is ambiguous: it can mean either "assault" or "inspect" and is not always a license for violence.

To make sure there was no doubt about the target, Salinas fired three grenades from his M-203 launcher, watching as they hit the structure he and Wuterich had singled out.

As they ran up a small incline between the IED site and the marked dwelling, Wuterich told the men to treat the house as "hostile."[20]

The word "clear" may have been imprecise, but there was only one interpretation of "hostile." It meant use all available force. To make sure the team understood, Wuterich added: "Shoot first and ask questions later."[21]

"Where Are the Bad Guys?"

The team reached the structure—subsequently labeled House One—without drawing fire. Gathering at the dwelling's front entrance, they looked to Wuterich for guidance. He hesitated for a only a second before kicking in the door and rushing inside with the others on his heels. Facing them in the entryway was an elderly man sitting in a wheelchair. Before he could react, one of the Marines fired a quick burst into his chest, killing him instantly. An elderly woman who had been standing at his side started to run, but Salinas fired a quick burst into her back, hammering her to the floor.[22] The man was later identified as 76-year-old Abdul-Hamid Hassan, the patriarch of three generations of family members who lived in the house. The woman was his wife, 66-year-old Khamisa Tuema Ali.

Stepping over the couple, Wuterich, Salinas, and Tatum lined up along the house's west wall. Mendoza, on the opposite side of the hallway, also turned his back to the wall while cautiously peering into a dimly lit room on his right. Despite the darkness, he could see the outline of an adult male. Stepping across the hallway, the low-ranking private first class approached Tatum, who outranked him by two steps.

"There's an Iraqi in the next room," he said.

"Well, he's the enemy," Salinas replied.

"Do I request permission to shoot?" Mendoza asked.

"Yes," Salinas answered.[23]

Mendoza went back to doorway and shot the man, killing him with two three-round bursts.[24] Mendoza next tossed a fragmentation grenade into the room, and then jumped through the door with his rifle set to maximum fire. On the other side of the hallway, Tatum and Salinas thought they heard an AK-47 being prepared for fire inside a room encased in shadow. They prepped the room with grenades before Wuterich and Tatum sprayed the interior with rifle fire.[25]

They found an open door at the rear of the house, which seemed to indicate someone had escaped and bolted to a second house a few yards away. One of the Marines yelled that he had seen someone run out the back door of the house into an adjoining dwelling, so the team ran to the next house, House Two. Instead of storming inside as they had at House One, the men paused and pounded on the door. "Wait until someone comes," Wuterich whispered to Mendoza, who was hovering at his shoulder, "then shoot."[26] When no one appeared, the group moved to the side of the house where there was a door with a glass upper panel presenting a view into an empty kitchen. Almost immediately, however, an Iraqi man peeked around a doorframe on the far side of the room. Mendoza fired through the glass, killing the man.[27]

Wuterich, Mendoza and Tatum hurried inside, leaving Salinas to stand guard outside. Following the practice developed in Fallujah, they used grenades and rifles to clear the rooms before moving through the dwelling.[28]

Later, following a body count, it was discovered that the team, in less than 30 minutes, had killed 20 Iraqis: five on the shoulder of Route Chestnut, seven in House One, and eight in House Two. The dead included six children, age 5 to 14, and four women. One woman escaped from House One, apparently through the back door, with her two-month-old daughter. Three children were wounded, including a 13-year-old girl who survived by pretending she was dead.

Exiting House Two, the men returned to the IED site to be greeted by a nervous Lt. Kallop. "I need to see the houses," he told Wuterich: "I need to make a report." With Rodriguez as a guide, Kallop traced the route the fire team had taken earlier. Rodriguez had not been part of the assault team, so he was as shocked as Kallop at what they found inside House One. The floors, walls, and even the ceilings were splattered with blood, pieces of flesh, and brain matter. A middle-aged man was sprawled in a pool of dark red liquid, his torso perforated by grenade fragments. Another man had only a red hole where an eye should have been. A woman of indeterminate age exhibited a yawning gunshot wound to her head. "What the fuck happened?" gasped Kallop. "Where are the bad guys?"[29]

The bodies were plentiful, but at first glance none of the dead appeared to be insurgents. No weapon was found, nor was there a device to indicate the IED might have been triggered by someone inside.

In House Two, there was only more butchery, the gore emphasized by the bodies of dead children. A five-year-old boy had bled to death after being shot in the arm. A three-year-old girl had a large hole in her chest, and her 14-year-old sister had been almost decapitated by gunshots to the head. The children had been clustered in the middle of a bed around two women—their mother and a visiting female relative.

When a visibly unsettled Kallop returned to the IED site, he was ordered to go immediately to the Palm Groves, a little more than a mile to the east, where a small band of armed insurgents was believed to be assembling. Min-

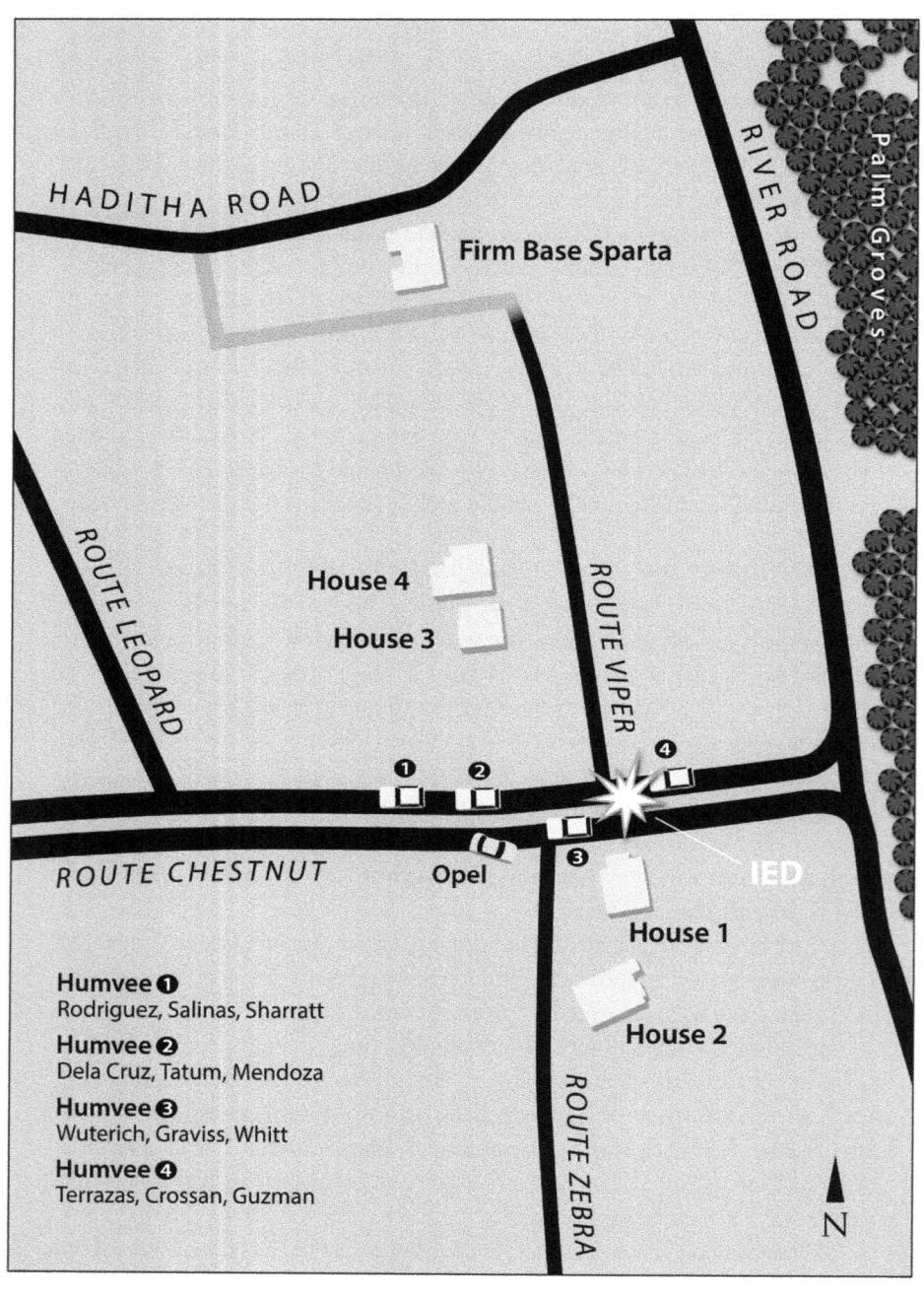

Ambush site (map by Steve McCracken).

utes later, the Kilo Company commander, Capt. Lucas McConnell, arrived with a small group from FB Sparta. They had set off from the headquarters almost as soon as they learned of the ambush. Traveling by foot, they had quickly covered the short distance, just missing Kallop and the QRF squad as they departed for what was expected to be the site of a new action.

McConnell surveyed the bodies of the men from the white sedan and was about to inspect House One when the watch officer in 3/1's headquarters radioed orders for him to press on to the Palm Groves as well. The interruption proved untimely because it negated the opportunity for a senior officer to get a firsthand look at the interior of the dwellings. So far, the only officer to go inside had been Kallop. Another second lieutenant would lead a body collection detail into the houses later in the day, but he and Kallop would be the only officers to view the path of destruction until the battalion civilian affairs officer visited several days later to examine the houses and determine if the families of the dead Iraqis were entitled to compensation.

3. Collateral Damage

Battalion 3/1's radios hummed day and night with a muted steadiness: calm voices transmitted the multitude of details necessary to keep a 1,200-man infantry unit functioning efficiently. To the men in the command operations center buried in the Haditha Dam, it was elevator music, reassurance that their limited world was operating as it should. That composure was shattered at about 0720 Hours when FB Sparta radioed news of the attack on the convoy. Casualties were not mentioned in the first report, so the officer in charge (OIC) saw no reason to interrupt the battle update brief (BUB) Lt. Col. Chessani was receiving from the battalion intelligence officer, Capt. Jeffrey Dinsmore.

Ten minutes later, Chessani and five other officers under his command sauntered into the COC, as yet unaware of the ambush. Dinsmore, a seasoned veteran who had served as an enlisted man before earning his commission, was the first to grasp the significance of the report. Coming instantly alert, he ordered the launch of a ScanEagle unmanned aerial vehicle (UAV). As quickly as the UAV could get airborne, it began to circle the Route Chestnut–River Road intersection transmitting video of the scene to an array of monitors inside the COC.

Because it arrived at the site a considerable time after the ambush, the video reflected a tranquil scene with Marines in a defensive position but no discernible activity. The situation was precisely what Dinsmore had expected. When he warned the battalion a few days earlier about the arrival of a group of terrorists from Syria, he had predicted there would be not just one blow but a series of orchestrated attacks. The IED that killed Terrazas had been the opening move—a distraction. The next phase, he felt, would start in the Palm Groves. Following his intuition, he guided the ScanEagle to the east. Almost immediately, his theory seemed to be borne out. The ScanEagle was just crossing River Road when its camera picked up a blue sedan turning off the thoroughfare onto a dirt road that plunged into the trees.

While Chessani and his staff watched, the sedan halted in a clearing, its shape barely detectable in the thick forest. As soon as it came to a stop, eight men piled out and hurriedly began retrieving several bundles that had been stashed among the palms. The men loaded the packages in the sedan's trunk before they jumped back into the car, which reversed its course and headed back to River Road. It traveled south for only a short distance before once more veering into the date plantation. A few minutes later, it stopped at a house that was almost totally hidden in the shadows. The men jumped out, recovered the packages from the trunk, and hurried into the dwelling.

The IED attack had taken place almost two hours earlier, and it seemed obvious to Dinsmore that the insurgents were setting up for another attack, part of a "coordinated" plan he had forecast. This time there would be no hidden bomb, but a *mano-a-mano*, Old West–style shootout that almost certainly was going to end with casualties on both sides. In the meantime, the Scan-Eagle's camera continued to function as the COC's eye in the sky, dutifully recording the arrivals of Lt. Kallop and his QRF team, as well as those of Capt. McConnell and his men from FB Sparta, at the edge of the Palm Groves.

"They're Turkey Peeking"

While the possibility of a confrontation in the Palm Groves grew, 1st Squad was not yet out of the picture. Shortly before Wuterich returned to the IED site from houses One and Two, Dela Cruz's fire team came back from its mission north of the blast point. Kallop had given "clear" orders to Dela Cruz as well as Wuterich, sending Dela Cruz to explore the other side of Route Chestnut. Unlike Wuterich's team, Dela Cruz's team did not fire a shot.

Some three hours after the IED explosion with no additional developments occurring, the men of 1st Squad were beginning to relax. They had established an observation post in an empty house some distance from the Vehicle Four wreckage, both to escape reminders of the traumatic event and to provide a better view of the surrounding buildings. They had not been there long when a photographer from FB Sparta arrived. Sgt. Justin Laughner showed up lugging cameras and a laptop computer, saying he had been sent by his boss, Lt Andrew Grayson, to photograph the dead Iraqis so their images could be compared to those stored in a Department of Defense insurgent database. Laughner and Grayson were members of the small Human Exploitation Team (HET) detailed to K Company. They were intelligence personnel trained to work with the local population to ferret out information on insurgent movements and locations of IEDs. With Tatum as a guide, Laughner's first stop was the white Opel. From there the two went to houses One and Two. Tatum, who had been a member of the fire team that assaulted the two houses, was as shocked as Rodriguez and Kallop had been by the results of the assaults. The number of dead—especially the bodies of the children—the nature of their wounds and the amount of gore in every direction left the men shaken and speechless.

While Laughner and Tatum completed their inspection of the bodies, Lt. Kallop returned from the Palm Groves. Chessani had decided that McConnell had enough men to assault the insurgents in the orchard, so he told Kallop to go back to the Chestnut/Viper site in case there was another attack there. As they waited, Kallop surveyed the area from the new vantage point. A house on the east side of Route Viper caught his eye because it was liberally decorated with anti-coalition graffiti. Neither he nor any of the other men in the squad could read Arabic, but several had learned to recognize the more common derogatory scrawls. The house, Kallop mused, was ideally situated to serve as a hiding place for an insurgent with a detonator waiting for a convoy to appear along Route Chestnut. It was worth checking out, he thought, dispatching Wuterich, Sharratt, Salinas and Tatum to investigate. The house was empty and there were no signs it had been recently used. Wuterich, Sharratt and Salinas returned to the observation post, leaving Tatum as a guard in the event anyone showed up.

At mid-afternoon—some eight hours after the ambush—Wuterich spotted suspicious activity around a house northwest of the OP. Several men of indeterminate age were playing whack-a-mole with 1st Squad. A head appeared above a wall and then disappeared, only to be replaced by another head a few yards away. "They're turkey peeking," Wuterich told Kallop, using Corps slang for a familiar Iraqi practice of observers bobbing up and down to take a quick look at the situation without risking long-term exposure. Kallop nodded, ordering Dela Cruz to fire a training round from his grenade launcher in the general direction. The object was not to damage or kill but to see what the reaction might be. The Iraqis vanished for several minutes but soon reappeared, continuing their bouncing movements. Kallop told Wuterich, Sharratt and Salinas to explore the situation.

When they approached the location they discovered that it was not one house but two, one so closely behind the other that from a distance it looked like a single dwelling. A teenage boy, a few women and an infant were the only ones inside the first building, subsequently to be known as House Three. When Wuterich asked where the men were, one of the women pointed to the rear door, which opened onto a narrow courtyard separating the structures. Wuterich ordered Salinas to remain in House Three while he and Sharratt inspected the rear building: House Four. Wuterich was armed with an M-16 while Sharratt had a SAW. He also carried an M9 he had borrowed from a corpsman in another squad before they departed on the TCP mission.

Sharratt entered first, walking into an empty room. After an exchange of glances, the two formed a "stack" against one of the walls. When Sharratt peeked around the doorjamb he came face to face with a man holding an AK-47 rifle. He raised the SAW and pulled the trigger, but it did not fire. "Jam!" he yelled, reaching for the pistol. His shot hit the man in the head and he immediately dropped to the floor. To Sharratt's surprise, a second man appeared and he also was holding an AK-47. Sharratt again used the pistol, firing until the 15-round magazine was empty.[1] Hollering to Wuterich that he was out of ammunition, Sharratt stepped back so Wuterich could move ahead. Jumping through the door, Wuterich emptied his M-16 into the room, killing two more men.[2] It was later learned that the four were brothers.

Before leaving, Wuterich and Sharratt scooped up the two rifles, which was standard operating practice. A quick search of the house also uncovered a suitcase containing Jordanian passports and wad of Jordanian and Syrian currency. After stowing the suitcase and the rifles in the rear of an Explosive Ordnance Disposal (EOD) Humvee that had brought bomb experts to study the IED site, they returned to the OP. Ostensibly, the material was to be taken to 3/1 headquarters, where it would be logged and protectively stored.

Chessani Leaves His Lair

During a six-hour span beginning when the ScanEagle first picked up the blue sedan traveling along River Road until the McConnell-led team subdued the insurgents (about the time Wuterich and Sharratt killed the brothers in House Four), Chessani had not left the COC. Instead, he spent the interval glued to the desktop monitors on which the ScanEagle images were being displayed, engrossed in the developments occurring before his eyes.

With McConnell in pursuit, the insurgents retreated from the first house, running to a second house where one of the men ran inside, then quickly came out with a child under each arm. The fighting finally ended at a third house after the McConnell team attacked with M-16s, M-203 grenade launchers, and AGM-114 Hellfire missiles fired from a support helicopter.[3] At midafternoon, with no appreciable progress toward overpowering the entrenched insurgents, Chessani called for a fixed-wing aircraft, which flattened the house with two 200-pound bombs. Just to make sure the insurgents were not going any farther, two M1A1 Abram tanks arrived prepared to reduce the mostly demolished house to gravel. A search of the rubble revealed four bodies. However, three others—including the man who picked up the children—escaped during the chase. Six of McConnell's men were wounded, two of them seriously.[4]

At about 1630 Hours—some two hours after the fighting in the orchards ended—Chessani and the battalion's ranking enlisted man, Sgt. Maj. Edward Sax, drove to the Palm Groves so Chessani could inspect the scene. He and McConnell spent about three hours amid the date palms—officially designated Site X-380—trekking from one location to another, examining where the insurgents had first gathered, the spots where several IEDs had been discovered, the locations where the McConnell team had exchanged gunfire with the insurgents, and, finally, to the house that had been destroyed by bombs.[5]

At about 1930 Hours, Chessani, McConnell and Sax left the Palm Groves for the short drive to FB Sparta, passing the Route Chestnut intersection on the way. Once they were at Sparta, McConnell briefed Chessani on what he knew about the IED attack, which was very little. Likely, it was the first information Chessani had received about the incident since the first report some 12 hours earlier. Among the bits of information McConnell passed along was his impression that 1st Squad had been receiving heavy fire from several houses before Wuterich led the assaults.[6] During his abbreviated stop, Chessani did not inquire about the welfare of the men from 1st Squad. Nor did he ask to interview the men, or direct McConnell to investigate the incident.[7] As Chessani and Sax were leaving Sparta, Chessani suggested a detour to the IED site but Sax dissuaded him, saying it was dangerous "to be outside the wire" at that hour.[8]

A crescent moon threw little light on the desolate landscape on the trip to the Haditha Dam, where they arrived sometime shortly after 2000 Hours. Almost immediately, Chessani got on a secure phone with Col. Stephen Davis, commander of RCT-2 and Chessani's immediate superior. Chessani mentioned that "women and children" had been killed at Chestnut and Viper and that Marines had assaulted several houses. Davis, who was preoccupied with another operation at the time, did not seem unduly perturbed by the news, probably because there were no numbers to indicate the seriousness of the event. Davis's parting remarks to Chessani were "to look into [the civilian deaths] further."[9]

After hanging up, Maj. Samuel Carrasco, the battalion operations officer, handed Chessani a draft of Journal Entry Note (JEN) 20-007. Chessani glanced at it and scrawled his approval.[10] Chessani and almost everyone in 3/1 was convinced that the Palm Groves conflict had been the "major attack" predicted by Dinsmore. McConnell supported this conclusion the next morning at Chessani's daily BUB by presenting a PowerPoint production that consisted almost entirely of ScanEagle video. There was no mention of civilian casualties at Chestnut and Viper. Neither Chessani nor any member of his staff asked about the IED attack.

The next afternoon, some 30 hours after the Chestnut/Viper events, Chessani, Sax and the battalion executive officer, Maj. Kevin M. Gonzales, drove to the IED site. It was Chessani's first and last appearance at the scene. Although he had devoted three hours to examining details in the Palm Groves, he spent less than a half hour at Route Chestnut, where his sole interest was in the demolished Humvee. He did not ask questions or inspect the houses.[11]

Collecting the Dead

Second Lieutenant Max Frank, a squad leader form another platoon, was assigned the grisly task of recovering and officially tallying the mangled bodies at Chestnut and Viper. Frank quickly ran into problems: there were not enough latex gloves for every man in the squad and there were not enough body bags to accommodate all the corpses. In the end, they were forced to stuff the dead into large, white trash bags.[12] Frank's men rebelled at the body-collection chore, leaving the undertaking to the squad leader and another Marine.

No one noted when the mission began, but it was approaching 1900 Hours—12 hours after the incident—by the time Frank drove the bodies to Sparta. When he got there, a gunnery sergeant separated them into two groups: one of women and children and another of men. Frank then made a second trip to deliver the bodies to the Haditha General Hospital. The sight of the mutilated, decomposing corpses was so horrifying that even the hardened morgue workers had to look away. One took a quick glimpse and vomited.[13]

Communications among 1st Squad, Kilo headquarters and the 3/1 COC were so tangled that no one knew precisely how many Iraqis had been killed until Frank made his report. Neither did anyone know how many of the dead were noncombatants and how many were suspected insurgents. One early report said there were eight insurgents among the dead; another claimed 15. At some point, an allegation was floated saying that the Chestnut/Viper incident had involved not only the IED attack but also a fierce firefight between the men of 1st Squad and insurgents entrenched in the homes, where they were holding the occupants as hostages. The first documented report of casualties came in a Journal Entry Note filed by the battalion COC to Regimental Combat Team-2 (RCT-2), the battalion's superior command. It traveled over a secure Internet-like system called the Secret Internet Protocol Router Network (SIPRNet), which was superior to radio or secure landlines. Numbered JEN 19-008, it correctly said that one Marine was killed and two wounded. However, it also incorrectly reported that five insurgents had been killed and one wounded. Curiously, it added that one of the enemy killed in action (EKIA) was carrying a map and $2,000 in U.S. currency.[14] The next JEN—number 19-019—said nothing new except that Vehicle Four was damaged beyond repair.[15] The day's final update—JEN 20-007—contained a wealth of information, almost all of it incorrect:

> There was a total of (8) EKIA (Enemy Killed), (1) EWIA (Enemy Wounded) who was medevaced out, and (15) NKIA (Neutrals Killed in Action), and (2) NWIA medevaced. Post engagement assessment has determined that a combined patrol [of 1st Squad and Iraqi soldiers] was attacked as it was moving past a group of [neutral Iraqis]. The ensuing blast and TIC [troops in contact] contributed to the number [of civilian dead]. [Anti-coalition] elements then engaged [coalition troops] from within residential structures in the area further adding to the [number of dead civilians] as a result of returned fire [by coalition forces]. Commanding Officer 3/1 moved to the scene to conduct a command assessment of the events.[16]

The source of the information was never revealed, but there were several noteworthy items in the communiqué. Besides the wildly incorrect casualty count, there was never substantiation of the existence of a "combined patrol," much less of the claim that the group was attacked by insurgents hiding in an unspecified number of houses in unnamed locations. More importantly, there was no evidence of a firefight occurring at Chestnut and Viper. The mention of "troops in contact" also was significant. Carrasco made this declaration when he was the OIC in the COC, apparently while Chessani was visiting the Palm Groves although the time cannot be verified. The term "troops in contact" has special relevance because it is official recognition that opponents are actively shooting at each other. However, as it ultimately played out, the most damaging statement in the JEN was this sentence: "Commanding Officer 3/1 moved to the scene to conduct a command assessment of the events."[17]

Whatever the source of the claims, they were substantial enough for the 2nd Marine Division to issue a news release on November 20 that solidified the Corps' position on what occurred:

> Camp Blue Diamond, AR Ramadi, Iraq—A U.S. Marine and 15 Iraqi civilians were killed yesterday from the blast of a roadside bomb in Haditha. Immediately fol-

lowing the bombing, gunmen attacked the convoy with small arms fire. Iraqi Army soldiers and Marines returned fire killing eight insurgents and wounding another.[18]

The author-of-record for the release was the division's public affairs officer, Capt. Jeffrey Pool. But it remains unclear who was responsible for the erroneous document. Unit protocol required that both the division operations officer—Col. J. Holden—and the commander's chief of staff—Col. R. Gary Sokoloski—review Pool's draft releases. It was rare, Pool said later, that changes were not made to his original submissions, but since the original could not be found, the issue was never resolved. Nevertheless, the release reveals a lot about the credibility of the information the Corps was distributing to the media. When questioned later, Pool and Sokoloski said the primary consideration in sending the release was to cement the Corps' spin on the event before the insurgents could reveal whatever information they had, possibly a video.[19] As far as the 2nd Division was concerned, the veracity of the release was immaterial. "Exact details of how the civilians were killed were not deemed important," Pool said.[20]

Apparently, domestic and foreign media ignored the release. United States newspapers and broadcast reports in the period surrounding the incident were filled with stories about the economy, high gasoline prices, and the continuing fallout from Hurricane Katrina. Iraq was still top headline material, but the non-combat stories mainly were focused on the country's two elections, on President Bush's refusal to commit to a timetable for U.S. withdrawal, and on military deaths in Iraq hitting the 2,000 mark. However, there also were stories about the turmoil surrounding the war. On November 21—two days after Haditha—there was a piece about U.S. troops shooting and killing five members of an Iraqi family, allegedly for failing to stop at a checkpoint.[21] On November 29, insurgents kidnapped a female German archeologist and her driver.[22] But the most shocking story was datelined Fallujah, where ten 2nd Division Marines were killed and 11 wounded in a roadside bomb attack.[23] Curiously, the announcement of the attack came from Washington rather than from Pool's office in the 2nd Division.

Amid the Tumult

The hours and days after the incident were jammed with episodes that for the most part remained undocumented or unexplained, their existence known only because of reports from others external to 3/1, occasional notations that they occurred, or as they were recalled later by the participants.

- The night of the incident, Maj. Kevin Gonzalez, the battalion executive officer, asked Chessani if a formal investigation might be in order to clarify the events surrounding the civilian deaths. "I have it for action," Chessani replied dismissively.[24]

- Also that night, Kilo Company held a memorial for Terrazas. The men were allowed to grieve for their friend, but there was no discussion of what had occurred. As far as is known, 1st Squad members were never debriefed, so there is no record of how the men reacted to the events.[25]

- Before the last JEN was sent, Dinsmore, who never visited the site, began constructing a "story board"—Corps jargon for a sanctioned narrative of the events of the day.[26] One of the defects of the document was that it did not give details of NKIA casualties. Nevertheless, it was used as the official account of the Chestnut/Viper event for months to come.

- While Kilo Company continued to sort the bodies, an officer from RCT-2 contacted the battalion Information Operations officer asking for photographs of the dead Iraqis for use in a possible IO campaign.[27] IO is a Corps propaganda arm whose duty is formally described as "the integration, coordination, and synchronization of all actions taken in the information environment to affect a target audience's behavior in order to create an operational advantage for the commander."[28] The apparent intent was to use the photographs to demonstrate the insurgents' brutality.

- The day after the incident, two Haditha residents complained about the assaults to an unreceptive Dinsmore, who dismissed them in the belief that their grousing was inspired by sympathy for the insurgents.[29]

- Kallop recommended Wuterich for a Navy and Marine Corps Achievement Medal with a V for valor, crediting the sergeant with initiating a "counterattack" that "turned the tide of the ambush and killed a number of insurgents still attempting to fight or attempting to flee the area."[30] The incident, Kallop wrote, was part of a "complex attack" that included the IED detonation and was followed by a "high volume" of automatic weapons fire from "several houses" in the area. To Kallop, it was enough to prove that the incident "was a planned and orchestrated attack by insurgents, and the Marines were responding in accordance within their [Rules of Engagement]."[31]

- Major General Huck, the division commander, visited the IED site on November 22. As had Chessani, Huck spent no time examining the scene. Carrasco briefed him on the official version of what had occurred, explaining that the deaths were the result "of the enemy's choice to fight amongst [civilians]."[32] Huck, also as had Chessani, asked no probative questions, did not inspect the houses, did not ask for photographs, and did not request interviews with the men of 1st Squad or McConnell. As far as is known, no one from RCT-2 went to the scene, interviewed anyone from 1st Squad, asked for photos of the carnage, or inspected the interior of the houses.

- On November 27, Chessani met with the Haditha City Council, a group in no mood to be placated. Instead, the group asked, both in writing and orally, for a formal investigation and requested that the Corps take the blame for the incident. This apparently infuriated Chessani, who accused the council of inflating the casualty count, apparently with the intent of extracting monetary compensation from the Corps. Chessani responded by telling the council it was the group's fault that civilians had been killed because the local populace sheltered insurgents.[33] Despite this, he said, he would take what action he could to arrange payments for the affected families.

- Two days later, Chessani sent his civil affairs officer, Maj. Dana Hyatt, to inspect the houses to determine if the Iraqis were entitled to reparations under the Commander's Emergency Response Program (CERP), a system created to provide a way for military authorities to shuttle funds to Iraqis who had suffered because of the war. Hyatt was the first (and last) officer to go inside the houses, which had not been inspected since the Kallop and Frank visits on the day of the incident. Even ten days after the bodies had been removed, the scene was enough to make Hyatt gag. "The walls were black [with grenade scorches]," he said, "and I think there were bullet holes in another room. It looked like hair and stuff in the ceiling, blood on the floor. It was the most blood I'd ever seen."[34]

- On December 22, five weeks after the incident, Chessani, acting on Hyatt's recommendation, authorized $38,000 in condolence payments to the families of those killed in Houses One and Two ($2,500 for each individual killed in Houses One and Two and $250 for each of the two children injured in House One).[35] Three families whose houses were damaged in the raid also were given $1,000 each for repairs, bringing the total to $41,000.[36] It was an unusually large amount to be paid under the circumstances, but it received only minimal scrutiny. Chessani later also authorized $10,000 to the family of the four brothers killed in House Four, but that money came from a different fund, called solatia.[37]

Table 1
Incident Timeline

Time	Event
0630	Convoy departs FB Sparta.
0700	Convoy leaves COP.
0716	IED explodes under Vehicle 4.
0730	White Opel arrives.
0734	Wuterich kills five men from the Opel.
0737	Kallop arrives at blast site.
0745	Dinsmore orders ScanEagle launch.
0750	Kallop orders Wuterich to "clear south!"
0753	Assault on House One, seven killed.
0800	Assault on House Two, eight killed.
0815	Dela Cruz team clears houses north of Chestnut without incident.
0900	Fighting begins in Palm Groves.
1045	Wuterich and Sharratt kill four brothers in House Four.
1430	Fighting ends in Palm Groves; nine Marines wounded, none mortally.
1630	Chessani begins Palm Groves inspection.
1930	Chessani visits FB Sparta; does not ask to talk to 1st Squad or view photographs.
2000	Chessani decides not to go to IED site; returns to Haditha Dam headquarters.
2100	Body count completed at IED site; twenty-four civilians dead.
2300	Chessani tells RCT-2 commander, Colonel Davis, he has visited IED site.

Note: Some times are approximate.

4. The Lid Comes Off

Moving into 2006, the underlying and unexpressed concern was whether an investigation was needed to determine what had happened on November 19 at routes Chestnut and Viper. There were 24 Iraqis supposedly killed, most of them, according to the Corps command in Iraq, in an explosion and firefight. The Corps contended the dead included eight insurgents. If there had been a firefight, why were there no casualties among the men of 1st Squad? Six Marines were wounded in the Palm Groves under conditions described as almost identical to those that took place at the blast site: well-armed insurgents fighting from within dwellings. Where were the weapons of the Chestnut and Viper fighters? Even the two AK-47s allegedly recovered in House Four were never logged in at FB Sparta or at 2nd Division. Neither was the suitcase supposedly containing foreign passports and currency. The Palm Groves jihadists fought from houses empty except for themselves. Why was each male who died at Chestnut/Viper killed along with his family? It did not add up, but no one noticed or cared. The Corps was happy with the way things stood.

These questions and others shadowed Battalion 3/1 for months. Some, such as Col. Sokoloski, Capt. Pool, Col. Davis at RCT-2, his top legal officer (Maj. Carroll Connelly), Chessani (*especially* Chessani), Dinsmore, Frank and other junior officers, were content with the story board resolution. Those higher up the chain, such as Huck and his bosses at MNF-W and MNF-I, knew only what they had been told by their subordinates, and every briefing was based on the story board.

However, not everyone was satisfied with the official version.

An engineer with the battalion's Headquarters Company asked his commander if it was true that four college students had been among the dead. When the officer confronted McConnell with the question, Kilo's commandeer replied that the men from the Opel had been wearing chest rigs and were armed with weapons and grenades.[1]

A week after the incident, 1st Sgt. Alberto Espinosa, the man responsible for maintaining Kilo's casualty reports, said he was sufficiently concerned about the unusual number of dead civilians to corner Capt. Randy Stone, the battalion staff judge advocate, in the battalion COC to ask why an investigation was not underway. Stone told him not to worry about it because the issue was being handled at a higher level.[2] McConnell gave him the same answer, Espinosa added.

Apparently, the only doubter with any clout was Maj. Thomas Osterhoudt, the 2nd Division comptroller. Suspicious about the exceptionally large CERP payments made to the families of those killed in houses One and Two, Osterhoudt asked if the incident had been reported as a Commander's Critical Information Requirement (CCIR)—a bureaucratic procedure designed to help a commander determine the nature of an engagement. Osterhoudt was worried about making CERP payments for losses caused by insurgents because that was prohibited under the CERP process. Osterhoudt also went a step farther by suggesting that the incident be reported to legal officers as a possible violation of the Law of Armed Conflict (LOAC), which outlaws operations against noncombatants.[3]

Not content with not-to-worry replies from Chessani and Stone, Osterhoudt went over their heads to the division staff judge advocate, saying he felt more details were needed. This resulted in an exchange of e-mails involving the division SJA, Chessani, and Stone. It ended when Stone forwarded the information from the story board.

Purely by Accident

Because of the stresses on correspondents in Iraq, *Time* magazine rotated its people in Baghdad at regular intervals. Early in January, more than two months after the incident, correspondent Tim McGirk, based in Pakistan, arrived in Iraq for his scheduled in-fill. He had just settled in for his five-week tour when the editor of the magazine's world section passed him an assignment. President Bush had said in a recent speech that an estimated 30,000 Iraqis had been killed thus far in the two-and-three-quarter-year-old war. The editor wanted McGirk to try to find out how many of those civilians had been killed by U.S. troops.[4]

To comply, *Time* sent feelers to its contacts throughout Iraq. Quickly, they had a response from a man named Taher Thabet, who said he represented an organization called the Hammurabi Organization for Human Rights and

Democracy Monitoring. Thabet gave McGirk a VCD (video compact disc) showing the mutilated bodies of Iraqi men, women, and children, and the blood-splattered interiors of two homes. Thabet said he had been trying for weeks to get the Arab media interested in the video, but no one had taken any notice.[5] Thabet explained that he had been visiting relatives in Haditha in November 2005 and was awakened on the morning of the 19th by an explosion powerful enough to break the windows of the house in which he was staying, even though it was a considerable distance from the IED site. Running outside, he saw a huge cloud of dark smoke and several Marines running toward a group of houses on the south side of Route Chestnut. "They went into one house. I heard gunfire, explosions and screams. Then they came out and went into another. I could only stand and watch," he told McGirk.[6] Thabet said the next morning he went to the morgue where the bodies were being prepared for burial. "I didn't know what I was recording. I just felt I had to record everything I could see."[7]

Immediately realizing he had powerful material that seemed to be evidence of a Corps massacre, McGirk contacted *Time*'s headquarters in New York. However, News Editor Howard Chua-Eoan was suspicious. "Go slow," he said; "get verification."

On January 24, after his interview with Thabet, McGirk e-mailed Maj. Neil F. Murphy, the public affairs officer for Multi-National Force–West (MNF-W)—the top Corps command in Iraq. Murphy pooh-poohed what McGirk told him and scornfully accused the correspondent of being suckered by "poorly constructed" insurgent propaganda.[8] Another *Time* correspondent, Aparisim "Bobby" Ghosh, also contacted Murphy and was similarly derided. Murphy, said Ghosh, was "incredibly hostile" and also blamed the news magazine for "buying into enemy propaganda."[9] Despite his scorn, Murphy sent the information down the chain, through Col. Sokoloski, the 2nd Division chief of staff, where it ended up on Chessani's desk.[10] Chessani's response is not part of the public record but, judging from later developments, he answered Murphy with details from the story board.

However, *Time*'s request did not go completely unnoticed. Soon after receiving the appeal, members of Chessani's staff tried to arrange a visit from McGirk so he could talk directly to the men of Kilo Company. When it seemed as if McGirk might actually travel to Haditha, two of Chessani's staff officers—majors Kevin Gonzales and Samuel Carrasco—gingerly mentioned to the battalion commander that an investigation might be in order. The proposal enraged Chessani, causing him to scream: "My men are not murderers!"[11] He later apologized.

At the time McGirk was considering traveling to Haditha, Anbar Province was an extremely active insurgent area and the reporter's boss, Chua-Eoan, fearing for McGirk's safety, didn't want him to go. "[McGirk] was on his way when Chua-Eoan called to tell him to turn around," said writer Lori Robertson.[12] Instead, "*Time* arranged for some witnesses to come to Baghdad. McGirk spoke to a few people by phone and interviewed others, including the mayor of Haditha, by e-mail."[13]

"If It Bleeds, It Leads"

In lieu of a personal visit to Haditha, McGirk e-mailed a half-dozen questions he had about the incident. Again, the list went to Chessani, who delegated a panel composed of Gonzales, Kilo commander McConnell, and 1st Lt. Adam Mathes, Kilo's executive officer to draft a reply. Their suggestions were published on the National Public Radio Web site, but the response was simply listed as "panel" and there was no indication of which individual had made the statement.[14] The responses, however, revealed both the Corps' widespread antipathy toward the media and the depth of the resentment felt by members of 3/1 when asked to provide clarification for an issue they considered closed.

> McGirk: How many Marines were killed and wounded in the IED attack that morning?
> Panel: "If It Bleeds, It Leads." This question is McGirk's attempt to get a good bloody gouge on the situation. He will most likely use the information he gains from this answer as an attention gainer.[15]

The panel conjectured that McGirk's follow-up would be to ask if there were any officers involved. In the group's opinion, McGirk was trying to spin the story to reflect badly on the Corps, the Bush administration, and the motivations for the war. The panel said:

> By asking if there was an officer on scene the reporter may be trying to identify a point of blame for lack of judgment. If there was an officer involved, then [McGirk] may be able to have his My Lai massacre pinned on that officer's shoulder. Unfortunately for McGirk, this is not the case. In the reporter's eyes, military officers may represent the U.S. government and enlisted Marines may represent the American people. Given the current political climate in the U.S. at this time concerning the Iraq War and the current administration's conduct of the war, the reporter would most likely seek to discredit the U.S. government (one of our officers) and expose victimization of the American people by the hand of the government (the enlisted Marines under the haphazard command of our "rogue officer.")[16]

In response to a question challenging the Corps' contention that insurgents were attacking the squad after the IED explosion when residents repudiated the claim, the panel said:

> Our Marines are trained to recognize the crack of small arms fire as it flies over their heads since their earliest days as recruits in boot camp.... We have experienced and professional Marines who know how to distinguish the sound of incoming automatic weapons fire from the clamor of combat. The Marines identified the origin of the enemy fires to the north and south of their position and returned fire.... Of course, the locals denied that the insurgents were using their homes and their children as sandbag bunkers in their attacks against coalition forces. If they did not deny it, they would fear being killed by the insurgents.[17]

The next question hit a sore spot.

MCGIRK: How many Marines were involved in the killings?

PANEL: First off, we don't know what you're talking about when you say "killings." One of our squads reinforced by a squad of Iraqi Army soldiers were engaged by an enemy-initiated ambush ... that killed one American Marine and seriously injured two others. We will not justify that question with a response.[18]

When McGirk asked if weapons had been recovered at the scene, the panel reacted angrily:

> Again, you are showing yourself to be uneducated in the world of contemporary insurgent combat. The subject about which we are speaking was a legitimate engagement initiated by the enemy.... Your reference to this event is a simple misnomer, and one that we would appreciate you being more precise and referring to an enemy engagement in the future.[19]

The panel also repeated the incorrect information contained in the final JEN on November 19:

> Yes, we found weapons on the confirmed terrorists in the houses that day. We found (8) AK-47s in the houses where we engaged the enemy who was honorably [*sic*] hiding behind women and children while firing AK-47s at our Marines.[20]

The panel anticipated that McGirk, by referring to House Four where two AK-47s reportedly were recovered, would ask if it were not permissible under then-existing Iraq law for homeowners to keep rifles in their homes for self-protection. It said:

> Each 18-year-old is allowed to have an AK-47 in his house. We confirmed the existence of terrorists in the house by observing that the "potential terrorists" were aiming and shooting their personal weapons at the Marines.[21]

Panel members again grew touchy after McGirk asked why the fire team had been unable to tell they were shooting at women and children in a daylight assault. It responded:

The Marines did, in fact, distinguish women and children from the terrorists.... The Marines know the difference between children and terrorists. The insurgents chose to take up firing positions from the bedrooms and living rooms of houses occupied by innocent civilians. Once they began to fire on our Marines, our Marines identified the insurgents' fighting positions and returned fire.[22]

At the time, Maj. Gen. Zilmer had not yet announced that the NCIS had been asked to investigate the incident, so McGirk asked if a probe seemed likely. "No," the group responded: "the engagement was a bona fide combat action against a group of insurgents who callously used innocent civilians as their human shields."[23] It added:

> By asking this question, McGirk is assuming the engagement was in fact a LOAC violation and that by asking about investigations he may spur a reaction from the command that will initiate an investigation. He assumes that "no" is not a good enough answer.[24]

At the end of McGirk's list was a query about whether the Marines involved in the incident were still serving in Iraq. The panel took exception to the use of the word "serving," by responding:

> Yes, we are still fighting terrorists of Al Qaeda in Iraq in Haditha.... The American people will side more with someone actively fighting a terrorist organization ... than with someone who is idly "serving," like in the way one "serves" a casserole.[25]

The suggested responses were presented to Chessani, who composed an official reply to McGirk. The text of Chessani's e-mail was not made public.

Command Intervention

Obviously unsatisfied with Chessani's response and unable to get a useful explanation from the 2nd Division public affairs officer, McGirk went around the Corps' Iraq command by sending a copy of the Thabet video to the American forces' top military public affairs representative: Army Col. Barry Johnson, a well-recognized public interpreter of the status of the war.[26]

Apparently, Johnson was so affected by the images that he passed the VCD to his boss, Lt. Gen. Peter Chiarelli, chief of the Multi-National Corps–Iraq (MNC-I). In 2005, Chiarelli had commanded the 1st Cavalry Division but returned in January 2006 as second in command to Gen. George W. Casey, Jr., commander of Multi-National Force–Iraq (MNF-I). The difference between "Corps" and "Force" in these organizational names was often confusing. Under the peculiar nomenclature, "Corps" was the unit responsible for strategic decisions while "Force" handled tactical issues. Casey's duty was long-term planning; Chiarelli handled day-to-day operations for war fighters, including the Marines, whose top man in Iraq was Maj. Gen. Richard Zilmer, commander of MNF-W.

After viewing the video, Chiarelli e-mailed Zilmer asking if an investigation had been conducted into the incident to determine if there was a LOAC violation.[27] Not surprisingly, Chiarelli's e-mail caught Zilmer off guard. He was even fresher to Iraq than Chiarelli, having taken command of MNF-W only ten days earlier. Because he knew nothing about the incident, he referred the query to Maj. Gen. Huck, the 2nd Division commander.[28] Huck, who also knew next to nothing about the events at Chestnut and Viper, forwarded a copy of the story board (which did not mention civilian casualties and was unaccompanied by Sgt. Laughner's photographs), adding that no investigation had been initiated because there was nothing to investigate.[29] If Chiarelli replied, his response is not in the public record. Nevertheless, on February 14, Chiarelli risked the Corps' ire by dispatching one of his investigators, Col. Gregory A. Watt, to Haditha with authorization to conduct an informal probe under Army Regulation 15-6, a narrowly structured provision permitting a non-criminal inquiry.[30]

Normally, the branches do not interfere in each other's operations, and there was a danger the Corps would perceive Chiarelli's action as an insult. Still, Chiarelli outranked Zilmer and had responsibility for all armed forces in the country, including the Marines. He also had a reputation as someone who was not afraid to poke at the military's cover-your-ass attitude. The Corps could take some satisfaction in the knowledge that Watt's investigatory scope was limited by the parameters of the regulation; he could look only for information that could help a commander make an informed decision on a possible next step. He could *not* dig into possible criminal activity; only the Corps could do that. In essence, Watt was restricted to searching for substantiation that Chessani was justified in his failure to conduct an investigation.

Watt spent more than a week in Haditha talking to 3/1 Marines and selected civilians before writing and submitting his report to Chiarelli on March 3.[31] The document that eventually was released to the public was a skimpy eight-page report containing considerable duplication. Overall, it mostly matched the story board version.

Wuterich and Dela Cruz shot the men from the white sedan, Watt said, because they "failed to comply with orders ... and proceeded to run away."[32] Furthermore, the Iraqis' response "was not what would be expected of normally prudent [military aged males] in combat ... and it was reasonable for the Marines to consider [them] to be legitimate military targets."[33] House One,

Watt continued, was aggressively assaulted because of "hostile actions" by the occupants and because the 1st Squad team could hear a rifle being prepared to fire. As a result, the team was compelled to use "offensive room-clearing techniques," including the use of "fragmentary grenades."[34] As for House Two, Watt said it was assaulted only after the team began receiving small arms fire from the dwelling while they were still in House One.[35] "This forced the Marines to approach, conduct a forced entry," and use the same house-clearing techniques they had used in House One.[36]

Additionally, Watt said, insurgent resistance necessitated the shootings at House Four:

> While Marines took a tactical pause in a house used to watch over the area, they started receiving small arms fire from the northwest. Marines returned fire with small arms and fired [a grenade] to cover their movement toward [House Three]. While inside House Four, Marines identified four [military-aged males], two with weapons, and engaged and killed them.[37]

In conclusion, Watt found that the amount of force used in the conflicts "was proportional and provided overmatch in order to insure mission accomplishment ... without putting Marines at risk."[38] He said:

> Indications are that insurgents fought from homes occupied by non-combatants and used these homes for cover and concealment. Statements by numerous Marines support that they received hostile [small arms fire] from [houses One, Two and Four] (as well as a house identified as a possible trigger house). Marine statements indicate that those [insurgents] did not distinguish themselves from non-combatants.[39]

Despite his support of 1st Squad's actions, Watt suggested a more thorough investigation. At the same time, however, he was pessimistic about what a second probe might accomplish. "Obtaining more prosecutable evidence will be extremely difficult," he observed, given the amount of time that had elapsed, the fact that condolence payments had been made, and that renovations had altered the interiors of houses One and Two.[40]

Chiarelli Unconvinced

Although Watt substantiated what Capt. Dinsmore had written in the story board, Chiarelli was unsatisfied. Less than a week later he summoned one of his top staffers—Maj. Gen. Eldon Bargewell—and told him he was going to Haditha. One of Chiarelli's concerns about Watt's findings may have been that the colonel's investigation was not as successful as he had hoped because his rank and level of experience were not sufficient to make an impact on MNF-W's commanders. Chiarelli decided to kick it up a notch. This time, he was sending a two-star officer.

In the meantime, MNF-W did an about-face on the need for an investigation. On March 12, about the time Bargewell set up shop in Haditha, Maj. Gen. Zilmer announced that he had asked the Naval Criminal Investigative Service (NCIS) to begin a criminal probe, as opposed to the non-criminal search headed by Bargewell.[41]

Although Bargewell had only a handful of aides to help with the mission, the NCIS fielded more than 60 agents and contractors in an examination that spread to the United States as well as Iraq. It was the largest NCIS contingent investigating a single incident involving a Marine since 1987, when a sergeant named Clayton Lonetree was accused of spying for the Soviets. A guard at the U.S. embassy in Moscow, Lonetree was seduced by a KGB operative and began supplying her with classified information. The incident led Secretary of Defense Caspar W. Weinberger to recall all of the embassy's 28 Marines and send a hundred agents to State Department offices around the world to make sure there were no more information thieves. Lonetree was convicted on 12 of 13 counts of espionage and sentenced to 30 years in prison.[42]

Remarkably, the MNF-W had kept the Haditha incident under such tight control that the Pentagon and the war-promoting White House was caught by surprise when *Time* published McGirk's story on March 19, 2006.[43] It was 2,400 words long—an extraordinary length for a piece in a weekly news magazine. McGirk paid little attention to whatever information he had obtained from Chessani and laid the blame for the shootings directly on 1st Squad. He wrote:

> According to eyewitnesses and local officials interviewed over the past ten weeks, the civilians who died in Haditha on Nov. 19 were killed not by a roadside bomb but by the Marines themselves, who went on a rampage in the village after the attack, killing 15 unarmed Iraqis in their homes, including seven women and three children. Human-rights activists say that if the accusations are true, the incident ranks as the worst case of deliberate killing of Iraqi civilians by U.S. service members since the war began.[44]

It quoted one of the two survivors in House One—Eman Waleed—at length. "First, [the Marines] went into my father's room, where he was reading the Koran ... and we heard shots," the 9-year-old girl told McGirk. "I couldn't see their faces very well—only their guns sticking into the doorway. I watched them shoot my grandfather, first in the chest and then in the head. Then they killed my granny."[45]

Three days earlier, CNN had hinted about a coming scandal in Iraq, announcing that the military had begun a criminal investigation into the deaths of an unspecified number of Iraqi civilians in Haditha, but the network and other media reports were vague and unverified.

Incredibly, not only had MNF-W kept the incident secret from the world, but also commanders had not told the Pentagon or Bush administration officials. *Washington Post* reporter Thomas Ricks, the author of a book about the early days of the invasion, published a piece on the front page of the newspaper's June 4 edition saying that Secretary of Defense Donald Rumsfeld and the chairman of the Joint Chiefs of Staff—Gen. Peter Pace, the first Marine to ever hold that position—had not been informed about the incident until March 10, three months and 20 days after it occurred and only nine days before McGirk's story appeared.[46] According to Ricks, Rumsfeld and the military chiefs of staff were shocked. After the meeting, a Rumsfeld aide told Ricks that the news was "really, really bad—as bad or worse than Abu Ghraib."

Undoubtedly, Rumsfeld immediately got on the line to the White House while the Corps—worried about what affect the news might have on Corps appropriations—rushed a team of politically connected Marines to the Hill to begin briefing influential congressmen. The message: "Something highly disturbing had happened in Haditha, and its repercussions could be serious."[47] Almost certainly Representative John Murtha, a Democrat from Pennsylvania, and Representative John Kline, a Republican from Minnesota, were among those who received briefings. While Kline was only beginning his second term, Murtha was in his 16th. Both were known for their sympathy to the Corps' funding needs and both always came through. Both were decorated, retired Corps colonels and both had served in Vietnam: Kline as a helicopter pilot and Murtha as an intelligence officer. Murtha, the first Vietnam combat veteran to be elected to Congress, was awarded two Purple Hearts and a Bronze Star medal with a combat V.[48] Kline, who for a time flew Marine One, the presidential helicopter, had four Legion of Merit awards, a Meritorious Service Medal, and a Defense Superior Service medal.[49] Kline was on the House Armed Services Committee and Murtha was the top Democrat on the House Defense Appropriations Subcommittee.

A few days after the March 10 meeting, Rumsfeld directed the Corps commandant to "say nothing to anyone" about the Haditha incident.[50] But the barn door was open: the Corps had been to Congress, whose members demonstrably were unable to keep secrets. Soon, Murtha became the first lawmaker to publicly address the Haditha issue, and he had no good words for the Corps.

Part II: Repercussions

5. Kicking the Ant Hill

The *Time* story was particularly unwelcome in Washington, where the administration was trying to put a good face on an increasingly unpopular war. On March 16, 2006, CNN broadcast the results of its most recent public opinion poll showing that only 54 percent of Americans felt a victory in Iraq was either certain or likely—a drop of 40 percentage points from a similar poll taken three years earlier. "Moreover," CNN said, "41 percent of the respondents ... said the prospect of a U.S. victory is unlikely or certain not to happen." More cynical was the poll determination that the number of people who thought the war was morally justifiable had dropped 26 percentage points.[1]

While news about the Haditha incident almost certainly would increase the public's negativism, the administration was able to temporarily limit the damage to what *Time* had exposed. At first, reporters were frustrated by the Corps' wall of silence and the inability to conduct on-scene examinations on their own because Haditha was still a dangerous area. *Time* had learned about Watt's probe and his conclusion that the civilians were killed by Marines and not by the IED, as the Corps maintained. *Time* also knew about the CERP payments, but no one in the media was aware yet that Chiarelli had ordered a second 15-6 investigation or that the Corps had adamantly refused to conduct an investigation on its own until pressured by Chiarelli. And only the Corps knew that the civilian death toll actually was 40 percent higher than what had been alleged. What caused Maj. Gen. Zilmer to do a complete turnaround on Haditha, dramatically altering his "nothing to investigate" stance to one of admitting that something illegal might have occurred, remains a mystery. Likely, his decision was influenced by Watt's report and Chiarelli's persistence. The secretary of defense and the chairman of the Joint Chiefs of Staff, who had just been enlightened about the situation, also may have urged an investigation.[2]

During the weeks following the *Time* disclosure, the media teased out minor bits and pieces of the broader story, but no one had yet put the components together. *Time* provided some specifics about the units involved, but those details had not yet been tied to a decision by Lt. Gen. John F. Sattler on April 7 to relieve three unit commanders—Lt. Col. Chessani, Captain McConnell of K Company, and, inexplicably, Capt. James S. Kimber of I Company—of their duties. It is unknown why Kimber was included. India Company was based at Haqlaniyah, which was some distance from Haditha; no information was ever disclosed showing that the unit had been involved in the November 19 events. Kimber was not mentioned again.

Also unreported at the time was that a separate NCIS investigation was underway to determine if the death of a retired Iraqi policeman in Hamdania, a small town in Anbar Province distant from Haditha, had been a homicide. It was not until May 28 that the *Los Angeles Times* published a story saying that seven Marines and a corpsman from the 3rd Battalion, 5th Marines, were suspected of assassinating a man named Hashim Ibrahim Awad and trying to camouflage the crime by claiming he had been shot when he was discovered digging a hole for an IED.[3] Members of the unit suspected in the Hamdania case had no connection with the Haditha Marines except that both units were in the 1st Marine Division, which was a subordinate unit of the I Marine Expeditionary Force. As such, the I MEF legal division would be responsible for prosecuting both cases.

"In Cold Blood"

One of the better-known national politicians of the day was Representative John Patrick Murtha, a crusty Pennsylvania Democrat known among other things for his loyalty to the Corps and his hawkish position on military affairs. A retired Corps colonel with medals awarded for combat in Vietnam, Murtha had been in the House for 31 years and had the confidence of the Corps' top command because of his unstinting support whenever the institution sought financial help from Congress. However, those ties were indelibly damaged after he asked lawmakers in November 2005 to support a proposal to withdraw troops from Iraq. "Our military's done everything that has been asked of them," he told startled reporters. "The U.S. cannot accomplish anything further in Iraq militarily. It's time to bring the troops home."[4]

Not surprisingly, conservative politicians reacted scornfully. House speaker J. Dennis Hastert, a Republican of Illinois, accused Murtha of delivering "the highest insult to the troops" and of adopting a policy of "cut and run." Majority leader Roy Blunt, Republican of Missouri, said statements like those made by Murtha "only embolden our enemies," adding: "Democrats undermine our troops in Iraq from the security of their Washington, D.C., offices." Neither Hastert nor Blunt are veterans. Representative Geoff Davis, Republican of Kentucky, an Army veteran, said Murtha and those who agreed with his "shameful statements" had committed treason.[5] The most savage berating, though, came from freshman Representative Jean Schmidt, Republican of Ohio, who attacked Murtha from the House floor.

> A few minutes ago I received a call from Colonel Danny Bubp.... He asked me to send Congress a message: Stay the course. He also asked me to send Congressman Murtha a message that cowards cut and run, [but] Marines never do.[6]

Boos and catcalls resonated throughout the chamber. The public responded in indignation, and Schmidt was lampooned on *Saturday Night Live*. The *Cincinnati Enquirer*, which had supported Schmidt's run for Congress, scolded her, saying that she was "way out of line." Bubp, a Corps Reservist officer and an Ohio state legislator, denied his comments to Schmidt were meant as a criticism of Murtha. "We never discussed anyone by name and there was no intent to ever disparage the congressman or his distinguished record of service for our nation," he said. Schmidt, known in her congressional district as "Mean Jean," soon apologized. "There's no way that I remotely tried to impugn his character," she said. Her intent, she contended, was to say she thought U.S. troops should remain in Iraq. "First and foremost," she added, "I support the troops. They dodge bullets and bombs while I duck only hateful words."[7]

The furor over Murtha's bring-the-troops-home stance abated somewhat over the next year, but it erupted with even more force on May 17, 2006, after Murtha called another news conference to expand upon his views on Iraq. Reporters went to the event expecting to hear more from Murtha about troop withdrawal, but this time Murtha had an even more shocking message. Since the *Time* story almost two months earlier, Haditha had virtually disappeared from public view. Reporters, frustrated by the wall of silence surrounding the incident, had not been able to advance the story beyond the details revealed in the news magazine. Murtha changed that situation dramatically and irrevocably with a direct attack on the established Corps version of what had happened on November 19, 2005. While the Corps maintained that more than a dozen Iraqis had been killed in the IED explosion or in a firefight, Murtha said that was not true. "There was no firefight," Murtha said. "There was no IED. Our troops overreacted because of the pressure on them, and they killed innocent civilians in cold blood."[8]

Murtha was vague about his sources, saying only that his information came from "the top," which was not an improbable claim because Murtha was recognized as a Corps insider with unlimited access to the institution's hierarchy.

The public understandably was shocked; Murtha's disclosures were devastating. Immediately, there were demands for him to explain his contentions. Within days, he began appearing on television news programs to define his position.

On ABC, Charles Gibson asked Murtha why he seemed so sure that his recriminations were true. "The Commandant of the Marine Corps was in my office last week, so ... I know there was a cover-up someplace," Murtha replied. "[The Corps] knew about this a few days afterwards, and there's no question the chain of command tried to stifle the story."

> GIBSON: The commandant told you that this was a case of murder?
>
> MURTHA: The commandant said it was a very serious incident. He was not going to tell me it was murder, but everything looked to him just like it looks to me. He didn't say that in so many words, but he told me exactly what happened. A taxi pulled up, they killed [the men inside] in cold blood. They went into the houses and killed.... [The commandant] didn't say it was murder ... but what is it, Charles?[9]

CNN's Paula Zahn pressed Murtha to be more specific about the charges.

> ZAHN: You are accusing Marines of committing murder against innocent civilians in cold blood, even before the investigation is over. What's your evidence?
>
> MURTHA: Well, Paula, the highest level of the Marine Corps came to me. First, I started hearing stories in the Marine Corps ... then, in March, *Time* magazine came out with a story [in which the situation] became confused, and I think confused on purpose. This happened six months ago. Two days later, [the Corps] knew exactly what happened. They know that there was no hostile fire.[10]

It was more or less the same scenario on *CNN Morning with Soledad O'Brien*, except Murtha was more forthcoming about a Corps cover-up.

> O'BRIEN: You have said that you believe that, in fact, there was a cover up. How high do you think this goes, sir?
>
> MURTHA: Well ... Soledad, this is what worries me. We're fighting a war about America's ideals and democracies ideas and something like this happens and they try to cover it up. They knew the day after this happened that it was not as they portrayed it.

Just how bad was it? O'Brien asked. "It's as bad as Abu Ghraib, if not worse," Murtha replied.

> If I remember the circumstances [of My Lai], you're out in the field and they killed civilians, but they used the excuse that they looked like they were the enemy. Here,

there were no shots fired. There was no enemy action at all ... and [the Corps tries] to cover it up saying they were killed by an IED to confuse the message. They're still trying to confuse the message. There's no way you can confuse something like this. You just get the facts out; you get them out as quickly as you can."[11]

The story also was playing out in Washington, where reporters asked Press Secretary Tony Snow about President Bush's reaction. "I think anybody who's heard the story has a personal interest and it's impossible not to [be concerned]," Snow said. "But the president also is allowing the chain of command to do what it's supposed to do."[12]

It moved deeper into politics when Murtha appeared on *Meet the Press* and Tim Russert showed him a video of a Karl Rove interview in which Rove slammed Murtha and the Democrats, saying they couldn't be depended upon. "They may be with you at the first shots, but they are not going to be there for the last tough battles," Rove said. Murtha's face reddened. "[Rove] is sitting in his air-conditioned office on his big, fat backside, saying, 'Stay the course.' That's not a plan," Murtha responded.[13]

What prompted Murtha to utter such stunning accusations months before the Corps would admit that crimes *may* have been committed is not known and probably never will be because Murtha died without going into more detail and without revealing his sources.

BootMurtha

Predictably, the Congressman's comments had the effect of an exploding grenade: shrapnel flew everywhere in a haphazard pattern. Recognizing the dangers this could present, the Corps moved to contain possible leaks. Roughly simultaneously to the publication of the *Time* story—"around March 2006," according to the Corps—Col. David Lapan, director of public affairs, and Brig. Gen. Kevin Sandkuhler, staff judge advocate to the Corps commandant, distributed a "guidance" memo warning Marines to keep silent about the incident. "Refrain from commenting on any aspect of the case before the investigations are complete," the notice said. In the meantime, "All must actively avoid comments which appear to send signals 'down the chain' that indicate desired or expected results." If it was deemed appropriate, the document continued, "selected Marine Corps spokespersons and officials will release information to the public and respond to media queries."[14]

While conservatives at the national level strove to temper their remarks, there were no such restraints on the right-wing bloggers who flooded the Internet with invective. Virtually overnight, the web blossomed with new sites dedicated to denouncing Murtha. They went by such names as "BootMurtha," "CensureMurtha," "MurthaLied," and "MurthaMustGo!" The sites were rife with accusations that Murtha accepted bribes, committed treason, and did not earn his Vietnam combat medals. The bloggers had two motives for damning Murtha: They were livid because he accused Marines of murder, and they also were enraged because the congressman was vociferously against the Iraq War.

The mood carried over to conservative evening talk shows, such as those on Fox TV. Unlike Russert, O'Brien, Gibson, and Zahn, who questioned Murtha only about his statements, the conservative TV personalities denounced Murtha on a personal level. Bill O'Reilly accused Murtha of "bomb throwing" and casting aspersions on all U.S. military personnel. "I'm mad about it," O'Reilly said, castigating Murtha for not "[having] the stones to come on this program and back up what he says."[15] Glenn Beck labeled Murtha a "nightmare," adding that the Congressman had "put an umbrella over all of our troops and [tried] to make them all look like they were involved in something as horrific as this."[16] Neil Cavuto, another popular conservative personality, reviled Murtha for "trying to create another Abu Ghraib prison scandal."[17] Veteran talk-show guest Ann Coulter told a Denver radio audience that Murtha was "the reason soldiers invented fragging," adding, "If he did get fragged, he'd finally deserve one of those Purple Hearts."[18]

A year after Murtha made his statements, he was still under attack. "Uncle Jimbo," posting on the web site "Black Five," proposed the formation of a "National Committee to Horsewhip Murtha."

> John Murtha is not a bright man, he is not a noble man, he has not accomplished great things in Congress, or even many small things. He is a perfect representative of the swine who wallow in our Parliament of Whores.... He has been nominated for the disgrace of being the 2nd ex–Marine (Lee Harvey Oswald being the first), and now he has brought his meager intellect to the service of losing this war.[19]

Given the degree of anger expressed publicly and privately against Murtha, it was inevitable that the Congressman would be taken to court. Therefore, it was not a surprise when Wuterich sued Murtha for libel in a federal district court in Washington three months later. According to the document authored by high-profile Washington attorney Mark S. Zaid, Murtha used information that he "had no legitimate need-to-know" to "spread false and malicious lies about [Wuterich]." The information, the suit said, was "inaccurate and false" and was deliberately leaked to Murtha so he could attack innocent Marines. It did not say who provided the information or why Murtha may have been purposely lied to.[20]

Normally, members of Congress are protected from libel and slander suits by laws that give them considerable leeway in what they say or write as long as they are expressing themselves in an official capacity. Murtha's defense was that he was speaking as the ranking Democrat on the House Appropriations defense subcommittee when he made the Haditha statements. Wuterich's suit, however, contended Murtha had been talking as an individual and had therefore made himself vulnerable to legal action.

Because of Murtha, the suit said, Wuterich had been "embarrassed, mortified, and humiliated before the general public and has suffered emotional distress." The "loyal and caring soldier has been seriously harmed and will now always bear a stain of being associated with the Haditha incident," the document said.[21] The suit asked for $7,500 in damages, a public apology, and "an injunction prohibiting future publication of any allegations regarding [Wuterich]."[22]

Interestingly, Murtha had not been the only Congressman to question the behavior of the Haditha Marines. Representative John Kline, Republican of Minnesota, came to the same verdict as had Murtha after being briefed by a Corps commander. "This was a small number of Marines who fired directly on civilians and killed them," Kline said. "This is going to be an ugly story," he told *Time*.[23]

Kline was a member of the House Armed Services Committee and, like Murtha, a retired Marine colonel. Although conservative blogs repeatedly battered Murtha, there was no mention of Kline. Yet the Republican Congressman's remarks did not go unnoticed. After filing suit against Murtha on Wuterich's behalf, lawyer Zaid contacted Kline, saying he would file suit against him as well if he did not retract his statement. Zaid also told Murtha he would drop the suit if he would concede he had been wrong. Murtha refused, but Kline surrendered. On August 14—12 days after Wuterich's suit was filed— Kline issued a public apology:

> As a retired Colonel in the U.S. Marines, I am especially proud of the sacrifices our men and women make day in and day out, especially in combat situations. And as a Marine officer, I would never want to publicly insinuate, implicitly or explicitly, that I have prejudged what took place that day on the battlefield or afterwards.[24]

Congressional Investigation

Murtha's disclosures had the affect of an exploding grenade: shrapnel flew everywhere in an unpredictable pattern. The media, which had not been able to make any discernible progress because of the Corps' cloak of silence, was newly blessed with offers from dozens of previously zip-lipped sources who now appeared willing to talk because the congressman had opened the door. The *Washington Post* reported that the number of dead noncombatants had been 24 rather than the 15 originally listed by the Corps.[25] The *New York Times* quoted anonymous officials as saying they thought murder charges eventually would be preferred against some of the Marines.[26] And the *Los Angeles Times*—which circulates heavily in the Camp Pendleton area—said there was apparent photographic evidence showing the Iraqis were shot "execution style."[27] The newspaper also quoted an unnamed official as saying Marines "suffered a total breakdown in morality and leadership, with tragic results."[28]

By the end of May, media reports had gone far beyond the bare bones details published in *Time*; Haditha was an international story appearing in newspapers and on the top of news broadcasts around the world.

More ominously for the Corps, the incident also was drawing special, unwanted attention in Washington. Republican House Armed Services Committee chairman Duncan Lee Hunter, who represented a district in the shadow of Camp Pendleton, told the *Washington Post* his panel would hold oversight hearings on the issue.[29] Senator John Warner, Republican of Virginia, said he also planned to schedule hearings in the Senate Armed Services Committee.[30] Even Gen. Peter Pace, the first Marine chairman of the Joint Chiefs of Staff, expressed a desire to get to the bottom of the issue. "We need to make sure that we in the Armed Forces and those who observe us understand that, if that were ... if that did happen, it's an anomaly," he told NPR's Margaret Warner.[31]

On June 6, Senator Warner wrote Defense Secretary Donald Rumsfeld saying he wanted to bring the issue before the committee as soon as possible. By stressing the need for speed, Warner was expressing the frustration he had experienced in earlier unsuccessful attempts to get prompt hearings on Abu Ghraib. "Congress and the American people are entitled to a timely disclosure of the official findings," Warner wrote. "Delays in getting out the official findings of fact due to a protracted review process will mean a mixture of information, misinformation and unconfirmed facts will continue to spiral in the public domain."[32]

It is unknown how, when, or if Rumsfeld responded. In any case, Warner's request and Hunter's declaration dropped into an abyss. Hearings were never held in Congress; there were no explanations, and the media did not pursue the issue. This, perhaps, was one of the largest failures in the history of the Haditha episode. The apparent squashing of hearings, either by Rumsfeld or someone higher, deprived the world of its first and most credible opportunity to learn what happened at Haditha and why.

In actuality, the possibility of hearings chaired by either Warner or Hunter was dim from the get-go. Warner—a former Marine and secretary of the Navy under President Nixon—was a loyal Republican and faithful supporter of President Bush. If the administration did not want hearings, it is unlikely that Warner would persist. Duncan Lee Hunter—renowned in Congress for his hard-right stances—was an even less likely candidate to direct hearings into activities by the Haditha Marines. At the time, his son and eventual successor—Duncan Dwayne Hunter—was a captain in the Marine Corps Reserves and a veteran of the First Battle of Fallujah. Military votes were crucial to the father/son congressional ambitions since the district they represented—California's 52nd—stretched from the huge Navy/Marine complexes around San Diego to just south of Camp Pendleton.

As the result of congressional inaction, the responsibility for delving into details of the incident and assigning accountability fell solely on the Corps, which continued to ignore requests for a public explanation. On June 7, the Corps commandant, Gen. Hagee, confirmed to reporters at a 14-minute Pentagon news conference that investigations were underway into events in Haditha and Hamdania. However, he refused to divulge specifics, proclaiming what had become—and what would remain—the Corps mantra: "I cannot comment." He did not hesitate, though, to say what the consequences might be. "Make no mistake," he added, "a Marine who has been found to have violated our standards will be held accountable. It is an important part of who we are, and all Marines expect it. High standards and accountability define Marines."[33] Hagee retired from the Corps six months later, so he was not available for comment about accountability when the legal proceedings ended in 2012.

Glimpses into the Void

Although the Corps remained resolute in its refusal to provide information about the incident, persistent reporters filled the gap by scouring their Rolodexes and calling in favors from government sources cultivated over the years. National publications such as the *Washington Post* and the *New York Times* were best equipped because of connections in the capitol. The same could be said on the West Coast because of the *Los Angeles Times*' inroads into the sprawl of military facilities that dot southern California from Coronado Island to Camp Pendleton, some 60 miles to the north. Included in that arc are at least a dozen major bases, either Navy or Marine Corps.[34]

Josh White scored a coup for the *Washington Post* with a June 11 story quoting Neal A. Puckett, Wuterich's top civilian trial attorney. Even though Wuterich had not yet been charged, Puckett wanted to give his client's point of view in advance of the Corps' version, when and if that was ever articulated. "It will forever be his position that everything they did that day was following their rules of engagement and to protect the lives of Marines. He's really upset that people believe that he and his Marines are even capable of intentionally killing innocent civilians."[35]

Lawyers for two other members of 1st Squad who also were potential targets were quick to declare their clients' lack of involvement in possible criminal activity. Kevin B. McDermott, representing Capt. McConnell, said all his client was told on the day of the attack was that 15 civilians had been killed by a "mixture of small-arms fire and shrapnel as a result of grenades" following an attack from a nearby house. It was a curious statement in that McConnell led a Quick Reaction Force team that traveled on foot to the site of the IED explosion soon after the ambush was reported. McConnell said he was summoned to the Palm Groves before he could inspect the houses, but it is hard to grasp how he missed seeing the bodies of the five Iraqis from the white sedan, which were sprawled next to their vehicle only yards from the bombed Humvee. "It wasn't a situation that dawned on him ... where it was like, 'Okay, guys, we need to conduct a more thorough investigation,'" McDermott said.[36]

Gary Meyers, an attorney representing Lance Cpl. Sharratt, said the main issue facing Camp Pendleton lawyers when evaluating possible criminal culpability would be the ever-changing rules of engagement that prevailed at the time. "What this case comes down to," Meyers said, "is what were the rules of engagement and were they followed?"[37]

The *Los Angeles Times* chimed in ten days later with a story claiming that Army Maj. Gen. Bargewell concluded from his AR 15-6 investigation that commanders up and down the chain of command made the mistake of not recognizing the seriousness of the incident and failing to call for an investigation. Bargewell was sent to Haditha on March 9 to conduct a more thorough probe than that of his predecessor, Col. Watt. Operating with a larger team and the advantage of wearing two stars as opposed to a colonel's eagle, Bargewell and his group spent three months interviewing individuals and sifting through records maintained by Battalion 3/1, RCT-2, and the 2nd Division. The story said Gen. Chiarelli was still reviewing Bargewell's report, but an anonymous Department of Defense official read a portion of the executive summary to reporters over the telephone. "Virtually no inquiry at any level of command was conducted into the circumstances surrounding the deaths," the official quoted Bargewell as writing. "No follow-up actions regarding the civilian casualties were deemed necessary by the senior leadership of MNF-West [Gen. Stephen T. Johnson's command responsible for all Marines in Iraq]. Initial reports of K Company and its subordinate units were untimely, inaccurate and incomplete. They were conflicted, poorly vetted and forgotten once transmitted."[38]

If the rendition was accurate, the report was a condemnation of Corps operations that sucked in two two-star generals (Johnson of MNF-West and the 2nd Division's Huck), a colonel (Davis of RCT-2), a lieutenant colonel (3/1's Chessani), at least one captain (McConnell of K Company), a lieutenant (Kallop of Kilo's 3rd Platoon), and any number of enlisted personnel. The story's authenticity could not be verified for ten months because the Corps, which received the report in mid-summer, stamped it "Classified" to keep it secret.

However, the depiction was given credence by a similar story in the *New York Times* some two weeks later. Headlined "General Faults Marine Response to Iraq Killings," reporters Eric Schmitt and David S. Cloud quoted anonymous sources who had been briefed on Gen. Chiarelli's copy of the Bargewell report as saying "senior officers failed to follow up on inaccuracies and inconsistencies in the initial reporting of the incident that should have raised questions."[39]

Aggressive reporting kept the story alive over the summer, but media reports continued to lack verification. Until the Corps began to loosen its "no comment" policy or until reporters had actual documents they could sink their teeth into, the story could not move to the next level. Media efforts so far had focused on the "big picture" and a number of less-than-earthshaking developments were overlooked, ignored, or given short shrift. One was the disclosure that Wuterich, despite his alleged deep involvement in the Haditha killings, had been promoted during the interval. It seemed incongruous that while a captain and a lieutenant colonel had been relieved of their commands, the man allegedly at the heart of the incident had been promoted from sergeant to staff sergeant and given a $283-a-month pay raise. Apparently the only major outlet pointing this out was *Time*, which was scratching to hold onto its reportorial dominance of the story. Sally Donnelly wrote that the promotion had been in the works since October 2005, a month before the incident, and was routinely granted. Wuterich's new rank had become effective on January 1, 2006, two and a half months before *Time*'s original story.[40]

A development that received virtually no attention but that would later become highly significant was the Corps commandant's decision to designate the commander of Marine Corps Forces Central Command (MARCENT) as the Consolidated Disposition Authority for "disciplinary and administrative actions" stemming from the Haditha incident.[41]

Under a system that represses interpretation by almost anyone other than a military lawyer, what the commandant's action did was set up an unambiguous line of legal authority for the forthcoming prosecutions. The Corps—as do the other military branches—has provisions for an officer obligated to supervise more than one command at the same time. Called "dual-hatting," the arrangement bifurcates a commander's official duties. It applies in the Haditha situation in that the high-ranking officer called the Convening Authority (CA)—a.k.a. the "Consolidated Disposition Authority" or CDA—was mandated to walk a fine line when making court-martial decisions.

The Convening Authority for the Haditha and Hamdania cases was the lieutenant general commanding the I Marine Expeditionary Force/Marine Forces Central Command (I MEF/MARCENT). As the CA, the three-star officer wielded immense power over the court-martial process, including the authority to approve what criminal charges would be preferred and against whom. Under the system, a team of military lawyers directed by a staff judge advocate is responsible for examining accusations against individual Marines and then deciding which of them—in their professional judgment—should be accused of crimes appropriate for trial at a General Court-Martial. It is the second step in the process that often causes confusion, which proved particularly true in the Haditha cases. The system requires that the leader of the legal team—the SJA—submit the group's recommendations to the Convening Authority, who makes the final decision. What complicated the Iraq cases was that the I MEF chief was dual-hatted: he also was the MARCENT commander.

The commands are more than 2,000 miles apart; the I MEF is garrisoned at Camp Pendleton north of San Diego, while MARCENT is based at MacDill Air Force Base in Tampa, Florida. The I MEF operates independently, while MARCENT is subordinate to the U.S. Central Command (CENTCOM). The I MEF is composed of thousands of Marines but CENTCOM has no troops of its own. Instead, it is responsible for deciding how many troops will be deployed, and from which branch. When CENTCOM calls for troops, the affected "CENT" command—in this case MARCENT—becomes responsible for providing the bodies.[42] In other words, the I MEF is responsible for training and supplying Marines who are then consigned to

MARCENT, which arranges for their deployment according to CENTCOM's plan.

What would come to cause discord in the Haditha cases was that the I MEF and MARCENT both had legal staffs headed by a staff judge advocate. The commandant's June proclamation stipulated that the MARCENT SJA would be responsible for making court-martial recommendations to the Convening Authority. This was critical because it removed the I MEF SJA from the Haditha/Hamdania legal decision-making processes—a judgment that would become a major factor in the Chessani prosecution.

At the time of the commandant's June decision, the Haditha/Hamdania CA was Lt. Gen. Sattler, who had commanded the I MEF/MARCENT for almost two years. But he was scheduled for rotation in August; his replacement would be Lt. Gen. James Mattis, then the head of the Marine Corps Combat Development Command at the Pentagon. The change of commands—given its future significance—may have been the most unrecognized and underreported development of the summer. Apparently unmindful of the role Mattis would play in the Haditha cases, the national media made no note of his taking command. The only big-city newspaper to acknowledge the changing of the guard was the *San Diego Union-Tribune*, which sent a reporter to the ceremony at Camp Pendleton. However, the story on the event didn't mention Haditha until the 16th paragraph of a 22-paragraph story, and then it was brought up only in passing: "Marine commanders and enlisted men at the base are ... awaiting a report by the Naval Criminal Investigative Service on the actions of [a] Camp Pendleton squad that led to the deaths of 24 Iraqi civilians in the city of Haditha last November," it said.[43]

6. Charges

On March 13, 2006, a small contingent of NCIS agents arrived in Haditha, the vanguard of a force that eventually would grow to 65 men and women with headquarters both in Iraq and Washington. It would become the largest complement of investigators delegated to probe a single incident since a worldwide search was conducted for possible Marine spies in the wake of the Clayton Lonetree incident in 1986.[1]

Investigators had only two weeks to question Battalion 3/1 Marines in Iraq because the unit returned to Camp Pendleton on March 28. Nevertheless, the inquiry continued for more than four months, often at considerable physical risk to the agents because of the persisting violent unrest in Anbar Province. The agency submitted a preliminary report to the Corps on August 2, an inconvenient time to expect quick action because of the change of command at I MEF. The current commander, Lt. Gen. Sattler, was already either settling in as the new director of strategic plans and policy for the Joint Chiefs of Staff or packing his bags to report to the Pentagon. It is not known if his replacement, Lt. Gen. Mattis, was at Camp Pendleton, because he would not formally assume his new role until August 14. The final report, said to total some 3,500 words, would not be finished until November.

By mid-summer, the Corps had two documents dealing with the Haditha incident locked in its filing cabinets: the NCIS' Quick Look summary and the narrative compiled by Maj. Gen. Bargewell, the Army two-star dispatched to Haditha by Lt. Gen. Chiarelli after the Corps indicated it had no plans to investigate the incident. The Corps declared both documents "Secret" so they could not fall into the hands of the media.

Despite the Corps' efforts to conceal information about Haditha, it was inevitable that there would be leaks. In June, Wuterich's lead lawyer, Neal Puckett, told the *Washington Post* his client did not deliberately kill civilians. "It will forever be [Wuterich's] position that everything [his squad] did that day was following their Rules of Engagement and to protect the lives of Marines," Puckett said. "He's really upset that people believe that he and his Marines are even capable of intentionally killing innocent civilians."[2] Also in June, the *Los Angeles Times* published details said to be from a report compiled by Maj. Gen. Bargewell. The story quoted unnamed officials saying that, according to Bargewell, commanders in Multi-national Force–West were asleep at the wheel when it came to investigating the Haditha incident. "Virtually no inquiry at any level of command was conducted into the circumstances surrounding the deaths," Bargewell allegedly wrote. "There were, however, a number of red flags and opportunities to do so."[3]

July was quiet, but the media came roaring back in August. First, the *New York Times* had its turn with the Bargewell report. Reporter David S. Cloud went to print with an article claiming the Kilo Company log book—theoretically a meticulously kept document designed to record unit activities daily—was missing the pages that were supposed to contain entries for November 19, 2005, the day of the incident. Also quoting anonymous sources, Cloud wrote that Bargewell disclosed that Wuterich had been on duty in Company K's operations center where the log book was kept. "No conclusions are drawn about who may have tampered with the log," Bargewell is said to have written.[4]

The next day, Thomas E. Ricks had a story in the *Washington Post* quoting Chessani as saying he was not concerned about the incident because he considered it a legitimate combat action. Attributing the information to "a person sympathetic to the enlisted Marines involved in the case," Ricks quoted Chessani as saying, "I thought it was very sad, very unfortunate, but at the time, I did not suspect any wrongdoing from my Marines."[5] The newspaper said the quote came from Chessani's statement to NCIS investigators on March 20, 2006, eight days before the unit returned to Camp Pendleton. "The statement provides the first public look at comments from a key commander who oversaw the action there and bolsters the defense argument that troops involved in the Haditha incident saw the events as part of the normal course of combat," Ricks wrote.[6]

The *Post* struck again five days later with a story claiming the HET photographer who documented the IED scene soon after the incident did not see anything to make him believe the events had been anything other than a legitimate response to an insurgent attack. The information, the newspaper said, came from a source "sympathetic to the enlisted Marines facing scrutiny for the shootings."[7] Most likely, it was the same source quoted by Ricks.

According to the source, Sgt. Justin Laughner was questioned by two unnamed colonels for more than a half hour about his impressions when he photographed the scene. Laughner was said to reply that the action taken by the men of 1st Squad seemed to fit in with what he had been told by members of 1st Squad—that the assaults had been triggered by insurgent fire coming from a house near the IED blast. When they entered the house, Laughner said, they believed they heard someone "racking" an AK-47, which would be justification for aggressive tactics. "From what the Marines had told me and from what I understood from them, that I can't say I wouldn't have done the same thing in their situation," Laughner allegedly said. "If I hear somebody racking AK rounds, and I don't know how many guys are there, I'm going to protect me and my guys."[8]

Charges Announced

Lacking any outstanding developments to report, the media took an autumn holiday from Haditha. From Labor Day to December, the media was more interested in the prosecution of the war and its effect on the public. On September 25, 2006, CNN announced that a new poll showed that opposition to the conflict had reached a new high. Only 35 percent of respondents said they favored the hostilities while 61 percent were in opposition.[9] There also was considerable attention on the forthcoming U.S. Senate elections and, after November 8, news of the resignation of Defense Secretary Rumsfeld.

However, Haditha leaped back into prominence in December—four and a half months after the NCIS submitted an abbreviated report to the Corps and 13 months after the incident. On Thursday, December 21, reporters jammed into a meeting room at Camp Pendleton at 1:30 p.m. in response to a summons saying the Corps was going to make a significant statement about Haditha. It was the first and last time the Corps addressed the case as a whole.

At center stage was Col. Stewart Navarre, chief of staff for Marine Corps Installations West. Skipping preliminaries, Navarre read an 800-word prepared statement announcing that criminal charges had been preferred against eight Marines from Battalion 3/1 in connection with the Haditha incident.[10] Four officers, Navarre said, were accused of various crimes ranging from dereliction of duty to obstruction of justice. Among the four was Lt. Col. Chessani, the former commander of Battalion 3/1, in limbo since being relieved of his command eight months earlier. Also included was Capt. McConnell, former commander of Company K, who had been relieved at the same time as Chessani, only a few days after the battalion returned from its Haditha deployment. The other two officers were virtual strangers to the media: Capt. Randy Stone, the battalion's former lawyer, and 1st Lt. Andrew Grayson, commander of K Company's Human Exploitation Team. The remaining four were enlisted men, all former members of 1st Squad. Heading the list was Wuterich, who was accused of 19 counts of unpremeditated murder. The others were Sgt. Sanick Dela Cruz and Lance Cpls. Justin Sharratt and Stephen Tatum. Dela Cruz had been with Wuterich at the "white sedan" confrontation; Sharratt had been present at the assaults on all three houses; Tatum had participated in the assaults on houses One and Two. An interesting point was the Corps' confession that it had botched the November 20, 2005, news release saying 15 civilians were killed in he IED explosion or in a firefight with insurgents. "We now know with certainty the press release was incorrect, and that none of the civilians were [sic] killed by the IED explosion," Navarre said.[11] The Corps rarely admits making a mistake.

Navarre hurriedly left the room after reading the statement, refusing to answer questions or elaborate upon the charges. "In order to preserve the integrity of that investigation, and to ensure fair and impartial legal proceedings, we will not discuss evidence or specific findings of the investigations," he said.[12]

Inexplicably absent from the list were Cpl. Salinas and Pfc. Mendoza—both of whom took active roles in the assaults on houses One and Two—2nd Lt. Kallop, who gave the "clear" order, and any member of RCT-2 or the 2nd Marine Division.

The death penalty was not on the table because the Convening Authority—Lt. Gen. Mattis—had not deemed it applicable. For a number of complicated reasons, military death sentences are rare and executions even rarer. At the time the Haditha charges were announced, there were only six service members on military death row; the last execution had been in 1961 when Army Pfc. John A. Bennett was hanged for raping an Austrian girl.[13]

Table 2
Accused and Charges

	Charges	Punishment		
		LWOP	Yrs	Mos
Lt. Col. Jeffrey Chessani	Willful dereliction of duty.	—	—	6
	Willful dereliction of duty.	—	—	6
Capt. Lucas McConnell	Willful dereliction of duty.	—	—	6
	Willful dereliction of duty.	—	—	6
Capt. Randy Stone	Violating a lawful order.	—	2	—
	Two counts of negligent dereliction of duty	—	—	3
	Willful dereliction of duty.	—	—	6

	Charges	Punishment		
		LWOP	Yrs	Mos
1st Lt. Andrew Grayson	Obstruction of justice.	—	5	—
	Two counts of willful dereliction of duty.	—	—	6
	Three counts of making a false statement.	—	5	—
	Two counts of attempting to illegally separate from the Corps.	—	5	—
Sgt. Sanick Dela Cruz	Five counts of unpremeditated murder.	x	—	—
Staff Sgt. Frank Wuterich	Eighteen counts of unpremeditated murder.	x	—	—
	Two counts of soliciting another to make a false statement.	—	5	—
	Making a false statement.	—	5	—
Lance Cpl. Justin Sharratt	Three counts of unpremeditated murder.	x	—	—
Lance Cpl. Stephen Tatum	Aggravated assault.	—	8	—
	Reckless endangerment.	—	1	—
	Two counts of unpremeditated murder.	x	—	—
	Four counts of negligent homicide.	—	3	—
	Assault.	—	8	—

However, there was still the threat of significant punishment. If each of the Marines was convicted as charged and the maximum sentences imposed, the results would be long prison terms, fines, and dismissal from the Corps. Wuterich could be sentenced to 19 terms of life without possibility of parole (LWOP), plus 15 years for the other offenses. Tatum could get two life sentences, plus 20 years; Dela Cruz, five LWOP terms plus five years, and Sharratt, three life terms. Officers would not have to serve as long in prison, but conviction could result in dismissal from the Corps.[14] This would be devastating for Chessani, a Corps "lifer," who could lose his pension, plus possibly be sentenced to three years in prison. McConnell could be sentenced to one year; Stone to two and a half years.[15] Even though military lawyers had more than four months between the end of the NCIS investigation and the leveling of charges, they still bungled the process. Charges against Grayson were amended a week later to include two counts of violating a UCMJ article entitled "Attempts." The Corps declined to explain the charge, but it later became apparent that the former HET intelligence officer was accused of "attempting" to get a discharge from the Corps to which he was not entitled. If convicted of all charges against him, Grayson could be sentenced to 20 years in prison.

Civilians have a tendency to view dereliction of duty as a relatively minor offense, although that is not true; the military treats dereliction as a very serious offense punishable by prison time, fines, and dismissal. The UCMJ breaks "dereliction" into two categories: the more serious offense is willful (intentional) dereliction, which is punishable by a bad-conduct discharge, forfeiture of all pay and allowances, and up to six months' confinement. However, negligent dereliction—exhibiting "a lack of ... degree of care which a reasonably prudent person would have exercised under the same or similar circumstances"—is punishable by forfeiture of two-thirds pay per month for three months and confinement for three months. Chessani, Grayson, and McConnell were accused of willful dereliction; Stone with both willful and negligent dereliction.

In the months and years ahead, charges were added, modified, or dismissed, but as the accusations stood at the beginning of 2007, the outlook from the Marines' point of view was disheartening: the list of charges and potential punishments seemed formidable. This appeared to be especially true for Chessani and Wuterich, the men in the spotlight. Wuterich was the leader who allegedly had encouraged the killings, and Chessani was the battalion chief allegedly so out of touch with events in his command he had been unable to recognize a potential war crime. Going into 2007, there was the assumption that they would be the main targets of a hand-picked team of prosecutors called Team Charlie, said to be the "best of the best."

The NCIS Report

The announcement that charges had been preferred did little to satisfy the fact-hungry media; there were still too many secrets, too many unanswered questions. By refusing to disclose even minor details and locking up documentation, the Corps set itself up to be a media target. Among the important unreleased documents were two reports dealing with the incident, both of which had been in the Corps' possession for months. One was the chronicle compiled by Maj. Gen. Bargewell; the other was the NCIS report. Apparently, the Corps intended to keep those hidden permanently. However, the Corps failed to reckon with media ingenuity.

The *Washington Post* achieved a major breakthrough only 16 days after the Corps announcement when it published a 3,000-word story based on a copy of the NCIS report that the newspaper had obtained from an unidentified source.[16] Some of the items mentioned in the story were known, but there was an abundance of new information as well, details that could have come only directly from the voluminous report. *Post* writer Josh White, quoting from the document, revealed how one of the Iraqi soldiers who had been passengers in the convoy's Vehicle Three—Sgt. Asad Amer Mashoot—reacted to the shooting of the men from the white sedan.

He told investigators he watched in horror as the four students and the taxi driver fell. "They didn't even try to run away. We were afraid from Marines and we saw them behaving like crazy. They were yelling and screaming."[17]

More damaging for the Marines was the suspicion among NCIS investigators that the men of 1st Squad failed to follow the Rules of Engagement (ROE) requirement that positive identification of suspected insurgents is necessary before opening fire. If that were to be proved, it could seriously damage the Marines' defense since the ROE are regarded as the battlefield bible; they define combat zone conduct, setting forth specific circumstances when Marines may use their weapons and against whom. One of the stipulations unambiguously warns against targeting civilians. In an apparent attempt to demonstrate how this rule may have been violated, White paraphrased a section of the report in which investigators recorded a statement from one of the survivors in House Two, a 13-year-old girl named Safah Yunis Salem:

> She said she played dead to avoid being shot. Her sister Aisha, 3, was shot in the leg and died; her brother Zainab, 5, was killed by a shot to the head. She said she lost five other members of her family in the room, including her mother. "[A Marine] fired and killed everybody. The American fired and killed everybody."[18]

According to White, the report provided a comprehensive narrative of events beginning at reveille in Firm Base Sparta and running throughout the day. However, White said that the document was often inarticulate, wandering from one point to another without creating a unifying narrative. It contained transcripts of "hundreds of interviews with Marines, Iraqi soldiers and civilian survivors," White pointed out, but it also "presented a fragmented and sometimes conflicting chronicle of the violence that day."[19] It also revealed that the stories of the Haditha Marines were not of a piece: the men disagreed on some vital issues and seemed genuinely confused about others. Some of the men believed they were taking fire from a house south of the IED site; others said they were unaware they might have been under attack. In an interview with investigators, Wuterich admitted he told the fire team to use force. "I told them to treat it as a hostile environment.... I told them to shoot first, ask questions later."[20] Once they were inside House One, the report said, the men thought they had further justification to use violent tactics because one of them—Tatum—reported hearing a rifle being prepared to fire—"racked," in military terminology. They assaulted House Two "after suspecting that insurgents might have escaped." They used the same methods in House Two that they had applied in House One—prep the environment with grenades, then open fire with their M-16s. "I fired because I had been told the house was hostile and I was following my training that all individuals in a hostile house are to be shot," Mendoza told investigators.[21] "The documents," White wrote, "show that Marines ... reported the incident to their base as it was happening and made clear that there were a significant number of civilian casualties." He also wrote, "Though at first the Marines classified eight of the civilians as insurgents, they quickly reported that at least 15 civilians had been killed in what they called 'crossfire' with the enemy.... The hectic nature of the day caused some early reports to be confused and inaccurate."[22]

One of the unanswered questions from the earlier stories had been whether McConnell, the company commander, had questioned the members of 1st Squad in the wake of the incident to get details while they were still fresh in the men's minds. He had not. "Investigators wrote that McConnell did not want to question his Marines on a day they lost a comrade but that he informed his superiors about the civilian deaths."[23] Normally, such a debrief is routine and vital to the compilation of an After Action Report. Such documents, the Corps feels, "support training and planning for both exercises and operations, and the warfighting capability development process."

As for Chessani's decision not to call for an investigation, the NCIS report said the battalion commander was told by his immediate superior, Col. Davis of RCT-2, that a probe was not necessary. "There was nothing out of the ordinary about any of this, including the number of civilian dead, that would have triggered anything in my mind that was out of the norm," Davis told the NCIS. There is nothing about this incident that jumped out at any point to us."[24] According to the report, Maj. Gen. Huck concurred. "Nothing in the brief [about the incident] caused any concern to me. I do not recall if the brief discussed the number of Iraqis killed that day, but I do recall the brief discussing Marines clearing houses following the IED attack."[25] Huck also was quoted as saying that he summarily dismissed the queries from *Time* out of hand because he believed they originated with the insurgents.

The Corps was not happy with the fact that the *Post* had been slipped a copy of the report. Neither were attorneys who had been hired to defend some of the Marines. Two days after the story was published, Houston lawyer Jack Zimmerman, representing Lance Cpl. Tatum, and Neal Puckett, Wuterich's lead civilian counsel, complained to Lt. Gen. Mattis, demanding an investigation to determine who had leaked the material. "I think whoever did it should be severely sanctioned," said Zimmerman. "[The information in the story] hasn't been subject to cross examination."[26] It was never disclosed if an investigation was conducted or if the leaker was found.

7. Outflanking the Corps

"I shot them," Staff Sergeant Wuterich admitted to millions of viewers tuned in to the popular current events program *60 Minutes* on the third Sunday of March 2007, one day shy of a year since *Time* exposed the incident in Haditha. Speaking calmly and impassively, Wuterich readily acknowledged his actions on Route Chestnut. "They were trying to run away," Wuterich said, referring to the five men from the white Opel sedan that arrived at the IED site immediately after the explosion, "so I shot them."[1]

"They were running away?" interviewer Scott Pelley asked in feigned shock.

"Yes," Wuterich replied.

"So you shot them in the back?"

"Yes."

Followers of *60 Minutes* watched spellbound as Wuterich, appearing in brilliant high definition on TV sets around the world, patiently recounted his memories of the events that occurred on November 19, 2005. Hundreds of stories had been written about the incident, but no reporter—until Pelley—had been able to get an on-the-record interview with Wuterich. His presence on the well-respected program represented a major coup for CBS. It was Wuterich's first interview and would be his last for five years.

Far from being uneasy on international TV, Wuterich—whose only known previous public oratory had taken place when he was on a stage as a member of his high school drama club—looked as comfortable as if he and Pelley were old friends chatting away over a freshly drawn latte. Wearing a patterned tie and a dark sports coat to hide a gruesome tattoo depicting a line of skewered fingers and eyeballs that streamed down his left arm, Wuterich stared unblinkingly into the camera, exuding an air of choirboy innocence. "Everyone visualizes me as a monster ... a baby killer ... cold-blooded ... that sort of thing," he said softly. "That's not accurate. And neither is the story that most of them know of this incident. They need to know the truth."[2]

Wuterich's version of the truth was not complicated. He and 11 fellow members of 1st Squad had been returning to their headquarters from an early morning mission when their convoy was attacked with an IED. The blast had been horrific, Wuterich said, reducing Terrazas's body "to a pile of flesh." He described the sight: "[Terrazas] was missing one of his arms, his legs were completely severed from his body, but they were still attached because for some reason his Cami's didn't rip completely."

Wuterich said he was still trying to absorb that vision into his consciousness when the Opel pulled up. "My first thought," Wuterich continued, "was that it might be a car bomb." Either that or one of the occupants may have been the insurgent who remotely triggered the IED. Wuterich eyed the men suspiciously as they obeyed Lance Cpl. Dela Cruz' rough order to get out of the vehicle. They stood looking at him, he said, and he could not understand why.

> Normally, the Iraqis know the drill.... They know if something happens, they know exactly what to do. Get down, hands up, and completely cooperate. These individuals were doing none of that. They got out of the car [and] as they were going around [it] they started to take off, so I shot at them.[3]

Pelley asked Wuterich—for the benefit of members of the audience who might not be familiar with warzone regulations—to explain the significance of the alleged attempt by the men to flee.

Wuterich nodded. First there was the Rules of Engagement (ROE), he said—a concise list of restrictions governing conduct on the battlefield. The prime commandment was the need to establish positive identification, or PID. "It means that you need to be able to positively identify your target before you shoot to kill," Wuterich explained. Once that was accomplished, a service member was allowed to open fire if he felt threatened. It also was permissible, Wuterich added, to shoot anyone displaying "hostile intent." Hostile intent trumped PID. "That was the biggest thing, "Wuterich said. "If they had used a hostile act against you, you could use deadly force."

Pelley looked puzzled. How could fleeing men be interpreted as a demonstration of hostile intent? Wuterich explained:

> Because [it demonstrated] hostile action, if they were the triggermen, would have blown up the IED, which would also constitute hostile intent. But also at the same time, there were military-aged males that were inside that car. The only vehicle, the only thing that was out, that was Iraqi, was them. They were 100 meters away from that IED. Those are the things that went through my mind before I pulled the trigger. That was Positive Identification (PID).[4]

Had his suspicions been justified? Pelley asked. Did a search of the vehicle turn up any indication that the men were insurgents?

WUTERICH: "As far as I know, there wasn't anything found."
PELLEY: "And they were unarmed?"
WUTERICH: "Yes."[5]

Turning to the assault on House One, Pelley asked Wuterich why he suspected there were insurgents inside the dwelling.

"Shots!" Wuterich replied quickly. "Sporadic shots. I think I heard two or three, two or three shots from the south," which was the direction of houses One and Two.

"Why that specific house?" Pelley inquired.

"This building was right in the line of sight of this explosion," Wuterich said, although he admitted he had no visual proof that someone inside was shooting at the squad.

PELLEY: "You did not see fire coming from the house, correct?"
WUTERICH: "I did not see muzzle flashes coming from the house, correct."
PELLEY: "If you didn't hear rounds coming from the house, how did you identify the house as a threat?"
WUTERICH: "Because that was the only logical place that the fire could come through seeing the environment there."[6]

Pelley asked Wuterich how he knew the procedure for assaulting a structure if he had never participated in in any previous house-clearings. Four of the men in his squad were veterans of Fallujah, Wuterich said, and they knew how to approach a house that was occupied by armed insurgents.

"Help me understand," Pelley implored. "You're in a residence. How do you crack a door open and roll a grenade into a room?"

"At that point, you can't hesitate to make a decision," Wuterich said. "Hesitation equals being killed, either yourself or your men."

PELLEY: "But when you roll a grenade into a room through the crack in the door, that's not Positive Identification. That's taking a chance on anything that could be behind that door."
WUTERICH: "Well, that's what we do. That's how our training goes."[7]

"Didn't you think you might have killed civilians?" Pelley asked.

Wuterich said he recalled seeing multiple bodies when he peeked into a bedroom in House One. "I remember there may have been women ... may have been children ... in there." However, that was not enough to convince him to call off the attack because he was still worried about the safety of his men.

After employing Fallujah-style tactics to clear House One, the fire team turned to House Two, which they decided to assault because they thought an insurgent had escaped through an open rear door.[8] They used the same clearing method in the second house that they had used in the first, Wuterich said. "We went through that house much the same [way], prepping the room with grenades, going in there, and eliminating the threat and engaging the targets." He paused. "There probably wasn't [a threat], [but] now that I look back on it ... there—in that time—yes, I believed there was a threat."

After learning that all those killed had been noncombatants, Pelley asked Wuterich if he wished he had acted differently.

"No," Wuterich said firmly. "I would make the same decision today."

"You can't mean that!" Pelley exclaimed. "Think of the women and all the children."

"What I'm talking about are the tactics," Wuterich explained. "It doesn't sit well with me that women and children died. We reacted to how we were supposed to react to our training and I did that to the best of my ability." He continued:

> You know the rest of the Marines that were there, they did their job properly as well. Did we know that civilians were in there? No. Did we go in those rooms, you know, it would have been one thing, if we went in those rooms and looked at everyone and shot them. You know, we cleared these houses the way they were supposed to be cleared.[9]

Pelly then addressed an issue that had been raised in numerous media reports. Did the fire team kill the civilians because they were trying to avenge the death of Terrazas and the wounding of Guzman and Crossan? Pelley asked:

> The accusation is made that your men went berserk [after] you got hit by an IED; one of the favorite guys in the squad was cut in half and lying in the road and your guys went nuts. You dropped the five guys next to the car because they happened to be there and then you went to the closest house and then you went down the hallway throwing grenades and shooting and you just killed everybody you could find.[10]

"That's absolutely untrue," Wuterich said. "My emotion was pushed back; my training came into play. But going completely crazy and acting wild, I don't know who came up with that, but it's false."

Pelley asked bluntly: "Was it a massacre?"

"No! Absolutely not!" Wuterich replied. "A massacre in my mind, by definition, is a large group of people being executed, being killed for absolutely no reason and that's absolutely not what happened here."[11]

Consequences

The Corps must have been hugely embarrassed by "Killings in Haditha." Pelley and a crew from *60 Minutes* had breached the command's regulations regarding media contacts and spent a day or more filming an interview with the one Marine that the Corps wanted most to keep under cover. When the program was shown on prime-time television, it apparently was a total surprise to the Corps. Unbelievably, no one in the I MEF/MARCENT command had anticipated that the media would go to such extraordinary lengths to get any of the Haditha Marines, particularly Wuterich, on tape. It is interesting that none of the other accused talked on the record to reporters. True to form, no Camp Pendleton commander explained the lapse in allowing Pelley's access to Wuterich. Clearly, Puckett, Wuterich's wily civilian attorney, engineered the CBS plan. As a retired Marine colonel and former judge, Puckett was well familiar with how to evade the Corps' bureaucracy, slipping into and out of Wuterich's house without raising official suspicion or risking comeback.

The Corps' ears may have been red, but in actuality there was nothing the Corps could have done to stop *60 Minutes* other than putting a guard on Wuterich's door or tossing him in the brig, neither of which was feasible. Civilians undoubtedly wondered why Wuterich wasn't behind bars to begin with. Although he had not yet been charged when the interview was taped in November or early December 2006, he was suspected of being involved in the murder of almost two dozen Iraqi civilians. He and Puckett were aware that Wuterich was in the prosecution's sights; witness the libel suit he filed against Representative Murtha in August. If Wuterich had been a civilian suspected of participating in the deaths of 18 women and children, he almost certainly would have been in jail or out on bail and under court-imposed restrictions. But Wuterich was not a civilian and those killed had been foreigners—not Americans—and they had died in a foreign country during a war.

One thing that makes the military society different is the armed force's attitude toward incarceration: the military is considerably more hesitant to order pretrial incarceration than civilian authorities. Considering the dissimilarities in the societies, this is understandable. For one thing, service members live in a disciplined, tightly regulated community whose members generally are law-abiding. For another, base jails are overcrowded, and commanders would rather use the available space to house service members who already have been convicted. Finally, pretrial incarceration involves a heavy commitment for prosecutors who would otherwise be required to spend significant amounts of time keeping up with the paperwork in order to comply with restrictions involving hearings, time clocks, and the requirements to provide for a speedy trial. Generally, the military does not order pretrial confinement unless they feel the service member is either a flight risk or potentially dangerous to himself or others. Wuterich did not meet those qualifications, so he was not confined to the brig. Conversely, the initial convening authority for cases involving seven Marines and a Navy corpsman from another unit—the 3rd Battalion, 5th Marines—handled the situation differently. The men from Battalion 3/5—referred to in the media as the Pendleton 8—were accused of killing a retired Iraqi policeman in the village of Hamdania (which was east of Haditha but west of Baghdad), and then trying to cover up the episode.[12]

The Hamdania murder occurred on April 26, 2006, five months *after* Haditha. Unlike the Haditha incident, the Hamdania event was discovered almost immediately. The men suspected of the killing were arrested in Iraq and flown under guard back to Camp Pendleton. Once they arrived, they were incarcerated and remained in the brig until the trials were completed 14 months later. The Corps never explained why the men composing the group known as the Pendleton eight were jailed while the Haditha accused were not.

When charges were preferred against the Hamdania group in June 2006, the convening authority was Lt. Gen. John Sattler. Presumably, he was the one who ordered the confinements. Some three months later, Lt. Gen. Mattis replaced Sattler as commander of I MEF/MARCENT, inheriting the job of convening authority for criminal cases stemming from the wars in Iraq and Afghanistan. It was never explained why Mattis did not order incarceration for the men of Battalion 3/1 or the release, pending trial, of the men from Battalion 3/5. Whoever made the decision (apparently Mattis) that kept the Haditha Marines out of the lockup apparently did not consider the consequences. Because Haditha was a hot media topic and Hamdania was not, the media more than likely would focus on the Haditha accused, especially Wuterich. If putting him behind bars—provided such an act could have withstood a challenge from the staff sergeant's defense team—was the only foolproof way of keeping him away from the media, it might have been worth it. His appearance on prime-time television would haunt the Corps in ways that no one anticipated; it proved to be a major contributing factor in the bungled attempts to bring Wuterich quickly to trial.

The Winners

Wuterich's appearance on *60 Minutes* was notable in two ways. One, as a Marine suspected of slaughtering Iraqi civilians, he had not appeared in the media as a sympathetic figure. This assessment shifted dramatically after his interview was broadcast. Because he remained unflustered when questioned by a skilled interviewer on a program renowned for being tough on guests—

and because he gave intelligent-sounding answers to Pelley's less-than-in-depth queries—he was viewed as amiable by those in certain sections of the population. One of the goals Wuterich's lawyers had hoped to achieve when arranging the interview was to shatter the popular view of the staff sergeant as a hardhearted killer. Instead, they wanted him to be seen as a victim of a sensationalist, liberal media and as a target of a bureaucracy that was looking for a scapegoat. As far as changing Wuterich's public image, the *60 Minutes* presentation probably was more successful than its planners had projected. During his 29 minutes of air time, Wuterich came across as the boy next door: a down-to-earth, dedicated Marine who simply was trying to do his job so he could return safely to his pregnant wife and two young daughters. Uncounted thousands of viewers were so impressed by his performance that they sent donations to help cover his legal fees. However, it was never disclosed how much was collected or how the money was spent. Generally overlooked was the fact that it was a remarkably self-serving exercise: Wuterich had nothing to lose but a lot to gain by seeming forthcoming, congenial and innocent. In reality, the interview was not an interrogation of the type one normally would have expected from a *60 Minutes* host. Pelley's role was limited to expositions of shock and dismay; his arsenal lacked fact-based rejoinders to Wuterich's answers. Wuterich guided the interview, not Pelley.

A much more serious consequence of the interview was the damage it inflicted on Wuterich's prosecution: it led directly to a series of legal maneuvers that delayed Wuterich's trial for almost two years. His lawyers' strategy in circumventing Corps regulations regarding media access to Wuterich put Corps prosecutors in a predicament. If CBS had followed Corps protocols by asking the Camp Pendleton Public Affairs Office for permission to interview Wuterich, the request unquestionably would have been refused. However, if it had *not* been rejected, the Corps would have made sure a lawyer and a videographer were present throughout the Pelley interrogation. If the Corps had been able to make its own tape of the process, the problems that later surfaced might have been avoided.

When prosecutors examined a transcript of the interview, they noted significant differences between what Wuterich told Pelley and what he had told NCIS investigators several months earlier. The discrepancies were in the prosecution's favor, that is, Wuterich admitted to actions he had not disclosed to NCIS agents—admissions that could be used against Wuterich at trial. On further consideration, prosecutors grew curious about what additional admissions Wuterich may have made that did not make it on the air—statements that may have been left on the cutting-room floor during the film-editing process. In other words, what statements from Wuterich had film editors deleted when preparing the finished product that also might be used against the staff sergeant in his court-martial? The attempt to obtain these clippings—called "outtakes" in the industry—evolved into a major prosecutorial quest.

An overall evaluation of the interview showed that Wuterich and Puckett emerged as the clear victors. The program not only helped change public opinion, it set the stage for a drawn-out legal battle between the Corps and CBS that proved of enormous benefit to Wuterich's defense. Even better, the defense could remain aloof from the fight, standing aside while the government and lawyers for CBS expended considerable amounts of money, time and energy on a process that ultimately provided almost nothing the prosecution could use in court.

While the defense slipped into a wait-and-watch mode, the team undoubtedly was considering what it could gain from Wuterich's comments to Pelley about how he and the men in 1st Squad had performed in following the Rules of Engagement during the Haditha assaults. Although Pelley did not go into the subject in detail during the interview, Wuterich could have been correct when he said that he ordered his men to treat houses One and Two as "hostile" and that the assaults that followed may have been conducted within the boundaries of the ROE. According to the ROE in effect at the time, Marines were prohibited from "firing into civilian populated areas or buildings *unless the enemy is using them for military purposes or if necessary for your self-defense*" (author's emphasis). That rule, No. 1 (d), apparently supersedes rule No. 1 (a), which says PID "is required prior to an engagement." PID is defined as "a reasonable certainty that the proposed target is a legitimated military target." The ROE document is brief enough to be printed on both sides of a wallet-sized card, but its complications lie in the service member's ability to recognize a situation in a split second, and then in applying the rules immediately and correctly. Whether the men of 1st Squad followed the ROE would be fodder in the forthcoming court battles.

8. The Bargewell Report

Major General Eldon Bargewell was counting the weeks until retirement when Lt. Gen. Chiarelli asked him to temporarily leave his job as chief of operations for coalition forces in Iraq to go to Anbar Province to investigate the Haditha incident. After a 38-year career that began as a Special Forces staff sergeant in Vietnam—where he was wounded seven times and earned a drawerfull of awards including four Purple Hearts and the Distinguished Service Cross—the 59-year-old Bargewell was universally viewed as incorruptible, evenhanded, and impervious to pressure.[1] After Vietnam and his commissioning as a second lieutenant, Bargewell rose to command the Special Forces Operational Detachment–Delta (the shadowy unit commonly referred to as Delta Force) and Special Operations Forces in Europe, and to serve as operations chief for the U.S. Special Operations Command, a strategic unit designed to execute global operations against terrorist networks. He went to Baghdad as Gen. Casey's right-hand man in April 2005.

Bargewell and his team arrived in Haditha at about the same time as the first of the NCIS investigators. Although the groups would be conducting parallel investigations, their goals differed widely. NCIS—which eventually would flood the field with more than five dozen agents—focused on searching for evidence of misconduct that might lead to courts-martial. Bargewell's team—which probably consisted of only a handful of members—operated under the limitations of the AR 15-6 regulation that forbids probing for unlawful activity. As directed by Chiarelli, Bargewell had three objectives: (1) Determine what training the Marines received in southern California before deploying and whether the instruction had been sufficient to help them complete their mission; (2) determine if they understood the importance of following the OE and LOAC, and (3) critique the way information about the incident was transmitted up the chain: Was battlefield data transmitted to commanders at battalion, RCT-2, 2nd Division, and MNF-West efficiently, and was it accurate?

Bargewell submitted his report to Chiarelli in mid–June, three months after his team began its scrutiny. Except for determining that, MNF-W apparently did not try to cover up the Haditha incident, the document was not pleasant reading for the Corps. Bargewell found that members of the Iraq command stumbled and blundered so egregiously after the IED attack that a clear evaluation of the incident was virtually impossible. The errors committed within MNF-W were so numerous that the list of the mistakes covered three and a half pages in the report. Faults uncovered by the Bargewell team included an inability at the company level to accurately determine the number of casualties, falsified reports sent up the chain of command, an incapacity by commanders to comprehend the seriousness of the situation, and the development of a division-wide view that Iraqi civilians were of so little consequence that it wasn't necessary to investigate the deaths of noncombatants.

Apparently rocked and embarrassed by the report's finding, the Corps was not enthusiastic about sharing it with the public and the media. Records are not available, but the Corps apparently received the report in mid-summer 2006, roughly about the same time it was handed a preliminary report on the NCIS investigation. The Corps classified both reports to keep them out of the public domain. Nine months later, the Corps changed its mind; it released the Bargewell report without explanation in April 2007 but retained the classified status for the NCIS report. The declassification decision may have been related to an announcement by the *Washington Post* that it had received a leaked copy. The headline over the *Post* story read: "Report on Haditha Condemns Marines."[2]

For the most part, the report as it was posted on the Internet[3] was a meticulous recounting of the team's conclusions, although it also raised questions about several events that remained puzzling. For example, even though the team established that there were five sets of photographs taken at the scene of the IED blast, they could not understand why McConnell chose not to send any of them to Chessani's headquarters. Why did Wuterich decide to employ Fallujah-style house-clearing methods at houses One and Two rather than the nonviolent approach used by a second team ordered to clear the houses north of Route Chestnut? How much did an apparent lack of command-level interest in following the ROE affect action in the field? The most critical question, though, dealt with the neglect by anyone in MNF-W to order an investigation. The team could not understand why, given the circumstances, no commander asked what had happened and why. "I found," Bargewell wrote, "that there were several obvious indicators ... that, at a minimum, should have triggered the professional curiosity and duty to pursue an investigation by the officers and senior enlisted leadership."[4]

Compared to the voluminous NCIS report, the Bargewell document is tiny—only 104 pages, which includes ten pages of references to statements and documents perused by the investigators during the probe. There were 193 references listed, but none of these were attached to the declassified version. Despite its brevity, the report reflected a thorough examination of every facet of command operations from the time of the incident until Maj. Gen. Zilmer's decision to order an investigation in March 2006. Probably because of the need to have the report done quickly, the document is somewhat disorganized and its nuggets are scattered throughout the text. Still, it presents the best available resource for explanations of actions within MNF-W from the squad level to the top.

1st Squad

Early news reports indicated that Wuterich viewed Kallop's order to "Clear south" as authority to use Fallujah-style techniques on houses One and Two. Bargewell, however, debunked this concept by pointing out how a second fire team responded to an identical order.

> After the IED explosion, one team headed south (led by Sergeant Wuterich), and Lance Corporals Graviss and Dela Cruz went north to clear houses. [Graviss and Dela Cruz] encountered numerous noncombatants and military aged males ... while clearing houses at approximately the same time as Sergeant Wuterich and his men. [Dela Cruz and Graviss] cleared at least seven houses, encountered numerous women and children, detained approximately 13 [men], and did not fire a single shot. [Graviss and Dela Cruz] separated [men] and women, found items of interest, and transported detainees. This action is in stark contrast to how Sergeant Wuterich and his team handled a similar situation.[5]

Overall, Bargewell said, pre-deployment training in house-clearing techniques was adequate, but mistakes surfaced when the methods were put into practice. "Some of the Marines' statements indicate confusion," the report said. "Specifically, some of the Marines said that if you are receiving [small arms fire] from an area or house, it can be deemed a 'hostile house' and everyone [can be] killed." Lance Corporal Tatum, Bargewell said, succinctly explained the misunderstanding: "He noted that these Marines knew that mistakes were made ... but he and all of them are putting it off on training, [and] not [taking] personal responsibility for their actions."[6]

At one point, the report came close to deviating into an unauthorized search for criminal activity by pointing out suspicious, possibly criminal, behavior. "There is evidence," the report said, "that two Marines conspired to fabricate accounts intended to make the killings appear legitimate."[7] After identifying the men as Wuterich and Dela Cruz, the report added: "[Dela Cruz] told NCIS investigators that he and Sgt. Wuterich on four separate occasions discussed lying about specific events related to their involvement in some of the killings. Such a conspiracy," the report concluded, "...inevitably impeded accurate reporting and follow-on action."[8]

Kilo Company

According to Bargewell, mistakes at the company level started almost as soon as the smoke cleared. "The immediate reports ... were untimely, inaccurate, and incomplete," the report said. "They were also conflicting, poorly vetted, and forgotten once transmitted to 3/1."[9] As the hours passed, the oversights built up. "After the day's combat actions had ceased, the report continued, "there was little or no apparent effort by Company K to evaluate or clarify to higher headquarters the details of the incident."[10]

Throughout the day, the company was never able to get a handle on the number of civilian casualties. Although the figure remained consistent at 15, Bargewell's team was unable to find where the calculation originated. Bargewell speculated that 1st Lt. Adam Mathes, the company executive officer, might have been the source. But when questioned, Mathes was unable to recall where he got the number. "At some point," Bargewell said, "[Mathes] reported to 3/1 eight EKIA [enemy killed in action] and seven NKIA [neutrals killed in action], which corresponds to the number '15' he recalls hearing sometime during the day."[11] Later, after the bodies were recovered, the number of dead was incorrectly given as 23. "Intuitively," Bargewell said, "it is possible that once the total KIA was determined at 23, simple math was applied based on the report by [Mathes] of 8 EKIA—that is, 23 minus 8 EKIA equals 15 civilians killed."[12]

Other details, such as the civilians being killed in the IED blast or in a firefight with insurgents, were fictions created in the battalion and RCT-2 COCs. Nevertheless, neither McConnell nor anyone else in Company K tried to correct the misapprehensions, although they could have been straightened out if McConnell had debriefed the men from 1st Squad. It also might have been set right once the bodies had been collected and taken to the morgue, but no one in the company pushed the issue. "There were attempts to distinguish and identify civilian casualties from [insurgents]," the report noted, but "because of confusion and frustration by the Marines ... there was no further inquiry at the Company level. As a result, there was no apparent rational basis for the distinction made in Battalion reports between civilian casualties and [insurgents]."[13]

In fact, Bargewell said, a large part of the problem was that there was no leadership. "It is apparent that no one person was in charge throughout the day or was assigned or assumed overall responsibility for bringing the incident to a close."[14]

The team did not focus entirely on the deaths in houses One and Two, but also looked at the killing of the Iraqis from the Opel sedan.

> [Kallop] questioned what had happened immediately upon seeing five men dead beside a car. [But] despite being given an account, which provided a questionably lawful basis for killing these individuals and despite later inspecting the first house in which there were at least six dead and two wounded children, 2d Lieutenant Kallop did not raise any further questions about or propose any inquiry into the circumstances of any of the killings.[15]

The team seemed baffled by Wuterich's decision to go in shooting in houses One and Two. McConnell "clearly understood and articulated house-clearing concepts," the report said, and repeatedly explained that Haditha was not Fallujah.[16] Kallop also stressed this point. It was a mystery why their instructions were not followed.

The report did cut the company a little slack—but only a tiny amount—by conceding that November 19 had been a busy day, with engagements taking place at different sites and at different times. The morning began with the IED attack, and then the action shifted eastward to the Palm Groves, where running gun battles were fought over a period of several hours. "This could have interfered with their ability and reduced their incentive to isolate parts of the sequence for detailed fact verification and evaluation," the team acknowledged.[17]

Among the more serious blunders Bargewell found were some related to record keeping. No matter the seriousness of the situation, the Corps demands two things from its company-level personnel: one, an accurate and up-to-date log of all radio traffic, and two, a written record—called a watch log—of all company activities. Kilo Company muffed both tasks. "Documentation of reports received from the IED site or submitted to higher headquarters was non-existent," the report said. "Company K's 19 November 2005 radio log showed no entries between the hours of 0633–1153 and there were no entries made in the watch log all day."[18] These were significant omissions that could have resulted in punishment for responsible individuals. Unfortunately, the flaws did not stop there. "Archived chat records were unavailable," the report said, "[and] there was no record of accounting or verification of weapons reportedly seized or of the number of [insurgents] or civilians killed."[19] Keeping such records is considered mandatory.

Battalion 3/1 and RCT-2

The Bargewell report was no less harsh in evaluating the performances of Company K's two superior commands, citing them specifically for delays in reporting the incident to higher headquarters. Company K reported the incident to Battalion 3/1 almost as soon as the IED exploded at 0716 hours. But it was almost three hours later—only after Company K had sent two updates to battalion—that Chessani's COC notified RCT-2. By the same token, RCT-2 did not inform the 2nd Division until six hours after *that*, roughly nine hours after the attack. Incredibly, it was another five hours before the division relayed the information to MNF-W, the command responsible for all Marines in Iraq. And two more hours passed before MNF-W advised Chiarelli's headquarters at MNC-I. Improbably, it was another four hours before MNC-I relayed the information to MNF-I, the command responsible for all coalition troops in Iraq. It appeared almost unbelievable that Lt. Gen. Casey's headquarters was not informed until 0300 on November 20, some 20 hours after the incident.[20]

In addition to sluggish reporting, battalion and RCT-2 also peppered their reports with incorrect information, which made it even more difficult for superior officers to assess the situation.

> The 3/1 staff's additions to information received from the Company, based on apparent assumptions as to what took place (e.g., a "group of Iraqis was passing by"), rather than facts obtained, further clouded the picture received at higher headquarters and may have obscured the high number of and questionable circumstances surrounding noncombatant casualties.[21]

The battalion operations officer, Maj. Samuel Carrasco, suspected the accuracy of the reports he was getting from Company K almost from the beginning, mainly because he did not believe the insurgents could muster the number of forces that would have been consistent with the number of claimed jihadist deaths. But he apparently did not act strongly enough on his suspicions. "The later reports that broke down the dead into eight [insurgents killed in action] and 15 [civilians killed] were accepted [by the battalion] without further questioning."[22]

The apparent breakdown in efforts by those at both the battalion and RCT-2 levels to demand more details from Company K was mentioned often in the Bargewell report. In the Executive Summary, which appeared in the first few pages, Bargewell noted that both commands "failed to adequately scrutinize information reported by Company K that was untimely and incomplete and of obvious questionable accuracy."[23] Making it worse, the report said, was the addition of "unverified information to give their reports a misleading appearance of completeness." In other words, battalion and RCT-2 staffers deliberately inserted false information to enhance the credibility of their reports with the 2nd Division and MNF-W. Seemingly sadly, Bargewell added that commanders in both 3/1 and RCT-2 ratified these fictions.

Bargewell also questioned whether officers in Company K and Battalion 3/1 had deliberately misled the team. Pointing out that the two commands had "failed to adequately review or reliably report combat actions associated with this incident," Bargewell said he suspected this was because of "inattention and negligence, in certain cases willful negligence."[24]

> There is evidence of intentional false reporting on the part of two individuals involved in the killings. Intentional false reporting or non-reporting on the part of other individuals can not be ruled out, particularly in view of the questionable candor displayed by numerous individuals during the investigations of this incident.[25]

2nd Division

Surprisingly, Bargewell did not particularly condemn the inaccurate news release distributed by the division's Public Affairs Office. Instead, he wrote it off as an "overly simplistic view" created in an attempt to meet the demands of the Information Office, the Corps' propaganda department. However, the problem arose when the division made a wrong decision about whether to correct the information. After the *Time* story was published, insurgents began using it as a propaganda tool to make the coalition forces look bad. But the division—rather than backing away from the statement—continued to support it in the mistaken belief that to make changes would be a form of "giving in" to the insurgents. This was an ill-advised move, Bargewell said:

> The Division's continuing inability to separate the insurgent's use of the incident from its factual validity, that is, to entertain the possibility that they had the facts wrong—despite having no indication that the facts had been definitively ascertained in the first place—reflected, a short sighted view of IO [Information Office] issues and their implications.[26]

Overall

If Bargewell had been grading the command's performance on an academic scale, it probably would have received a low D. Ranking high on

Bargewell's list of negatives was the discovery that an attitude prevailed at all levels of command that Iraqi lives were not as important as American ones. In turn, this may have discouraged strict compliance with battlefield regulations. "[Iraqi] deaths," the report said, were viewed as "just the cost of doing business, and that the Marines need to get 'the job done' no matter what it takes."[27] This, Bargewell said, would have the effect of desensitizing Marines by "portraying all [Iraqis] as the enemy even if they are noncombatants." Commanders at every level through MNF-W remained unaware of the repercussions of such an attitude. "The tenor of a number of the comments was to blame the insurgents for what happened, and as a result of the insurgents' tactics, the Marines were relieved of the responsibility of applying the ROE."[28]

As with the alleged incident with Wuterich and Dela Cruz, the report came close to stepping over the AR-16 restrictions by hinting at another UCMJ violation. "There was evidence," Bargewell said, "from which one could draw the inference that Marine commanders and staff members were guilty of dereliction of duty in failing to request, recommend, or direct that an inquiry into the incident be conducted."[29]

At the end of the text section of the report, Bargewell made a half-dozen recommendations. Five of them were suggestions for procedural changes that might help prevent such mistakes from reoccurring. The sixth, however, was a pointed piece of advice to the Corps to consider preferring criminal charges.

> I recommend the appropriate Marine Corps Commander review this report in conjunction with the NCIS investigation to determine the possibility that MNF-W commanders and staff down to Company K, 3d Battalion, last Marines were derelict in their duties and professional responsibilities. I also recommend the Marine Commander review the conduct and statements of individuals during the course of this and related investigations for the purpose of evaluating whether they met their professional and legal obligation of candor and cooperation.[30]

It is not known if the Bargewell report influenced the decisions made by Mattis and the prosecutors from Camp Pendleton's Legal Services section. However, the report was available to the Corps months before the complete NCIS report, so it may have played a role. On the other hand, there was nothing in the report implicating the men eventually charged except for Wuterich and Dela Cruz and—indirectly—Chessani and McConnell. The version that was released did not include the statements referred to in the final pages of the report, so there may have been details not available to the public concerning Capt. Stone or lance corporals Sharratt and Tatum. It would later be revealed that some of the charges preferred against Lt. Grayson apparently resulted from a complaint filed by Col. Watt after his contact with the Haditha Marines early in February 2006. There is no way to cross-reference the Bargewell report with the one from NCIS, because the latter remains classified and not available for public examination.

Table 3
Comparing Reports

Author	Completed	Length	Declassified	Comments
Watt	March 3, 2006	7 pages	March 9, 2006	Generally supportive of the Marines but recommends a more thorough examination.
Bargewell	June 15, 2006	104 pages	April 27, 2007	Highly critical of Battalion 3/1; finds an investigation should have begun immediately; does not look for criminal violations.
NCIS	Nov. 2006	+/- 3,500 pages	Remains classified	Agents found evidence supporting accusations of violations of the UCMJ.

Despite the Corps-imposed limitations on availability, the 97 pages that made up the text of Bargewell's report were jammed with nuggets such as these:

> Our interviews disclosed no evidence of a criminal cover-up ... the preponderance of the evidence shows that the overall deficiencies in reporting and follow-on action—while sometimes perplexing—were not the result of an extensive and orchestrated criminal cover-up throughout the chain of command....[31]

> There was evidence of an attitude within [the command] to presume all Iraqis to be the enemy or supporters of the enemy, or at least to the extent that noncombatants were not necessarily innocents....[32]

> At the outset of this investigation, the state of the evidence on the underlying events indicated that the Iraqi civilian casualties suffered near the intersection of Routes Chestnut and Viper in Haditha ... were caused by a negligent or, at worst, reckless application of the ROE, by Marines from Company K, [Battalion] 3/1.[33]

> There was an observed preoccupation with friendly casualties. Understandable and laudable, but it contributed to a thought process in which the loss of a Marine eclipsed other reportable and actionable details. The most significant event to most readers of the reports of this incident was the FKIA, despite the fact that noncombatant losses were 20 times higher.[34]

> I found that all commands from the Battalion to the MNF-I level effectively validated inaccurate information in immediate reports by failing to make adequate attempts to verify the untimely and incomplete reports originating from Company K.[35]

> I found that the duty to inquire further [into the incident] was so obvious in this case that a reasonable person with knowledge of these events would have certainly made further inquiries.[36]

The man gate going into Marine Corps Base Camp Pendleton, the 125,000-acre facility located an hour's drive north of San Diego. The base is the Corps' largest expeditionary training facility on the West Coast and houses almost a dozen Marine, Army, and Navy units ranging from a dental battalion to the 25,000-person I Marine Expeditionary Force. A small courtroom on the southwest side of the facility was the venue for legal proceedings stemming from criminal violations in Hamdania and Haditha (author's photograph).

Failure to verify the number of EKIA and distinguish that number from noncombatants, failure to verify weapons seized, and failure to systematically question and evaluate actions taken in the clearing operation resulting in the deaths of 24 Iraqi civilians all demonstrate a lack of awareness or unwillingness to confront what had happened within the battlespace and the command.[37]

Upon viewing some of the photographs, we were convinced that they were at least relevant to reporting and follow-on actions because we thought anyone viewing the pictures would be compelled to question the account of the killings that had been officially reported and conclude that further reporting and investigation was essential.[38]

The most remarkable aspect of follow-on action with regard to the civilian casualties ... was the absence of virtually any kind of inquiry at any level of command into the circumstances surrounding the deaths. There is no indication that the "15 NKIA" reported in spot reports even registered or caused hesitation with anyone from the MNF-W level and above.[39]

Part III: The Hearings

9. Captain Randy Stone

When prosecutors assigned to the Haditha cases pounced, their first target was a fellow lawyer, Capt. Randy Stone, Battalion 3/1's judge advocate. His Article 32 hearing began on May 7, four and a half months after he was accused of violating a lawful order by refusing to call for an investigation, plus dereliction of duty. If convicted and given the maximum sentences, Stone could spend two years and nine months in the military prison at Fort Leavenworth, Kansas.

Media interest, already acute, was further heightened when Stone's civilian defense attorney, Charles Gittins, announced that he intended to summon Maj. Gen. Richard Huck, former commanding general of the 2nd Marine Division, and Huck's former chief of staff, Col. R. Gary Sokoloski, as witnesses. Although neither Huck nor Sokoloski had been charged, both were under fire for failing to adequately respond to the incident.[1]

Perhaps to take the edge off any unfavorable publicity that could result from Huck's or Sokoloski's testimony, the Corps—which up to then had refused to divulge any information beyond notifying that charges had been preferred—released a number of files revealing how the top officers at division and regimental headquarters reacted, including details on how they responded to queries from *Time*'s McGirk.[2] Not incidentally, the information confirmed the conclusions Maj. Gen. Bargewell had laid out in his report, declassified only three weeks before, that commanders throughout the division had exhibited an extraordinary lack of curiosity about the incident. Among the declassified files were transcripts of March 2006 interviews with Huck, Sokoloski, Col. Davis of RCT-2, and Stone. Particularly interesting was the interview with Sokoloski in which he was asked about the erroneous news release he approved on the night of November 19 claiming that seven civilians in houses One and Two had died either in the IED explosion or in a crossfire resulting from an insurgent attack. "At the time, given the information that was available to me and the objective to get that out for the press, it was correct," Sokoloski told investigators.[3] His plan, he said, was to beat the insurgents to the punch: provide a positive spin on the incident before the insurgents could distribute their propaganda. Sokoloski did not say why the release was allowed to remain unchallenged for 13 months. When Gittins—an Annapolis graduate and a former member of a military appeals court—told reporters about his plans to call Sokoloski, he did not foresee that the colonel would refuse to honor the subpoena. Just before the hearing started, Sokoloski announced that he would take advantage of his Fifth Amendment right and not take the stand.[4]

Twenty-two witnesses testified during the weeklong hearing but, bafflingly, there was minimal mention of Stone. Instead, the focus was on the mindset of the major participants and their reactions to questions submitted by McGirk. This was less puzzling when considering the big picture. Realistically, Stone was only a minor player who had the bad luck to be caught up in a pivotal event. His position as Battalion 3/1 judge advocate had been strained from the beginning. He held the job only because the Corps had decided it would be beneficial to have a legal perspective on developments at the battalion level. In effect, Stone was a guinea pig in a Corps lab experiment. As a late addition to Chessani's staff, he was the odd man out. The others had all trained together before being deployed and had worked out their particular pecking order. Stone was a stranger, and the other staff members were not sure what to do with him. To make matters worse, Stone was given very little authority. As a company-grade officer, he was two ranks below Chessani and one under his immediate superior, Maj. Carroll Connelley, the RCT-2 deputy staff judge advocate. Both Chessani and Connelley were field-grade officers, which indicated they were on the career track. The hurdle from captain to major—from company-grade to field-grade—is a high one fraught with hazard. Only about 80 percent make the leap. All it would take was one bad fitness report to wreck Stone's dreams of earning his livelihood in the Corps, provided that was his goal. It would have been asking a lot to expect Stone to go around his superiors, especially when Chessani, a very strong-willed commander, had announced his opposition to an investigation. Stone's presence among the accused, given lack of authority and influence, raised the question of why he was being charged.

Kallop and Dela Cruz

First Lieutenant Kallop was the prosecution's lead-off witness. Young, inexperienced and evidently naïve, Kallop—who had never seen combat or its aftermath before November 19, 2005—seemed not to have fully recovered from the shock he experienced when he walked into House One soon after the attack by Wuterich and his team. He was sickened by the amount of gore resulting from the violence inflicted on six adults and three children. He was even more unsettled, he said, when he realized that two children had improbably survived the onslaught. "I saw one breathe," he said. "That's how I knew. The little boy ... was about six or seven and when I touched him, the little girl jumped up. She was about 11."⁵

Kallop had been the leader of the platoon that included 1st Squad and, on November 19, was detailed as the commander of the primary Quick Reaction Force (QRF). After the incident, Kallop was the first officer to arrive at the scene. Within minutes of his arrival, he testified, he ordered Wuterich to "clear south" because he was under the impression that the men were being fired upon. "I pointed to a group of buildings and said, 'Flush them out, try to find the trigger man.'"⁶

When Stone's attorney got the opportunity to cross-examine, he asked Kallop if he thought the Marines had done anything wrong that day. "No," Kallop replied tersely, "I thought that was within the rules of engagement because the squad leader was about to kick in a door and walk into a machine gun nest."⁷

Kallop was followed the next day by Sgt. Dela Cruz, who stunned spectators with a tale about how Wuterich cold-bloodedly gunned down the five men from the white Opel while they stood passively on Route Chestnut's southern shoulder. "They were just standing, looking around, had hands up," Dela Cruz said.⁸ "Then I saw one of them drop in the middle [of the group]. I didn't know what was going on. [I] looked to my left, saw [Wuterich] shooting."

Dela Cruz' statement sharply contradicted what Wuterich had told Scott Pelley during the *60 Minutes* interview when he earnestly claimed that he shot the men because they were running away. Dela Cruz said he had followed Wuterich's lead by immediately running to the bodies and shooting them again. "I knew they were dead," Dela Cruz said, "[but] I wanted to make sure."⁹

Eyebrows shot up when Dela Cruz told how he unzipped his fatigues and urinated into an open wound in the head of one of the men. "I know it was a bad thing. I shouldn't have done it. But at that time I was angry because [Terrazas] had died and I pissed on one of their heads."¹⁰ Still not finished, Dela Cruz, who along with Wuterich also was charged with making false statements, testified that Wuterich tried to convince him to lie when and if he was ever questioned by investigators. "He told me that if anybody asked, [to say] they were running away and the Iraqi Army shot them."¹¹

Huck Takes the Stand

Not surprisingly, the hearing's headline attraction was Maj. Gen. Huck. By the time of the hearing, Huck was long gone from Iraq, posted to the Pentagon as assistant deputy commandant for Plans, Policies, and Operations. Even though the public received a preview of what Huck might say a few days before the hearing opened, thanks to the declassified files, reading excerpts from a transcript was not the same as hearing him tell the story from the witness stand.

According to the recently released files, Huck swore to investigators some three months after the incident that he knew civilians had died but had not been told the circumstances. At the time, he said, he had been overseeing several combat situations and was too preoccupied to focus on what was happening in Haditha. If he had been told about the civilian deaths, he added, he probably reckoned they were insurgents and therefore did not give it another thought.[12]

Even though Huck blamed his failure to grasp the significance of the situation by saying his staff, notably Col. Sokoloski, had let him down, he admitted he had become aware that civilians had died after he visited the site. The deaths of civilians was not unusual in the type of warfare being waged in Iraq, Huck said, where insurgents wore no uniforms and tried to blend in with the general population. "I had no suspicion that a Law of Armed Conflict violation had been committed. In my mind's eye, I saw insurgent fire; I saw Kilo Company fire. I could see how 15 neutrals in those circumstances could be killed."[13] He had not been told until February, Huck added, that *Time* was investigating a possible massacre.

He said he angrily confronted Sokoloski, demanding to know what was happening. "I was highly irritated," he exclaimed, accusing Sokoloski of withholding information from him.[14] "Am I the last guy in this outfit to find out about [the questions from *Time*]?" Rather than hearing the news from his chief of staff, Huck said he had to learn about McGirk's queries in an e-mail from Army Lt. Gen. Chiarelli, who asked if the Corps was investigating the incident. Huck did not know the details of what happened at Haditha, and when he asked his staff, he was given the information that had been included in the misleading news release. Apparently not realizing how weak the Corps' story was, Huck told Chiarelli: "I support our account [of what occurred] and do not see a necessity for a further investigation."[15] Huck said he later questioned junior officers who may have had the opportunity to challenge the veracity of the news release, but not one of them suspected anything had occurred other than what would be expected in a combat situation.[16]

First Lieutenant Adam P. Mathes, who had been Kilo Company's executive officer at the time of the attack, took the stand on the fourth day. Because Mathes had not been at the scene and had no conspicuous role afterward, he had no significant details to offer. The young officer, however, had played a part in Chessani's search for advice on how to handle McGirk's questions since he was a member of the group the battalion commander delegated to help him form a response to the *Time* reporter. In his opinion, Mathes said, McGirk was simply trying to besmear President Bush and the Corps.[17] Testifying electronically from Kuwait, where he was on another deployment, Mathes said McGirk's questions were "sensationalistic and based on information that was factually inaccurate." To him, Mathes said, "it sounded like a really bad negative spin." Asked by Gittins if the reporter's questions had made anyone suspect that a possible Law of War violation occurred and that an investigation was called for, Mathes replied: "To do an investigation after being prompted by the press would be some kind of admission of guilt."

Unexpected Support

Major Jeffrey Dinsmore, a former enlisted man who made it to field-grade officer after 21 years in the Corps, supported Stone by saying there was no reason for the judge advocate to believe the raids had not been legitimate. Connected to the courtroom by telephone from Iraq, Dinsmore said, "It's well-established that this was a [Troops in Contact situation], and the civilians were unfortunately collateral damage."[18]

Major Thomas McCann, the hearing's presiding officer, asked Dinsmore, "If there had been 150 [civilian] bodies that day where would we be, in your mind?"[19]

Dinsmore slipped around a direct answer by saying that it was rarely evident who was a civilian and who was an insurgent because of the nature of the war. While admitting he had not interviewed the men of 1st Squad, nor had he studied their reports, he recited as fact that insurgents were firing at the Marines after the IED explosion. "The reality is then and the reality is now, [that if] you let loose Marines in a [Troops in Contact] against a hostile situation—taking small-arms fire—they don't have the training nor do they have the presence of mind to differentiate between civilians and insurgents," Dinsmore said.[20]

As battalion intelligence officer, Dinsmore had been responsible for creating an in-depth report on the incident—the story board—that would serve as the official version of what had occurred. Under questioning by Gittins, Dinsmore admitted he kept hidden from anyone up the chain that the civilians, except for the ones who had been killed along the road, died in their homes. If that had been reported—perhaps to Stone—it might have prompted queries about the accuracy of the news release. "I said women and children were killed in that particular engagement," Dinsmore said firmly. But, he added, "it isn't a requirement of combat reporting" to disclose where they died.[21] Dinsmore also admitted he had shrugged off the complaints from the Haditha City Council, made in a document published about a week after the incident. The council had referred to the incident as a "massacre" and asked for a formal investigation. "My assessment was the City Council was being used as a tool of insurgent propaganda," Dinsmore said. "They would take grains of truth and add details that were false and it would end up looking like a wild allegation."[22]

When Maj. Connelley, Stone's immediate superior, took the stand, he testified he had been in an operation on the Syrian border when the reports about the incident came in. Echoing Huck, Connelley said he had his hands full with what he was doing and did not pay a lot of attention to the JENs. From what he had skimmed, however, he did not think anything unusual had occurred.

"What was your basis for drawing that conclusion?" McCann asked.

"I can't think of any," Connelley replied.[23]

Some six weeks later, he continued, after he had been promoted to RCT-2 staff judge advocate, he reread the Haditha documents and, again, nothing jumped out at him. No one was talking about an investigation, he said, so he was not surprised that Stone had not taken the initiative.[24]

Major Dana Hyatt, the battalion civil affairs officer, said he, like Kallop, was shocked when he examined the houses even though his visit came ten days after the incident, and the mangled bodies had been removed and buried. The purpose of his visit, he said, was to see the scene so he could prepare a report for Chessani to be used in determining payments to the Iraqis. "The walls were black," Hyatt said. "Obviously a grenade had gone off and I think there were bullet holes in another room. It looked like hair and stuff on the ceiling; blood on the floor. It was the most blood I'd ever seen."[25]

Nevertheless, he did not feel an investigation was necessary. Apparently, he based his judgment on what he had been told by a member of 1st Squad, whom he did not identify but who probably, judging from later testimony, was Lance Cpl. Sharratt. The squad member told him, Hyatt said, that he heard a weapon being prepared for firing —called "racking"—when he barged into

House One. If so, that would have justified the viciousness of the assault. "It made sense. It sounded OK," said Hyatt, who subsequently suggested payments totaling more than $40,000 to the families of the Iraqis who were killed.[26]

While witnesses danced around Stone's possible culpability, it was not until Col. John Ewers, the I MEF staff judge advocate, took the stand that the captain's role was addressed head-on. "Unfortunately," Ewers said, it was his belief that Stone had been "set up to fail."[27]

Ewers said that Stone should not be held criminally responsible for his alleged inaction. "[Stone] didn't cover himself with glory, but without being asked by his commander to do an investigation, I didn't think [his failure to do so] rose to the level of criminal dereliction [of duty]."[28] Nevertheless, Ewers added, he was "astonished" that an investigation had not been ordered. There was "plenty of responsibility to go around [for that decision]," he said.[29]

Investigation Proponents

Although a number of witnesses testified that they did not think an investigation should have been ordered, two voiced contrary opinions. First Sergeant Alberto Espinosa, the man responsible for maintaining Kilo's casualty lists, said he noticed something was not right within hours of the attack because the company log book was not being kept up to date, an issue that led to a dispute with Mathes, the company executive officer.[30] The lack of attention to procedure became more noticeable the next day, Espinosa said, when he discovered log entries still had not been made. When he complained to Mathes, the lieutenant told him the matter would be taken care of. Not content with Mathes' responses, Espinosa went first to Capt. McConnell, the company commander, and then to Stone. "Don't worry about it," he quoted Stone as saying. "Battalion will handle it."[31] Espinosa said he left Iraq on emergency leave soon afterward and when he returned, he assumed an investigation had been conducted because condolence payments were in the pipeline.

Major Samuel Carrasco, the battalion operations officer, said he began to have doubts about the legitimacy of the action when he saw McGirk's list of questions. "[McGirk's e-mail] hit me in the chest like a baseball bat," Carrasco said.[32] Although he believed the questions "were not based in reality," they made him wonder if there was more to the incident than he was aware of. "I was of the belief that where there's smoke, there's a little bit of fire."[33] He was concerned enough, he said, to raise the issue during a meeting with Chessani and the battalion's executive officer, Major Kevin Gonzalez. The three were in Carrasco's quarters in the Haditha Dam, Carrasco recalled, when he brought up McGirk's e-mail. "These allegations are pretty serious," he recalled telling Chessani, "probably something we want to look at." Chessani lashed out. "My men are not murderers!" he shouted. Soon afterwards, Chessani apologized for his outburst and promised a review, although he never followed through.[34]

At the end of the hearing, Stone took the stand in his own defense, making an unsworn statement under the rule permitting him to present his comments safe from cross-examination. "I have never lied and have worked at all times to assist as best I could to shed light on what I knew and when I knew it," Stone said.[35] "The most frustrating thing," he continued, "is the reality that even looking at this whole matter through 20/20 hindsight, I know I was trying to help. My firm belief—that there was no Law of Armed Conflict violation—was the foundation for what actions I did take as well as action I did not take." This was a rather surprising admission, considering that one of the planks in his defense was that Connelley told him that there was no need to examine the situation more closely. His statement suggested—contrary to what Connelley had said—that he had gone to Connelley expecting to be told an investigation was necessary rather than that there was nothing to investigate.[36]

Other than the pre-hearing announcement by Sokoloski that he was claiming his right of self-protection under the Fifth Amendment and the chilling testimony from Dela Cruz, the proceeding offered few surprises. It did, however, expose a number of unanswered questions. A primary one, despite voluminous testimony, dealt with the issue of insurgents in either House One or House Two. Although Dinsmore, the battalion intelligence officer, had said, "It's fairly well established through the [unmanned aerial vehicle] coverage that there were insurgents in those homes," that was unsubstantiated. Neither the prosecution nor the defense followed up on Dinsmore's claim by showing the video secured by McGirk. In addition, photos of the dead Iraqis were processed in a Department of Defense database, and there were no hits for known or suspected terrorists, which indicated that the reports of insurgent deaths were fictitious.

The hearing also seemed to clarify the strategy the Corps would follow in subsequent proceedings. Five of the witnesses were given immunity to testify: Dela Cruz, Kallop, Hyatt, Dinsmore, and Connelley. That seemed to signal that the prosecution was eager to overlook the possible sins of others to nail one or more men thought more likely to be convicted. It was not yet clear who those targets might be, except for Wuterich, who was definitely in the crosshairs. By freely handling out grants of testimonial immunity (eventually there would be 17), the Corps appeared to be trying to cover up mistakes made in deciding who should be charged.

Testimony during the hearing also appeared to reveal how dedicated the members of Battalion 3/1 were to the script laid out in the news release. Witnesses related as fact items that already had been proven to be either untrue or close to it: aspects such as the claim that the men of 1st Squad were receiving hostile fire; that the dead Iraqis were collateral damage; that someone in House One had a weapon that he planned to use against the raiding team; that there were insurgents in one or both houses, and that McGirk was on some kind of mission to damage the administration and the Corps.

The IO's View

Major McCann—a judge advocate from the 3rd Marine Aircraft Wing at nearby Miramar—submitted a 54-page report to Lt. Gen. Mattis on June 8, 24 days after the hearing ended. Roughly half of the report was a summary of witness testimony; the other half was McCann's analysis of the charges. Clearly, the evidence presented against Stone did not sway McCann. "There are not reasonable grounds to believe [Stone] failed to obey a lawful order," McCann wrote, adding, "There are not reasonable grounds to believe [Stone] knew or should have known a possible, suspected, or alleged law of war violation existed."[37] He also doubted that Stone was derelict in the performance of his duty. In actuality, McCann said, there was no good reason to expect Stone to go over the heads of his superiors by ordering a probe.

> No reference, legal authority, or testimony was presented which established a duty of the battalion judge advocate to initiate an investigation. [Stone's] fitness report billet description did not empower him to initiate investigations, nor was it the routine practice with the battalion or [Regimental Combat Team].[38]

Stone's position within the command was not well defined. He was regarded as an "overstaff" inserted into the battalion at the last minute and was not a full-fledged member of the theater's judge advocate chain of command. For example, McCann pointed out, "There is no evidence [Stone] ever met the division staff judge advocate or that he ever received any direct guidance from him."[39] Chessani, McCann said, did not consider Stone part of his "inner circle of advisors and [Stone] does not appear to have advised [Chessani] directly on any issue. His role was described as more of a 'super adjutant' than command legal advisor."[40] As a result, McCann said, Stone's "knowledge of his technical chain of command was most likely lower than other judge advocates participating with battalions."⁴¹

Probably the most startling segment of McCann's report was his stated suspicion that Stone had been charged because he was convenient, not because he was responsible for the lack of an investigation. McCann wrote:

> Other information presented during the hearing indicated [Stone] was selectively singled out for prosecution. Despite significantly more experience and access to the same information, officers senior to [Stone] have not been charged. Each of these officers is under the same duty as [Stone] to report law of war violations.⁴²

McCann was referring to officers who appeared to have much more knowledge about the event and possessed the power to take action. As examples, McCann listed the battalion intelligence officer (Dinsmore), Hyatt and, indirectly, Connelley, who at the time was the deputy staff judge advocate at RCT-2. Rather than being charged, McCann said, both men were given immunity to testify against Stone. Echoing Bargewell, McCann said that, in his view, the situation got out of hand almost immediately after the IED explosion. "The incident represents a structural failure of the reporting and verification system in the commander, operational, and judge advocate channels."⁴³ He added:

> No weapons were found in the objective area and none were reported in the journal entry. How the 7 [enemy killed in action] were assessed as enemy was never established. Additionally, the number of civilians killed by the IED blast compared to those killed in the crossfire was not evaluated. While not a law of war violation on its face, this even should certainly have raised questions regarding the use of force.⁴⁴

In conclusion, McCann found "reasonable grounds" to believe Stone erred in not being more forceful with his superiors. "While it was not within his authority to order an investigation or initiate one on his own, he should have at least been in contact with [his superiors] providing them the information he did have to assist them in assessing the next step."⁴⁵ However, McCann determined that the situation in which the Corps found itself was not directly attributable to Stone. He wrote:

> Based on all evidence presented, it appears to be a cascading series of events aggravated by a structural failure of three separate reporting channels, specifically—the command, operational, and judge advocate chain of command. The failure is not only within each independent chain, but in a failure of interaction between the respective chains.⁴⁶

McCann recommended that the criminal charges against Stone be dismissed and that Lt. Gen. Mattis handle his case in a procedure called nonjudicial punishment (NJP). Article 15 of the UCMJ, NJP provides an avenue for a Convening Authority to discipline an individual in his command without the stigma of a court-martial, although a court-martial is an option. Punishment can range from short-term confinement to forfeiture of pay.

Among other aspects noted by McCann and reported to Mattis, not all of which related directly to Stone, were the following:

> Col Ewers stated that the Bn level judge advocate should be able to spot issues, but if we really wanted them to be advisors we would not put junior captains into that billet.[47]
>
> There are not reasonable grounds to believe [that Stone] committed this violation.[48]
>
> [Dinsmore] appears to have detailed knowledge of the circumstances surrounding the civilian deaths. Specifically, his testimony indicates he was aware the civilian authorities included women and children and that they were all killed inside their homes with no accompanying evidence of insurgent activity. He has not been charged despite his knowledge of the incident.... He was granted immunity from prosecution.[49]
>
> The Division SJA did not consider it to be a Law of War violation and did not inquire into the matter.... The RCT judge advocate failed to ask any questions ... or consider the possibility of an investigation. The same theory of liability which applies to [Stone] can therefore be applied to both the division and RCT-level judge advocates, yet the RCT judge advocate has ben granted immunity ... and no other judge advocate in the chain of command has been charged.[50]
>
> Evidence revealed a complete failure of the judge advocate technical chain to evaluate this even through a use of force analysis. The use of force in this incident was not a peripheral consideration but was instead the central issue. The failure to analyze the incident from a legal perspective directly contributed to the lack of accurate and complete information provided to the chain of command. Each level of the judge advocate technical chain bears some measure of responsibility for this failure as it relates to dereliction of duty. This includes the accused.[51]
>
> [Stone's] failures are not the result of willful acts or malfeasance, but instead flow from negligence manifested as a failure to act.... [Stone] never asked a single question, even informally. He never contacted the RCT judge advocate staff nor discuss the matter with anyone.... His failure to discuss the events ... in any capacity, with his higher judge advocate headquarters directly contributed to the stagnation of information flow up the judge advocate chain of command.[52]
>
> There were ample opportunities for this event to be questioned and verified, and there was a failure to do so at every level.[53]
>
> [Stone] clearly failed to perform as a reasonable battalion judge advocate in these circumstances. He failed to take even the smallest affirmative step. This indicates, at a minimum, a negligent dereliction of duty.[54]

Mattis was under no obligation to accept McCann's suggestions. However, two months later—on August 8—he dismissed the charges against Stone. There is no mention in the record of NJP. On the same day, the base public affairs office issued a release that quoted Mattis as congratulating Stone for the way he handled the job under "difficult circumstances as a staff member of an infantry battalion engaged in combat operations. It is clear to me," Mattis added, "that any error of omission or commission by Capt. Stone does not warrant action under the Uniform Code of Military Justice."[55]

10. Lieutenant Colonel Jeffrey Chessani

Wednesday, May 30, 2007, was the kind of day Southern Californians live for. At Camp Pendleton, an hour's drive north of San Diego, temperatures were in the mid–60s; the sky was cloudless, and a gentle northwest breeze carried the briny scent of the nearby ocean.[1] The allure, however, was lost on the herd of reporters corralled in the Media Center, the inflated term for the expensively renovated Vietnam-era barracks adjoining a warehouse complex on the southeastern side of the sprawling base. From a seat at one of the black-painted metal tables that stretched from wall to wall in the center, a reporter could follow the Chessani Article 32 proceedings on an overhead monitor displaying a back-to-front view of the courtroom a quarter-mile away. The purely utilitarian courtroom was about the size of a tennis court, enclosed within tan-colored walls and a low, acoustical-tile ceiling. There were no windows and no decorations except for a section of faux oak paneling behind the bench. Flags demonstrating allegiance to the United States and the Corps lent the only color to the pallid area. Spectator seating consisted of 16 tightly packed chairs, only slightly more roomy than an airliner's coach section.

The closed circuit broadcast system was fed by a single camera mounted at ceiling height in the rear of the room, focused on the bench and the witness box. At center screen was Col. Christopher Conlin, the investigating officer (IO) charged with assessing the strength of the evidence presented by the defense and prosecution. Conlin was not a judge; in fact, he was not even a judge advocate. He was the only non-lawyer among the five IOs chosen by Mattis to preside at the Article 32 hearings. Apparently, Mattis felt Conlin's battlefield experience outweighed his lack of legal training, given the circumstances of Chessani's case. The Uniform Code of Military Justice does not require that an IO be an attorney; it stipulates only that the designee be of a higher rank than the accused and, in a situation involving a non-lawyer, that a judge advocate be appointed as an advisor. A Conlin-Mattis connection went back at least to the Iraq invasion in 2003, when Conlin commanded Battalion 1/7 on its march to Baghdad and Mattis, then a major general, led the 1st Marine Division. Conlin's battalion was one of the division's subordinate units. Ironically, so was Battalion 1/5, in which Chessani was serving as operations officer.

The Enigmatic Commander

Unlike Wuterich, who had become a familiar figure because of his legal action against Representative Murtha and his appearance on *60 Minutes*, the world knew little about Chessani.

In October 1983, a year after Chessani graduated from high school in Rangeley, a small town in northwestern Colorado not far from the Utah border, a Muslim suicide bomber drove a truck packed with explosives into a barracks at the Beirut International Airport, killing 220. The incident inspired Chessani to join the Corps, which he did four years later after graduating from the University of Northern Colorado. Not long after signing up, Chessani was plucked from the enlisted ranks and sent to Officer Candidate School. He graduated in 1988 and was commissioned a second lieutenant. His first assignment was to Panama, where he joined some 26,000 other American troops on a mission to depose President Manuel Noreiga. In 1992, he was posted to Saudi Arabia, where he sat out the First Gulf War (Operation Desert Storm). Soon afterwards, he was selected to attend the Corps' Command and Staff College, where he earned a master's degree in military studies.[2]

Moving steadily upward, Chessani was promoted to captain and posted to the Marine Corps Recruit Depot at Parris Island, South Carolina, where he commanded Kilo Company in the 3rd Battalion. It was there that he crossed paths with author Thomas E. Ricks, who was researching a book on the Corps' recruit training program. The contact between the two apparently was fleeting, but noteworthy enough for Ricks to mention Chessani in his book *Making the Corps*, describing him as a "tight-lipped, gray-skinned man whose face is chiseled in a way that makes him appear older than his 32 years."[3] Ricks also noticed a more revealing side of Chessani that would emerge later and lead others to see him as an intense, humorless man whose sole interests seemed to be his religious faith and the Corps. After spending weeks following Platoon 3086 through the rigors of boot camp, Ricks stood next to Chessani as they attended the graduation parade and subsequently wrote:

Watching the ceremony, Captain Chessani ... worries about what will happen to the recruits on boot leave. "Something I've seen as a platoon commander out in the Fleet is that the Marines who get in trouble are the ones who hang out with civilians," he says. He worries that some recruits will fail to cut their ties to their old friends.[4]

In other words, Chessani was anxious that the recruits, after 13 weeks of living like hard-driven monks, would forsake the discipline that had been drilled into them and return to their old drinking, partying, sinful ways.

Almost ten years later, William Langewiesche, writing in a *Vanity Fair* article published after the Haditha incident, pointed out the same character traits. Chessani, Langewiesche wrote, was viewed by the men in the Battalion 3/1 as "a strange guy" who "had a reputation of being standoffish, intensely religious, and uncommunicative." The men, Langewiesche added, felt that Chessani knew them "only by the nametags on their chests, and they felt he offered them little guidance at best."[5]

Chessani was deployed to Iraq a second time in 2004, first as a staff officer with Battalion 1/5—the unit he had served with during the invasion—and then as operations officer for RCT-1, which played a crucial role in Operation Phantom Fury during the Second Battle of Fallujah. Reportedly, Chessani did much of the planning for the team's role in the operation, which may have been the reason he was nominated for a Bronze Star.

Chessani pinned on the silver oak leaves of a lieutenant colonel early in 2005 and soon afterwards was given command of Battalion 3/1.[6] There is nothing in the public record to show why Chessani was chosen for the coveted post; promotion board actions are tightly guarded secrets. Nevertheless, it was a high honor. The Corps has only 35 infantry battalions and more than 1,700 lieutenant colonels, so competition for a command is fierce. Commanding an infantry battalion during a war often opens doorways to promotion, so it seemed that Chessani was destined for a colonel's eagle and possibly a star. However, those dreams disappeared after he was accused of two counts of deliberate dereliction of duty. Even if the charges were dismissed or he were to be tried and acquitted, the best future Chessani could hope for was to hang onto his rank and sit it out until he could retire. Another possibility was that he could be convicted of the charges, sentenced to a year in Fort Leavenworth, and kicked out of the Corps.

The Opponents

Conlin's reputation was solid, but so were the reputations of the lawyers fighting over Chessani's fate. Because of Corps policy not to reveal personal information about service members, the backgrounds of the Marine participants were largely unknown. Sitting at the prosecution table to Conlin's left were lieutenant colonels Paul Atterbury and Sean Sullivan, who had directed the government's case against Captain Stone 15 days earlier. Other than the Corps' admission that both men were reservists called to active duty specifically to help with the Haditha cases, their histories were obscure. Sullivan apparently had been in private practice in Chicago, but there were no details available about Atterbury.

Crowded around the defense table to Conlin's right were five men: the accused, his two detailed judge advocates, and two civilian lawyers provided by the Thomas More Law Center (TMLC), a not-for-profit, faith-based firm in Ann Arbor, Michigan. Since the TMLC's métier is freedom of speech and religious rights litigation, it appeared evident that its president and chief counsel—Richard Thompson—was intrigued enough by the Chessani case to offer the organization's services free of charge.

The experience of the two Marines on the defense team was no better articulated than that of the prosecutors. Media reports said Lt. Col. Jon Shelburne had been teaching at the Roger Williams School of Law in Rhode Island when he was summoned to serve as a defender, while Capt. Jeffrey King already was on active duty as a member of the Camp Pendleton Legal Services Support Section (LSSS).[7] According to available information, Robert Muise, the lead defense attorney, spent 13 years in the Corps, four of them as an infantry officer.[8] After participating in Operation Desert Storm in 1991, he enrolled in law school at Notre Dame, graduating at the top of his class. He resigned from active duty in 2000 to open a firm specializing in constitutional law but remained active in the Marine Corps Reserves. Shortly before signing on to the Chessani defense, he returned to Iraq for Operation Desert Shield.

Brian Rooney, Muise's civilian assistant, was the grandson of the founder of the Pittsburgh Steelers pro football franchise and the brother of a Republican congressman from Florida. He dropped out of Florida State University to join the Corps in 1998. In 2004, he deployed to Anbar Province as a member of the 3rd Marine Air Wing, 11th Marine Expeditionary Unit, which was part of Mattis's 1st Division. After Mattis took command of I MEF/MARCENT, he asked Rooney—then a captain and a senior prosecutor in the legal office at the Marine Corps Air Station in Miramar—if he would join the Haditha prosecution team. For unexplained reasons, Rooney turned down the offer and left active duty, only to reappear on Chessani's defense team.[9]

"Execution Style"

Sullivan rocked the courtroom even before the first prosecution witness could take the stand. Minutes into his opening statement, he caused a stir by revealing that two of the men and three of the women killed in the assault on House One had been shot "execution style." It was information that had not previously been disclosed, and it reflected badly on Chessani, who had endorsed the position that the civilians who died in the two houses were killed in a wild firefight between the men of 1st Squad and insurgents who had taken over the dwellings. Anticipating that the defense would argue that it was the jihadists who murdered the civilians, Sullivan delivered the knockout blow. The fatal shots were made by 5.56-mm rounds—the type fired by U.S. military weapons and a different caliber than that used in the insurgents' AK-47s.[10] The implication was that Chessani would have known this fact if he had called for an investigation, maybe even if he had immediately gone to the scene and viewed the bodies. One of the women, Sullivan continued, was killed by a shot to the base of her skull administered while she was in a "cowering position" with her arm around a young boy, who also was shot in the head.[11]

Initially, prosecutors planned to call 16 witnesses, but Col. Davis of RCT-2 and Tim McGirk of *Time* were scratched because they claimed protection under the Fifth Amendment, as Sokoloski had done at the Stone hearing. Of the remaining 14, only five appeared "live"; the testimony of eight was videotaped because of deployments and one was allowed to testify by telephone.

The day's first witness, whose testimony was presented on tape, was Lt. Max Frank—the young Marine who had been in charge of the body-collection detail. Frank spoke without emotion, but the tale he told was horrifying. "It was gruesome," he said. The bodies of six children were clustered on one bed and each body was riddled with "multiple [bullet] holes"; one of the children was headless.[12] The situation was made worse for the Marines, Frank said, because they did not have enough body bags and latex gloves to go around—a condition he angrily reported to McConnell, the company commander. The body bags were used for the adults, he said, while those of the children were stuffed into white trash sacks.[13]

Responding to a question from Sullivan, Frank said he never considered the possibility the killings may have been deliberate. "It was unfortunate what happened, sir, but I didn't have any reason to believe that what they had done was on purpose." Pushed to explain how he came to that conclusion, Frank said: "From my perspective at the time, my assumption was my Marines were doing the right thing. I rationalized it to myself as they were taking fire. The

Marines could have come in, yelled at them to come out, and when they didn't come out they cleared the room with a fragmentation grenade."[14] Asked how the Marines explained the incident to the families of the dead civilians, Frank said Lt. Mathes, the company executive officer, suggested there should be no apology. Instead, they were to say, "This is what happens when you let the terrorists use your house to attack our troops."[15]

William Hays Parks, called on the second day, was the first witness to give in-person testimony. A highly respected expert who wrote the first official manual on investigating Law of War violations, Parks served in Vietnam as an infantryman and then as a senior prosecuting attorney for the 1st Division. Later, he was a congressional liaison officer for the secretary of the Navy and chief of the Law of War Branch for the judge advocate general of the Navy. By the time of Chessani's hearing, he had worked for the DOD either in the military or as a civilian for more than 35 years. Under direct examination, Parks was specific about the responsibilities of commanders in a Haditha-like situation. "If the men on the ground lose sight of the 'big picture'" and do not report "possible, alleged or suspected violations of the Law of War, they take the risk of losing the public's support," he said.[16] The rule of thumb, he added, should be, "when in doubt, report." Parks also was adamant about the importance of the disclosure Sullivan made at the hearing's opening: "The substantial number of head shots does not suggest a resisting force." Under prompting from Atterbury, Parks added: "The fact is, a crime appears to have been committed. How could you not investigate that?"[17]

Major General Huck took the stand on the third day, testifying by video teleconference from his desk at the Pentagon as a witness for the defense. He surprised many by appearing at the Stone hearing because it was highly unusual for an officer of his rank to give evidence in a criminal procedure. This made his attendance at the Chessani hearing even more of a rarity. As commander of the 2nd Division, Huck could have ordered an immediate investigation, but—like Chessani—he showed little interest in what had occurred. Both men visited the IED site after the incident, but neither asked questions, talked to the men from 1st Squad, or inspected the houses.

Although Huck repeated much of what he had said earlier, he was more specific about his view of Chessani. During the Stone hearing, he strongly criticized Sokoloski, his former chief of staff, for not keeping him informed. This time, he singled out Chessani. "The question becomes, did [Chessani] report everything he knew, and I have some questions about that." For example, he continued, Chessani did not mention that five men had been shot on the road. "That should have been reported," he said emphatically. Even more serious, though, was Chessani's failure to disclose that he had met with the Haditha City Council in the wake of the incident—a fact Huck said he learned only days earlier. The council, Huck said, had formally requested an investigation in a plea written in English. "If that document was presented, [that] needs to be reported and the commander should be thinking, 'Perhaps I should get an investigation started.'"[18]

Lieutenant Mathes, Kilo Company's former executive officer, and Lt. Kallop, the leader of the platoon that included Wuterich's 1st Squad, both appeared on videotape but neither offered new material, essentially repeating what they had said at the Stone hearing: neither had viewed the incident as a LOAC violation.[19] Mathes, however, caused a small stir when he said he had overheard Chessani and McConnell, Kilo's former commander, discussing how to "spin" the incident. Muise quickly interjected that Mathes was not correctly remembering the event.[20]

While much of the testimony echoed what was said at the Stone hearing, there were a few unexpected comments. One was a statement by Capt. Dinsmore, the former battalion intelligence officer and one of Chessani's staunchest supporters, who blurted in the middle of a heated exchange with Sullivan that he thought the Corps had drummed up the charges against his boss because the command was looking for a whipping boy. "Politically, the Marine Corps made a decision to hang Col. Chessani out to dry," he exclaimed.[21] He did not elaborate.

Another unexpected turn came when Maj. Carrasco, the former battalion operations officer, explained why Chessani had remained in the battalion COC rather than going to the IED site immediately after the attack. He and other members of his staff had convinced Chessani that it would have been "prohibitively dangerous" for him to go into the field. As a defense witness, Carrasco was prompted by Muise to add: "I was of that opinion that day and still believe that ... we thought he could best serve the battalion by staying in the COC."[22]

Conlin, who had said little during the testimony, interrupted. How would he have felt if he had been a company commander and his battalion chief had stayed at his desk while men were being attacked? Conlin asked Carrasco. "In that case," Carrasco admitted, "I would have been upset." But the IO did not want to let the matter drop. No matter what subordinates advise, Conlin lectured, a battalion commander is supposed to "do the commander thing" and go to the scene of the fighting. Somewhat sheepishly, Carrasco acknowledged the staff may have been wrong. "In hindsight," Carrasco said, "should we have allowed [Chessani] to go out there? Absolutely."[23]

Although called by the defense, Maj. Connelley's testimony favored the prosecution's case. The former judge advocate for RCT-2 recapitulated his Stone testimony, saying there had been nothing in the report from Chessani's headquarters on the night of the incident that caused him to think that the squad's action may have been illegal. However, Connelley, who was promoted to RCT-2 staff judge advocate not long after the incident, elaborated on what he had said earlier. "My understanding, at least at the time, was that [the civilians] were out in the open. [The report] says they were out moving past the vehicles." He said he would have viewed the incident in a different light if the initial report had said that the majority of the civilians were killed inside two houses and that no weapons or dead insurgents were found. "It would have raised questions. I would have asked for an investigation. It was something different than what I had always pictured," he added.[24]

Staff Sergeant Justin Laughner, the HET photographer who made the *in situ* photographs at the IED site shortly after the attack, was the prosecution's final witness. Apparently called in the expectation of buttressing the contention that Chessani showed no interest in knowing what had happened at the IED site, Laughner could only shrug when asked how Chessani reacted to the images; he did not know if Chessani had ever seen them. However, he added, he *did* know what happened to his photographs soon after the incident: his immediate superior, 1st Lt. Andrew Grayson, ordered him to erase them from his work computer.

"How did you feel about that?" Sullivan asked, affecting dismay at Laughner's statement.

"Not good," replied Laughner, who was testifying under a grant of immunity. "I knew it was wrong. I just kind of looked at [Grayson] with shock; it just didn't seem right."[25]

The fate of the photographs had no connection to Chessani or with the battalion commander's alleged dereliction, but it did fit into the prosecution's case against Grayson.

"Did you feel you had just obstructed justice with Lt. Grayson?" Sullivan asked, taking advantage of testimony he planned to revisit although Grayson's Article 32 was still months away.

"Yes," Laughner said.[26]

"A Godly Man"

Despite the assumption that Muise and Rooney would put up an aggressive, lively defense, their case was remarkably lackluster. Although they called eight witnesses in the first eight days of the hearing, most of them, like Huck, Carrasco, Connelley, and Dinsmore, contributed more to the prosecution's case than to Chessani's. Defense witnesses in the last two days had little impact as well, consisting almost exclusively of a string of military personnel willing to say positive things about Chessani and how he had been an inspiring leader regardless of what had been said about him during previous testimony.

Sergeant Major Edward Sax, the battalion's former top enlisted man who drove Chessani to the Palm Groves and to FB Sparta on the afternoon of the incident, testified that Chessani had wanted to visit the IED site late in the afternoon of the incident, but he had talked him out of it. Sax professed strong admiration for Chessani, calling him "by far the strongest moral leader I have ever served with in my life." Asked if he thought Chessani would have ordered an investigation if he suspected wrongdoing, Sax replied firmly: "Without batting an eye."[27]

First Lieutenant Mark Towers, Chessani's former adjutant, called Chessani a "godly man" who spent a half hour each morning reading the Bible. However, when asked if he thought the last sentence in JEN 20-007, in which Chessani said, "Commanding officer 3/1 moved to the scene to conduct a command assessment of the events" implied he had been there, Towers replied, "Yes, sir."[28]

Colonel Brennan Byrne, a longtime associate of Chessani's, testified by phone from a deployment in Saudi Arabia, "He's a Christian; an upright man," Byrne said. "As a Marine officer, he has shown impeccable integrity. I would trust him with my life."[29]

Chessani took the floor on the tenth day of the hearing, making an unsworn statement, which could not be challenged by the prosecution or by Conlin. "I understand that I am accountable for my decisions," Chessani said in a firm, emotionless voice, "but I do not believe my decisions and actions were criminal, sir."[30] Standing stiffly with his hands clasped behind his back, Chessani continued: "Hindsight is 20/20 [but] I will tell you the decisions I made, the actions I took, were made in good faith."[31] Turning to one of the critical issues of the proceedings, Chessani said he did not go to the IED site because he was focused on the action in the Palm Groves. It had been a day of "nonstop action," and he was more concerned about the firefights in which his men were actively engaged. After a lengthy pause, he added: "[It] was the single most devastating [day] of my life ... as a battalion commander [I was] at the pinnacle, the top of my career."[32]

Chessani did not explain why he did not question the men of 1st Squad; why he did not ask for photos of the engagement; why he did not inspect the houses when he went to the site the next day; why he gave Col. Stephen T. Davis the impression he had gone to the scene; or why he did not provide more information to Maj. Gen. Huck.

On June 8, the next-to-last day of the hearing and the day before Chessani made his statement, the *New York Times* published previously undisclosed details about an alleged sworn account Chessani had made to military investigators in March 2006. The newspaper did not say whether Chessani had been talking to the NCIS or members of Bargewell's team, but reporter Paul Von Zielbauer, who had been covering the hearing, wrote:

> Colonel Chessani said he never suspected that the killings were improper under the American laws of war, because they followed an attack by insurgents that, he believed, were intended to provoke lethal return fire by Marines in a residential area. "I believe the enemy picked the ground where he wanted to attack us," Colonel Chessani said in a statement dated March 20, which has not been officially released. "They were—they had set this up so that there would be collateral damage." He later added, "Enemy had picked the place, he had picked the time and the location for a reason. I believed he made a definite choice in where it was and thought that, you know, he wanted to make us look bad."[33]

It was assumed that Chessani's statement would end the hearing, but prosecutors caught the defense off guard by announcing they intended to amend the charges against Chessani in a fashion that would make him more susceptible to a longer prison term if he were convicted. The government, Sullivan said, intended to dismiss the two original charges of dereliction of duty and replace them with a single charge of willful dereliction and one of "violating a lawful order by wrongfully failing to accurately report and thoroughly investigate a possible, suspected, or alleged violation of the Law of War by Marines under his command." Under the original charges, Chessani could have been sentenced to a maximum of one year in prison, but under the amended charges, he could face as many as two and a half years behind bars.

Not unexpectedly, the defense was furious. Following some back and forth with Conlin, Rooney told the IO that if prosecutors wanted to change the charges, the defense should be entitled to call additional witnesses in rebuttal.

How many people was he talking about? Conlin asked.

Rooney and Muise did a quick calculation: "Thirteen," Muise responded.[34]

That seemed excessive to Conlin, but he was unwilling to slam the door in the defense's face. Take some time, he said, get together with the prosecutors, and come back with a compromise. He left the session open, saying he intended to reconvene in the near future after the lawyers had a chance to confer.

The Defense Spin

The defense took a considerable number of lumps during the ten-day hearing, and there was little doubt, judging from media reports about Conlin's reactions during the testimony, that the IO was going to come down hard on Chessani. First, there had been the disclosure that five of the civilians were killed by what appeared to be deliberate gunshots to the head. Parks had heightened the impact of this revelation when he said this should have alerted the command that an investigation was needed, yet nothing had been done. Huck dealt a damaging blow by testifying that he had qualms about Chessani's veracity. Even defense witnesses such as Connelley and Carrasco seemed to have impaired Chessani's case more than they helped.

Unwilling to admit the weaknesses in its case, the defense tried to put a positive spin on Parks' testimony by claiming that the Law of War expert had actually supported Chessani. A "news release" issued by the TMLC five days after Parks testified read:

> A key expert witness for the government last week ended up being a great witness for Marine Lieutenant Colonel Chessani and the Thomas More Law Center. William Hays Parks, a lawyer with the Department of Defense who wrote the Directive on the "Law of War," was called by the prosecution to bolster their case against Lt. Col Chessani, the battalion commander of the Marines charged in the Haditha case. Instead, Mr. Parks testified that when he wrote the Directive, he did not envision that battalion commanders would investigate Law of War violations. They would merely report any suspected violations up the chain of command.... Mr. Parks stated that he wanted combat commanders in the field to focus on the fight, while those higher in the chain of command decided whether to investigate. Mr. Parks believed that it would be improper for the battalion commanding officer to investigate his own men in this situation.[35]

The statement continued:

> It is clear from M. Gen Huck and the others that have testified that all officers in Chessani's chain of command in the 2nd Marine Division had knowledge that civilians were tragically killed in Haditha, but as seasoned combat veterans they knew that this can regrettably occur in war when you face an enemy that specifically fights behind women and children.[36]

The 800-word statement ended with a quote from Thompson, the TMLC president:

> It is insane that we are pulling effective combat commanders off the battlefield in response to enemy propaganda, and to appease the liberal media and anti-war politicians with a scapegoat. We at the Thomas More Law Center believe that we should be honoring these brave men instead of trying to criminalize their actions to placate

anti-war politicians and their anti-war friends in the press who have already announced the verdict."[37]

Conlin's Report

Thirty-one days after the conclusion of Chessani's Article 32 hearing, Col. Conlin submitted an explicit recommendation that the case against the lieutenant colonel be referred to trial. The blistering eight-page report cited a long list of mistakes, omissions, and misjudgments allegedly committed by Chessani ranging from imprudence and neglect to remaining in the COC when he should have been in the field. Conlin wrote:

> Choosing where to be is always an art, but it rarely is in your Main [command post]. In this case, the commander remained in his Main CP from the initiation of all contact at 0716 [Hours] ... through the kinetic hostile contact [at the Palm Groves] until moving to the X-380 site between 1630 [Hours] and 1730 [Hours]. We can command and control via communications media, but we must lead by physical presence.[38]

Rarely do IOs denounce an accused so witheringly. Conlin blamed Chessani for neglecting the "absolute and unmitigated responsibility to investigate what a reasonable commander would deem as a 'possible' or 'suspected' Law of War violation"[39]; for letting down the junior officers in his command by not giving them better guidance; and for sending a "virulent response" to *Time* reporter McGirk in response to his questions about the incident, accusing him of being "uneducated" and "muckraking" while embellishing a false report of the day's activities.[40] In Conlin's view, "the command climate was such that the incident was quickly blamed on others and anyone who disputed the Battalion's version of events was considered inherently suspect."[41]

Such action, Conlin said, was not conducive to the United States' announced intentions in Iraq: "You cannot win popular support by killing over twice as many civilians as insurgents in one day's engagement, and then attempting to lay the blame at the feet of that same population and their leader, regardless of how corrupt you may perceive them to be."[42]

What particularly enraged Conlin was Chessani's response to Col. Davis on the night of the incident that implied he had inspected the IED site. "To say that the most senior officer in the Battalion has physically gone to a battle site to do a personal assessment—a senior field-grade officer screened for his high level of judgment and decision making—is to attribute a 'gold standard' to any facts quoted."[43] It was evident from JEN 20-007—the final JEN of the day—Chessani added, that this was not the case. "This statement was wrong as were many facts in the JEN."[44] That single transmission, Conlin determined, was the impetus for many of the mistakes that followed.

> It became the zealously guarded collective "truth." With the apparent stamp of approval from Lt. Col. Chessani's personal "command assessment," the numbers and actions in this message became the primary source for the subsequent Story Board presentation.... A classic "Groupthink" scenario developed as the Battalion summarily dismissed challenges and inquires by the Haditha City Council, 6th Civil Affairs group ... Mr. McGirk from Time magazine, and eventually MNF-I.[45]

Conlin continued his attack on Chessani and his staff, writing:

> The day's events were taken at face value based on the reports that the Bn COC received and the JENs and Story Board they sent to RCT-2. Those Higher Headquarters reports became 'gospel'... [which] meant that even as late as mid–February ... there was still the perception that many of the civilian casualties resulted from the IED blast and open crossfire between Marines and insurgents as they were moving through the area. But this is not what occurred.[46]
>
> [Chessani] did not personally go to this particular battlefield for over 30 hours after the last shots were fired at the Chestnut and Viper intersection. When he did, [he] analyzed the scene without including any of the participants and without going beyond the initial IED blast site.[47]
>
> The mere fact that one Fireteam was solely responsible for 24 deaths in all direct-fire actions should have solicited more than passing interest from the senior leadership.[48]
>
> To not recognize the potential for this event to reverberate far beyond the confines of Haditha is not to be in touch with the current nature of the conflict.[49]

All things considered, Conlin wrote, Chessani exhibited severe lapses in his obligations:

> In this case, [Chessani] failed to do his duty. He failed to thoroughly and accurately report and investigate a combat engagement that clearly needed scrutiny.... He failed to accurately report facts that he knew or should have known and inaccurately reported at least one fact he specifically knew: his claim to have "moved to the scene [of the IED attack]" to conduct a command assessment of the events to his higher headquarters.[50]

In summary, Conlin said: "I believe from my investigation that these actions represent a violation of [the dereliction of duty article]."[51]

The Defense Reacts

Fifteen days later, Chessani's defense team sent a single-spaced 22-page letter to Lt. Gen. Mattis complaining about Conlin's report. The document, which was almost three times as long as Conlin's, began by asserting that Conlin's report was "factually inaccurate, legally deficient, and grossly misleading in so far as the opinions and recommendations are not supported by the evidence of the law."[52] The report, the defense claimed, was a "tendentious view of the evidence, mischaracterization of the facts, and misapprehension of the legal issues" all of which "call into question the legitimacy of the entire Article 32 proceeding."[53]

The defense went into considerable detail about what it considered errors in Conlin's interpretation of testimony, including a seven-and-a-half-page, paragraph-by-paragraph breakdown of the report. Much of the defense argument centered on what Conlin allegedly had deliberately omitted from his report, especially testimony from witnesses who had praised Chessani's performance and those who had said they did not see a need for an investigation. Several times, the document mentioned that Conlin's references to Chessani being bound to investigate incidents of multiple civilian deaths were incorrect. Asserting that was "one of the greatest oversights of the IO's report," Chessani's lawyers said that such an order was not put into place until April 2006; therefore it was not relevant to what happened in 2005. "This fact demonstrates that there was no legal duty for [Chessani] to conduct such an investigation," the defense said, adding:

> In the final analysis, given the overwhelming evidence in this case, it is absurd to conclude that [Chessani] is criminally liable for not suspecting a LOAC violation.... [His] actions were consistent with those of a reasonable and prudent commander, particularly in the light of the fact that ... [Davis] advised him ... that no investigation was required because it was a "bona fide combat action" and ... [Huck] never requested a formal investigation.[54]

Additionally, the complaint challenged Conlin's contention that Col. Davis' direction to "look into this further" was an order and argued, in fact, that it may not even have been issued. "This is no simple oversight," the defense contended. "The record shows that during an 'actual-to-actual' conversation ... [Davis] told [Chessani] that because it was a bona fide combat action, no investigation was necessary."[55]

Davis could not clarify this because he refused to testify at the hearing. The defense also maintained that Conlin was being unfair by emphasizing a JEN and picking at a communication that essentially was correct.

> It is ironic and disappointing that the IO recommends a [General Court-Martial] for an approximately 85 percent accurate JEN drafted in the midst of an ongoing battle in Haditha, and yet [Conlin] significantly misstates critical evidence after having three weeks to ponder, draft, and review his narrative with the aid and assistance of an experienced judge advocate[56] [formatting in the original].

The defense also criticized Conlin for trying to second-guess Chessani's decision to remain in the Haditha Dam headquarters throughout the incident at Route Chestnut and Viper and the skirmishes in the Palm Groves:

> For the IO to disagree as a fellow commander with [Chessani's] choice of where to fight the battle is one thing. But for the IO to disagree with this decision ... and allege criminal wrongdoing goes beyond the full and fair hearing mandated [by the UCMJ].[57]

During the testimony phase, the defense had been quick to claim that William Hays Parks, the grand old man of LOAC investigations, had presented a more accurate interpretation of Chessani's reactions and—although a government witness—his statements should be carefully considered by Mattis as supportive of Chessani.

> [Parks] testified [that] the battalion commander's duty is not to investigate LOAC; he reports the incident and continues the fight. The duty rests with higher headquarters to determine whether a LOAC investigation is required or needed.[58]

It was not, they argued, Chessani's responsibility—as Conlin maintained—to make decisions contrary to those made by his superiors. "To imply that the duty to conduct a criminal investigation rested with [Chessani] is to ignore [Park's] testimony and the great weight of evidence."[59] The defense also picked at Conlin's contention that Chessani had been derelict because he had not made an effort to debrief the men from 1st Squad. "[Conlin] makes the absurd assertion that [Chessani] should have personally interviewed the shooters. A battalion commander relies on his chain of command, he does not subvert it."[60]

Overall, the defense grievances appeared to be more of a personal attack on Conlin than on the substance of the colonel's report to Mattis. Chessani's lawyers were particularly indignant about Conlin intimating that their client was more interested in his personal safety than in fulfilling his duty as commander of a combat battalion. "[Conlin] essentially insinuated that [Chessani] was a coward," the defense fumed. "Whether [Conlin] thinks he would have done it differently and better is not relevant to the proceedings and certainly should not factor into whether criminal charges are warranted in this case."[61]

The Second Phase

Two weeks later, Conlin reconvened Chessani's Article 32, which had been in recess since the prosecution announced it was filing additional charges.

Predictably, the prosecution and defense said they had not been able to reach agreement on how to handle the issue.

Visibly perturbed, Conlin indicated that his patience had run out and he was in no mood to sit through long arguments. He opened the session on the morning of August 8 and closed it a few hours later. He refused to call six of the witnesses the defense had requested because he "found absolutely no relevance to their testimony."[62] Two officers whose testimony he did consider appropriate testified over the telephone. Conlin denied three others because he considered their testimony to be cumulative, and a fourth—a captain who had since left active duty—refused to appear. "[He] declined an invitation to testify and informed the government that any further contacts with him would need to go through his attorney," Conlin said, somewhat sourly.[63] When the defense objected to Conlin's decisions about the witnesses, Conlin angrily told them to take it up with Mattis.[64] A week later, he filed a two-page-long amended report saying nothing had been said to make him feel he should soften his stance. "I continue to believe that [Chessani's] actions represent a violation of Article 92 ... and he was derelict in the performance of his duties."[65] He recommended a court-martial for the second time.

As it had done after Conlin filed his original report, the defense sent another complaint to Mattis. It was only eight pages long—about a third of the length of its first protest.[66] It, too, criticized Conlin's action but expressed resignation about its position. "It is evident that the defense will never get a full opportunity to defend against these additional charges at an Article 32 hearing," the defense said.[67] Chessani's lawyers suggested two possible remedies to solve the impasse: Mattis should dismiss the charges against Chessani and allow him to retire from active duty or convene a Board of Inquiry to evaluate Chessani's performance. "To proceed with criminal charges against Lt. Col. Chessani under these circumstances would be patently unjust," the defense argued.[68]

If the defense arguments impressed Mattis, it was not evidenced in his decision. On October 19, he referred two charges of dereliction of duty against Chessani to trial.[69]

11. Captain Lucas McConnell

Someone was watching over Luke McConnell. The former commander of Kilo Company, who was relieved of his duties by Lt. Gen. Mattis on April 7, 2006, because of his alleged involvement in the reporting process following the Haditha incident, was suddenly and unexpectedly the beneficiary of the general's largess.

McConnell had no advance notification of what might be coming when the Corps announced on September 18, 2007, that Mattis had dismissed all charges against him six days previously. The only explanation Mattis offered for his action was contained in a brief news release from the Camp Pendleton Public Affairs Office:

Charges Dismissed Against Marine Officer in Haditha, Iraq Investigation

CAMP PENDLETON, Calif. (Sept. 18, 2007)—Charges against Capt. Lucas M. McConnell stemming from the command response to the death of Iraqi civilians in Haditha, Iraq on Nov. 19, 2005, were dismissed on Sept. 12, 2007. A Grant of Immunity and Order to Cooperate with All Parties were issued to McConnell in order to further the fact-finding process into the incident.

McConnell was charged Dec. 21, 2006, with dereliction of duty for allegedly failing to ensure the incident was reported accurately to higher headquarters and for failing to ensure the incident was immediately investigated.

McConnell was the Commanding Officer of Company K, 3rd Battalion, 1st Marine Regiment, at the time of the incident.

Lt. Gen. James Mattis, Commander, U.S. Marine Corps Forces, Central Command and the Consolidated Disposition Authority for cases related to the Haditha incident, ordered the dismissal of the charges.

Lt. Gen. Mattis determined that administrative measures are the appropriate response for any errors or omissions allegedly committed by McConnell. This determination is based upon a thorough consideration of information developed from rigorous investigations by Marine, Army, and Naval Criminal Investigative Service investigators, as well as evidence produced in previous Article 32 hearings relating to the Haditha incident.

McConnell's civilian defense attorney, Kevin McDermott, said the notification came as a surprise. "The dismissal occurred without discussions and the [immunity] grant came without our approval or request," McDermott said.

With the exception of Cpl. Dela Cruz, McConnell had been the only one among the Marines who had never been assigned an investigating officer. The only reason for Mattis's decision, McDermott reasoned, was that Mattis had seen the video from the ScanEagle and deduced that it conformed to the action report McConnell gave to Chessani. "The [Scan]Eagle began recording [at the Palm Groves)] within 30 minutes of the IED. You could observe the insurgents fleeing through the palm farm and rearming before they hit the final firefight," McDermott said. Before going to the Palm Groves, McConnell led a second Quick Reaction Force, which arrived at the IED site not long after the explosion and managed the evacuation of the wounded. He might actually have inspected houses One and Two if he had not been called away to join in the Palm Groves skirmishes. Although the news release about the dismissal of charges hinted that "administrative measures"—likely in the form of a non-judicial punishment hearing before Mattis—might later be scheduled, it is unknown if this ever came about. Subsequently, McConnell was promoted to major and deployed to Afghanistan.

Mattis's decision to dismiss the charges against McConnell simply added to the puzzle. There was never an explanation for the reasoning involved in deciding who was charged and who was not; questions about why the eight accused Marines had been singled out for prosecution while others both up and down the chain of command were not were never answered. Why, for example, was McConnell charged and not others on a sizable list of Marines who were involved? Lieutenant Kallop—who gave the order to "clear south," which was interpreted by Wuterich as justification for an aggressive assault on House One —was not accused, nor was Capt. Pool—the author of the news release that triggered the *Time* article. Also not charged were Pfc. Mendoza and Cpl. Salinas, the two squad members who took part in the assaults on houses One and Two, although three others—Wuterich, Sharratt and Tatum—were. Chessani was accused, but his superiors—Col. Davis and major generals Zilmer and Huck—were not, even though they did not override Chessani's decision not to order an investigation. There may have been sufficient reasons for these discrepancies, but the Corps did not explain and refused to entertain media questions seeking clarification.

While superior officers in the Iraq command were not criminally accused, that did not mean that no one was punished. On September 5—a week before Mattis announced his decision on McConnell—Navy Secretary Donald C.

Winter wrote letters of censure to Huck, his chief of staff, Col. Sokoloski, and Davis.[1] Censure is not a finding of criminal liability, but in the Corps, such action is a certain career-killer. All three men retired shortly afterwards. Zilmer, who had not assumed his post as MNF-W commander until two and a half months after the incident, was not censured.

Winter's letters made clear that he was disappointed with the three high-ranking officers. The issuance of such reprimands is not commonly announced, and even more rarely is the text disclosed. In this case, however, a partial text of the secretary's letter to Davis was leaked to the media. "Even when made aware of the serious allegations raised by the *Time* magazine journalist," the communication read, "your response to higher headquarters was to forward incomplete, inaccurate, and inconsistent materials provided by a subordinate unit, rather than to initiate a thorough inquiry into the incident."[2] It is likely that the other letters were similar if not identical.

Even though details were not made public, the letters apparently were written over Mattis's objection. The Camp Pendleton Public Affairs Office issued a statement evidently designed to moderate Winter's harsh words soon after they were announced. "[Mattis] did not find any evidence that these senior officers intended to cover up the incident," the statement said, adding, "He did determine that their actions, or inactions, demonstrated lack of due diligence on the part of the senior commanders and staff."[3] Included in the statement was a lengthy quote from then-commandant Gen. James Conway: "While these three officers have served their country and Corps exceedingly well for decades, their actions, inactions and decisions in the aftermath of the Haditha incident did not meet the high standards we expect of Marine senior officer leadership," he said. "These administrative sanctions will affect officers who have dedicated their lives to our Corps and country, but they are necessary actions in light of what happened on November 19, 2005, and in the weeks and months following."[4]

12. Lance Corporal Justin Sharratt

In *No True Glory,* which to date is the definitive book about the Corps' struggle to gain control of the Anbar Province city of Fallujah, former Marine infantry officer Bing West writes movingly about how the troops fought house to house, often hand to hand, against entrenched insurgents who would rather die than surrender.[1] It was a type of combat the Corps had not experienced or trained for since Vietnam, so the men of 1st Squad had to learn the hard way about the viciousness required in give-no-quarter urban warfare. According to West, an outstanding example of how the infantrymen learned to cope was the fight for a nondescript two-story residence that came to be known as the House from Hell, or, simply, Hell House. A unit from Kilo Company, Battalion 3/1, was ordered to capture the building, which was occupied by a group of resolute jihadists. The Marines succeeded, but two were killed and 11 wounded in the struggle. Among the survivors were lance corporals Justin Sharratt and Stephen Tatum.

The struggle for Hell House occurred on November 13, 2004. One year and six days later, Sharratt and Tatum—both still with Kilo Company—were in the convoy that was hit by the IED on Route Chestnut. Neither was injured in the blast, but both played prominent roles in the raids that followed. Tatum was a member of the team that assaulted houses One and Two, in which 15 Iraqis died, and Sharratt was at House Four, where four brothers were killed. When the Corps announced the names of the men who had been charged in connection with the Haditha incident, both Sharratt and Tatum were on the list. Sharratt was charged with three counts of unpremeditated murder; Tatum with two counts of unpremeditated murder, four counts of negligent homicide, and one count of assault. Given their history of sharing unpleasant experiences, it seemed natural they were assigned almost the same dates for their

Article 32 hearings, which would both be conducted by Lt. Col. Paul Ware, who was summoned from a base in Hawaii to help the overloaded lawyers at Camp Pendleton.

Sharratt was called first, on June 11, 2007. He was accused of killing three of the four men in House Four. Staff Sergeant Wuterich was accused in connection with the fourth death. For Sharratt, conviction on even a single count could result in a life sentence.[2]

At the heart of the prosecution's case were accusations by the widows and a teenage son of the men Sharratt was said to have killed that challenged Sharratt's claim of shooting the men only after being threatened with AK-47s. They had not actually witnessed the incident because they were kept under guard in House Three while Wuterich and Sharratt went alone into House Four. Nevertheless they denied there was a confrontation: they contended that Sharratt and Wuterich forced the men into an isolated area where Sharratt executed them with his Beretta M9 pistol.

Observers predicted that the military would have a tough time validating its allegations against Sharratt because of a lack of evidence. The investigation into the Haditha incident did not begin until four months after the event, so crime-scene analysts had virtually nothing to work with. In keeping with religious conventions, the brothers were buried without being examined by a pathologist or anyone trained to gather evidence that could be used in court. The only witnesses to the deaths in House Four were Sharratt and Wuterich, and their stories did not waiver: they maintained they shot the brothers during an armed confrontation. Although Sharratt and Wuterich said they recovered two rifles from the house, the weapons could not be found when investigators searched for them months later.

The purpose of the hearing was to establish that the prosecution's case was strong enough for Ware to recommend that the charges against Sharratt be brought to trial. The convening authority—Lt. Gen. Mattis—would make the decision on a court-martial.

In essence, the prosecution's case rested almost entirely upon the videotaped testimony of the Iraqi family members, which was entered into evidence but not played before Ware.

Different Faces, Different Challenge

Witnesses in the Stone and Chessani hearings had been mostly officers, but that changed dramatically in the Sharratt proceeding. Fourteen men and women were called to the stand during the five-day hearing, but only two were Corps officers while another was an Air Force pathologist. Among the remaining witnesses, four were NCIS special agents, two were Iraq experts, and one was a former lance corporal who had been in the ill-fated convoy.

Michael S. Maloney, an NCIS forensic consultant who inspected the room where the men were killed, supported the prosecution's case. He testified that blood splatters on the walls indicated two of the four brothers had been "crouched or sitting" when they were shot, implying that they were passive during the shootout despite Sharratt's claim that the men were actively threatening him when he killed them. However, Maloney conceded under cross-examination that one of the men might have been moving when he was shot, either toward Sharratt or in the direction of a closet, which might have contained a weapon.[3]

Two prosecution witnesses—Lance Cpl. James Prentice and former Lance Cpl. Trent Graviss—attacked Sharratt's integrity, insinuating that he may not have been telling the truth when he told investigators he had been acting in self defense. A Fallujah veteran who had been posted to Kilo Company in Haditha, Prentice—who had not been in the IED attack—testified for the prosecution that Sharratt told him that he had shot an Iraqi in the head, then invented a "story" for investigators claiming the victim had pointed a rifle at him. On cross-examination, Prentice admitted he wasn't sure that Sharratt had been serious.[4]

Graviss was a more weighty witness because he had been riding in the Humvee with Wuterich when the IED exploded. He was at the scene the entire day, but he did not participate in the assaults. Testifying for the prosecution, Graviss said he and Sharratt were standing outside the battalion's Haditha Dam headquarters waiting to be interviewed by investigators when Sharratt told him about an NCIS agent who boasted that he could tell when a witness was lying. According to Graviss, Sharratt said he challenged the agent to determine if he was being truthful. "I'm a good liar," Sharratt said, adding that he tested the agent by deliberately spinning a tale. "Do you have an opinion regarding Lance Cpl. Sharratt's reputation for honesty or dishonesty?" the prosecutor asked. "Until that day," Graviss replied, "I thought [Sharratt] was pretty honest. But when he said he was lying to the NCIS agent, I then started to question his honesty." Under cross-examination, Graviss conceded that Sharratt had a reputation for being a braggart and that he often made things up, implying that Sharratt fabricated the story about the investigator in an attempt to impress him.[5]

Because the Iraqis were quickly buried and the families refused requests for exhumation, there was a marked absence of the kind of forensic evidence that would have been presented in a major murder trial. Except for bloodstains found at the scene, the only verification that four men had died of gunshot wounds was found in photographs of the bodies taken by a Corps photographer. However, the cameraman's primary interest had been in recording the faces of the dead so they could be compared with images in a DOD database of known and suspected insurgents, not to document conditions that could be used at a trial. The bodies all were clothed, and the only visible wounds were those to the men's heads, which made it difficult for examiners to make determinations that could be accepted as evidence. The best Air Force Lt. Col. Elizabeth A. Rouse, a pathologist who conducted the analysis for the Corps, could say was that the wounds had been inflicted by a weapon fired no closer than two feet away.[6] This did little to help the government support its allegations the Iraqi brothers were murdered "execution style" and not killed in a legitimate combat action.

The prosecution suffered another blow when NCIS Special Agents Nayda Mannle and Mark Platt described questioning the Iraqis in their homes in late March and early April 2006. Because neither could speak to the Iraqis in their native language, they relied on an interpreter named Amir al-Kaysey. Knowing the defense would challenge the Iraqi's truthfulness, al-Kaysey testified that he required them to tell the truth "in the eyes of their god."[7] However, an Iraqi called by the defense—Barak Salmoni, deputy director of the Marine Center for Advanced Operational Cultural Learning and an expert on Middle East culture—said the oath demanded by al-Kaysey would not guarantee honesty. To be more certain, Salmoni said, al-Kaysey should have required that the Iraqis testify before local religious authorities and Iraqi court officials.[8]

During cross-examination, Mannle affirmed that Sharratt had been non-deceptive when he told a polygraph examiner that the brothers had threatened him with rifles.[9]

Sharratt Explains

On the last day of the hearing, Sharratt read a prepared, unsworn, five-page statement detailing his experiences in Iraq, about a third of which was devoted to Fallujah. When he got to Haditha and November 19, Sharratt—who was decorated for conduct at Fallujah—said he and Wuterich entered

House Four through the front door. He shot and killed three men, he said, and Wuterich shot the fourth.

In his view, Sharratt said, the men were insurgents who posed an armed threat. "We did not execute any Iraqi men," Sharratt said. "When an insurgent pointed [an AK-47] at me from behind a door, I shot him in the head."[10] After he shot the first man, he said, he heard a weapon being racked in the room in which the first man had been standing, so he rushed through the door, shooting two more men who were inside. "I kept firing until I used my magazine because I didn't know if they had body armor on or suicide vests. As I fired at the other insurgents in the room, I felt as though they were coming toward me," he said.[11]

In a strong voice, Sharratt said he performed precisely as he had been taught. "I am a disciplined Marine.... I did exactly as I was trained to do." He had no regrets, he said, because he was convinced he acted correctly. "In the end, no matter how much I second-guess myself, I would not change any of the decisions that I made that afternoon." He concluded his statement with a maxim repeated frequently in the Corps: "I'd rather be tried by a jury of 12 of my peers than carried in a casket by six of my friends," he said.[12]

Although Ware would summarize his conclusions in a report to Mattis a month later, he gave an early indication of his mood by reprimanding the prosecution. "The account you want me to believe does not support unpremeditated murder," Ware told the lead prosecutor, Maj. Daren Erickson, before adjourning the procedure. "Your theories don't match the reason you say we should go to trial. To me it seems the most important issue is whether the Marines perceived a hostile threat," Ware said, adding, "It comes down to credibility to determine if this case should go to trial."[13]

Despite the lack of supporting evidence, prosecutor Erickson urged Ware to support the government's request for a trial, saying a court-martial was needed because of the strength of the contradictory positions. Sharratt's leading defender, civilian Jim Culp, however, argued that the evidence presented during the hearing reinforced his client's claims. "He charged into that room at great risk to his own safety and killed those men before they killed him. He deserves a medal," Culp said.[14]

Culp also raised the question of the role played by politics in the decision to prefer charges against eight Marines, particularly Sharratt, who was dragged into the chaos for reasons beyond his control. After *Time* exposed the incident, Culp said, the public became polarized and was sharply divided on the issue of the conduct of the war. "This is a new kind of war, and this case is a result of the new kind of warfare," Culp said. "There's also politics involved here, and the politics of the war is tearing at this nation."[15]

The Controversial IO

The Corps is unwilling to say how, why, or by whom Lt. Col. Ware was recommended or selected to preside at the Article 32 hearings for Sharratt, Tatum and Wuterich. Technically, he was the choice of Lt. Col. Mattis, or at least Mattis had to sign off on his appointment. However he got to that position, Ware turned out to be the most controversial courtroom official participating in the lengthy Haditha judicial proceedings. While it was unusual to assign one man to preside at Article 32 hearings for all three of the enlisted, it was not unprecedented. At the time, Camp Pendleton's Legal Services Support Section was under considerable stress because of the demands stemming from the war, perhaps explaining why Mattis had to reach out to a judge in Hawaii to fill a courtroom vacancy. However, the choice of Ware was curious in that he did not have a record that would indicate he would be selected to be the IO in the three most important legally related civilian-slaying cases of the war.

Detailed information about Ware's career is almost nonexistent: the Corps would not release information about his combat history or his record as a senior judge. What little is available reveals that in 2000, when Ware was a captain, he was awarded a Combat Action Ribbon after serving for two months at an undisclosed location in the Middle East.[16] Most likely, he was part of a force sent to Yemen after the bombing of the USS *Cole* on October 12.

Ware's Military Occupational Specialty code indicates he was a communications officer and, at the time of his Mid-East deployment, was posted to the Marine Corps Air Station in Miramar, California.[17] According to the available record, Ware, by then, had finished law school at the University of San Diego and had served in a variety of positions ranging from civil law officer to staff judge advocate, although details including units and dates are missing.[18] After he returned from the Middle East, he was promoted to major, probably in 2002. In 2003, he was posted to the Corps' Western Judicial District, which encompasses Camp Pendleton. During the next three years, according to the single releasable document including background material, Ware presided at more than 400 Special and General Court-Martial cases, "including 38 contested cases."[19] The record, however, does not break down the number of each type, which would be an important factor in gauging Ware's experience because Special Courts-Martial handle misdemeanor cases while General Courts-Martial are reserved for felony cases. Neither does the record list the contested cases. The Corps refused to elaborate, citing privacy. Overall, judging from what information is available, it does not appear that Ware's service was remarkable. He retired on July 31, 2009, after 20 years, 2 months and 20 days as an active duty Marine.[20]

Ware filed his report on Sharratt on July 6, three weeks after the hearing concluded. It was 18 pages long and included the names of witnesses and a list of 107 items entered into evidence, although the items themselves were not attached. Two pages summarized the testimony, and four and a half pages were devoted to a meticulous dissection of what witnesses said, much of it written in crisp, disaffected terms. However, Ware also was prone to drift away from lawyerly language and segue into personal opinion, creating the impression that he was writing in a personal journal. At one point, he peevishly sniped at the prosecution's alleged audacity in suggesting that the Iraqis had been executed, writing:

> It is difficult, if not impossible to believe, that trained and experienced Marines would decide to execute 4 unarmed men by leading them into a house, moving them to a back room with no light (curtains were closed) and allow them to move about the room while trying to shoot them with the least effective weapon in their arsenal.[21]

He also made it clear that he felt that the Iraqis had been mendacious in asserting that the Sharratt and Wuterich were murderers, citing greed as a possible motive. "Shortly after making these claims, the Ahmed family was paid $10,000 in solatia payments," Ware noted, pointing out that the complaints about how the men were killed did not surface until they learned that families of the dead in houses One and Two had been paid.[22]

In a section headlined "Timelines of Interviews" Ware derided the value of the oaths taken by the Iraqis, emphasizing that their statements did not meet American standards for perjury. To prove his point, he referred to testimony from the Middle East expert, Salmoni. In the expert's opinion, Ware said, the Iraqis' statements would not be considered solemn declarations in Iraqi courts. In addition, Ware said, testimony from women and children was felt to be less reliable than that of men under Iraqi law. Maintaining that was not his personal belief, Ware nevertheless added:

> Although such discrimination is not recognized in our society, the fact that these Iraqis have this cultural understanding suggests that they believe United States authorities would likewise view their statements as less reliable and may suggest they would feel less need to be fully truthful.[23]

In other words, they likely would lie because they did not feel they were going to be believed anyway.

Ware was particularly critical of defense witnesses Prentice and Graviss, brushing off their testimony as vague or inaccurate. Prentice, Ware contended, denied telling NCIS that Sharratt "made up a story." Splitting hairs, he said he had told investigators only that Sharratt had a "story," not that he had fabricated one. Blaming this at least partially on what he believed was an NCIS tendency to add material to what a witness said, Ware commented: "Regardless of which version is true, [Prentice] is now on record as providing two contradictory sworn statements."[24] As for Graviss, Ware said it was unclear whether "this conversation between [Graviss] and [Sharratt] was an admission that [Sharratt] lied about the events in House four ... or whether this was simply [Sharratt] bragging and or exaggerating the truth."[25]

Sharratt, on the other had, was believable because his claims were "fully supported by independent scientific evidence." He defended his conclusion by quoting NCIS agent Maloney, who "conceded that [Sharratt's] account of what occurred is the most reasonable and plausible explanation supported by forensics." Ware added: "Although science will never be able to remove all doubts, with a high degree of certainty, the science supports the statements of [Sharratt] as the most plausible, possible, and most likely."[26]

It was clear Ware did not believe Graviss' testimony supported the prosecution's case. In a one-paragraph section headlined "Evidence Offered Against Reasonable Grounds" Ware said Sharratt's testimony had added believability because it was supported by independent scientific evidence.[27]

Ware's first recommendation was to change the wording in the charges against Sharratt, adjusting the accusations to make them non-capital offenses. This could be accomplished, he said, by deleting the words "intent to kill or inflict great bodily harm" from each of the counts. However, he also recommended adding a fourth count accusing Sharratt of murdering a single Iraqi, although he did not say who that Iraqi might be.[28]

Ware made it clear that he had little appreciation for the testimony of the Iraqis.

> I find that the Iraqi witnesses' statements are unsupported by scientific evidence and are incredible for the following reasons:
> 1. Evidence Not Consistent with an Execution—None of the victims received defensive wounds to their hands or arms nor did they receive wounds to their backs or rear of their heads. Each was shot facing forward, from a distance, and with a 9mm pistol, which I find inconsistent with an execution or persons reacting to an execution.
> 2. Witness Accounts Are Not Credible—The Iraqis' first statements to NCIS were taken in a group setting, five months after the events occurred and with knowledge that other families in Haditha had received monetary compensa-

tion from the United States for events that occurred on 19 November 2005.... Although $10,000 does not appear to be a large amount of money, testimony from Maj. Hiatt suggested that such a sum of money was equal to 4 times the average annual salary of a typical resident of Haditha.

3. Timeliness of Interviews—[T]he family's unwillingness to allow NCIS to exhume bodies and conduct an autopsy prevents the defense from discovering exculpatory evidence. Failure to examine the bodies does not in itself raise reasonable doubt, but coupled with inconsistencies in statements and apparent fabrications in the Iraqi witness statements the government's version is seriously deficient.

4. Government Evidence of Confessions or Admissions—None of the statements offered comes close to being a confession or admission that the actions of LCpl Sharratt on 19 November 2005 were criminal. Although I suspect LCpl Sharratt has not been entirely truthful concerning all the events on 19 November 2005, the statements submitted by the government are rife with rumors, hearsay within hearsay, and unclear, confusing and often inadmissible opinions.[29]

The more important of Ware's recommendations, though, was to dismiss all charges against Sharratt. This would solve the problem of a trial because—in his view—a court-martial was unnecessary. He explained:

> The crux of this case centers on the question of whether the government has sufficient evidence to support a finding that there are reasonable grounds to believe that the killings were unlawful and if unlawful, whether they were done with premeditation.... A reasonable ground is commonly argued as being similar to probable cause. The test is whether there is more evidence for than against. Another commonly used test is a set of circumstances, which would satisfy an ordinary, cautious and prudent person, that there is reason to believe an offense has been committed.[30]

In the long run, Ware maintained, it was simply a matter of which version was more convincing.

> It is clear that these accounts are radically different, the government version describing a deliberate execution and LCpl Sharratt's account describing a lawful use of deadly force in either a combat situation or a clearly perceived threat of hostile intent on the part of the Iraqi men. If the government version is true, a charge of premeditated murder with 4 specifications is warranted. If the defense version of events is true, dismissal of the charge is justified.[31]

Ware shot down prosecutor Erickson's argument that a trial was needed to settle the differences between the opposing camps. "To adopt [the prosecution's] position that because there are two different accounts, a General Court-Martial is warranted is an abdication of the necessary process of determining whether reasonable grounds exist to warrant a court-martial," he said.[32]

If the government wanted a trial, it had to make a reasonable argument that it had produced enough evidence to make a credible case. And, this, in his opinion, the government had not done.

> The government version is unsupported by independent evidence and while each statement has within it corroboration, several factors together reduces the credibility of such statements to incredible.... To believe the government version of facts is to disregard clear and convincing evidence to the contrary and sets a dangerous precedent that, in my opinion, may encourage others to bear false witness against a Marine as a tactic to erode public support of the Marine Corps and its mission in Iraq.[33]

"Even more dangerous," Ware continued, "is the potential that a Marine may hesitate at the critical moment when facing the enemy."[34]

As for the four brothers, Ware said it was his perception that either they were insurgents or they were trying to defend their house against the "uninvited and unannounced" arrival of the Marines. When one of the brothers stepped forward with a rifle in his hands, Ware said, Sharratt "perceived him as a threat." What followed was what one would expect:

> Using his training, he responded instinctively, assaulting into the room, emptying his pistol. Whether this was a brave act of combat against the enemy, or tragedy of misperception born out of conducting combat with an enemy that hides among innocents, LCpl Sharratt's actions were in accord with the rules of engagement and use of force.[35]

Reaction and Disposition

Ware's report infuriated Lt. Col. G.W. Riggs, the staff judge advocate at Marine Forces Central Command, which also was under Lt. Gen. Mattis as well as I MEF, although the two headquarters were more than 2,000 miles apart. Because of complicated bureaucratic protocol, it was Riggs who was tasked as Mattis's legal advisor on all issues dealing with the Haditha and Hamdania prosecutions. Although it was never disclosed exactly what Riggs said to Ware, the Associated Press claimed he strongly criticized the IO for being too "harsh" in determining the government had not made its case. Apparently, this so angered Ware that he retorted by sending e-mails to several judge advocates calling Riggs's comment "inappropriate and impudent," adding he was "offended and surprised" by Riggs's reaction.[36] Riggs countered by recusing himself from any future action in Sharratt's case.[37]

Mattis apparently remained aloof from the Riggs/Ware dispute but he accepted Ware's recommendations. On August 9, he dismissed the charges against Sharratt.³⁸ A statement issued by the Camp Pendleton Public Information Office quoted Mattis as saying the Marines' job in Iraq was made more difficult because the insurgents took refuge behind civilians.

> The experience of combat is difficult to understand intellectually and very difficult to appreciate emotionally. Where the enemy disregards any attempt to comply with ethical norms of warfare, we exercise discipline and restraint to protect the innocent caught on the battlefield. Our way is right, but it is also difficult.³⁹

The statement was curious because there had been no testimony mentioning the possibility of insurgents trying to mix with civilians at Haditha. That had been totally the creation of the inaccurate news release, which the Corps had conceded was deliberately false.

Sharratt's reaction was to file a civil damage suit against Representative Murtha, as Wuterich had done earlier. The document, filed in a federal district court in Pittsburg on September 25, 2008—a year after charges against him were dismissed—accused the congressman of violating the lance corporal's constitutional rights in his statements about the Marines' actions in Haditha.⁴⁰ The premise was shaky: Murtha did not mention Sharratt by name, but his attorney, Noah Geary, said the media was able to identify him.⁴¹

13. Lance Corporal Stephen Tatum

The prosecution opened its case against Lance Cpl. Stephen Tatum on July 16 before Lt. Col. Ware. It had been ten days since Ware submitted his recommendations on Lance Cpl. Sharratt's case to Lt. Gen. Mattis, but the convening authority had not yet acted on the report. While prosecutors had been able to study the investigating officers' submission and perhaps make minor adjustments in its presentation to meet Ware's peculiar methodology, the two cases were so dissimilar that a major change in tempo would be difficult. The prosecutors would have to proceed as they had been planning for months and hope they could satisfy Ware's demands.

While Sharratt had been accused in connection with the deaths of three men inside a single dwelling, the accusations against Tatum were more complicated. He was one of the raiders in both houses One and Two, along with Staff Sgt. Wuterich, Pfc. Mendoza, and Cpl. Salinas. After studying the evidence gathered by the NCIS, Mattis preferred charges of murder, manslaughter, aggravated assault, reckless endangerment, non-aggravated assault, and unpremeditated murder against Tatum. Specifically, he was accused of murdering two Iraqis in House One, as well as being involved in the deaths of two others in House One and one in House Two, plus the non-fatal of shooting an eight-year-old girl in House One. If convicted, Tatum could be sentenced to life in prison without parole for each of the murders and 30 years on the other charges.

Testimony from Iraqis had played a major role in Sharratt's hearing, but the emphasis on that would be less in Tatum's case. The Tatum witness list also differed from those in the Stone and Chessani hearings, which had been officer-heavy. For the first time in the continuing series of Article 31 hearings, a sizable number of civilians—primarily NCIS agents—were scheduled to be called. A lack of pertinent witnesses was a problem for the prosecution. The NCIS agents added heft to the list, but what they could say was severely limited. By the time investigators arrived in Haditha, it was too late for them to collect valuable evidence. Mendoza and Salinas would be the main government witnesses.

Mendoza was called first. Lt. Col. Paul Atterbury, the primary prosecutor, decided to focus on events that had occurred in House Two because that was the background for the most damaging testimony against Tatum. According to Mendoza, the fire team had just entered the dwelling in its search for the "runner" allegedly seen running away from House One when he found himself alone in the kitchen. While the others were clearing rooms in other areas of the house, Mendoza said he was attracted to a strange sound coming from behind a closed door across the hall from where he was positioned. Since the noise didn't appear to be threatening, Mendoza cracked the door open and peered inside. Facing him, he said, was a large bed, in the center of which were two women and four or five children who were huddling together in terror.

"They were scared," Mendoza said.[1] Realizing they were no threat, he quietly shut the door but remained at his post in the hallway while waiting for the others to arrive. Seconds later, Mendoza said, Tatum appeared. At the time, Mendoza, who was about five foot four and a private first class, said he looked up at the six-foot-two lance corporal, pointed at the closed door and told him in fractured English, "There's just womens [*sic*] and kids [inside the room]."

"Well, shoot them," he quoted Tatum as ordering.[2]

"Was he joking?" asked Atterbury.

"No sir, he was very serious," Mendoza replied.[3]

Mendoza said he persisted in trying to dissuade Tatum from assaulting the room. "There's no males, no threat, no hostile situation." At that point, Tatum pushed past him, Mendoza said, and went into the bedroom. "Next thing I know, I hear a lot of noise in the house."[4] Later, when he returned to the dwelling as part of a team collecting bodies, Mendoza said the bedroom was filled with dead people. "I found all of the womens [*sic*] and childrens [*sic*] dead. They got multiple wounds everywhere."[5]

Under cross-examination, Mendoza—who had been granted immunity in return for his testimony—admitted he initially lied to investigators about the details and did not disclose Tatum's involvement for almost a year. He lied, he said, because he feared he might be deported to his native Venezuela if he admitted he had been at the scene. When Tatum's lead civilian attorney, Jack Zimmerman, asked Mendoza if he had shown deception when asked during a polygraph examination about Tatum's involvement, Mendoza admitted he had.[6] In contrast, Zimmerman pointed out, Tatum cleared the test.[7]

NCIS special agent Matthew Marshall testified that Tatum admitted to him that he knew at least one of the people he shot in the darkened room was a child. Marshall said when he asked Tatum about the people in the room, he hesitated. "Then he said, 'That's the room where I saw the kid that I shot. Knowing it was a kid, I shot him anyway.' He was very emotional about it, very sorry to the point that he cried."[8]

Marshall said Tatum told him the child was "standing on a bed." He couldn't tell if it was a boy or girl, Marshall said, although the figure had "black hair and a white T-shirt on." Tatum, Marshall added, "was very remorseful about it, very emotional about it."[9] In a later interview, Marshall said, Tatum seemed to have to have rationalized his actions: "He stated that women and children can hurt you, too."[10]

On cross-examination, Marshall admitted that Tatum never reviewed or signed the transcribed copies of his interview, nor had Tatum been told he was a suspect in a homicide investigation.[11]

Forensic Frustration

Sergeant Dela Cruz, who had created a courtroom stir when he testified earlier that Staff Sgt. Wuterich had shot and killed the five men from the Opel without provocation, followed Mendoza to the stand with more previously undisclosed details about Haditha and Battalion 3/1's deployment.

Before the Haditha incident, Dela Cruz said, Tatum scoffed at another Marine who said they needed permission before shooting a suspected insurgent. Tatum said he believed Marines should be allowed to approach combat as incidents were recorded in the Bible, "where you just go in the city and kill every living thing."[12]

While searching the houses after the November 19 raids, Dela Cruz recalled, he and Tatum found a cache of 5,000 U.S. dollars. They were staring at the money, Dela Cruz said, when Tatum suggested they take it and send it to the family of Lance Cpl. Terrazas, who was killed in the IED blast, to help pay for his funeral. Tatum, however, did not take the money, Dela Cruz added.[13]

When Terrazas' squadmates gathered his personal items to send to his family, they put them in the lance corporal's pack, which all of them signed. Alongside his signature, Dela Cruz said, Tatum inscribed two dozen hash marks supposedly signifying the number of civilians killed in the incident. According to Dela Cruz, Tatum wrote: "This one's for you." Tatum's attorney, Zimmerman, said the inscription referred to a rosary that Tatum had attached.[14]

As with Sharratt, prosecutors were unable to link Tatum to the shooting forensically. Testimony from Lt. Col. Rouse, the Air Force pathologist, was almost identical to that she had given at Sharratt's Article 32: there was no smoking gun; the evidence was too thin.[15]

Special Agent Tom Brady testified that, from his examination of photographs from the House Two bedroom, it appeared that someone standing over a young boy might have executed him with a shot to the head. Tatum's attorney, Zimmerman, however, posited that the boy might have been huddled against his mother when Marines sprayed the room with rifle fire and was killed by a bullet that passed through his mother.[16]

Agent Nayda Mannle, who also had testified at Sharratt's hearing, added a new detail when she told how her superiors at NCIS headquarters in Washington had denied her request to tape record her interviews with Iraqis in the spring of 2006. When asked why she was turned down, Mannle said she was told that earlier interviews had not been recorded and her bosses "did not want any inconsistencies."[17]

Denies Murdering Civilians

As had Sharratt, Tatum made an unsworn statement at the end of the hearing, but unlike Sharratt, who had used written notes, Tatum spoke off the cuff. "There are some points I'd like to bring to light," he began. "The reason I fired in House One is that I knew small arms fire was coming from the south. I didn't see where it was coming from, but I saw [a round from a Marine grenade launcher] hit House One and [Wuterich] told me on the way to House One to treat it as 'hostile,'"[18] which, according to most interpretations of Corps regulations, meant everyone was a fair target.

Tatum said he heard gunfire from a Marine weapon almost as soon as he got inside, and he knew that Mendoza had "engaged a target." Then, he said, he heard an AK-47 being racked. He said he followed his training by entering the room and firing with his rifle on automatic. "The visibility was horrible," he said. "There was dust and smoke. I really couldn't make out more than targets." When one of the Marines yelled that he had seen someone run from House One, to another dwelling nearby, Tatum sprinted to House Two. "Before we entered, Mendoza [shot and killed] someone through the door. Inside, I was told to [toss a fragmentation grenade] into a room. When I saw that the room was clear, I heard another Marine engage in the next room," which apparently was the one containing the women and children. "My duty was to help that Marine, so I went in and engaged targets."[19]

Tatum denied being told by Mendoza that there were only women and children in the room. "I did not know [that] ... until I went back later. Otherwise, I would have physically stopped everybody in that room from shooting." Expressing contrition, Tatum added in a shaking voice, "I'm not comfortable with the fact that I might have shot a child.... That is a burden I will have to bear."[20]

Ware's Report

If prosecutors were hoping for more favorable treatment from Ware than they had received in his Sharratt submission, they didn't get it. Ware filed his 29-page report with Mattis on August 23, meticulously listing the names of 21 witnesses and 213 items either filed or attempted to be filed in evidence.[21] He dutifully included a summary of testimony and his guidelines for analyzing the evidence. He also noted the contradictory accounts of what may have occurred in House One.

Ware began his report by explaining his standard for analysis:

> The test I applied to determine if reasonable grounds exist is whether the set of circumstances would satisfy an ordinary, cautious and prudent person, that there is reason to believe an offense has been committed. Reasonable grounds must be more than suspicion or the ability to theorize a criminal act from a set of facts excluding all evidence to the contrary. Although the government does not have to prove the allegations are true at an Article 32 investigation, it must present credible evidence to support the conclusion that reasonable grounds exist to believe that a crime was committed.[22]

Before conveying his analysis, Ware clarified what he would be looking for—a definition that undoubtedly would have been helpful to prosecutors if he had pronounced it in advance.

> In a homicide case arising from actions by a Marine within a combat environment, the government may not rest on the normal presumption that killing is wrong and is therefore burdened with proving that the killing was in violation of the rules of engagement. The ambiguity that arises in this case is not what the rules of engagement require, but how those rules are applied for criminal liability.[23]

He began with House One and an exploration of whether Tatum had observed the ROE requirement to make positive identification (PID) before commencing aggressive action.

To use the government theory,... Tatum should have distinguished between hostile targets and innocents before firing his weapon into the room. The end result is that he would be required to expose himself to danger within the room in case there were non-hostile persons inside. Such restraint might be good practice for law enforcement or special operations forces conducting hostage rescue operations, but not in combat. In combat Marines are trained to neutralize the enemy with overwhelming force. If we adopt the theory of liability espoused by the government, we in turn are placing innocents in grave danger as they will become truly effective shields against our Marines engaging the enemy.[24]

Ware was convinced from what he heard that Tatum followed the ROE's PID requirement in House One.

[If] while inside a structure you hear a sound that you honestly and reasonably believe is an indication that a weapon is being prepared, that is positive identification of hostile act and or intent and no specific individualized positive identification is required within the room while employing deadly force to clear the room.[25]

However, in Ware's view, the evidence of what happened in House Two was not as well-defined. He admitted he was suspicious about Mendoza's claims that he warned Tatum that there were only women and children inside one of the bedrooms.

It is difficult to believe that ... Mendoza decided to protect his fellow Marines who he believed murdered seven women and children and only after he is given testimonial immunity for his actions, he decides he no longer wants to protect them and provides a version of events that implicates ... Tatum. More likely, he provided a version of events to his counsel and that was part of the negotiations with the government for testimonial immunity. Furthermore, his demonstrated malleability to the truth and ease of manipulation by counsel makes his credibility highly suspect and in my opinion, it is not prudent to base a prosecution primarily on his testimony.[26]

After considering the testimony, Ware said his top recommendation was to dismiss the charges.

There is insufficient evidence to find reasonable grounds for offenses charged based on events in house 1 and although there are reasonable grounds for charges arising out of the events in house Two, I do not recommend referral of those charges. The evidentiary hurdles are too great, and basing a prosecution on LCpl Mendoza's testimony is too weak a case to warrant referral to a trial.[27]

If that did not appeal to Mattis, Ware suggested an alternative plan in which charges would be reduced to cover events in both houses. Charges stemming from the deaths in House One would be downgraded to voluntary manslaughter and those in House Two would be changed to attempted murder, aggravated assault and reckless endangerment. However, he remained skeptical that convictions would be forthcoming on any charges except the latter.[28]

> Notwithstanding my belief that a case against LCpl Tatum is too weak to pursue, the charge of Reckless Endangerment may avoid the most significant evidentiary problems of proving cause of death and Iraqi witness production while ensuring a trier of fact could hold LCpl Tatum accountable in some way for his actions.[29]

Ware conceded that he was shaken by the photographs of those killed in House Two.

> [They] are heart wrenching, and the desire to explain this tragedy as a criminal act and not the result of training and fighting an enemy that hides among innocents is great. However, in the end, my opinion is that there is insufficient evidence for a trial. LCpl Tatum shot and killed people in houses One and Two, but the reason he did so was because of his training and the circumstances he was placed in, not to exact revenge and commit murder.[30]

In the end, he said, the death resulted from Tatum's training as a Marine and not because of a desire to kill Iraqis.

> I believe ... Tatum's real life experience and training on how to clear a room took over and his body instinctively began firing while his head tried to grasp at what and why he was firing. By the time he could recognize that he was shooting at children, his body had already acted.[31]

Mattis weighed Ware's recommendations for almost two months. On October 19—in essence following Ware's alternative recommendations—Mattis decided that Tatum would face a court-martial on two charges of involuntary manslaughter for the deaths in House One and one charge each of reckless endangerment and aggravated assault for the other deaths.[32]

Table 4
Evolution of Charges Against Tatum

Original	Ware's Recommendations	Referred to Trial
2 counts unpremeditated murder (House Two); 4 counts negligent homicide (3 in House One; 1 in House Two); aggravated assault for wounding an 8-year-old girl (House One).	3 counts voluntary manslaughter (House One); 7 counts aggravated assault (houses One and Two); 1 count aggravated assault; 1 count reckless endangerment	2 counts involuntary manslaughter (House One); 1 count reckless endangerment (House One); 6 counts of aggravated assault.

14. Staff Sergeant Frank Wuterich

"The day was chilly and the sky was clear," said Staff Sgt. Frank Wuterich, describing the morning 1st Squad departed Firm Base Sparta on what was expected to be a routine resupply mission to a southern outpost. "The city was ominously quiet,"[1] he said. But then came the roadside bomb. "[It was] an explosion louder than anything I have ever heard; [it] rocked the entire convoy. Clear skies suddenly turned brown, black and gray as shrapnel ... came plummeting down in front of me from hundreds of feet in the air."[2] That was followed by the unexpected appearance of the Opel sedan: "At this point, I realized my mission had changed," Wuterich said. "I heard yelling mostly from the west where [Dela Cruz] was shouting in broken Arabic and using expletives to the military-aged males who occupied the white car. His weapon was at the ready, as it should have been. They were not complying and in fact were starting to run in the opposite direction to the south. I took a knee in the road and fired. Engaging was the only choice. The threat had to be neutralized."[3]

After both Wuterich and Dela Cruz ran to the bodies and shot the men again—the customary "dead shots"—attention swiveled to a structure south of the ambush site, the dwelling later to be designated House One. Several men in the squad yelled that someone in or near the house was shooting at them with an AK-47. Under an order from 2nd Lt. Kallop to "clear" the area, Wuterich led a fire team in an assault on the home, killing seven Iraqis. From House One, the men ran to an adjacent residence—House Two—where they killed eight more Iraqis. Within a half hour of the IED explosion, men from 1st Squad had slain 20 civilians. Wuterich was a major participant in all three events. Later in the day, he also took part in another shooting at House Four, where four Iraqi brothers died.

"The exact details of clearing the first and second house will forever remain unclear to me," Wuterich told Lt. Col. Paul J. Ware, the officer authorized to determine if the accusations had enough merit for him to recommend that they be referred to trial.[4] At the time Wuterich gave his statement, Lt. Gen. Mattis, at Ware's suggestion, had dropped charges against Sharratt, but a decision on Tatum's charges, which Ware also proposed be dismissed, would not be forthcoming for almost two months. "I'll never be able to pinpoint exact shooting positions, exact chronology of events, who was where and when, or even what the exact layout of the houses were," Wuterich said. "What I do know is that we cleared those houses as we were trained using forced entry, grenade employment, followed with clearing by fire."[5] He concluded his unsworn account with a comment of modest regret. "I will bear the memory of the events of that day forever, and will always mourn the unfortunate deaths of the innocent Iraqis who were killed during our response to the attack."[6]

For more than five months the world had been anxious to hear additional details of Wuterich's experiences on November 19, 2005. In the interim between the disclosure of the incident and Wuterich's Article 32 hearing, the staff sergeant and his family appeared regularly in the news. His wife and father were guests of *Hannity and Colmes* on the Fox network[7]; Wuterich filed an attention-getting suit against Representative Murtha[8]; his promotion to staff sergeant was disclosed[9]; he was profiled in *Time*,[10] and he appeared on *60 Minutes*.[11] Much of the public focus was on the much-viewed interview with Scott Pelley, but that had been little more than a teaser. When Wuterich got an opportunity at his hearing, he expanded upon the squad's actions in a well-honed, four-page statement, which he read with the stagecraft and thoroughness one would expect from a former drama class star and high school honor student.

Wuterich was the last of the enlisted men to face an Article 32 hearing—an advantage because his defense team had heard much of what witnesses were going to say. On the day the hearing opened—August 30, 2007—the prosecution dropped the allegation that Wuterich murdered the fourth brother in House Four, an incident that had been the focus of the Sharratt hearing.[12] Because Lt. Gen. Mattis had tossed out charges against Sharratt, who had been accused of killing the other three brothers, the prosecutors apparently felt it was fruitless to pursue Wuterich. The decision, however, made little dent in the list of charges against him. He still faced 17 counts of unpremeditated murder, two counts of soliciting Dela Cruz to make false official statements, and one count of making a false official statement—collectively enough to send him to prison for several lifetimes upon conviction.

Days One and Two

Lance Corporal Mendoza, who had testified that Tatum ignored his warnings that there were only women and children in a back bedroom at House Two, essentially repeated the statement, adding that he had killed a man on Wuterich's orders when the assault team entered the dwelling. Mendoza had been a private first class at the time of the incident and was the lowest ranking member of the fireteam. Despite admitting that he killed men at both houses One and Two, Mendoza had not been charged. As an immunized witness for the prosecution, Mendoza said he shot the man at House One because he thought the man was reaching for a weapon in a closet. At House Two, he testified, he killed on a direct order from Wuterich.[13] According to Mendoza, the team gathered at the entrance of House Two before trying to enter the dwelling. As they were standing at the door, Wuterich told him he was going to knock but Mendoza was to hold his fire until someone responded. "Just wait until he opens the door and shoot," Mendoza quoted Wuterich as saying.

On cross-examination, Mendoza said he did not see Wuterich shoot anyone in either house, although the staff sergeant was accused of killing a woman and her six children in House Two, as well as ordering Mendoza to shoot the woman's husband.[14] When asked by Maj. Haytham Faraj, a military defense counsel, what he thought of the former squad leader, Mendoza expressed no hesitation in declaring his loyalty: "I think he's a great Marine, sir," he replied.[15]

Winding up the day's proceeding was Capt. Kathryn Navin, a judge advocate from Camp Pendleton's Headquarters Battalion. The prosecution called her to emphasize the need for positive identification (PID) while launching an assault. Although Navin had not coached the men of Kilo Company before their deployment, she outlined what she routinely tells Marines headed for overseas deployment: "I tell them to have knowledge to a reasonable certainty that the target you are engaging is a lawful military target."[16] In other words, make sure of the quarry before pulling the trigger. However, she softened her stance during cross-examination, admitting there were occasions when positive identification of every individual was not needed. She did not elaborate.

Sergeant Dela Cruz—the lead-off witness on the second day—repeated what he had said during the Stone hearing two and a half months earlier, claiming that the men from the white sedan were not running when Wuterich shot them. Instead, he said, they were standing by the vehicle, some of them with hands locked behind their heads, when Wuterich opened fire.[17] After the initial burst, Dela Cruz said, Wuterich ran to the bodies and shot the men again. "He went to each body and shot at them," Dela Cruz said. "The muzzle [of his rifle] was about a foot from their upper torsos."[18]

Before the defense could make its point that Wuterich had been operating within the then-existing Rules of Engagement if he had shot them while they had been trying to flee, Dela Cruz added that Wuterich had told him during an earlier conversation what he would do if he found himself in a situation such as an IED attack. "He made a comment that if we ever get hit again, that we should kill everybody in the vicinity to teach them a lesson."[19]

Prompted by the prosecution, Dela Cruz added that Wuterich had asked him to lie about the shootings if they were ever asked. "Just say they were running away," Dela Cruz quoted Wuterich as telling him.[20] Dela Cruz said he went along with the plan because he "didn't want to get into trouble."[21]

Ware, who had been following the testimony intently, asked Dela Cruz: "Did you think you could provide false information?"

"That was our plan, sir," Dela Cruz responded.

When asked to elaborate, Dela Cruz said the object was to "just lie in general."[22]

Dela Cruz grew heated when Lt. Col. Colby Vokey, the lead military defense attorney, asked him to comment on a statement made by an unidentified Marine alleging Dela Cruz kicked the head of a dead Iraqi when removing his body from the blast site. Quoting the unnamed Marine, Vokey said Dela Cruz mumbled, "I killed that [expletive]" when he delivered the kick.

Dela Cruz denied it. "If I had the guts to tell I urinated [on one of the dead Iraqis] and confessed about it, why would I deny this?" Dela Cruz said. "Pissing is worse than kicking."[23]

"Oh, is it?" Vokey retorted sarcastically.

Dela Cruz, apparently contrite, responded, "They're both worse, sir."

Vokey switched subjects, getting Dela Cruz to admit he had abused prisoners on an earlier tour in Iraq by kicking them in places where bruises would not be visible. When Vokey pressed Dela Cruz to explain why he shot the men from the white sedan if he thought they were already dead, Dela Cruz said he thought he could be prosecuted for the act.

"Was it your understanding that if you shot a dead body you could be charged with murder?" Ware asked.

"Yes, sir," Dela Cruz replied.[24]

"Shooting dead bodies is not murder," Vokey interjected. "Or maybe you were the first to shoot at them?"

"No, sir," Dela Cruz said emphatically.[25]

Winding Up

As the hearing progressed, there were fewer witnesses who had been involved in the Haditha incident and more of those who tried later to make sense of the events. The first witness on the third day was NCIS special agent Thomas Brady, who testified earlier at Tatum's hearing. Although the prosecution was hoping for clarification about what happened after the white Opel arrived on the scene, Brady only confused the issue.

From his examination of photographs, Brady said he concluded that the five Iraqis were struck by shots fired from both the north—where Dela Cruz was standing—and the east—where Wuterich was kneeling when he fired his M-16. However, Brady clouded the issue when he said that it seemed to him that the fatal shots had come from Dela Cruz' direction. This was puzzling because Wuterich admitted killing the men in his *60 Minutes* interview and again in his Article 32 statement. At no time did Wuterich mention Dela Cruz's firing his weapon before the men were already on the ground.

In his testimony, Dela Cruz also said the men had been standing beside the car with their hands in the air when Wuterich opened fire. Wuterich, however, said they had started to run, which was the reason he shot them. Brady may have helped clarify that issue when he told Ware that, in his opinion, four of the men had been stationary when they were killed. The fifth might have been moving, but he had not been not running when he was shot.[26]

Captain Alonzo Capers, an instructor at Marine Corps Air Ground Combat Center in Twenty-nine Palms, California, followed Brady on the stand. Capers had not taken the men of Kilo Company through the Security and Stability Operations (SASO) program in which they were lectured on how to react in varying situations involving actual or suspected insurgents, but was called to explain the training program. He testified that SASO instructors emphasized that no one had the authority to kill indiscriminately. However, he admitted situations got confused when an individual in a position of authority, such as a squad leader, told his men to "shoot first and ask questions later." According to Capers, such a statement could be interpreted to mean that everyone is a target. "You can't do that," he said.[27] Still, Capers was intrigued by what had happened at Chestnut and Viper, saying the actions fell into a large gray area in which it was unclear which rules governed behavior. It could be the ROE, which frequently were changed on a daily basis, or it could have been what the men had been taught during the urban warfare course, called Military Operations on Urbanized Terrain, or MOUT. Whatever caused the men to act as they did had to have a trigger, Capers said. The defense claimed the trigger was the contention that the squad was taking incoming fire from House One, which is what prompted Kallop to order the area cleared. Wuterich's understanding, according to his defense team, was that the "clear" order was the equivalent of declaring the house "hostile." This, Wuterich maintained, gave him the green light to use violent house-clearing methods.

Staff Sergeant Travis Fields, who had been with Battalion 3/1 on the day of the attack but was not in 1st Squad so he was not at the IED site, was the day's last witness. Fields presented a different picture of Wuterich than had been offered by the prosecution. "He was the least aggressive [of the 1st Squad Marines]," said Fields. "He was the calmest in the squad in interacting with Iraqis." Despite his apparent regard for Wuterich's temperament, Fields said he thought it had been a mistake to tell his men to shoot first. "It goes directly against what the Rules of Engagement say," Fields said.[28]

As the day's last item of business, prosecutors entered into evidence a report from Special Agent Mike Maloney, which also had been introduced during Tatum's Article 32. Malone had not been available to testify but his report consisted of a forensic analysis that identified three shooter positions in House Two. The Corps does not make evidentiary items available to the public, but the analysis, as described by Lt. Col. Ware in Tatum's Article 32 testimony, was that "the location of the shooters, angles of impact and resulting actions of the victims is logical, concise and convincing."[29] Mendoza, who admitted shooting the head of the household when they entered the dwelling, occupied one of the positions identified by Malone. But the identity of the other two shooters remained a mystery. One was believed to have been Tatum; the other may have been Wuterich, although this issue was never resolved. Tatum could not be called to present clarifying testimony because his case was still active.

The hearing ended on September 6 after only three days. It had been expected to go into a fourth day with a cross-examination of Dela Cruz, but the session was cancelled without explanation.[30]

Ware's Report

Ware submitted his 37-page report on October 2, less than a month after Wuterich's hearing ended. It was significantly longer than similar documents on Sharratt and Tatum, and it was unusual because Ware's writing style switched from the conventional to the highly individualistic. Military legal reports rarely vary from the conservative, but in his report on Wuterich, Ware made extensive use of boldface and italicized type, adding underlining and exclamation points at unexpected places. Although he had been sharply critical of the prosecutors in his previous reports, he stepped up his fault-finding comments in Wuterich's report, frequently falling back on his favorite word—"incredible"—to describe his feelings about the government's presentation of witnesses and evidence. It appears a half dozen times in the report, sometimes with an exclamation point.

Curiously, Ware was particularly agitated by Dela Cruz, unreservedly expressing his disregard for the veteran sergeant at considerable length. "[A]bsent immunity, [Dela Cruz] would likely find himself an accused at an Article 32 instead of a key government witness," Ware interjected at one point.[31] "Simply stated, [Dela Cruz's] demeanor and performance in the courtroom is poor. He is easily impeached and absent independent evidence to support his statements, wholly incredible."[32]

Pointing out that Dela Cruz twice lied to investigators and admitted urinating in the wound in the head of one of the five Iraqis killed on the Route Chestnut shoulder, Ware added:

> His reason for providing these "false" statements is because he wanted to ensure he would not be charged with murder because he shot into the dead bodies of the individuals. He believed that forensics would trace the bullets back to him. It is incredible to believe that he would confess to killing those individuals leaving SSgt Wuterich completely out of the scenario as part of a conspiracy to obstruct justice ... because he was worried he would be charged with murder.[33]

Because Wuterich had been involved in every event in which an Iraqi died, Ware meticulously divided his report into sections referring to the episodes as they occurred, beginning with the roadside confrontation. Reliable witness or not, Dela Cruz unequivocally placed Wuterich as a major participant in the shooting deaths of the five men from the white Opel. Wuterich himself admitted shooting the men, and Ware conceded that if he had he should be held "equally responsible, regardless of whether rounds from his, Sgt. Dela Cruz' or Sgt. Salinas' weapons caused the fatal injuries."[34] But there was a catch. "To hold [Wuterich] culpable," Ware said, "the government must prove he actually shot those individuals or by his actions encouraged others to shoot and kill these men."[35] Ware elaborated:

> The central issue [is] ... whether the killings were unlawful. [Dela Cruz's] testimony, if true, provides solid reasonable grounds for [the charges] to go forward. However, the Government impeaches [Dela Cruz's] testimony with other evidence.... Because the Government presented [Dela Cruz's] testimony and then impeached large portions [of it] ... my duty to seek the "truth of the allegations alleged" prevents me from recommending that [Dela Cruz's] testimony be believed.[36]

If Dela Cruz was not believable and there was no forensic evidence, Wuterich would be off the hook regardless of his admissions. Ware wrote:

On the whole of the evidence, I believe the actions of [Wuterich] were reasonable and lawful under the circumstance presented to him and the <u>Government has insufficient evidence to recommend referral [of the charges] to a court-martial</u>[37] [Ware's formatting].

The Houses

Surprisingly, Ware found reason to doubt Wuterich's testimony in his analysis of evidence relating to the assault on House One. The reason for misgiving was Wuterich's statement to investigators that he did not fire his rifle inside the dwelling. "I find it incredible that [Wuterich] chose to stand by while his Marines entered and engaged in clearing the House with grenade and rifle fire," Ware wrote.[38]

Despite this apparent misstatement by Wuterich, Ware's support of the former squad leader did not falter. This was particularly evident in the IO's backing of the defense contention that Wuterich and the members of his team followed the ROE and did not deviate on the PID issue.

> Government claims that [Wuterich's] advice to "shoot first and ask questions later" is a command to ignore the ROE. But this still remains a compelling story unsupported by evidence. [Wuterich] and his Marines didn't kill everyone in sight. They didn't celebrate the opportunity to kill. Their post-assault actions conform with behavior which is expected of Marines who have experienced combat and the absence of such a display of satisfaction in their actions works against the theory they were out to seek revenge.[39]

In short, Ware found the prosecution's case lacking.

> Certainly today, we can second guess [Wuterich's] assessment of the situation and conclude there were better alternatives, but it is imperative to objectively look at the situation as it existed at the time, not what was learned later. Marines will often make tactical decisions that are not always the best with the benefit of hindsight, but decisive action at the critical moment is the hallmark of our training. [Wuterich] acted decisively and in accord with how he was trained, not on a specific intent to murder innocent people in revenge for an IED assault upon his convoy. Accordingly, based on the ... analysis, <u>I find that the Government has failed in its burden to demonstrate reasonable grounds to believe SSgt Wuterich committed a crime within House 1</u>[40] [Ware's formatting].

When it came to scrutiny of evidence relating to House Two, Ware found a target almost as worthy of scorn as Dela Cruz: Lance Cpl. Mendoza, who had been a private first class at the time of the incident. Ware simply did not believe Mendoza's claims that he had warned Tatum that the rear bedroom of House Two contained only women and children. His testimony was "untruthful," Ware said, but his reasons for thinking this are unclear.[41]

> [Mendoza] claims to have told [Tatum] that there were women and children in the room! Incredible. Not only is this Marine clearly an accomplice in the shooting [of an Iraqi in House Two], making his testimony highly suspect, his explanations for his actions within House Two strike me as a desperate attempt to cover lies with more lies.[42]

Tatum did not testify at Wuterich's Article 32 hearing; only a week before the procedure began, Ware recommended that the charges against him be dismissed. Although he had not appeared as a witness, Ware said his lawyers might point to Mendoza as one of the Marines who killed the two women and five children in the House Two bedroom. Previous testimony had indicated there were two shooters involved. One allegedly was Tatum and the other was believed to be Wuterich, although there was no testimony supporting the allegation. Wuterich denied firing his weapon in House Two, just as he claimed was the case in House One. Ware questioned the veracity of the statement but found a way to excuse it:

> It is [Wuterich's] insistence that he did not participate in shooting inside House Two that causes great consternation. I am left with two alternatives. He either did fire inside House Two and the trauma of the event and through denial has convinced himself that he didn't, or he was woefully derelict in his duties.[43]

Even if Wuterich had indeed been the shooter, that, too, was pardonable to Ware. "This is not to say that [Wuterich] did not enter the room and formed a reasonable, honest, but mistaken belief that there was a threat inside the room." If that were to be true, it would give prosecutors grounds for a court-martial, the IO said.[44]

Ware glided over the other accusations, suggesting changes as he had with Tatum. In conclusion, he suggested that the murder charges be dismissed and replaced with less serious accusations.

> I believe, after reviewing all the evidence, no trier of fact can conclude that SSgt Wuterich formed the criminal intent to kill. The evidence is contradictory, the forensic analysis is limited and almost all witnesses have an obvious bias or prejudice. The evidence ... that he committed murder is simply not strong enough to prove beyond a reasonable doubt.[45]

All told, Ware did not have much hope that the prosecution was going to convict Wuterich of any crime other than dereliction of duty. Still, he recommended that the charges be referred to court-martial due to their "serious nature."[46]

Also, in the final pages of the report, Ware inserted a comment describing what he thought of the incident and how it might have occurred. Regarding the issue of the white car, Ware said he felt that the men did not actually have to be running; what was important is that Wuterich *thought* they were running. "One or more of the men started to move as [Dela Cruz] shot them," Ware said, indicating his support for Special Agent Brady's opinion that the fatal shots were fired by Dela Cruz rather than Wuterich.[47] The important factor, Ware said, was Dela Cruz's credibility. "The facts remain that these charges rest upon an immunized Marine whose character for truthfulness incentive to please the Government and obvious self interest are, in my opinion, obstacles too great to overcome."[48]

Ware did not believe Wuterich committed murder. "Although there are reasonable grounds to believe [Wuterich killed Iraqis] confusion as to how the events unfolded, coupled with the unique stresses of combat operations, will make proof beyond a reasonable doubt of murder or manslaughter unlikely. "The most likely [state of mind] ... is simple negligence."[49]

Despite Wuterich's disclaimer that he could not "pinpoint exact shooting positions, exact chronology of events, who was where and when" events occurred, Ware embraced the prosecution theory that the staff sergeant was in the House Two bedroom. "It is my opinion that [he] was in the back room of House two and his denial of any participation is born out of a lack of memory of the traumatic events, or a deliberate denial because he is aware he acted criminally."[50] If he was culpable, Ware added, it was because he failed to supervise the members of his fireteam and was "willfully derelict" in performing his duties.[51] Wuterich's main fault, as far as Ware was concerned, was his failure to report what happened.

> He had a duty to report accurately what occurred. If he witnessed these events but willfully failed to take action to accurately report these events to superiors he may be held liable under alternative charges ranging from accessory after the fact ... misprision [misunderstanding] ... and violating a lawful general order.[52]

The Outcome

As Lt. Col. Bill Riggs had been incensed by Ware's remarks about the Sharratt case, so prosecutors were infuriated by Ware's comments about a "trier of fact" and "reasonable doubt." Those are issues, the prosecutors contended, that should be decided by a jury, not by an investigating officer, and Ware erred by considering them in his analysis. The prosecutors also claimed that testimony from Dela Cruz and Mendoza, however flawed, was sufficient to meet Article 32 demands.[53] Their immediate reaction was to compose a letter to Mattis complaining about Ware. The text of the letter was never made public.

Early in November, roughly a month after receiving Ware's recommendations on Wuterich, Mattis abruptly departed Camp Pendleton for Norfolk, Virginia, where he had been detailed to head the U.S. Joint Forces Command and as NATO's Supreme Allied Commander for Transformation. The job specifications required a general to be in command, so Mattis had to wait until the Senate could confirm his promotion to a four-star officer. The vote was held on September 29 and was positive.

Table 5
Evolution of Charges Against Wuterich

Charges Preferred Dec. 21, 2006	Charges Dismissed Dec. 27, 2007	Charges Referred to Trial Dec. 28, 2008
18 counts murder; 2 counts soliciting another to lie to investigators; 1 count making a false official statement.	18 counts murder; 2 counts soliciting another to lie to investigators; 1 count making a false official statement.	9 counts voluntary manslaughter; 2 counts aggravated assault; 3 counts willful dereliction of duty; 1 count obstruction of justice.

As a result of Mattis' unexpected reassignment, the decision on referring Wuterich to trial was left to his replacement, Lt. Gen. Samuel Helland, a helicopter pilot and veteran of Vietnam and the 1991 Gulf War. Helland assumed command of I MEF/MARCENT on November 5, the day before Wuterich's hearing concluded. On December 28, just a tad shy of three months since Ware filed his report, Helland referred to trial a hodgepodge of charges against Wuterich that bore little resemblance to Ware's recommendations. The accusations included nine counts of voluntary manslaughter (eight for the deaths of all civilians in House Two, plus one inclusive charge for "killing one or more persons" from the white sedan); two counts of aggravated assault (for the attacks on houses One and Two); three counts of reckless endangerment (for firing his rifle in houses One and Two and for the Opel incident); three counts of willful dereliction of duty (one for failing to achieve positive identification of the men from the white car, one for failing to ensure that his men observed the Rules of Engagement, and one for failing to ensure positive identification of the man shot by Mendoza at House Two); and one count of obstruction of justice for asking Dela Cruz to lie about the Opel incident.[54] The only vestiges of Ware's recommendations that Helland retained included dismissing the murder charges, along with accusations of soliciting another to commit an offense, and making a false official statement. Helland's decision, as announced in a release from the Public Affairs Office, failed to include comments, which would have given a glimpse into the convening authority's thought process or the prosecutions' realigned strategy.

15. First Lieutenant Andrew Grayson

If media interest in the Article 32 hearings for the Haditha Marines were to be depicted on a line chart, the independent variable would be at its zenith for the Chessani and Wuterich hearings and at its nadir for 1st Lt. Andrew Grayson's proceeding. When Col. Michael Stahlman opened Grayson's hearing on November 13, only one print outlet was represented: the *North County (California) Times*, Camp Pendleton's hometown newspaper. That was bizarre, perhaps, but understandable. Of the eight Marines charged in connection with the incident, Grayson seemed to be the least likely candidate for a court-martial resulting from the Haditha Incident.

The 25-year-old Ohio native boasted an excellent record and, as the leader of a Human Exploitation Team (HET) Team detailed to Battalion 3/1, was about as far removed from the action as possible. He did not participate in the raids in which the Iraqi civilians were killed; he never visited the homes where they died; and he played no role in determining whether an investigation should be conducted. Unfortunately, however, he was trapped in one situation that put him crosswise with an Army colonel, another in which he was fighting Corps bureaucracy, and still one more in which he was faulted for not ordering an investigation. As a result, he was accused of making false officials statements (three counts), obstructing justice, and scheming to get a discharge to which he was not entitled. If convicted on all charges, he could be sentenced to as many as 30 years in prison.

Charges were preferred against Grayson, along with the other Haditha Marines, on December 21, 2006, but that was the extent of the similarity between his case and those of the others. In actuality, Grayson was not a formal member of Battalion 3/1. He commanded the HET unit that was detailed to Kilo Company—he and a subordinate, Staff Sgt. Justin Laughner. He had not trained with the others and was not in the battalion chain of command. HET members are intelligence personnel prepared to interact with civilians to try to identify insurgents and to try to prevent attacks such as that on November 19. They are most valuable when they are able to persuade Iraqis to warn of IED locations, which Grayson was able to do on the day of the attack, when he was credited with locating two other roadside bombs. As a result, he was nominated for a Bronze Star medal, the fourth highest award presented for performance in combat. Grayson was on his second deployment at the time of the Haditha Incident.

The only time Grayson's name had come up in the proceedings, prior to his Article 32, was when his civilian lawyer, Joseph Casas, announced that Grayson had rejected an offer from Lt. Col. Sean Sullivan, one of the more ubiquitous prosecutors, to remove his case from the court-martial list if he would agree to go before the convening authority in a proceeding called non-judicial punishment.[1] An NJP procedure is not a trial, and there is no record of a criminal conviction in a service member's file. It can, however, damage an officer's career. According to Casas, criminal charges against Grayson would be withdrawn if he confessed to trying to cover up the killings. Grayson flatly turned down the offer and sent an e-mail to the Associated Press reading: "I was asked by the prosecution to fall on my sword for the greater good of the Marine Corps. The prosecution wanted me to distort the truth to fit their end goal."[2] At the time Grayson made the offer public, the Wuterich hearing had just ended and Grayson's story was lost in the avalanche of coverage of his case.

Colonel Stahlman drew fire from the defense as soon as the hearing started. In appointing the investigating officers for the accused, Lt. Gen. Mattis originally had named Lt. Col. Tracy Daly to preside. But Daly recused himself as soon as he saw that the names on the prosecution's witness list included a close friend. Stahlman was Daly's last-minute replacement. However, Casas objected to Stahlman because the colonel had been the legal advisor to Col. Conlin at Chessani's Article 32. Stahlman rejected Casas' protest. "I concluded that my participation in the present case would not prejudice 1st Lt Grayson or otherwise adversely impact the proceedings," Stahlman wrote later in his report to Mattis.[3]

As Grayson's IO, Stahlman faced a situation unlike any confronted by the other investigating officers. Major McCann and Col. Conlin were required only to evaluate evidence of dereliction of duty against Capt. Stone and Lt. Col. Chessani, while Lt. Col. Ware concentrated on whether lance corporals Sharratt and Tatum and Staff Sgt. Wuterich were potentially responsible for the deaths of Iraqi civilians. But Stahlman was being asked to oversee a hearing in which multiple issues demanded analysis.

The Destroyed Photographs

As commander of the HET team attached to Battalion 3/1, Grayson had sent his subordinate—Staff Sgt. Laughner—to Route Chestnut to photograph the bodies of the dead civilians; the scene of the Opel confrontation in which five of the Iraqis had been riding; and the interiors of houses One, Two, and Four. It was a routine assignment designed to photograph the bodies so their images could be compared to those stored in a Defense Department database to determine if the dead were known or suspected insurgents. The photographs were not intended to be used as Corps documentation of the incident. Laughner made about 70 images, which were forwarded to intelligence officials for comparison. Grayson did not examine the photos before passing them up the chain. Soon afterwards, when he was informed there were no hits on the images, he ordered Laughner to destroy them because it was Corps policy not to keep photos that had no intelligence value.

Unknown to Grayson, Laughner transferred about half of the images to his personal computer before wiping them from the unit's computer. Some seven months later, Laughner was called as a government witness during the Chessani Article 32 hearing. When asked about the destruction of the photos, Laughner said he felt it was an attempt by Grayson to hide the slaughter of the Iraqi civilians.[4]

The photographs became an issue after Army colonel Gregory Watt, who had been sent to Haditha by his boss, Lt. Gen. Peter Chiarelli, to conduct a preliminary investigation of the incident, decided that Grayson had been lying when he said there were no photographs from the scenes although they had been erased before Watt arrived. When Watt was called as a prosecution witness on the third day of the hearing, he said Grayson had been arrogant and uncooperative. "[He] was not forthcoming in providing information in support of the investigation," Watt said, because he did not respond to his request for photographs. Watt said he did not learn until several weeks later that photographs by other Marines had been available at the time he was with Battalion 3/1.[5] "I gave Lt. Grayson multiple opportunities to provide photos," Watt said, but at least twice Grayson told him no pictures were available.[6]

Under cross-examination, Watt admitted that Grayson explained that there were no photographs because they had been wiped to comply with Corps policy. Evidently, Watt did not look beyond Grayson in his attempt to secure blast scene images. Major General Eldon Bargewell, who was sent by Chiarelli to perform a more thorough investigation, noted in his April 2006 report to Chiarelli that photographs of the victims were plentiful. But photographs were not all that was on Watt's mind. Before leaving the stand, the Army colonel also criticized Grayson for allegedly withholding information by not telling him that there had been a meeting between Chessani and members of the Haditha City Council within days of the incident. If he had known this, Watt said, he would have contacted Chiarelli immediately asking for a full-fledged probe.[7]

Seeking a Discharge

Another major issue facing Stahlman was how to evaluate accusations that Grayson had twice violated the UCMJ's Article 80—entitled simply "Attempts"—in an effort to get a premature discharge.[8]

Before Stahlman could delve into that contretemps, he first had to determine if Grayson was indeed an active duty Marine. Available records showed he had separated from active duty on June 1, 2007, five and a half months before the hearing. However, the Corps refused to define his duty status. According to a hearing fact sheet distributed by the Associated Press, "the Marine Corps disputes that Grayson has been deactivated and declined to explain why he had received discharge papers."[9] On the other hand, the prosecution contended that Grayson had lied about his service status to facilitate his separation. He could not have been discharged, prosecutors argued, because as a service member facing unresolved criminal charges he would have been on "legal hold"—a situation that would have prevented him from being released until the criminal charges were resolved.

Pushing Grayson's case into the realm of extreme unconventionality was a remarkable lack of testimony. Stahlman did not include a witness list in the report that was released, and the Corps refuses to disclose documents on Article 32s. The only available record was in the stories published by the *North County Times* and the Associated Press. According to the articles, only five witnesses were called: Watt, Laughner, Maj. Dinsmore, and Navy captains Michael Dubrule and Joseph Burke. Navy captains are equal in rank to Corps colonels.

Laughner repeated what he had said during his testimony at the Chessani hearing. However, he added an admission that he had lied to investigators about the copies of the Haditha photos on his personal computer. Dinsmore, the former Battalion 3/1 intelligence officer, testified as a defense witness, saying it had not been Grayson's job to order an investigation simply because he knew what the photos revealed. Grayson, Dinsmore said, was responsible for developing intelligence leads, not probing civilian deaths.[10]

Dubrule, director of training at the Navy-Marine Corps Intelligence Center, praised Grayson for his initiative and his successes as an intelligence officer. Grayson and members of his team were nominees for the Pentagon's Counter-Intelligence Team of the Year award, but their names were withdrawn because of the charges. While questioning Grayson's judgment in ordering the photos deleted, Dubrule added he did not think it was a lieutenant's job to "be the moral authority for the battalion."[11]

Unlike other accused, Grayson chose not to make a personal statement. Stahlman, who had been mostly silent during the hearing, waited until its conclusion to comment on the charge of willful dereliction of duty against Grayson. He did not understand, he said, why more senior officers had not been accused of the same crime. "I would have expected everyone in that battalion would have been charged and obviously that didn't happen," Stahlman said drily.[12]

Stahlman's Report

Stahlman's report was submitted to Mattis' successor, Lt. Gen. Helland, on December 3, 2007. It was distinctive because it was by far the briefest of the reports submitted in connection with the Haditha cases. It consisted entirely of a three-page executive summary and a two-page addendum, which was mostly boilerplate. Stahlman's report also was devoid of any personal opinions or substantial observations, stating only the bare-bones reasons for his recommendation that Grayson's case go to trial minus the dereliction accusations. "I do not recommend the referral of this charge," he wrote, speaking about dereliction. "The evidence presented at the proceedings failed to establish reasonable grounds to believe this offense was committed."[13]

Originally, Grayson faced two counts of attempted fraudulent separation from active duty, and Stahlman suggested the counts be consolidated.[14] He also recommended retaining and referring to court-martial the charge of obstructing justice and two counts of making a false official statement. "Reasonable grounds exist to believe [Grayson] committed" these offenses, he noted.[15] Lieutenant General Helland, only a few weeks on the job, adopted Stahlman's advice verbatim. On January 1, 2008, he ordered charges of obstructing justice, lying to investigators, and fraudulently attempting to get a discharge referred to trial.[16]

Grayson's hearing was the last for the Haditha Marines. The next move was to prepare for trials for the four men scheduled to be court-martialed: Grayson, Chessani, Tatum, and Wuterich. The seven-month period during which the Article 32 hearings were held had not been a glowing testimonial to the Corps' ability to plan and execute a series of critical prosecutions. Over the months, as many charges had been dismissed as were referred to trial. One of the issues that remained puzzling was why, so far, ten Marines had been immunized, including three former members of 1st Squad (Dela Cruz, Mendoza, Salinas), the commander of Kilo Company (McConnell); Laughner; three battalion-level officers (Stone, Connelly and Hyatt), Kallop, and Frank, who was in charge of the body collections. Five of them—Kallop, Mendoza, Salinas, Dela Cruz, and McConnell—possibly had information that would be vital at trial, but the reasons for immunizing the others were unknown.

Part IV: The Trials

16. The CBS Fiasco

By early 2008, trials appeared imminent for the four Haditha Marines whose cases had not been dismissed following an eight-month-long series of Article 32 hearings: Chessani, Tatum, Wuterich, and Grayson. Team Charlie—an unidentified group of judge advocates appointed by Mattis to direct the prosecutions—produced a trial calendar that appeared at first glance to be a reasonable and efficient schedule for rapid disposition of the Haditha cases. Under the plan, the courts-martial were to begin on February 28 with the trial of Staff Sgt. Wuterich. The other three trials were to follow at monthly intervals: Lance Cpl. Tatum on March 28; Lt. Col. Chessani on April 28, and Lt. Grayson on May 28. By setting such an ambitious timetable, the Corps seemed to be answering critics who were asking why procedures weren't moving more quickly. By the time Lt. Gen. Helland announced his decision on what charges Wuterich would face at court-martial, it had been 25 months since the incident, yet the Corps still was only *talking* about trials.

Based on the Corps' past performance in other high-profile cases, what was happening with the Haditha courts-martial was notably at odds with history. The last series of prosecutions in which Marines were accused of killing multiple noncombatants had been in 1970, near the end of the Vietnam War. In that case, five enlisted men from B Company, 1st Battalion, 7th Marines, were accused of murdering 16 women and children in an isolated village near Da Nang, South Vietnam, called Son Thang-4. One of the men was awarded immunity to testify against the others. Two of the men were convicted and two were acquitted. What was remarkable—other than it was the largest known civilian massacre in Corps history—was the efficiency of the proceedings. The time consumed—from the day of the incident to the final trial—was only six months.[1] More current examples were the prosecutions of seven Marines and a Navy corpsman accused of killing a retired Iraqi policeman in Hamdania, Iraq, on April 26, 2006. The first trial stemming from that incident was conducted within five months. Eight trials were conducted in a little less than ten months, and all accused were convicted. By the time of the last Hamdania trial, Haditha prosecutors were only halfway through the Article 32 hearings even though the Hamdania incident occurred five months after Haditha.

To take the Haditha trial schedule literally would mean accepting the presumption that the Corps was making an honest effort to get back on the timetable expected from the touted Legal Services Support Section (LSSS). In reality, the announced schedule was only bluster; it fell apart less than two weeks after it was published. The first sign it was not going to work came on January 16, 2008, when the Haditha prosecutors subpoenaed CBS for unaired footage recorded by Scott Pelley's crew in connection with the *60 Minutes* interview. What the prosecutors were looking for was some four hours of video that had been cut by editors when they were putting the program together—material commonly known as "outtakes."

Lieutenant Colonel Jeffrey Chessani, center, chats with his military lawyer, Lieutenant Colonel John Shelburne, on their way to a proceeding in a Camp Pendleton courtroom. Chessani, the former commander of the 3rd Battalion 1st Marines, was accused of dereliction of duty for not ordering an investigation into the incident in Haditha. Behind Chessani and Shelburne are Chessani's two civilian lawyers, Robert Muise, left, and Brian Rooney. Charges against Chessani were dismissed (Reuters/Fred Greaves).

The Disputed Material

The Wuterich interview was broadcast on March 18, 2007. As expected, prosecutors quickly compared what Wuterich said in the interview to what he had told a military investigator a year earlier. Just as quickly, they found relevant discrepancies between what Wuterich said during the 2006 investigation and what he had told Pelley. Hypothesizing that there were more discrepancies in the material they had not seen, prosecutors subpoenaed CBS in an effort to force the broadcaster to relinquish the unaired video. The subpoena was submitted on January 16, 2008—some ten months after the broadcast and only six weeks before Wuterich's trial was scheduled to begin before Lt. Col. Jeffrey Meeks.[2] Thirty-seven days later, CBS asked Meeks to quash the subpoena, claiming the material was protected under the First Amendment's guarantee of freedom of the press. "It is not easy for journalists to have witnesses, who are central witnesses in cases such as these, to sit down and share their story with the general public," CBS attorney Seth D. Berlin argued at a hearing before Meeks on February 22. "If we become viewed as an arm of the government, nobody is going to do that."[3]

The judge agreed with CBS, declaring the subpoena invalid. It was, he said, a "fishing expedition" driven by over-reaching prosecutors. The government, he added, had enough evidence to make its case at trial, and anything else they could get from CBS would be "cumulative." If prosecutors wanted to purse their search, he said, they would have to go to sources other than CBS.

Meeks was an experienced judge advocate with 25 years in the Corps, most of it in defense-related positions. He was certified as a judge in July 2004 assigned to the Corps' Western Judicial Circuit, which includes Camp Pendleton. According to a biography on his civilian firm's web site, Meeks presided at trials ranging from recruit abuse at Marine Corps Recruit Depot, San Diego, to murder cases resulting from alleged violations in Fallujah and Hamdania as well as Haditha.[4] He was the judge in three Hamdania cases: those of Pfc. John Jodka III, Lance Cpl. Jerry Shumate, and the most prominent member of Hamdania Eight, Sgt. Lawrence Hutchins III. Jodka and Shumate pleaded guilty to charges relating to the murder of a retired Iraqi policeman in Hamdania in April 2006. Hutchins—the leader of the unit that killed Hashim Ibrahim Awad—was convicted in August 2007 and sentenced to 15 years in prison.[5]

Given his experience, it was puzzling why Meeks—in his decision to quash the subpoena—issued an order with two gaping holes. First, he had not addressed CBS's main point about First Amendment protection; second, he decreed the information in the outtakes was duplicative even though he had not viewed the material. The reason he had not was that he didn't have it. CBS had not provided it, because the company considered it privileged.

A week after Meeks quashed the subpoena, prosecutors asked the Navy-Marine Court of Criminal Appeals (NMCCA) for a reversal. The appeal did not mention CBS's claim to First Amendment protection, but the broadcaster itself brought the issue before the court in a cross-appeal a few days later. CBS's aggressive action was the first of several components that complicated the outtakes argument and led to more than two and a half years of legal wrangling.

Wuterich joined CBS in its plea to the NMCCA, broadening the affair into a three-party fight in which each party was seeking a different result. The prosecutors wanted the appeals court to revoke Meeks's order and compel CBS to turn over the video. CBS, on the other hand, wanted the NMCCA to rule that the outtakes were protected by the First Amendment. This would serve a dual purpose: not only would it make the outtakes unavailable but it would establish a precedent extending newsgatherers' rights into military courts, which did not recognize the alleged privilege. Wuterich had a different motive: his lawyers wanted to muddy the waters as much as possible and delay a court-martial that was only days away when Meeks quashed the subpoena. Under military law, a trial could be delayed by filing an appeal even if it strayed from issues directly related to the case. The decision to join in the CBS plea was classic lawyer double-talk. Wuterich's argument was that an appeal was delaying his Sixth Amendment right to a speedy trial, but by participating in the CBS appeal he essentially was contributing to the delay. Because of the legal mess, Wuterich's trial was on indefinite hold.

Consider the situation: the trials of the Haditha Marines had not even begun and already they were mired in gridlock. In addition to the government's appeal of Meeks's subpoena decision, CBS's separate plea to the NMCCA and Wuterich's intervention, prosecutors also had formally complained to Meeks that Marines it was planning to call as witnesses at Wuterich's trial—the staff sergeant's squad mates—were refusing to cooperate. According to the lead prosecutor, Capt. Nicholas Gannon, the most adamant violator was Lance Cpl. Tatum, who himself was scheduled for trial on March 28, only a month away. "They are grudging witnesses," Gannon told Meeks. "There are a lot of inconsistencies in their testimony."[6]

The Battle Begins

At first, it appeared that Wuterich's trial delay might be short-lived. On June 20, just a little more than two months after CBS and Wuterich appealed, the a three-judge NMCCA panel voted unanimously in the prosecution's favor.[7] Slim by appeals court standards—only 11 pages—the ruling addressed three topics. First, it kicked Wuterich into the cold: "We conclude ... that the appellee lacks standing," the court said abruptly, meaning in the court's view, he had no right to participate in the plea.[8] Second, it criticized Meeks for not viewing the video before making his ruling. "Unfortunately," the court said tartly, "[Meeks] was at a disadvantage in assessing that which he had not seen."[9] It also ungraciously pointed to Meeks's abrupt denial of a prosecution request to examine the material. "Indeed," the court said, "in this case the Government requested an in-camera review of the undisclosed audio-video material, but [Meeks] summarily denied it."[10] The court also piled on Meeks for calling the government request "fishing," saying his decision was "arbitrary."[11] Third—and importantly because it looked as if it might move the case along—the court reinstated the subpoena. In effect, this legitimized the government request for the outtakes, and if CBS complied, proceedings could commence without haste. What the court did not do was rule on the issue of First Amendment privilege, passing the burden back to Meeks by ordering him to assess whether "'newsgathering' privilege" applied.[12] It declined to delve into the claim because it did not consider the question to be "ripe" for review. In addition, the court declined to examine it independently because "it would exceed our scope."[13]

The opinion left Meeks in a bind. Although he had been commanded to review the outtakes, he could not examine material he did not have. Inexplicably, the NMCCA had not mandated that CBS surrender the material, and CBS continued to refuse to do so without a court order. Making Meeks's predicament worse was that the instruction to take on the privilege issue was packed with risk. Meeks may have

Lieutenant General James Mattis, commander of the I Marine Expeditionary Force and Marine Forces Central Command, during testimony at a 2007 hearing of the Senate Armed Forces Committee to determine if he should be awarded a fourth star and named commander of the Joint Forces Command and Supreme Allied Commander Transformation in Norfolk, Virginia. He later took command of the U.S. Central Command (CENTCOM) (Reuters/Yuri Gripas).

disregarded CBS's claims on purpose because it was such a touchy subject. The claim of reporters' privilege is raised fairly often in civilian courts, especially in civil cases, but it had never come up in a court-martial. Some civilian courts recognized it; some did not. But the military is a much smaller community, and by issuing a possible precedent-setting decision, Meeks chanced setting a standard that could not work to the Corps' advantage. There also was the question of whether he was qualified to determine if a Constitutional right existed.

More Appeals

Undoubtedly, the Haditha prosecutors were happy to have the subpoena back in force, thanks to the NMCCA ruling. But Wuterich and CBS did not share the enthusiasm. Three weeks after the NMCCA issued its opinion, the broadcaster and the staff sergeant turned to the military's highest court—the U.S. Court of Appeals for the Armed Forces (CAAF)—by filing a petition seeking determinations on two issues: they asked the court to decide on whether Meeks's ruling was the proper basis for a pretrial appeal, and whether Meeks should have quashed the subpoena without first viewing the disputed material, which seemed redundant because the NMCCA already had ordered him to examine the outtakes.

The CAAF responded in a rambling, 68-page opinion on November 17, 2008.[14] However, before getting to the meat of the issue, the court ruled almost offhandedly that the NMCCA erred in saying that Wuterich had no status in the appeals. "It was not appropriate to deprive him altogether of the opportunity to participate in appellate litigation having direct consequences on the prompt disposition of criminal proceedings brought against him," the opinion said reprovingly.[15]

After a multi-page technical discussion on the underlying reasons for pretrial appeals and the differences between the civilian and the military codes in allowing them, the court determined that, considering the situation, "a ruling quashing a subpoena is appealable" under the UCMJ.[16] The court echoed the NMCCA decision when it zeroed in on whether Meeks should have viewed the material before making his ruling. The court said he should have and his failure to do so was an "abuse of discretion."[17] To correct the error, the court ordered Meeks to first look at the video in his chambers and then decide if an open hearing would be "the appropriate forum for consideration of issues pertinent to a motion to quash the subpoena."[18] However, as had the

NMCCA, the CAAF waffled on the important question of First Amendment privilege. It dodged the issue by writing:

> On appeal, the parties have referred to the question of whether a newsgathering privilege should be recognized in the military justice system, but they have not asked this court to resolve whether the subpoena in this case should have been quashed on a qualified newsgathering privilege. Under these circumstances, we do not decide here whether such a privilege should be recognized in the military justice system.[19]

Less than four months after the CAAF ruled that the prosecution's appeal of Meeks's decision to quash the subpoena had been permissibly filed under military law, Wuterich's lawyers took the issue to the U.S. Supreme Court.[20] The staff sergeant's March 10, 2009, request for high court action was permissible but highly unusual and stood little chance of success. According to one judge advocate writing on a web site devoted to military legal issues, it had been 13 years since the Supreme Court had heard a military case.[21]

The request—formally known as petition for a writ of certiorari—challenged the CAAF's authority to make decisions about which pretrial appeals were permissible under military law. The CAAF's ruling, Wuterich's lawyers argued, was "overly expansive" and could have results contrary to the designs of the authors of the UCMJ.[22] The drafters of the military code—the petition said—did not intend to allow for frequent government interlocutory appeals that would "disrupt trial dockets" and "interfere with military operations and other activities [that] would impose a heavy burden on appellate courts and counsel."[23] If the practice were to continue, Wuterich's lawyers warned, "such stays can have devastating consequences on service members charged with UCMJ violations, such as prolonging their military enlistments and lengthening pre-trial restraint."[24] Although Wuterich was approaching the end of his latest enlistment, he could not be discharged as long as criminal charges were pending.

Not surprisingly, the request went nowhere. The court denied the request without comment on October 5, 2009, almost seven months after it was filed. The attempt to get the Supreme Court involved played no role in Wuterich's proceedings in the Camp Pendleton judicial district, but was strong evidence of the delaying and obfuscating tactics that would be used throughout the proceedings.

Back to the NMCCA

CBS surrendered the outtakes to Meeks for his exclusive viewing on March 11, 2009, the day after Wuterich's request to the Supreme Court and more than a year after the judge quashed the outtakes subpoena. Three days after receiving the material, which had been burned on eight CDs, Meeks called the lawyers together. It was his opinion, he told them, that the video revealed nothing that was not already available to the prosecution. "All the statements are consistent with prior statements [Wuterich] has made. It might be nice [for the prosecution] to have [the material], but it's not critical," he said, sticking to his original decision to void the subpoena.[25] Also, in a more timid repeat of the statements he had made in February 2008, Meeks said CBS enjoyed a "qualified newsgatherers' privilege," which it exercised by refusing to turn over the outtakes videotape.[26] Borrowing words from CBS's original motion to quash, Meeks said, "The press has an interest in being able to prepare and preserve stories without being an investigative arm of the government."[27] However, he did not explain what he meant by "qualified privilege," and he did not describe the material he determined should not be reviewable.

It was Meeks's last act as a Corps trial judge; two days later, he retired. His exit from the case may have been a surprise to the public, but it definitely was not to the Corps. Military retirements are not spur-of-the-moment events. First, a retirement request must be submitted months in advance so it has time to work its way up the chain of command. In addition, pre-retirement physicals must be completed at least six months before separating. On top of that, the retiring officer is obligated to attend a series of briefs and seminars, which are drawn out for a period of weeks if not months, immediately before his or her departure from active duty. The Corps undoubtedly knew the exact date Meeks was leaving even before the CAAF's November 2008 ruling.

Because the Corps traditionally reveals as little as possible to the public, there was no announcement of Meeks's retirement—either before or after he left active duty—nor was there a statement concerning a replacement. Evidently—as seen from subsequent developments—the Corps did not have a plan to have someone ready to take Meeks's place when he retired, because there was no action in the case for another year. It was not until late March 2010—a full 12 months after Meeks retired—that the public learned that Wuterich had a new judge: Lt. Col. David Jones, who was brought in from a base in Okinawa. The Corps did not announced Jones's appointment; it was made public only because his name was mentioned as Wuterich's judge in media reports on a court proceeding involving Wuterich. The fact that the convening authority—Lt. Gen. Joseph Dunford, who had replaced Helland in May 2009 to become the third man to hold that job since the Haditha proceedings began—had to go outside I MEF/MARCENT to find a judge suggested that the command still had not come to grips with a lawyer shortage stemming from the Iraq War cases. It contributed to a situation that had persisted since late 2006 when Lt. Gen. Mattis had to look to Hawaii to find a presiding officer for the Article 32 hearings for Wuterich, Tatum and Sharratt.

Within days of Meeks's ruling, the prosecution filed its second appeal within a year to the NMCCA demanding to know if there was such a thing as reporter's privilege and, if so, whether it applied in military courts. Finally, the government wanted to know if Meeks had mistakenly used First Amendment rights as an excuse for twice tossing out the request for outtakes. The court, which heard the appeal sitting *en banc* (that is, as an 11-member court), responded in a unanimous opinion five months later that reversed Meeks's order recognizing a reporter's privilege and employing that as a reason for rejecting the government's attempt to secure the outtakes.[28] Although the judges all agreed on those points, they were sharply divided over how the

Neal A. Puckett, lead civilian defense attorney, and Staff Sergeant Frank Wuterich on their way to the Camp Pendleton courtroom in January 2012 where Wuterich was on trial for multiple crimes in connection with the deaths in Haditha. Wuterich's trial was postponed for more than five years—longer than any other in U.S. military history. It ended when he pleaded guilty to a misdemeanor (author's photograph).

UCMJ—specifically its Article 62—could be used in decisions for quashing subpoenas. It was a plurality vote: 3-2-3-3. Three agreed on all points; two judges mostly concurred but disagreed on a technical issue (whether the correct UCMJ Article was cited as a basis for appeal); three agreed in general but diverged over a different technical issue (whether the appeal should have been based on "discoverability" of material or its "admissibility" at trial), and three abstained. Two of the judges had been on the panel that issued the June 20, 2008, opinion, one of whom was among the three who did not take part.

From the perspective of non-lawyers—that is, those not interested in the parsing of legally technical issues such as discoverability and admissibility— the fascinating parts of the 24-page document dealt with the court's research into the existence or non-existence of a Constitutionally sanctioned reporter's privilege. In short, the court said such rights did not exist although four out of the 12 federal Circuit Courts of Appeal have recognized such rights in criminal cases involving non-confidential material.[29]

The core of the court's research on newsgatherer's rights was a 37-year-old Supreme Court decision in a case involving three reporters covering non-related news events who refused to testify about their sources before grand juries, citing First Amendment protection. After hearing arguments in a consolidated case titled after one of the reporters—Paul Branzburg of the Louisville *Courtier-Journal*—the court ruled 5–4 against the existence of reporter's privilege under the Constitution.[30]

The case—*Branzburg*—was dissimilar in many respects from the issues raised in the CBS fight, but the court said it was the closest match it could find. Some of the more interesting points that featured in the NMCCA's fractured decision included these:

> The United States Supreme Court has held that "neither [reporter nor source] is immune, on First Amendment grounds, from testifying against the other." ... According to the majority of the Court ... the only testimonial privilege for unofficial witnesses that is rooted in the Federal Constitution is the Fifth Amendment privilege against compelled self-incrimination.[31]
>
> The First Amendment, of course, makes no explicit mention of a reporter's privilege in either the federal courts or in military courts-martial. It provides simply that "Congress shall make no law ... abridging the freedom of speech, or of the press."[32]
>
> *Branzburg* represents the Supreme Court's sole consideration of the reporter's privilege, and the Court declined to recognize it as a broadly based First Amendment protection. We conclude that *Branzburg* is controlling precedent on this aspect of our analysis.... We, therefore, must adhere to the conclusion ... that there is no ... reporter's privilege.[33]
>
> We conclude that there continues to be "substantial controversy" over the legit-

imacy and parameters of the reporter's privilege in the federal courts.... In reaching this conclusion, we need not delineate precisely what is required in order to be "generally recognized." This is because we find it incongruous to characterize as generally recognized in criminal cases any privilege over non-confidential news material, when such a privilege is recognized in only four [federal] circuits and when an equal number of circuit court opinions hold otherwise.[34]

As did the Supreme Court in *Branzburg*, we recognize the important interest of maintaining a robust and free press. Nonetheless, in this case, we decline to align ourselves, as did [Meeks], with those few circuits recognizing the reporter's privilege for non-confidential material in criminal cases. This is because the privilege asserted is not commonly recognized, and because the policy considerations in those cases that did not recognize it are inapposite to the facts before us.[35]

The opinion effectively ended the outtakes mêlée, but it was 18 months in the making. It was another year before CBS actually surrendered the material, but that dovetailed neatly with the entrance of Lt. Col. Jones as Wuterich's new trial judge. Jones's arrival was first noted in a story in the *North County (California) Times* in late March 2010 in relation to a motion filed by Wuterich's lawyers. Anyone who thought a resolution in the CBS affair meant that Wuterich would soon go to trial was mistaken. Jones's action on the latest motion was only the signal for the start of another long series of fights conducted in large part in the appeals courts.

One of the unmentioned downsides of the prosecution's outtakes victory was that it exposed serious weaknesses in the government's case. The fact that Team Charlie was so desperate to wrest the material from CBS indicated it had a dearth of potent evidence it could use against Wuterich. Still haunting the prosecutors was Capt. Gannon's grouse to Meeks that witnesses against Wuterich were not being forthcoming. Not easily forgotten, too, were Lt. Col. Ware's criticisms of the prosecu-

Haytham Faraj, a defense attorney for Staff Sergeant Frank Wuterich, in January 2012 during Wuterich's trial on multiple charges. Faraj was one of Wuterich's original military lawyers in 2006 and joined the defense team as a civilian after he retired from the Corps in 2008 (author's photograph).

tion's presentations in the Wuterich Article 32 hearings and the IO's prediction that the government did not have enough proof to convict Wuterich of anything except dereliction of duty. It also probably was worrying the Corps that the Camp Pendleton Legal Services Support Section had been battered during the CBS encounter. Two appeals courts had criticized Meeks—one of the Corps' senior judges.

Table 6
Outtakes Timeline

2007

Mar. 18	Wuterich appears on *60 Minutes*.

2008

Jan. 16	Prosecutors subpoena CBS for outtakes.
Feb. 22	Lt. Col. Jeffrey Meeks, at CBS's request, quashes subpoena.
Feb. 28	Wuterich's trial postponed indefinitely pending decision on the outtakes issue.
Apr. 7	Government asks the NMCCA to reverse Meeks's ruling voiding the subpoena.
Apr. 11	Wuterich and CBS, acting as a "non-party," ask the NMCCA to dismiss the government's appeal.
June 20	NMCCA sends case back to Meeks with three directives: conduct additional fact-finding; determine if the disputed material is relevant; and address the issue of newsgatherers' rights.
July 10	CBS asks CAAF to reverse the NMCCA decision.
Nov. 17	CAAF votes 3–2 to send case back to Meeks without ruling on the reporter's privilege issue.
Dec. 12	CAAF denies petition seeking reconsideration of its Nov. 17 decision.

2009

Mar. 10	Wuterich files a petition for a writ of certiorari with the U.S. Supreme Court, asking for a review of the statutory jurisdiction of the military's appellate courts.
Mar. 11	CBS delivers outtakes to Judge Meeks for in-camera viewing.
Mar. 13	Meeks rules CBS has "qualified reporter's privilege" and is not required to surrender material.
Mar. 14	Meeks retires.
Apr. 20	Government asks the NMCCA to rule on Constitutional privileges.
Aug. 31	NMCCA reverses Meeks's reporter's rights ruling saying CBS does not have Constitutional privilege to withhold outtakes.
Oct. 5	U.S. Supreme Court denies Wuterich request for a writ of certiorari.

2010

Sept. 12	CBS delivers outtakes to prosecutors.

17. Unlawful Command Influence

In mid–February 2008, some ten weeks before Lt. Col. Chessani's court-martial was scheduled to begin, the former battalion commander's attorneys bombarded Col. Steven Folsom with a stack of motions ranging from one seeking a new Article 32 hearing to one seeking permission to question Representative Murtha under oath about his discussions with Corps commanders on the Haditha Incident.[1] The motions submitted by Robert Muise and Brian Rooney stood little chance of winning the approval of Chessani's judge, but were noteworthy because Chessani's team had been publicly silent since filing a pair of lengthy complaints about Col. Conlin's Article 32 recommendations with Lt. Gen. Mattis the previous summer.

As expected, Folsom, quickly denied the motions.[2] But less than a month later, Muise and Rooney rebounded with two more motions. One accused the prosecutors of choosing Chessani as a target while leaving higher-ranking officers untouched because he was high enough in the Iraq command "to sacrifice at the political altar so as to appease the anti-war politicians and media."[3] The second motion had far more serious potential consequences.[4] The 31-page document was disjointed and sometimes nearly incoherent, bouncing from one subject to another. One ten-page section, for example, was devoted to statements Murtha made to talk show hosts about the Haditha incident. Another hinted at a spurious conspiracy involving Lt. Gen. Mattis; Navy Secretary Donald Winter; the then-current Corps commandant, Gen. James T. Conway; his predecessor, Gen. Michael Hagee; the prosecutor; and two staff judge advocates. Even its goals were vague. At one point, the documents' authors contended that charges against Chessani should be tossed out because of excessive pretrial publicity, or because Navy Secretary Winter had interfered with the judicial process by censuring three of Chessani's superiors. However, what grabbed the attention of the prosecutors and Judge Folsom was an assertion that lieutenant generals Mattis and Helland had violated the UCMJ's ban against unlawful command influence, or UCI.

While it means nothing in the civilian legal world, an accusation of UCI screams trouble to military lawyers. Damned as a "mortal enemy of military justice" by the country's highest military appeals court, a proven claim of UCI means certain death for a prosecution's case.[5] It is so menacing that even the suggestion of its presence can be catastrophe to the prosecution.[6] Because it has such potential for irreparable harm, a claim of UCI alone triggers a process that overrides all other issues. Mindful of his obligations to resolve the affair before proceeding with Chessani's court-martial, Folsom ordered a hearing for May 7—nine days after the former battalion commander's trial had been scheduled to convene—to see if the accusations had merit.

Grounds for the Confrontation

Chessani's accusation was based on subjects that had not previously been discussed in the proceedings, so it caught most Haditha-watchers by surprise. The claim stemmed from events that took place in Iraq and had been festering for more than two years. The principal character in the unfolding drama was an unknown in the Haditha proceedings: Col. John Ewers, the I MEF staff judge advocate.

As the story progressed, it was revealed that Ewers had worked as a Marine liaison officer with Army Maj. Gen. Eldon Bargewell during his March 2006 investigation of the Haditha incident.[7] Bargewell's probe, which was conducted independently of the NCIS investigation, had been authorized under Army Regulation 15–6, which prohibited a search for criminal activity. Bargewell's job had been simply to determine the internal reaction in Battalion 3/1 to the IED explosion and to decide if its men had been adequately trained to meet such an emergency. Ewers, however, went over the line. Convinced that Chessani had been derelict in his duty by not initiating an examination, he told the battalion commander that he was a suspect in a criminal matter and read him the military version of his Miranda rights.[8] This blunder, which preceded the Corps' charges against Chessani by nine months, led to Ewers being formally categorized as "tainted"—an offense punishable by being prohibited from attending any meetings dealing with the Chessani prosecution.[9]

According to Chessani's lawyers, both Mattis and Helland committed UCI by ignoring the ban against Ewers' participation in Chessani-related discussions, inviting him to numerous Haditha prosecution-planning sessions in which all the Haditha cases were discussed, including Chessani's.[10]

In actuality, there were other, more subtle layers to the issue that included overtones of cronyism and extreme command arrogance.

Ewers's history did not begin in Haditha. During the May 7 hearing—which was closed to the media although arguments were regurgitated at a later open session—it was learned that Ewers and Mattis had a strong working relationship that stretched to the period before the launching of Operation Iraqi Freedom in 2003, when Mattis commanded the 1st Marine Division and Ewers was his staff judge advocate.[11] While the division was waiting to invade Iraq, Mattis and Ewers dreamed up a unit called RIAT, an acronym for Reportable Incident Assessment Team.[12] Basically, RIAT was a program designed to protect the commander in a battlefield situation in which LOAC violations were suspected. If such a scenario developed, a RIAT team—in this case headed by Ewers—would rush to the site to determine if violations had occurred and how the commander should react if questioned by his superiors or the media.[13] Ewers had been on just such a mission soon after the invasion when he was so seriously wounded he had to be evacuated to the United States for treatment and rehabilitation.[14]

Ewers returned to service in 2006 and was detailed to work on a reconstruction project in Anbar Province.[15] He was snatched from that job to work with Bargewell. When the probe ended, Ewers was redeployed to the United States, where he was eligible to take the I MEF SJA job when it was offered by Mattis, who only recently had become the unit commander.[16]

Ewers did not assume the I MEF SJA job until February 2007, by which time the planning of the Haditha prosecutions was already well underway.[17] Nevertheless, according to testimony at the initial UCI hearing, Mattis had come to rely heavily on Ewers and apparently wanted him close at hand when making legal decisions. Ironically, this opened another issue.

As commander of a joint command called I MEF/MARCENT, Mattis was responsible for directing the courts-martial of all Marines on charges stemming from alleged battlefield violations in Iraq and Afghanistan.[18] That was part of his job as unit commander. However, since very few commanders of combat units are also active judge advocates, the Corps designates legal advisers. In this case, Corps headquarters picked the SJA at MARCENT—Lt. Col. G.W. Riggs—as the officer Mattis was obligated to turn to for legal advice on the Haditha proceedings.

This created an additional dimension to the Chessani challenge. Not only had Mattis and Helland ignored the ban against Ewers, they had also gone around the order that specified Riggs should be the one providing the generals with legal advice by allowing Ewers—who had no formal standing in the proceedings—to effectively take over Riggs's job.

Judge Folsom's Position

Ewers was the only witness at the May 7 hearing. Although the meeting was closed to the media, a transcript was available as part of an appeals court document.[19] Speaking to the group over a staticky telephone connection that sometimes faded altogether, Ewers denied that he had acted inappropriately during any phase of the proceedings. He admitted attending more than 20 of Mattis's meetings in which pending cases, including Chessani's, were the major if not the exclusive subjects under discussion.[20] However, he was vague about why he was there, saying only that Mattis invited him. When asked by Muise why the convening authority might ask him to attend meetings in which he could not participate, Ewers replied, "I think he just wanted me there."[21]

MUISE: "Wanted you there for what?"

EWERS: "As I say... I specifically told Mattis when I got back [from the Iraq deployment] that I couldn't give him advice. But he still asked me to come to the meetings. So I can't really say why he wanted me there."[22]

Despite several attempts, Muise was unable to get Ewers to confess that he had advised Mattis on the Chessani prosecution. "The reason I couldn't give him advice is because of the statutory and regulatory prohibitions. I just didn't think it was a particularly good idea for me to get involved because I had been involved in the [Chessani] investigation [while on the Bargewell team]."

"Well, why wouldn't it be a good idea? Muise pressed.

Ewers replied: "Just because from the appearances, in a nutshell."[23]

While remaining unshakable in his denial of acting as an adviser, Ewers nevertheless confirmed that he performed other tasks that could be considered violations of the prohibitions that governed his actions. He replied affirmatively to a question from Muise about whether he had engaged in private discussions with prosecutors about the Haditha proceedings, and maybe about Chessani's case. "It was certainly possible" that he had talked about Chessani's situation, he said.[24]

He also acknowledged he had appeared briefly on a nationally televised program with others discussing the Haditha incident. An episode of *Frontline* on PBS first aired on February 19, 2008, consisted of a series of interviews with more than two dozen men, including a few Iraqis talking about what happened in Anbar Province more than two years previously.[25] Ewers appeared on camera for only 12 seconds, but the crux of the defense's criticism was that he appeared at all. Ewers did not mention Haditha in his abridged debut, but he was identified as I MEF staff judge advocate "who was involved early in the Haditha investigation."

Asked why he did not address the Haditha affair, Ewers said it was "because there were cases pending, and I just thought it would be a bad idea for me to get on television and talk specifically about it."[26] He added that Mattis and possibly Helland were aware of his appearance but neither mentioned it to him, and neither did anyone else in his chain of command.

"Is it your understanding," Muise asked, "that nobody from the Marine Corps has ever issued any public statement clarifying any of your comments that were made during the course of that nationally televised show?"

"Not that I am aware of it," Ewers replied, "and I probably would be aware of it if they had."[27]

When questioned by Judge Folsom about his presence in the meetings that dealt with MARCENT rather than I MEF cases, Ewers became defensive. "Despite the fact that I told [Mattis] and he understood and acknowledged that I should stay out of Haditha because it wasn't my jurisdiction, he still asked me to come [to the meetings] and I wasn't inclined to decline."[28]

"Did you offer any advice, opinions, or input at any time when [Chessani's] case was discussed?" Folsom asked.

"I did not," Ewers replied resolutely.

"Have you had any personal discussions with [Mattis] about [Chessani] or any aspect of his case?"

"No."

FOLSOM: "Have you reviewed any defense memoranda, requests, briefs, any sort of legal documentation and provided an opinion or any advice to [Mattis] while he was in command of I MEF?"

EWERS (emphatically): "No."[29]

On May 20, almost two weeks later, Folsom e-mailed the attorneys saying that he felt that the defense had made a strong enough case for him to move to the next step in the UCI procedure: the convening of a second hearing to allow the prosecution to refute the defense allegations.[30]

Folsom's decision signified a major victory for Muise and Rooney. It shifted the burden of proof to the prosecution, putting Team Charlie in an uncomfortable position.[31] At the next hearing, set for June 2, prosecutors would be required to establish three things: (1) Certify that the facts presented by the defense were wrong; (2) confirm that the facts did not constitute UCI, and (3) demonstrate that even if UCI did obtain, it would not prejudice Chessani's trial.[32] The challenge for the prosecutors was the need to satisfy Folsom to the high standard of "beyond a reasonable doubt"—the same difficult one demanded of a jury in civilian criminal trials. If the government failed to meet the requirements, Folsom could find in favor of the defense.

Team Charlie was under considerable pressure. Chessani and Wuterich were the principal targets in the government's efforts to secure convictions related to the Haditha killings, so, if the charges against Chessani were to be dropped, it would be the most severe setback for the government in its 18-month-long struggle, which so far had produced no results. The "beyond a reasonable doubt" requirement was a major hurdle, but there was one thing in the government's favor: prosecutors could summon as many witnesses as they wanted and take as long as they needed to defuse the defense threat.

18. The Grayson Debacle

The media—diverted to other stories because of the slow-motion progress in the Haditha proceedings—all but ignored the trial of 1st Lt. Andrew Grayson even though it was the first of what had been expected to be a series of courts-martial. When the court convened on May 28, 2008, 17 months after charges were preferred, the number of reporters present could be counted by ticking off the fingers on one hand.

In reality, there was little in Grayson's case to stimulate the excitement of assignment editors. It was generally accepted that Grayson was the least likely of any of the Haditha group to be convicted. As the leader of a HET team detailed to Kilo Company, Grayson had not played a direct role in events before, during, or after the incident. He had not gone to the scene; he had not inspected the houses; and because of his rank and position, he had no input toward determining if an investigation should have been held. He did hold two distinctions, however: his trial was the only one of four scheduled courts-martial to begin on time, and his file was the only one with a clean appeals-court record.

The 26-year-old native of Springboro, Ohio, joined the Corps in May 2003, some two months after the invasion, following in the footsteps of his older brother, a captain posted to the Marine Corps Recruit Training Depot at Parris Island, South Carolina, when the trial opened. By the fall of 2005, when Grayson's team joined K Company, Grayson already had served one tour in Iraq and had earned a reputation as a competent, promising young officer. He also had earned a sterling reputation in Battalion 3/1 because of his team's proficiency in dealing with the local Iraqis and collecting sources willing to tell him about hidden IEDs and plans for forthcoming insurgent attacks. After the attack on 1st Squad, Grayson's sources tipped him off about two other bombs planted in the Palm Groves in time to have experts disarm the devices before they could kill any more Marines. That performance won him a nomination for a Bronze Star medal. The award was never presented because of the criminal charges.[1]

Eight months before his trial, Grayson's civilian attorney, Joseph Casas, told the Associated Press that his client had rejected an offer from Lt. Col. Sean Sullivan, one of Grayson's prosecutors, to dismiss the criminal charges if he would confess to trying to cover up the incident. According to Casas, Sullivan offered to make arrangements for Grayson to appear at a non-judicial punishment hearing rather than being court-martialed. NJP proceedings are conducted by commanding officers and do not include trial.[2] If Grayson had agreed to the proposition, he probably would have received only a reprimand or a fine. Instead, he faced a mishmash of accusations, including three counts of making false official statements, one of obstruction of justice, and two others under an obscure UCMJ article called "Attempts" that were based on prosecution claims that Grayson lied in an effort to be released early from active duty. On December 31, 2007, Lt. Gen. Helland dismissed a charge of dereliction of duty against Grayson without explanation. Still, if convicted of the remaining charges, Grayson could be sentenced to 25 years in prison and dismissed from the Corps.

A Textbook Trial

In contrast to the proceedings involving other Haditha Marines, Grayson's trial progressed calmly and swiftly. There had been some legal maneuvering in the weeks before when Casas asked Grayson's judge, Maj. Brian Kasprzyk, to approve a series of motions that would have changed the structure of the case and reduced the severity of the accusations. One motion asked Kasprzyk to separate the fraudulent discharge complaints from the other charges—a seemingly rational plea since Grayson's tussle with the Corps had nothing to do with Haditha. Another requested that the charges be dismissed because Grayson had not been granted a speedy trial. Two involved witnesses. Casas wanted Kasprzyk to order both Lt. Col. Chessani and Representative Murtha take the stand. From a tactical point of view, the most interesting petition would have forced Grayson's chief accuser, Army Col. Gregory Watt, to attest that he had failed to advise Grayson of his constitutional rights before telling him he was a suspect. Kasprzyk rejected all the motions on May 19.[3]

By the time the court-martial began, there were no impediments to hold up the process. Not even jury selection—often a time-killing bugbear in civilian courts—slowed the proceedings down. A colonel, four lieutenant colonels, a major and a captain—all combat veterans—were picked to hear the evidence within hours of the trial's onset.[4]

"The Corps is using Grayson as a fall guy," Maj. William A. Santmyer, Grayson's detailed military defense lawyer, contended in his opening statement. "He is [a] convenient [target] for the government, pure and simple."[5] Grayson steadfastly adhered to Corps policy throughout his involvement, Santmyer continued. As soon as he was told about the ambush, he sent his photographer, Staff Sgt. Justin Laughner, to the scene to document everything in sight: bodies, the houses, the white sedan. Laughner returned with some 70 images on his camera card, which he downloaded onto the office computer. Without looking at the photos, Grayson passed them to intelligence analysts so they could be compared to photographs of individuals stored in a special Department of Defense database dedicated to suspected and known insurgents. It was Corps policy, Santmyer said, to destroy photos of individuals who do not pop up in the database. So, after being told there were no hits on the photos of the Haditha dead, Grayson ordered Laughner to wipe the images.

When Laughner took the stand soon afterwards as a prosecution witness, he repeated what he had said at Chessani's Article 32 hearing a year earlier. "I knew I had done something wrong with those photographs [by erasing them]," Laughner said. Asked why he had felt that way, Laughner replied, "It seemed to me like November 19 [2005] might be an important date [so] the photos might help explain the Marines' actions later."[6]

Under cross-examination by Casas—a former Navy judge advocate— Laughner admitted he did not permanently erase the images, as Grayson had ordered. Instead, he downloaded about half of them to his personal computer—a fact he had denied when questioned by five different investigators. It was only after an NCIS agent threatened to seize his laptop that Laughner came clean.[7] In courts-martial, members of the jury are allowed to question witnesses, and Laughner's testimony prompted a flurry of queries, most of which dealt with why he refused to cooperate with investigators. The staff sergeant said it was because he feared he would charged and sent to prison.[8] Although Laughner had been granted immunity to testify against Grayson, the privilege did not extend to the computer security violations. It is unknown if he was ever charged.

Colonel Gregory Watt

It was the prosecutor's plan to present Laughner as a warm-up for its star witness: Army Col. Gregory Watt, who they hoped would seal Grayson's fate by convincing the jury that the lieutenant obstructed justice by repeatedly lying about the existence of on-scene photographs of the Haditha dead.

Watt had arrived in Haditha on February 16, 2006, under orders from Lt. Gen. Chiarelli to conduct an AR 15-6 investigation into the incident. Chiarelli sent Watt to the scene after he was unconvinced by statements from Maj. Gen. Huck that the incident was not worthy of a probe. Watt spent about a week with the battalion, taking statements from civilians as well as members of the battalion. His report to Chiarelli generally supported the battalion's version of events, but he suggested a more thorough investigation.

Grayson and Watt got off to a bumpy start because Grayson refused to sign a pre-interview form Watt said was needed for his report.[9] Grayson told Watt he could not add his signature because it was against Corps policy for HET operatives to do anything that might expose their identities. As intelligence-gatherers, they were prime targets for insurgents and could not risk having their names revealed.

The personalities clashed more conspicuously when Grayson spurned Watt's demands for photographs taken at the scene of the IED attack. Grayson told him he could not comply because he had no images he could share. Evidently, this irritated Watt so much that he complained to investigators, saying Grayson had been "uncooperative" and "untruthful."[10] This could not be confirmed because the NCIS report is classified, but it apparently was the basis for the obstruction charges.

On the stand, Watt said he asked Grayson three times about photographs, and twice Grayson denied any existed. The third time, Watt said, Grayson told him the photos had been deleted, although he did not mention that they were erased because, under Corps policy, they had to be destroyed if they had no intelligence value.[11]

Under cross-examination, however, Watt seemed to contradict his earlier testimony.

"Did you ever specifically ask Lt. Grayson to provide photographs?" Casas asked.

"No," said Watt.[12]

It is unknown if Watt added photographs he may have obtained from other sources to his report to Chiarelli. Although a few pages of Watt's report were released on March 3, 2006, the attachments were not made public.

Surprisingly, Judge Kasprzyk allowed Casas to broaden his cross-examination of Watt to areas beyond the Watt-Grayson confrontations. In an attempt to blacken Watt's character, Casas asked the colonel about allegations that he had threatened to kill one of his junior officers because he reported that Watt was conducting a sexual relationship with a subordinate, a female staff sergeant. Watt did not admit to the assignation, but he acknowledged that he had been relieved of duty a few months before Grayson's trial pending completion of a probe into the allegations.[13] The investigation had not been completed at the time of Grayson's trial and the results are unknown.

"While [Watt's alleged affair] has nothing to do with Haditha, it clearly goes to Watt's truthfulness," Casas explained.[14]

Obstruction Charge Tossed

On June 3, the trial's fifth day, Kasprzyk announced that he was dismissing the obstruction of justice charge against Grayson.[15] The judge did not explain his decision, but Casas told the *North County Times* that Kasprzyk realized the charge was groundless because of a technicality. Grayson could not be charged with a criminal offense stemming from his connection to Watt, if Watt had not been authorized to conduct a criminal investigation.[16] Watt's probe was conducted under a regulation (AR 15-6) that did not permit a search for criminal activity. Whatever the reason for the dismissal, it was a major victory for Grayson. With the obstruction accusation out of the way, the Haditha-related case against Grayson effectively collapsed. Casas still had to address the service-related matter, but Kasprzyk's decision meant that Grayson no longer had to worry about the five-year prison sentence he could have received had he been convicted on the obstruction charge.

By the same token, the judge's action significantly increased the pressure on the prosecution. To rescue what remained of the case, prosecutors had to convince the jury that Grayson had violated the UCMJ by making false official statements and fraudulently separating from the Corps—accusations totally unrelated to Haditha. If convicted, Grayson could be sentenced to up to 20 years in prison. At the heart of the case was the prosecution's contention that Grayson illegally took advantage of an error by the Corps' Separations and Retirement Section to get out of his service commitment. The office that oversees discharges, the prosecution said, mistakenly sent Grayson a Certificate of Release or Discharge from Active Duty, called a DD-214, advising him that he was eligible to return to civilian life. Apparently office personnel did not notice that Grayson's personnel file had been flagged with a notice that he was not to be allowed to leave the Corps until the criminal charges against him had been resolved—a warning that Grayson was on "legal hold" pending disposition of the criminal charges. Realizing the blunder, the Corps tried to correct it by sending Grayson a companion form, a DD-215, which is issued to correct errors in the DD-214. Only later did the Corps grasp that a DD-215 could not be used to cancel a DD-214; its purpose was to fix inaccuracies before a DD-214 was issued. The prosecution contended that Grayson was aware of the gaffe but did not inform the Corps of its oversight. That, the prosecution said, was a criminal act.

When asked what Grayson had done to correct the slip, Lt. Col. Kevin Woodard, one of Grayson's detailed defense lawyers, replied, "Nothing." Grayson, he claimed, had no legal or ethical obligation to try to rectify the inaccuracy; it was the Corps' mistake, not Grayson's.[17]

Lieutenant Colonel Paul Atterbury, the lead prosecutor, attempted to save the government's case in an hour-long closing argument in which he accused Grayson of lying to investigators and being a willing participant in an attempt to avoid responsibility. "[Grayson] was not a 'fall-guy,'" he said, cynically using Casas's description of his client. "Lieutenant Grayson is not some victim of a botched investigation [brought] by media pressure. He's a liar. He has a motive to lie and a desire to avoid accountability."[18]

Grayson's lawyer, Casas, argued that the case against Grayson flowed from what Watt told NCIS investigators in an effort to retaliate against the lieutenant. "[Watt] was miffed at Grayson and he had an ax to grind," Casas said.[19] Comparing the trial to a football game, Casas picked up a pigskin that had been sitting on the defense table. "We stopped their offense," Casas told the jury, waving the football. "We don't need to score. The government had to make a touchdown on each and every element of the charges, but we stopped their offense."[20]

The case went to the jury late Thursday, the trial's sixth day. Members deliberated for five hours before finding Grayson not guilty on all counts.[21] There was no announcement about the breakdown of the vote; in courts-martial, unlike in civilian trials, the verdict does not have to be unanimous. Under the UCMJ, two-thirds of the seven members of Grayson's panel would have had to vote to convict to avoid a mandated not-guilty verdict.

Cases in Chaos

From the prosecution's point of view, Grayson's trial was a fiasco. Its two main witnesses were effortlessly demolished, and the allegation that Grayson had cheated his way to a discharge crumbled under the weight of testimony regarding Corps regulations. Particularly hurtful to the prosecution's reputation was the knowledge that the government had 18 months to prepare for the trial, yet had failed to make a halfway persuasive argument or properly vet its witnesses.

Prosecutors made three crucial mistakes in preparing and presenting their case against Grayson. The first was the failure to anticipate that Laughner's testimony could be dismantled so easily. The second was in adopting a strategy that called for heavy dependence on Watt, whose credibility was ruined by testimony relating to his personal life. It is interesting that Kasprzyk allowed this information to be presented to the jury, but it is even more interesting to speculate about how the defense knew about it while the prosecution apparently did not. The third mistake was even more mystifying. While the prosecution was intent on convicting Grayson of successfully gaming the system to get a discharge, apparently no one on the prosecution team dug deep enough to determine that Grayson had not, in fact, successfully pulled off the virtually impossible act of scamming his way out of the Corps.

In a brief meeting with reporters after the verdict was announced, Casas criticized the government's handling of the proceedings, saying it was his feeling there would be no significant prosecutions even though the cases against Chessani and Wuterich were pending. "I think [Grayson's trial] sets the tone for the overall whirlwind Haditha has been," he said. "It's been a botched investigation from the get-go."[22]

19. Chessani Resolution

The prosecution opened the June 2 hearing to determine if the prosecution could discredit the defense's UCI accusations with a shocker. Although Team Charlie could have called as many witnesses as it wanted, it settled on only two: Gen. Mattis and Col. Ewers. Even Judge Folsom seemed surprised. Ewers already had testified, and what he had to say the second time around likely would not deviate greatly from his earlier statements. But calling Mattis was risky. It was rare for a four-star officer to be subpoenaed as a witness in a criminal case, and his reaction to being placed in a position in which he did not have complete control was touchy. Most civilians—especially those who have come of age in the post-conscription era and have never served in the military—have little conception of a full general's power. An officer with four stars is like a prince, maybe the closest thing in contemporary American society to royalty. As such, they are hardly ever contradicted and almost never have to explain their actions. Mattis was not famous for his humility or his appreciation of politically correct speech. In 2005, before he took command of I MEF/MARCENT, he was mildly reprimanded by the Corps commandant after blurting that "it was fun to shoot some people" at a conference in San Diego. Mattis was speaking about Afghanistan's Taliban but the statement seemed inappropriate before a mixed audience. Afterwards, Gen. Michael Hagee counseled him to choose his words "more carefully."[1]

Because it was a prosecution case, Lt. Col. Sullivan opened the questioning, throwing softball queries to the impatient Mattis.

Mattis said the strategy sessions, which began in August 2006, soon after he inherited the duty of Convening Authority and some four months before charges were preferred, quickly worked into a routine. Depending on his travel schedule, he chaired one or two meetings a week, the vast majority of them in his Camp Pendleton office. The meetings normally ran about two hours but could last as long as four or five. Mattis said the most pressing cases were addressed first, and when the presenters were finished, they gathered at a round table in the back of the room. Ewers's place usually was at the rear table, where he was said to have remained silent for the duration of the session. "The only people talking were the ones who were responsible for those cases," Mattis said.² Riggs, the MARCENT SJA and Mattis' official legal adviser, attended the conference if he was in California, or he patched in by video teleconference. Sometimes, he sent his assistant SJA. Mattis said he had never questioned the contention that the Haditha cases were under MARCENT's jurisdiction and that Ewers was prohibited from taking part in the discussions. "We considered him tainted because he'd been an investigator [under Bargewell] but secondly, he was the I MEF SJA and [Haditha] was under MARCENT," Mattis said. "[Ewers] had no role to play advising on anything to do with the MARCENT issue."³

"At any time, did [Ewers] ever provide you legal advice with regard to any of the Haditha cases?" Sullivan asked.

"Never," Mattis replied briskly. "And I would not have asked for any. But he never offered it and I never heard any from him."⁴

He didn't need Ewers's counsel, Mattis said, because he had informational dominance in matters relating to Haditha. He spent his holiday time in 2006 reading reports about the incident so he would have a full grasp of the details. "I maintained a page count," he said. "I read over 9,000 pages of testimony, of evidence, of statements of investigation reports from NCIS." He also read the Bargewell report, but he discarded it from his calculations because he felt it did not have enough information.⁵

"Why did you feel it was important for your own personal review?" Sullivan asked.

Mattis replied:

> The environment in which [the Marines in Battalion 3/1] were operating I considered to be the ethically most challenging environment that I'd experienced in over 35 years of service. I did not want to have information filtered to me through lenses other than my own. And by doing this, I was able to bluntly challenge the trial counsels and the staff judge advocate as I maintained an independent view of what these investigations were revealing.⁶

When asked if he had received advice or direction from the Corps commandant, the secretary of the Navy, Congress, or other officers of the same rank, Mattis firmly said no. "I make my own decisions," he said, as if offended.⁷ The possibility that others would think he might have succumbed to outside influences seemed to anger him.

> The idea that someone would approach me on that, while I suppose it could happen because I don't control others, it never happened. I would not have tolerated it....

The first thing I would have done had somebody even approached me ... is I would have reported it to the trial counsel, defense counsel, and my SJA immediately.[8]

Defense Plays Rough

As expected, Muise was more aggressive in his questioning than Sullivan, who had tiptoed around his major witness. Also as expected, Mattis was more contentious in his responses. While somewhat verbose with Sullivan, Mattis replied to Muise's queries in as few words as possible.

The defense attorney began his cross-examination with questions about the directive designating MARCENT as the CA/CDA for the Haditha cases.

MUISE: "[Ewers] could have nothing to do with [the Haditha cases] based on the authority that was provided in that letter. Isn't that right, sir?"
MATTIS: "That's correct."
MUISE: "There was nothing unclear about that at all to you. Is that right, sir?"
MATTIS: "No, there was nothing unclear."[9]

Pointing out that Ewers had testified earlier that he had been invited to meetings in which no I MEF cases were discussed, Muise asked if the staff judge advocate's statements had been correct. "I can't imagine he would have been invited if it wasn't a I MEF case," Mattis said. "I mean, the only reason [for him] to be there was if he had something on our agenda."

In an apparent contradiction, when asked if it would have been improper for Ewers to attend meetings in which only the Haditha cases were being discussed, Mattis said it would not.

"Why not?" Muise asked, puzzled.

"Because he had no input," Mattis said. "He was not asked for his opinion, nor did he offer any, nor would I have accepted any on things that he has nothing to do with."[10]

On redirect, Sullivan went back to a subject he had raised earlier: possible outside pressure. Could he have been swayed by media reports of the proceedings? Sullivan asked. "I know it sounds like I'm asking the same question, [but] with this particular case and with Lt. Col. Chessani's case, did any of the media or publication ... ever influence your determinations with regard to Lt. Col. Chessani's case in any manner?"

"No," Mattis said, scoffing at the suggestion. "I was uninterested in the media's view."[11]

Judge Folsom picked up where Sullivan and Muise left off. Shuffling his notes, the colonel gazed at the four-star officer, his superior by four ranks. "So, sir," Folsom began, seemingly unintimidated, "Lt. Col. Riggs told you that Col. Ewers could not participate because he was tainted, and you didn't ask any detailed questions as to ... what his role [in the Bargewell investigation] was?" Mattis replied:

> I knew what his role was. I knew he'd been involved in Bargewell. I didn't—again, I didn't care if he was peripherally involved or fundamentally involved. I was not going to have anything to do with it. Plus, he was I MEF ... and he was not to have any involvement at all when it came to a MARCENT issue and he had none.[12]

Folsom's inquires covered much of the same ground already visited by Muise and Sullivan, but his questions seemed to be more acceptable to Mattis than those of the two lawyers. At times during his almost three hours on the stand, Mattis responded differently to his inquisitors. To Sullivan, he sometimes seemed condescending; to Muise, he often appeared arrogant and abrupt, taking on the aspect of Jack Nicholson's Col. Jessup in *A Few Good Men*.[13] However, his responses to Folsom were thoughtful and expository.

"How many legal meetings had there been and had Ewers attended all of them?" Folsom asked.

There were "dozens," Mattis said, but he did not believe Ewers had been in all of them.[14]

In light of Mattis's earlier statements that he was not concerned about what the media said or what was being reported to the public, Folsom asked his final question:

"Did anyone ... ever voice a concern to you ... that Col. Ewers' presence at military justice meetings where Haditha cases—and for [Chessani] in particular—were being discussed with you may not be proper or may create an appearance problem?"

"No," Mattis said emphatically.

> I mean, I was being considered to have an appearance problem just because I was dismissing charges on some people. I was charging others and as long as we maintained strictly by the book that he had no input whatsoever. I was more concerned with the reality of what was going on than what other people would draw for conclusions. I'd already been drawn and quartered in enough different newspaper articles that I was uninterested in that sort of thing.[15]

Details Omitted

Ewers followed Mattis on the stand, but, as anticipated, his testimony was much the same as he had given at the May 7 hearing.

When questioned by Sullivan, Ewers admitted he had showed up at meetings he was not supposed to attend, but he denied offering Mattis advice on the Haditha cases; therefore, his attendance did not break any regulations.

On cross-examination, Muise got to the point more directly. "Did you ever give [Mattis] any legal advice that it's not a good idea for you to attend any legal meeting discussing the Haditha cases?"

"You know," Ewers said, "I didn't give him that advice. I told him that I couldn't advise him on the Haditha matters, but I did not tell him that I shouldn't be at the meetings."

Then why attend? Muise pressed.

"I got the e-mail that announced the meetings, which I took as being an invitation," said Ewers.[16]

Under questioning from Judge Folsom, Ewers peeled back a layer that had not been previously discussed. What was the depth, Folsom asked Ewers, of his conversation with Mattis about why he was unable to offer advice on the Haditha questions—other than they were MARCENT cases?

"I told him I'd been a member of the Bargewell investigative team, and, therefore, I shouldn't talk to him about the Haditha cases," Ewers said, indicating he did not go into particulars.

Folsom picked up on the evasion. Was that the extent of your explanation? Folsom asked. Had he told Mattis that he had been a major contributor to the Bargewell report and had actually notified Chessani that he was suspected of a criminal violation?

"You know, I'm not sure I gave him chapter and verse on everything I did," Ewers said, backpedaling. "But in my mind, I was [just] an investigating officer."[17]

Folsom didn't want to let the matter go; he asked Ewers for more specifics about what he had told Mattis.

"I simply told him that I'd been part of the investigation.... I didn't go into detail into what my role was."

Why was that? Folsom prodded.

"I figured he'd be asking me questions, and I wanted to prepare him for the fact that I was going to have to decline to answer questions with respect to this issue."

Folsom: "Why did you believe that he would be asking you, as the SJA of I MEF, questions about MARCENT cases?" Ewers said:

> Oh, jeez. I guess I anticipated it—I didn't know whether he was going to ask me or not, but I anticipated it based on our history together; based on the fact I'm the senior SJA in terms of—in terms of, I guess, time as an SJA. So and—so I just anticipated that he'd want me to weigh in, and I wanted to make sure I couldn't.[18]

After a two-hour meeting the next day to give the lawyers from both sides the opportunity to summarize their points, Folsom said he needed time to consider what he had heard. He set a third session for two weeks later.

Fatal Mistakes

The judge picked a good breaking point. The day after he adjourned the Mattis/Ewers session, a seven-man jury acquitted Lt. Grayson, leaving the prosecution with a 0–6 record in the Haditha cases. By contrast, the Hamdania trials were completed ten months earlier with an 8–0 conviction rate. The disparity did not reflect positively on the Haditha prosecutors, even though several of them also had participated in successful Hamdania courts-martial. Why Team Charlie performed so well against the Hamdania accused and so miserably in the Haditha proceedings may have had more to do with the nature of the cases than with the judge advocates. NCIS agents jumped onto the Hamdania incident almost immediately, as opposed to the seven-month delay in Haditha before a probe was ordered. Also, in Hamdania, there was certainty about who should be accused, again opposed to Haditha, where questions were raised about who was selected to be charged. In the Haditha cases, charges against five of the six men whose cases had been addressed so far were dismissed without trials, two of them (Dela Cruz and Captain McConnell) without even Article 32 hearings. Finally, there were no time-consuming interlocutory appeals in Hamdania and no wholesale grants of immunity, like the 17 absolutions awarded to Haditha witnesses. Whatever the circumstances, the Haditha prosecutors could ill afford to let another case go down in flames. Yet that is precisely what happened.

An unsmiling Col. Folsom settled behind the bench on June 17, 14 days after listening to Lt. Gen. Mattis and Col. Ewers explain their actions. Facing him was a reinforced fire team of lawyers representing both sides in the fight to bring the former battalion commander to trial: Jamison and Sullivan for the prosecution; Muise, Rooney and Chessani's two detailed military counselors—Lt. Col. John Shelburne and Capt. Jeffrey King—for the defense.

He began with bad news for the defense team: their attempt to compel the prosecution to turn over additional evidence against Chessani had failed. He had denied the motion back in February, and the Navy-Marine Court of Criminal Appeals had only just informed him that it had rejected the plea. In addition, he reminded the defense that he had already pledged to deny its motion relating to selective prosecution. The unpleasant reports, though, had no effect on Chessani's case; Folsom's truly distressing news was for the prosecution.

"I am going to spare everyone the suspense," he said, turning to Sullivan and Jamison. "I am going to grant the defense motion for Unlawful Command Influence; I am going to dismiss the charges [against Chessani]."[19] He was taking the "drastic remedy," he added, because of the *appearance* of UCI.

After dropping the bomb, Folsom spent 45 minutes explaining his rationale. It was a long-winded, often repetitious lecture in which he expressed his disappointment with everyone connected to the events: Mattis, Helland, the prosecution team that presented the case, Riggs, and emphatically Ewers, whom Folsom seemed to hold in low regard, both professionally and personally.

The judge appeared to be particularly stunned by Mattis's disregard for Ewers's banned status and his apparent lack of vision in failing to see how the staff judge advocate's appearance at the meetings might look to the media and the public. "Although aware that Col. Ewers was 'tainted' as a legal adviser, Lt. Gen. Mattis did not require Col. Ewers to either not attend or to leave the room during these discussions," he said.[20]

In Folsom's opinion, Mattis, was "unconcerned with how the appearance of Col. Ewers at what were essentially MARCENT legal meetings would look to the outside."[21] To the judge, external appearances were vital to the maintenance of the criminal justice system. It was immaterial, the judge said, whether Ewers actually *offered* legal advice during the sessions; his presence alone was damning. That he did not actually *submit* advice, Folsom said, "is hollow comfort where the facts indicate that all present knew Col. Ewers' legal opinion on [Chessani's] guilt."[22]

In the judge's view, Helland's performance had not been much better. Despite knowing that Ewers was tainted, Helland allowed him "to attend at least half a dozen or more legal meetings ... at which this case and other related cases were discussed and legal advice was rendered." While Mattis denied accepting advice from Ewers, Helland apparently had no such qualms. "At least on one or more occasions [Helland] approached [Ewers] seeking legal advice on documentation submitted by defense counsel in a separate but tangentially related MARCENT Haditha case or cases."[23]

Folsom scolded both staff judge advocates for neglecting to speak up about the potential effect of Ewers's presence. "Although [Riggs and Ewers] knew of a potential appearance problem due to the ... presence of Col. Ewers at these meetings, not one person in that room full of lawyers advised Lt. Gen. Mattis of it."[24]

In addition to his poor opinion of Ewers's professional behavior, it also was evident that Folsom had little respect for the I MEF staff judge advocate, describing him as a "senior officer" whose "demeanor ... while on the stand, was at times frustrated and exasperated and occasionally mumbling under his breath prior to responding to a question that posed a differing version of the facts than his."[25]

The chief target of the judge's disdain, however, was the prosecution, which was unable to prove any of the three points required to refute the defense's claims of UCI. "Having found that the government has failed to meet their [sic] burden to rebut the presumption of either actual or apparent unlawful command influence, this court must now turn to an appropriate remedy," Folsom said. His findings, he added, while leading to draconian action, were nevertheless in accordance with previous rulings. "Courts have approved [such action] when they believed that it was absolutely necessary to not only remove the taint but to ensure that public confidence is continued in the military justice system and in a particular proceeding against any particular accused."[26]

Despite his morose assessment, Folsom did not view his findings as the last word in the drama. He left the door open for Team Charlie to pursue the issue by rejecting a defense plea that his findings be recorded "with prejudice," that is, that the charges could not be re-preferred. The prosecution, he said, could start the process anew as long as prosecutors began in a command other than I MEF, MARCENT, or the Joint Forces Command, which was headed by Mattis.[27]

Which Way Forward?

The prosecution's first step toward a possible revival of the case against the officer that they most wanted to court-martial was to file a 43-page appeal with the NMCCA.[28] The plea alleged that Folsom erred in numerous ways, ranging from an improper finding that Ewers influenced participants, including Riggs, in Mattis's meetings, to the contention that Mattis accepted Ewers's advice.

> On 21 different occasions, [Mattis] testified that he did not solicit input, nor received input, and would not have tolerated any input from [Ewers] on any Haditha-related matters. It goes without saying that no reasonable person would question [Ewers's] role in the Convening Authority's consideration of this case: [Ewers] played no role at all.[29]

Nine months later, a three-judge panel rejected the argument in a succinct and lucid ruling: "We find that a careful review ... reveals that [Folsom's] essential findings of fact are not clearly erroneous," the justices ruled, adding: "and we adopt them as our own."[30] Further in Folsom's favor, the court agreed with the judge that the government had failed to meet its burden of proof in its attempts to refute the defense allegations. "We are ... convinced that an objective, disinterested observer, fully informed of all the facts and circumstances, would harbor significant doubt about the fairness of this proceeding."[31] The court gently rebuked Folsom for including the entire Joint Services Command in his list of organizations banned from participating in any possible attempt to re-prefer the charges. Rather, the court implied, Folsom should have named only Mattis. Adding the JFC, the court said, "is not supported by factual findings ... and therefore is an abuse of [the judge's] discretion."[32]

The NMCCA opinion against the prosecution limited Team Charlie's options. Prosecutors could start the process once more by a new convening authority; they could ask the NMCCA for reconsideration by a full court; they could withdraw the charges; or they could ask for a review by the Court of Criminal Appeals for the Armed Forces.

Team Charlie's first choice was to go back to the NMCCA with a plea for an *en banc* hearing. The request was abruptly denied a few weeks later.[33] Next, they turned to the Corps commandant, Gen. James Conway, asking him to select another CA/CDA. Acquiescing to the request, Conway selected Lt. Gen. George Flynn, deputy commandant for Combat Development and Integration.[34] That approach didn't work either. Three months later, Flynn—apparently realizing the futility of an attempt to start from the beginning in an old case that had been botched from the beginning—announced that he was ending the pursuit of criminal charges against Chessani. Two years and eight months after charges were preferred and almost four years since the incident, the Corps formally dismissed the criminal accusations against the formal battalion commander.[35]

But that was not the end. While Flynn did not recommend starting from the beginning, he proposed that Chessani be required to face a three-member board of inquiry (BOI) to determine if Chessani should be retired as lieutenant colonel or if his rank should be reduced to major. It was a blatant attempt to punish Chessani monetarily. If his rank were reduced, his retirement pay and benefits also would be trimmed.[36]

A BOI is not bound by the same strict standard of proof as a jury in a court-martial, so Chessani had an advantage. While a jury must decide a case beyond a reasonable doubt, a BOI is required to judge only by preponderance of evidence, i.e., that the accusations against Chessani were more likely true than not true.

Chessani, who had said little in previous appearances in legal proceedings, was garrulous before the BOI at a hearing that convened on December 2, 2009, at Camp Pendleton. In an attempt to persuade the board that he alone was not to blame for not ordering an investigation, Chessani explained that he had kept his immediate superior, Lt. Col. Davis of RCT-2, fully informed. "I recall telling him we were subject to an [IED attack] and small-arms fire and had pursued the enemy and we regrettably had killed women and children," he said, adding that he repeated the same information to the division commander, Lt. Gen. Huck, when he visited the ambush site two days later.[37] Neither of the superior officers felt the situation was serious enough to order an investigation, Chessani pointed out, so why should he be the only one accused of criminal activity? In effect, it was a replay of the Muise and Rooney contention that Chessani had been selectively prosecuted.

He also told the board about a meeting with the Haditha City Council shortly after the incident during which the officials tried to hold his men responsible for the fatalities. Chessani angrily denied the council claim that the attacks had been unprovoked, telling the board that he thought the Council was more interested in monetary compensation for the families than in finding out what had really happened. The Council dropped its opposition, he said, after he agreed to pay the families with government funds.

Despite his newly found loquaciousness, Chessani could only shrug when asked why he did not inspect the houses in which the majority of civilians had died. "I can't honestly say right now," he said evasively.[38]

Eight days later, the board found that Chessani's performance in the wake of the incident had been "substandard" but it did not sink to the level of "misconduct," which would have been the necessary finding for Chessani to be reduced in rank. In effect, the board ruled that Chessani could retire with the full pay and benefits of a lieutenant colonel.[39] A little more than six months later, the secretary of the Navy—whose approval is required on BOI rulings—signed off on the decision.

Chessani retired honorably on July 16, 2011.[40] He was 46 years old and had been a Marine for 23 years.

"An American Hero"

The Thomas More Law Center, which paid for Chessani's defense, honored him in a 1,200 word statement, calling him an "American hero" who was "unjustly prosecuted" on a "trumped-up charge" to "appease the anti-war press and politicians." It said:

The Government did everything it could to convict LtCol Chessani. It spent millions of taxpayer dollars, employed over 65 Naval Criminal Investigative Service (NCIS) agents—the largest investigation in that agency's history—and granted immunity to scores of witnesses, all in their attempt to make [Chessani] and the "Haditha Marines" political scapegoats.[41]

Unlike Wuterich, Chessani never took his case to the public, at least not until after he retired, when Nathaniel R. Helms, a correspondent for the pro–Corps web site Defend Our Marines, wrote a deferential 8,000-word story telling Chessani's story in a tone similar to that adopted by Wuterich in his *60 Minutes* interview.[42]

"I'm not bitter," Helms quoted Chessani as saying. "I am not necessarily glad these things happened, but it worked out for the best," meaning he would have more time to spend with his rapidly growing family.[43] Chessani maintained his earlier position that the IED attack and the deaths of the Iraqi civilians could not be viewed as an isolated incident. The ambush was only the first phase of the larger plan that played out in the Palm Groves, he continued to insist, even though investigators ignored his analysis. The NCIS agents, Chessani said, were interested only in dead noncombatants, overlooking the organized resistance perpetuated by insurgents within minutes of the IED attack. By aggressively attacking the insurgents, Chessani said, "We took away the enemies' ability to attack my Marines and civilians."[44]

According to Helms, Chessani remained unable to explain why the situation developed as it did. "When I was in theater I heard the [Corps commanders] were briefing the President of the United States. I knew I was going to be relieved and probably charged. I even told my [executive officer] to be standing by if I was relieved. But I didn't expect what happened."[45] Viewing the situation fatalistically, Chessani said he probably would never know the government's motives in pushing the case against him so vigorously. Whatever prompted the charges, however, had been unfair to him and the men under his command. "My Marines had done nothing wrong," he contended. "I had done nothing wrong."[46]

As a result of the removal of Chessani and Grayson from the picture, Wuterich was the only accused still facing a court-martial. As of August 27, 2009—when the Corps officially abandoned its efforts to court-martial Chessani—it had been two years and eight months since Mattis announced that he had preferred charges against the Haditha Marines and three years and nine months since the incident. Proceedings against Chessani, from the time charges were preferred to his retirement, stretched for more than three and a half years. Wuterich's would continue for even longer. The staff sergeant's trial was delayed for almost two years by the outtakes dispute and was, on paper, ready to proceed. However, there was a problem: there was no judge assigned to his case. If the Corps had appointed a replacement for Lt. Col. Meeks, who retired on March 14, 2009, it had not been not announced. It was not until March 2010—almost seven months later—that the media reported a new judge's presence at a Wuterich-related public hearing.

Table 7
Chessani Timeline

2008

Feb. 19	Chessani's defense attorneys file five motions with Col. Steven Folsom, Chessani's judge, including a request to depose Representative John Murtha in a search for information they could use at trial.
Mar. 5	Folsom denies the deposition request and a plea for a new Article 32 hearing.
Apr. 1	Defense files motions with Judge Folsom asking for dismissal of charges; one raises the specter of unlawful command influence.
Apr. 15	Folsom refuses to dismiss charges based on allegation of selective prosecution.
Apr. 29	Defense asks the Navy-Marine Court of Criminal Appeals for "extraordinary relief" by forcing prosecutors to turn over more of its evidence against Chessani.
May 20	Defense convinces Folsom that allegation of UCI has merit; judge orders prosecutors to try to disprove defense's claims.
June 2	General Mattis testifies he neither asked for nor accepted advice from Col. John Ewers during a series of strategy sessions; Ewers admits attending meetings but said he took no part in discussions.
June 17	Folsom dismisses charges against Chessani, citing appearance of UCI.
July 28	Government appeals Folsom's decision to the Navy-Marine Court of Criminal Appeals.

2009

Mar. 17	NMCCA upholds Folsom's findings.
Apr. 17	Government asks NMCCA for an *en banc* reconsideration of its Mar. 17 ruling.
Apr. 29	NMCCA denies government plea for *en banc* hearing.
May 5	Corps announces no more appeals in Chessani case.
June 19	Corps commandant names Lt. Gen. George Flynn as the new convening authority in Chessani case.
Aug. 27	Corps drops charges against Chessani.
Aug. 30	Corps decides to send Chessani before a board of inquiry.
Dec. 11	Board finds Chessani's performance was "substandard" but he will be allowed to retire at rank of lieutenant colonel.

2011

July 16	Chessani retires.

20. Wuterich's Offensive

The Chessani battle, combined with the nearly two-year fight over the outtakes, had strained the prosecution's resources, sapping Team Charlie's energy when it still had a particularly daunting task ahead. Chessani was a major setback for the government, and the head-to-head with CBS ended in a draw. Although the prosecutors eventually got the sought-after material from the broadcaster, it was a Pyrrhic victory: the gains were negligible. Prosecutors accomplished little in either conflict except exposing the weak spots in their strategy. Wuterich's defense team remained aloof from the engagements, which gave it a tremendous advantage in the next struggle that started much sooner than the still-reeling Team Charlie would have liked.

The next challenge began on March 22, 2010, when Wuterich's defense team tested the standard set by Muise and Rooney in the Chessani case by filing a motion with Wuterich's new judge, Lt. Col. David Jones, asking that the staff sergeant's charges be dismissed because of unlawful command influence.[1] It had been less than seven months since the Corps dropped the charges against the former battalion commander because of the appearance of UCI, and the defense was eager to see how far it could go with an identical tactic.

Jones may have been the new man on the Wuterich case, but he was no stranger to the Iraq proceedings. This was at least the second official trip to Camp Pendleton for the Okinawa-based Jones regarding MARCENT prosecutions. In 2006, he had presided in the case of Pfc. John Jodka III[2]; in 2007, it was the case of Cpl. Trent D. Thomas (both members of the Hamdania Eight).[3]

Taking a page from the Chessani playbook, Wuterich's lawyers contended that Ewers unlawfully influenced Mattis and Helland in the staff sergeant's case, just as he had in *Chessani*. Despite the strong impression of déjà vu, Jones went through the moves required in cases of allegations of UCI. Following a day-long, closed-door hearing, Jones announced that the defense had presented enough evidence for him to order the prosecution to try to refute the defense's claims. He did not go into detail about what was discussed in the session, but he said he had heard enough to cause him concern about Ewers's presence in the strategy meetings.[4]

The hearing the following day was a virtual repeat of Chessani's June 2 session. The star witness, as before, was Gen. Mattis, who seemed to be reading from a transcript of the Chessani hearing: no, Ewers had not influenced him ("I don't recall a single time that anyone tried to influence me unlawfully"); no, he did not need Ewers's advice because he knew everything there was to know about the incident ("I intended to have a better grasp than anyone before I subject Marines to situations like we are in today"); and no, Washington brass did not interfere in his decisions ("I'm obligated to do my duty; I did my best").[5]

Although the same ground was covered, there were two significant differences between the UCI proceedings. First, Ewers did not testify at the Wuterich hearing. Two months after *Chessani*, he was reassigned as a judge in the Corps' Western Circuit, the same one in which Wuterich was being prosecuted.[6] Ewers's new job blocked him from being a witness, so the prosecution turned to Lt. Col. Riggs, the MARCENT SJA. Because the commandant selected MARCENT to be the CA/CDA, Riggs was the legal officer Mattis was obliged to consult for legal advice. He also was the one Ewers allegedly tried to subvert by taking over his duties as legal advisor to Mattis and Helland. Riggs did not testify at Chessani's hearing and he said little of import at Wuterich's. His appearance was brief and his testimony about Mattis laudatory. "General Mattis is one of the most single-minded commanders we have," Riggs said. "He doesn't give a damn what higher headquarters thinks. He's his own man."[7] The second difference was that the prosecution summoned Helland, who also had not testified during the Chessani hearing but was found blameworthy by Folsom because he asked Ewers for advice after he took over as commander of I MEF/MARCENT. He had retired in May 2009, so his knowledge of current developments was limited. He spent little time on the stand, and he—as had Mattis—swore that Ewers had no impact on his decisions.[8]

There was, moreover, a fundamental divergence between Chessani's and Wuterich's hearings. Ewers had played a major role in Chessani's case as far back as 2006 and was tagged as "tainted" because of his direct involvement with the former battalion commander. As far as is known, Ewers had no connection to Wuterich, although he may have been present when the staff sergeant's case was discussed in Mattis's long strategy sessions. As far as it is known, Ewers never talked to Wuterich, much less accused him of a crime, as he had with Chessani. There was no ostensible reason why Wuterich would have been affected by Ewers's presence at Mattis's meetings.

Despite this, Wuterich's team smelled victory when, at the end of the hearings' second day, Jones commented that there was a "possibility" the defense had made its point, i.e., that the prosecution had failed yet again to discredit the defense's contentions. However, three days later, Jones ruled in Team Charlie's favor, dismissing the defense request for a UCI ruling similar to the one in Chessani's case.[9] Charges against Wuterich would not be dismissed, Jones said, and the staff sergeant would have to face trial for voluntary manslaughter, aggravated assault, reckless endangerment, dereliction of duty, and obstruction of justice. "Any apparent Unlawful Command Influence did not and will not affect the proceedings," the judge added. Unlike Judge Folsom, who had been highly critical of the prosecution's UCI presentation in *Chessani*, Jones complimented prosecutors for their Wuterich presentation. "They 'overwhelmingly' refuted the defense allegations," he said.[10] It was a surprising about-face showing for Team Charlie.

At the end of the session, Jones set Wuterich's court-martial for September 13, a little more than five months in the future. In the meantime, however, there was a ruling in another case that also had nothing to do with Wuterich's but nevertheless profoundly affected developments.

The "Hutchins Motion"

Barely a month after Jones denied Wuterich's UCI motion and the clock was ticking toward his court-martial, the Navy-Marine Court of Criminal Appeals issued an opinion in the case of Sgt. Lawrence C. Hutchins III, of the 3rd Battalion, 5th Marines.[11] Hutchins had been the leader of a unit composed of six other Marines and a Navy corpsman, all convicted of involvement in the murder of an Iraqi civilian in the Anbar Province town of Hamdania in April 2006. Their cases, like those of the Haditha Marines, fell under the jurisdiction of the commander of I MEF/MARCENT—1st Lt. Gen. Sattler, then Mattis, then Helland.

Hutchins, the last of the "Pendleton 8" to be tried, was convicted in August 2007 of murder, conspiracy, and making a false official statement. He was sentenced to 15 years in prison, but ten months later, Helland, exercising his prerogative as CA/CDA, ordered Hutchins' sentence reduced by four years.[12] The specter of a similar fate for Wuterich apparently was a significant motivator for Wuterich's lawyers, who creatively drew a parallel between the two cases. What brought them together was the 5–3–1 vote of the full NMCCA court that overturned Hutchins's conviction because of a legal technicality originating in a complicated situation involving a Hutchins's military lawyer. Shortly before Hutchins's court-martial, one of his two detailed military defense attorneys separated from the Corps after his enlistment contract expired. Hutchins's judge—Lt. Col. Jeffrey Meeks (Wuterich's judge during the CBS dispute)—allowed the trial to proceed anyway. The majority of the NMCCA judges ruled that was a mistake, that Hutchins' conviction could not stand because the sergeant had been deprived of his right to a detailed (i.e., "assigned") defense attorney during his trial.[13] As a direct result of the ruling, Hutchins was released from prison after serving about one-fourth of his sentence.

The opinion opened the door for Wuterich's lawyers to claim that charges against their client should be dismissed for the same reason that Hutchins's conviction was tossed out: Wuterich, like Hutchins, his lawyers argued, was being deprived of his right to a detailed military counsel. This position was articulated in a document known as the "Hutchins Motion."[14] To understand it, one had to go back to the early days of the case against Wuterich. When charges were preferred against the staff sergeant in 2006, two military lawyers were named to defend him. They were Lt. Col. Colby Vokey and Maj. Haytham Faraj.[15] Each had more than 20 years of service in the Corps, and Wuterich's case probably would be their last. As is customary when veteran judge advocates are named as defense attorneys, each had to specify a planned retirement date. They agreed they would retire on February 1, 2008, some two years in the future.[16] By then, they reckoned, Wuterich's trial would be history. But it didn't work out that way. When their announced retirement dates came around, the fight with CBS over the outtakes from Wuterich's *60 Minutes* interview was just warming up, and Wuterich's case was on indefinite hold; there would be no court-martial trial for Faraj and Vokey to participate in. This, however, made no difference to the Corps bureaucracy: if Faraj and Vokey said they were going to retire on a given date, they had to live up to those commitments, trial or no trial. Still, the bureaucracy was not completely unyielding. Under the military system, their separation dates could be extended in one-month intervals. The catch was, those allowances were limited in number. After using three of their extensions, Faraj and Vokey were told they would have to retire regardless of the delays in Wuterich's trial because they had used all the postponements they were going to get. Faraj placidly accepted the decision and voluntarily left active duty in August 2008.[17] Vokey, however, resisted. This forced his superiors to issue a direct order for him to leave, which he did, under protest, in November 2008, three months after Faraj.[18]

As soon as he left active duty, Faraj went to work for Wuterich's lead civilian attorney, Neal Puckett, thereby maintaining his position as a member of Wuterich's defense team. Vokey, on the other hand, joined a firm in Dallas, Texas, that specialized in defending current or former service members.[19] Fortuitously for him and Wuterich—at least initially—Vokey's new boss assigned him to Wuterich's defense. Therefore, in effect, both Faraj and Vokey were back on Wuterich's team, except they were acting as civilian rather than military lawyers. So far, so good, until Vokey's presence on the team was challenged.

Two years later, early in September 2010, with Wuterich's trial some two months away, a problem developed regarding Vokey's position on Wuterich's defense team. When Vokey took the job with the Texas law firm, he paid little heed to the fact that that it also represented another Haditha Marine—former Sgt. Hector Salinas.[20] This landed Vokey in a jam. Salinas, who had taken part in the raids on houses One and Two, was never charged in connection with the incident, but he was scheduled to be a prosecution witness against Wuterich. This meant that if Vokey remained on the Wuterich defense team, he could be disbarred because of conflict of interest: a firm could not represent clients on opposite sides of the fence.

Judge Jones called for a closed-door Article 39(a) session to discuss the situation. At the end of the two-day hearing, on September 14, Vokey resigned from Wuterich's team.[21] At that point, thinking the conflict-of-interest issue was settled, Jones turned his attention to the Hutchins Motion. Some six weeks after Vokey's resignation, Jones denied the motion, issuing an 18-page findings of fact that was highly critical of the defense proposal.[22] Wuterich's lawyers, Jones said, had misinterpreted the NMCCA's *Hutchins* ruling as a permission slip allowing the defense to seek dismissal of charges any time a detailed military attorney left a case before trial. "The defense seems to believe that [*Hutchins*] means that a Court can never sever an [attorney-client relationship] for an attorney who is retiring or leaving active duty. This is an unnecessary and overboard reading of the case," Jones said.[23] The judge also scoffed at a defense request for a delay in Wuterich's court-martial until the issues could be resolved. "Abating the proceedings does nothing to assist [Wuterich] or the government because there is nothing to cure and nothing to wait for. Due to [Vokey's] ill-advised hiring [by the Dallas firm] he is now conflicted out of the case.... The unspoken reality is that the parties have had plenty of time to get ready for trial and [it] has been delayed long enough."[24]

Confusion Reigns

There is an acronym—FUBAR—often used in the military to describe a muddled situation. It means Fucked Up Beyond All Recognition. If there was ever a condition to which it could be said to apply, it was the status of Wuterich's case in October 2010. What had appeared to be a simple state of affairs eight months earlier evolved into a predicament that required a database to keep track of. Consider:

- In March, Judge Jones rejected Wuterich's claim that charges should be dismissed because of UCI.
- In April, the NMCCA issued its *Hutchins* opinion, which opened a new path for Wuterich's lawyers to explore.
- In August, Wuterich's team filed the Hutchins Motion.
- In September, Vokey resigned from Wuterich's defense team because of a conflict-of-interest threat.
- In October, Jones rejected the Hutchins Motion.
- Also in October, prosecutors in the Hutchins case asked the Court of Appeals for the Armed Forces to overturn the NMCCA *Hutchins* ruling.

And there was more to come.

Wuterich's trial was still up in the air. It had been set for September 13 but was postponed until November 1 because of an ankle injury suffered by a prosecution witness.[25] And that was only the beginning. Wuterich's team set the case in still another direction on October 28 when it filed a petition for a writ of mandamus with the NMCCA, bypassing Judge Jones.[26] The plea was an attempt to force Jones to immediately reinstate Vokey or halt proceedings until a way could be found to let Vokey again take a place on the defense team.

Requests for writs of mandamus are rare in civilian courts; in military courts, they are almost unheard of. A mandamus is an explicit order, or mandate, compelling the object of the petition (in this case Jones) to perform a specific task (reinstate Vokey). It is different from a normal request because it demands instant action, thereby speeding up what can be a poky process. However, it has definite downsides. Foremost, a mandamus can be issued only under certain, narrowly defined conditions, such as the need to demonstrate that the offending party (Jones) has committed a grievous error that could injure a specific party (Wuterich) and has refused to correct it. Because of the narrow restrictions under which a mandamus can be issued, it is frequently viewed as a measure of desperation. While it is unlikely to be granted, it can obstruct proceedings.

The request, perhaps as the defense planned, set off a battle that would not be resolved for almost a year. In the meantime, the CAAF did, in fact, overturn the NMCCA *Hutchins* ruling.²⁷ The result was that Hutchins, who had been released from prison, was sent back behind bars. The high court decision also effectively killed Wuterich's attempt to have the charges against him dismissed based on the NMCCA opinion; the Hutchins Motion was swept off the board. The mandamus request remained viable, however, but it was on life support. Four days before the CAAF *Hutchins* opinion, the NMCCA declined to rule on the petition, saying Jones's "findings of fact were supported by the evidence," meaning that the court placed no value on the mandamus request.²⁸

Unwilling to take no for an answer, Wuterich's lawyers went to the CAAF. In April, that court denied the writ request.²⁹ The ruling, however, left the door open for Wuterich's team to go back to the NMCCA, which it did.

By this time, the NMCCA evidently was fed up with Haditha. The mandamus plea was the ninth involving issues stemming from the incident it had been asked to consider since 2008 and the beginning of the fight over the *60 Minutes* outtakes. This time, the court seemed determined to wrap it up. On June 15, two months after the CAAF effectively dumped the mandamus petition back in its lap, the NMCCA ordered a halt in the proceedings. Then it held oral arguments on the matter. A snatch of dialog from the hearings provided insight into the judges' mindset:

According to an audio rendition available on-line, an unidentified member of the court posited: "What if [Vokey] had been killed by a truck on the day he retired?"³⁰

One of the lawyers, who also was not identified, replied: "Then we would have had to find a replacement. But he isn't dead and can be revived."

One of the judges harrumphed, "He is 'mostly dead' to the court [now]. What if he is recalled, then at trial sits there like a potted plant because he is afraid of being disbarred?"

The court debated the issue for two weeks before issuing a nine-page opinion tongue-lashing Wuterich's lawyers.³¹

"In short," the court said, "[Wuterich] seeks to burden the Government with a mandate to recall [Vokey] to active duty in order to remedy a malady of which they [*sic*] are not the cause."³²

It harshly rejected the defense team's allegation that Jones was biased, saying, "If there is any prejudice against [Wuterich] it was laid upon him through the actions of his defense counsel."³³

Finally, the court bluntly told Wuterich's defenders its patience had run out. "Put simply," the court said, "it is time to place this matter before a trial court for a verdict."³⁴

The CAAF sealed the decision a month later with a one-paragraph order denying a defense request for a re-hearing.³⁵

The upshot of the 18-month-long series of defense stratagems was that Wuterich's team had gambled and lost, especially with its mandamus request. It alone ate up 11 months and led to five postponements of Wuterich's court-martial. In any case, the CAAF decision not to revisit the NMCCA opinion made a court-martial unavoidable: Wuterich would have to go to trial, the sooner the better as far as the courts were concerned.

21. Court-Martial

On January 5, 2012—for the first time since Wuterich's arraignment almost exactly four years earlier—a criminal procedure involving the elusive staff sergeant began on schedule.

The trial's opening session had the character of a high school reunion for its participants: they were not friends, but they all knew each other from previous encounters in the record-setting prelude. The lead military counsel was Maj. Nicholas Gannon; his assistant was Lt. Col. Sean Sullivan, both veterans of other Iraq proceedings. The main defense attorneys were Neal Puckett and Haytham Faraj, retired Marines and abundantly familiar to Haditha watchers. Only the media were notably absent. Burned by years of delays, last-minute postponements, cancelled hearings, and Article 39(a) sessions that were closed to reporters, assignment editors had become extremely cautious about sending staff members on expensive trips to California that more often than not turned out to be dead ends. Besides, the public had long ago lost interest; there was no lack of breaking news in other areas to capture the attention of a fickle populace that had all but forgotten about Haditha. In addition, there was an expectation that the court-martial would not produce much in the way of startling testimony: what Wuterich had or had not done had been thoroughly covered in the Article 32 hearings, including Wuterich's statement at his own pretrial proceeding. And then there was his appearance on *60 Minutes*. If he took the stand—which seemed unlikely—the chances of him elaborating on what already was in the record were slim. On opening day, there were only a handful of reporters present, all of whom represented local publications. Reporters from national and international organizations that had followed the proceedings aggressively for about a year were markedly absent.

This non-appearance undoubtedly delighted Corps commanders. From their perspective, the less that was printed or broadcast about Haditha, the better. It had been the worst incident of its kind in the long Iraq War, and the most deadly of any known Marine–civilian clash in Corps history. The Corps would not have welcomed another rehash of how 24 Iraqi noncombatants were killed under suspicious circumstances. It would not have been good for the organization's carefully crafted image; it could hurt recruitment and— even more seriously—it could have a detrimental affect on congressional appropriations.

Wuterich's trial was expected to last a month, but that seemed an underestimate considering that the prosecution and defense lists of potential witnesses contained more than 50 names. Naturally, not all of those would be called. Some names were submitted merely to confuse the opposing side. Others would prove to be superfluous. Still, it was an impressive collection of active duty and retired military personnel, investigators, crime lab specialists, and civilians, including most of the former members of 1st Squad who had left the Corps since the incident. The prosecution had generously handed out 17 grants of testimonial immunity to men from Battalion 3/1, and some of those beneficiaries would almost certainly take the stand. Missing from the witness lists were the men with high ranks who had appeared at previous proceedings: the three- and four-star generals and those who had been in command positions in the Iraq theater in 2005–06. This was an enlisted man's trial, and Wuterich was a relatively low-ranking one at that.

Picking a Jury

Jones' first act was to dismiss charges of obstruction of justice and reckless endangerment because they were no longer applicable due to recent changes in the UCMJ. Despite this, Wuterich still faced nine counts of voluntary manslaughter connected to the deaths of eight persons in House Two and "one or more unknown persons" from the white sedan, plus three counts of willful dereliction of duty and two counts of aggravated assault.

The judge's next job was to oversee selection of a jury—a process that differs considerably from the one encoded in civilian law. The UCMJ—unlike the civilian system—does not mandate a specific number of jurors; it says only that there must be at least five. The military also has rules regarding jurors' ranks as they relate to the rank of the accused: all jurors must hold higher rank. At a General Court-Martial in which an officer is the accused, jurors also must be officers. But that does not hold for enlisted personnel. An enlisted accused may request a jury in which at least one-third of the panel also be enlisted. Wuterich chose that alternative.

In the civilian system, potential jurors represent a random selection of individuals, but there is nothing random about the process under the UCMJ. Military law specifies that potential jurors be nominated by the convening authority, in this case Lt. Gen. Thomas Waldhauser, the fifth three-star officer to serve in that position since the Haditha incident became publicly known. Nominations are based on a number of criteria, including education, Military Occupational Specialty (MOS), length of service, and experience, in this case having served in a war zone. The objective is to provide a pool of service members whose qualifications most closely approximate those of the accused. As a result, military juries are much closer to a panel of peers than those in a civilian trial.

In both civilian and military courts, the judge and lawyers from both sides question potential jurors to determine their suitability. Waldhauser nominated five officers and six enlisted men to the initial panel. All were combat veterans. After one and a half days of questioning, four officers and four enlisted were selected to hear the charges against Wuterich.[1]

A relatively small man at five foot six or seven, Wuterich sat stoically at the crammed defense table during jury selection. Usually speaking only when addressed, he spent most of the time staring trancelike into the distance through dark-circled eyes. Both Faraj and Puckett were conspicuous because they were the only ones not wearing uniforms. Faraj favored suits of conservative cut and conventionally colored ties, but Puckett, on the other hand, stood out like a rose in a snow bank. After he left the Corps, Puckett transformed into a dandy, a veritable peacock. Gone were the twice-a-day shaves and the high-and-tight hairstyles much loved by the Marines, along with the drab uniforms that allowed no room for sartorial individuality. Puckett appeared at Wuterich's side sporting a close-cropped goatee (the only facial hair in the vicinity) and moderately long hair swept behind his ears. He preferred bespoke suits, bright multi-colored silk ties, and designer eyeglasses. While the Corps-decreed uniform of the day called for short-sleeved blouses, Puckett opted for tailored shirts with sleeves on the other side of wrist length, meticulously turned French cuffs, and flashy links.

His wardrobe tastes likely were cultivated from his post–Corps years of roaming the globe—from England and Germany to Hungary and Spain—defending service members as a rambling legal gun for hire. One of his more notable cases involved that of Lt. Col. Allen West, a former Army battalion commander accused of using force and scare tactics to get information from a suspected insurgent in Iraq. If convicted of aggravated assault, West could have been sentenced to several years in prison. Puckett and his team convinced

Army prosecutors to forget about a trial and agree to let West be judged by his commanding officer at an non-judicial punishment (NJP) procedure. As a result, rather than being sent to Fort Leavenworth, West was fined $5,000 and allowed to retire at his then-current rank with full benefits.[2] Because an NJP is not a judicial proceeding, West's record was clean. After he retired, he was elected to Congress from Florida's 22nd Congressional District—a feat he probably could not have accomplished with a dirty trial on his résumé.

Down to Business

From the beginning, Wuterich's prosecutors faced an uphill battle. The predominant weakness in their case—an almost total lack of evidence—was exposed during the CBS battle when prosecutors stretched the outtakes struggle for more than two years. Even with the desperately sought material in hand, it would be an upset-of-upsets if prosecutors could win a conviction. There simply were too many factors working against the prosecution. Probably the most formidable was the obvious unwillingness of former squad members to testify against a fellow Marine. The Corps' often-touted bond of Marinehood was, in this situation, working against the prosecution. Despite the grants of immunity so liberally handed out by prosecutors, the Marines who trained and fought alongside Wuterich only grudgingly gave up details. Gannon, the lead prosecutor, candidly expressed his frustration early in the proceedings: "I can't think of a single witness desiring of being helpful to the government," he told Judge Jones.

There was the time-and-memory issue as well. In the six years since the incident, memories had faded and almost everyone involved in the events at Chestnut and Viper had gone on to lives far removed from Haditha; most undoubtedly were trying to forget what had happened in Iraq. The lack of physical evidence also presented a major problem for Sullivan and Gannon. Testimony from investigators during the Article 32 hearings was vague and lacked specifics. In each instance, analysts said they were called in too late to make technically supportable judgments. The dead already had been buried and requests for exhumation were denied. The houses had been patched up and the white sedan had mysteriously disappeared, along with the two AK-47s Wuterich and Lance Cpl. Sharratt said they recovered at House Four.

When he took the floor for his opening statement, Gannon sounded like someone trying to whip up enthusiasm for a story that had become hackneyed through repeated retelling. "Sergeant Wuterich," he began, using the rank

Wuterich held at the time of the incident, "had his squad kill 19 people." The prosecutor's motive was to depict Wuterich as an inexperienced rifleman who panicked in his first combat. "He never lost control of his squad, [but] he lost control of himself," the prosecutor said accusingly.

Pressing on, Gannon suggested that Wuterich's mood segued from hysteria to blood lust. "He killed five [Iraqis] along the roadside, six in House One and eight in House Two." Pausing to let that statement sink in, he added: "None of these victims was a threat; many of them were women and young children."

Video from Scott Pelly's interview with Wuterich—selections from the CBS material that had never been publicly displayed—flashed on a nearby screen as Gannon continued. In one segment, jurors could watch Pelley challenge Wuterich by asking how he felt after learning that the dead were all noncombatants. "You're proud of what your men did?" Pelley inquired in seeming incredulity. Wuterich, showing no contrition, replied that he was totally satisfied with his men's performance. "They did their job and they did it well," he responded.

To emphasize his contention that Wuterich was so overcome by anger, consternation and a desire for revenge that he ignored the ROE, Gannon described a hypothetical scene that may have occurred within minutes of the IED attack. "Wuterich moved back to the destroyed vehicle and he saw [Terrazas's] body. It was just a pile of flesh. One of his arms was missing and his legs were severed from his body. His face was completely mangled." Turning to Wuterich, Gannon said, "That is what influenced Wuterich's thinking."

When his turn came, Faraj maintained the defense position that Wuterich had acted within the restrictions of the ROE. The team assaulted houses One and Two because its members had been fired upon, which was sufficient justification for an armed attack. Wuterich shot the men from the white sedan because he thought they were fleeing—and this also was sanctioned by guidelines governing troops in Iraq at the time. Speaking so softly he could barely be heard, Faraj claimed it did not matter that there were no weapons or dead insurgents found inside either of the first two houses. It was immaterial, he said, if Wuterich's team came under small arms fire because the attack already had been initiated by the insurgents when they sprung the ambush. "The IED [constituted] an attack," he said, "and the first casualty was a Marine." The team picked House One as the target because it was the closest and the most likely place for insurgents to take shelter. "They didn't know there were noncombatants in that house," said Faraj. "They were responding to a threat."

Faraj's presentation got confusing, however, when he tried to argue that shell casings found in House Two were not from cartridges used in the weapons carried by the four-man fire team. Thirty percent of the casings found at the scene, he said, were from cartridges used in an AK-47 or were 9-mm casings consistent with cartridges by a Russian-made Makarov pistol. By making this an issue, Faraj wanted to plant the idea that the Iraqis were killed by insurgents rather than by the fire team. But his argument partially collapsed when Lance Cpl. Sharratt took the stand. Sharratt had not been part of the original fire team but had joined the group after they left House One. At the time, the former lance corporal was armed with a M240G medium machine gun, which he preferred over the standard-issue M-16. The weapon fires the same 7.62 mm rounds used in the AK-47 and not the smaller 5.56-mm cartridges used in an M-16. Sharratt said he also carried a Beretta M-9 pistol, which also fires a 9-mm round. Still, because Sharratt testified he never entered House Two, the casings alluded to by Gannon could not have come from his weapons.

Further damaging Faraj's theory was the fact that no insurgent weapons were recovered although houses One and Two were thoroughly searched after the assaults. The first squad nonmember to enter the dwellings was Staff Sgt. Justin Laughner, the HET photographer ordered to the scene by Lt. Grayson to take pictures of the dead so the images could be compared to those in the DOD database of known and suspected insurgents. Under cross-examination, Laughner backed off from a statement he had made earlier to investigators about seeing the suspicious casings. In retrospect, he said, the casings he was referring to were in the hallway of House Two, not in the rear bedroom where seven Iraqis were killed, six of them children under the age of 14. When pressed, Laughner further admitted he was not sure about the caliber of the casings, only that they appeared to him to be different from those used by the M-16.

"What about 9mm?" Faraj asked.

"I don't remember any 9mm," Laughner replied.

The Green Wall

As the trial progressed, it became even more obvious that the prosecution was not going to get the cooperation from its witnesses that it needed to make a strong case against Wuterich. Former Lance Cpl. Tatum—who had been accused of involuntary manslaughter, reckless endangerment, and aggravated assault before the charges were dropped and he was awarded immunity—was the first of Wuterich's former squad mates to testify. His reluctance to speak out against Wuterich had been evident from the beginning, when he had to be ordered to talk to prosecutors.

"Those houses were declared 'hostile,'" Tatum said defensively, alluding to the commonly held belief in Battalion 3/1 that a "hostile" house could be assaulted with impunity. "Anyone inside could have had weapons." For him, the danger intensified when he heard what he thought was a weapon being racked almost as soon as he entered House One. He tossed a grenade into the room and then rushed inside firing his M-16. "I was firing at silhouettes," he said, recalling that the visibility inside the houses was so poor that it was not possible to distinguish individuals. The air was so filled with dust and smoke from the grenade that he could not even guess about age or gender. By his testimony, Tatum implied that if he couldn't identify the targets, neither could Wuterich, so his former squad leader could not have willfully killed civilians.

Under cross-examination, in response to a question from Puckett, Tatum blamed NCIS agents for trying to make a mountain out of a molehill. The investigators had been so intent on accusing him of murder, he said, that they resorted to improper interrogation techniques. Tatum told how he was taken into a dank room in the lower levels of the Haditha Dam normally used to hold suspected insurgents. The room had no toilet and reeked of urine and mold, he said. He was obliged to add to the stench when interrogators ignored his pleas to leave the room to relieve himself, requiring him to urinate on the floor. The questioning went on for 11 hours, he said, ending only when the battalion sergeant major forced his way into the dungeon-like cubicle and demanded a halt to the procedure.

Tatum was followed on the stand by Dela Cruz, Salinas, and Kallop. All had testified during various Article 32 hearings and, when questioned by Sullivan or Gannon, they basically repeated their earlier statements. The most damaging testimony came from Dela Cruz, who reiterated how Wuterich had coached him to lie about the men from the Opel trying to run before Wuterich gunned them down. "They were just standing around," Dela Cruz maintained.[3]

Kallop verified again that he had told Wuterich to "clear" the area south of Route Chestnut, where houses One and Two were located. The houses were "legitimate targets," Kallop said, and the fire team members were responding correctly to a declaration that House One was "hostile." He did not mention that it was Wuterich who slapped the "hostile" tag on the house, not him. If he were facing a house that had been declared hostile, Kallop said, he would have "used everything from tanks to air assets" to complete the mission to clear the dwelling.[4] "I believed then and I believe now that my Marines followed the Rules of Engagement," added Kallop, whose only combat experience was in the Haditha incident. He took his discharge after the Haditha deployment.

In response to a question from Gannon, Kallop also admitted that he had ordered a second "clearing" procedure that morning. Soon after he ordered Wuterich to "clear south," he also told Dela Cruz to take a second fire team to "clear" houses north of the blast site. The mission, which was noted by Maj. Gen. Bargewell in his 2006 report, was accomplished without a shot being fired.

Earlier, there had been questions raised during some of the Article 32 hearings about what house-clearing techniques had been drilled into the men of Battalion 3/1 in preparation for the Haditha deployment in the late summer of 2005. Instructors responsible for training Marines awaiting deployment to Iraq and Afghanistan (but not those in Battalion 3/1) denied they had followed Commandant Hagee's post–Fallujah suggestion to assault every dwelling with grenades and small arms fire. In Fallujah, the Battalion 3/1 mantra had been "clear every room with a boom," a tactic Hagee heartily endorsed, later telling a conclave of officers that that was the secret to success in Iraq.

However, after Haditha, Corps commanders contended the Fallujah-method had never been a training standard. Former battalion Sgt. Maj. Edward T. Sax reinforced this notion when he took his turn on the stand. "What we did at Fallujah was something we never did again," he said, emphasizing that "Haditha was not Fallujah." The men of Battalion 3/1 were reminded about the Fallujah prohibition before they arrived in Anbar Province, he said, adding that instructions were that "[Haditha] was not going to be Fallujah."[5] However, even if Fallujah-like tactics were not part of the Corps training program, Wuterich said on *60 Minutes* that the Fallujah veterans in his squad offered the men in the squad their own opinions on how to "clear" a house.

At the end of Sax's testimony, prosecutors said they still had at least a dozen more witnesses waiting in the wings. By then, however, Team Charlie's case was sliding rapidly downhill; those who had already testified for the prosecution had been spectacularly ineffective. As a result, it seemed unlikely that second-tier testifiers would be able to prevent another ignominious defeat. Rumors had circulated since before the trial began that the prosecution was going to offer Wuterich a plea deal if they thought they could not get a conviction. By the trial's tenth day it seemed obvious that the time for a decision had arrived; it seemed inevitable that the government intended to cut its losses and take whatever it could get. Judge Jones gave credence to the possibility when he announced an unexpected 24-hour recess at lunchtime on Thursday, January 19.

Court-watchers were surprised when the trial resumed the next day without mention of an agreement. Nevertheless, the parade of witnesses continued normally through the rest of the day until Jones called the customary weekend break. The situation, though, changed drastically on Monday. Minutes after the session opened with expectations of testimony from the first of two crime scene reconstructionists, Jones impassively declared that Wuterich had pleaded guilty to a charge of negligent dereliction of duty. Although the plea was not a surprise, the charge was a bit of a shocker. To confess to a crime that would be the equivalent of a misdemeanor in a civilian court was a disappointment to many, considering that Wuterich had once been charged with 19 counts of murder.

Jones remained emotionless when he broke the news, but his anger seeped out the next day at the sentencing hearing. The judge properly had been excluded from the plea negotiations, which were carried out among the lawyers and Lt. Gen. Waldhauser. However, the consequences were conspicuous when it was time to allot punishment. Jones obviously had planned to assess the maximum allowable under the UCMJ—90 days in the brig, plus a fine and demotion to the rank of private. But before he could act, he was told that the agreement precluded a jail sentence. Staring fixedly at Wuterich, Jones, going as close as he could to expressing his displeasure, harshly said, "It's difficult for [me] to fathom negligent dereliction of duty worse than the facts in this case." In the end, he rejected a fine because Wuterich was a single father with three young daughters, so the only penalty left was reduction in rank. In actuality, this was meaningless because Wuterich was going to separate from the Corps as soon as the paperwork could be completed. He had long ago fulfilled his commitment to the Corps but had not been able to separate because of the pending charges.

Before the session adjourned, Wuterich offered another statement of regret about the deaths. It was his third: he had expressed similar sentiments during the *60 Minutes* interview in March 2007 and at the end of his personal statement at his Article 32 hearing a few months later.

> I wish to assure you that on that day it was never my intention to harm you or your families. I know that you are the real victims of November 19, 2005. For six years, I have had to accept that my name will always be associated with a massacre, with being a cold-blooded baby killer, an "out-of-control" monster and a conspiring liar. There's nothing I can do about whoever believes those things. All I can do is continue to be who I've always been: me. And none of those labels have ever been, or will ever be, who I am.[6]

It was impossible to judge his sincerity.

While the outcome failed by a long way to meet the prosecution's expectations, it proved to be a blessing in disguise. Because a guilty plea, no matter for how menial a violation, is recorded as a conviction, it saved the proceedings from being a total loss. It was the only success, no matter how limited, in eight tries, and it gave Team Charlie a conviction rate of 12.5 percent in the Haditha proceedings. If Wuterich's charges had gone to the jury, the verdict might well have been not guilty because of the shortcomings in Team Charlie's case. In contrast, the prosecution's conviction rate in the Hamdania cases was 100 percent and the Corps-wide average is above 93 percent.

Epilogue

Reaction to Wuterich's plea agreement was swift and polarized. The Iraqis, as expected, were outraged. "This is not new, and it's not new for the American courts that already did little about Abu Ghraib and other crimes in Iraq," said Khalid Salman, 45, whose cousin was among those killed.[1] The Haditha incident was a big crime against innocent civilians," said Ali al-Moussawi, a spokesman for the Iraqi government. "We will follow up all legal procedures and judiciary measures to seek justice in the case."[2] Many Iraqis viewed the climax of the Haditha prosecutions as another example of how the United States' justice system has failed to punish those accused of felonies committed in wartime Iraq, pointing to the cases of Army private Charles A. Graner, Jr.,[3] of Abu Ghraib infamy, and the 2007 murders tied to members of the contracting company Blackwater.[4]

Surprisingly, there was little feedback in the United States. Editorial comment about a story that dominated the news cycles in 2006 and 2007 was virtually nil and public response was remarkably restricted. *The North County Times*, the closest thing Marines at Camp Pendleton had to a hometown newspaper, brushed it off by saying that anyone who had not undergone the rigors of combat was destined to judge the incident from a weakened position. "That Wuterich was even facing criminal charges for his role in the tragic killing of civilians in Iraq is a mark of our country's commitment to notions of right and wrong," the newspaper said.[5] "Few nations in history have even viewed the killing of civilians in a war zone as wrong, much less something their troops should be punished for," the editorial continued. "That Wuterich's plea deal satisfied prosecutors and his commanding general is enough to convince us that justice was, however imperfectly, served in this case."[6]

Readers' comments in various media outlets were more outspoken but numerically underwhelming. Some felt the Wuterich finale was justifiable. "When you lose a comrade to a remotely detonated mine, it becomes difficult to believe that those observing civilians are not insurgents," said a *Christian Science Monitor* reader identified as "brandenbergtor." "Indeed some probably are. As a junior officer, I will conserve the lives of my men as my first priority after my mission, irregardless [*sic*] of what higher command tells me. I am the man on the ground and I will always have the faces of my dead in my dreams and on my conscience."[7]

Others found the plea deal contemptible. "This guy doesn't deserve to wear the uniform of the U.S. Marines," Ed Needham wrote to *Frontline*.[8] "He's a murderer who serves as a recruitment poster for anti–American violence. That he's let off just goes to show the rest of the world that we don't value the lives of others." What would be fair, he suggested, would be to extradite Wuterich to Iraq.

Foreign opinion followed the same divided path. "At last, some common sense. I hope this brave Marine gets back to doing what he does best, protecting the free world from our enemies," a reader identified as "Like it is" wrote to the *London Mail Online*.[9]

On the same day, another reader, "Poliphobic," wrote the *London Telegraph*: "This incident and its outcome epitomises the conduct of America as a nation generally, the behaviour of its armed forces particularly, and the lack of any respect for justice especially."[10]

A Former Marine

Wuterich separated from the Corps a month after the plea agreement with a General discharge under honorable conditions.[11] It was one level below an honorable discharge but not detrimental enough to keep him from getting a civilian job in computer technology, a trade he had learned in the Corps while waiting for trial. A few days later, he agreed to an interview with reporter Mark Walker, who covered developments from the beginning for the *North County Times*. It was Wuterich's first interview since his appearance on *60 Minutes* almost five years previously.

The former Marine admitted he was nervous about suddenly becoming a civilian after a dozen years in the Corps. His worries were conventional. What if he couldn't find a job to support himself and three daughters? What about his past? Would potential employers be turned off because they might tie his name to negative publicity? To compensate, he confided to Walker, he was thinking about legally changing his name. Was his reputation ruined forever? That depended, Wuterich reckoned, on how he was viewed in the light of the result of his court-martial. "I didn't go to Iraq and murder 24 innocent civilians. I am not some psychopathic, crazy killer—I'm just a normal guy," he told Walker.[12]

When Walker asked if he had any second thoughts about his actions after the IED attack, the closest Wuterich came to admitting wrongdoing was to acknowledge that he may have set the wrong tone when he told the fire team members to "shoot first and ask questions later" and to treat House One as "hostile." "I should have had a tighter rein on [the men]," Wuterich said. "I shouldn't have allowed or said anything to them to make think that it was OK to shoot whoever, to shoot first and ask questions later. I understand how that could have influenced the Marines to thinking that they could kind of do whatever they wanted."[13]

Why did he think he was singled out to be the first Marine in history to be accused of 19 counts of murder? It was the NCIS, Wuterich said. "[Investigators] were influenced to look at the case one way—that Staff Sgt. Frank Wuterich was the guilty man here and the only one. I think that they were a little closed-minded about the way they handled it."[14]

In one venue, at least, he still was still was regarded as a hero. On August 18, some six months after receiving his discharge, he returned to his hometown of Meriden, Connecticut, for the first time in two years. With transportation for him and his girlfriend[15] paid for by local veterans' groups, Wuterich was the guest of honor at a golf tournament and later at a celebratory dinner topping off Frank Wuterich Day.[16] "I wish there was something I could do that could change the perception of me ... [but] The only way is to live my life the best I can, be the best person I can," he said in a dinner speech.[17]

The story elicited mixed response from readers. "Can we get more notice next time before he comes to town," wrote Allthefacts. "That way we can lock our doors and keep the kids safe. Glad he lives in California." Another reader, connect, responded: "I do not know the Meriden Marine Frank Wuterich, but I believed from the start that he was being set up. I am so pleased to know that so many military groups stood by him and honored him the way they did this weekend. His parents raised a remarkable young man. God be with him always."[18]

Prosecution Strategy

Puckett, who had not succumbed to media requests for interviews until after the trial, told Maureen Cavanaugh on San Diego radio station KPBS a week after the trial on April 23 that what had happened in Haditha would always be a mystery. It might have turned out otherwise, he said, if prosecutors had used a different strategy:

> I believe if different decisions had been made in terms of dropping charges or dismissing charges or giving people immunity—I believe had all the Marines who fired their weapons that day been required to be charged and go through court-martial process, I think perhaps a truth would have come out of all those cases rather than waiting till the last one and you don't get a truth. I believe we would know the truth of what happened that day, and know either that the Marines who did fire their weapons in the rooms where there were women and children ... perhaps we would know whether or not those individuals either engaged in criminal acts or they didn't, or they followed the Rules of Engagement. But because the prosecution chose to basically let them off without trials, the truth-finding process of a court-martial was denied us.[19]

If the system seemed to have failed, he added, it was because "individual prosecutors" decided to drop the charges. He did not accuse individuals but he hinted that answers might be found if the Corps wanted to pursue the issue.

> I don't blame the justice system. I think it's wrong to blame the military justice system, but we may in an after-action report or lessons-learned situation may want to look at those decisions to see where the blame lies.[20]

If the prosecution had taken a different tack, Puckett said, Iraqis might have found the outcome more acceptable.

> Looking from the Iraqi perspective, it would appear that justice was not done because literally no one held accountable for what happened that day. Once again, I go back to had all the Marines who were charged been required to go to completion in their trials, I think we'd know a lot more. I can't hazard a guess as to the outcome, but I suspect that something closer to justice for the Iraqis would have already been obtained prior to staff sergeant Wuterich ever going to court martial.[21]

One of the things that neither the prosecutors nor defense attorneys talked about before Wuterich's trial was the defense's offer of a plea deal. Puckett said he had proposed a settlement as far back as 2010, before the deluge of motions that led to a year-and-a-half delay in proceedings. Wuterich agreed to plead guilty to *negligent* dereliction of duty, Puckett said, but Team Charlie turned down the offer, because it wanted a conviction of *willful* dereliction. There was not much difference between the two. A conviction on willful dereliction carries a possible jail sentence of six months; a conviction of negligent dereliction, three months, plus differences in fines. However, willful dereliction would have required Wuterich to admit he purposely—as opposed to unknowingly—ignored his duties. In the end, the defense won.

Not Quite Over

The Wuterich trial was history and all its documents may have been locked away in file cabinets, but the government was not yet finished with the Haditha Marines. Roughly three months after Wuterich's trial, Navy secretary Ray Mabus instructed Corps officials to discharge former 1st Squad members Dela Cruz and Mendoza. His examination of the files, Mabus said, "revealed troubling information about their conduct."[22] Both men testified against Wuterich under grants of immunity that precluded them being charged for crimes they admitted during their testimony. However, Mabus felt they should be punished for lying to investigators in the early stages of the probe. "Such conduct is wholly inconsistent with the core values of the Department of the Navy," Mabus said in a letter to Commandant Gen. Jim Amos. "You are directed to immediately initiate administrative processing for Sgt. Dela Cruz and Sgt. Mendoza for administrative separation in the best interest of the service."[23]

When questioned about the secretary's order during a second appearance on KBPS' *Midday Edition*, Puckett told Cavanaugh there were implications that generally went unrecognized. First, he said, he was surprised by Mabus's involvement. "Obviously he got some kind of after-action report or brief or post-trial investigation about this and was shocked to learn that they were relying on the testimony of lying noncommissioned officers."[24] However, he added, it had been clear to everyone involved from the beginning that the two Marines had been lying. "What's surprising is that the prosecutors themselves didn't refer these two sergeants for disciplinary action to their individual units immediately after [Wuterich's] court-martial." What bothered him more, Puckett said, was that it appeared Team Charlie was "sponsoring perjury" by calling Mendoza and Dela Cruz as witnesses. "[I] even confronted them about this," Puckett added, "and they seemed to sort of brush it off and talked around it and said we have an obligation to put all the evidence in front of the jury. Yet there, is an ethical obligation to prevent attorneys from ... putting up witnesses ... who they know are lying."[25]

Puckett emphasized that Mabus was not accusing Mendoza and Dela Cruz of perjuring themselves in their testimony; his complaint was that they had lied before they took the stand. "Something becomes perjury once there's testimony to a materially false statement under oath in a proceeding like court-martial," he said, adding, "There are also other charges, like false swearing and making a false official statement. But the bottom line from [Mabus's] point of view is that the individuals who are noncommissioned officers in the Marine Corps lied when it was their duty to tell the truth."[26] In his experience, Puckett said, it also was unusual for the Corps or its civilian head to pursue such an issue. "We find the military justice system rarely goes after people," because charges often are hard to prove. "But this was a really, really big case; went on for six years; a lot of money was spent in prosecuting Staff Sgt. Wuterich, and these people, these two noncommissioned officers, were people who helped the government make their case."[27] Mabus may have been motivated, Puckett speculated, because "he saw that as a way of maybe putting things right in the military justice system. [The proceedings] had been so tragically flawed from the investigation through the prosecution phase, and been so badly handled by the chief prosecutors."

Donning his lawyer's hat, Puckett also pointed out that Mabus's order was not the last word. Mendoza and Dela Cruz were entitled to hearings by a board at which prosecutors would have to present a case accusing the two of lying. A second step would be for the board to determine if they indeed had lied, and whether that was justification for expelling them from the Corps. Finally, it would have to be determined what type of discharge and benefits they would receive. Although it would be possible for Mabus, because of his position, to override the board, it would be unlikely for him to do so, Puckett added.[28]

Because the status of Mendoza's and Dela Cruz's cases are not considered public information by the Corps, it is almost certain that the results of Mabus's order will never be known unless Mendoza or Dela Cruz go to the media.

Conclusions

In retrospect, it is disconcerting to see the number of missteps, misjudgments, and outright mistakes that occurred in the six years between the Haditha incident and the day when prosecutors offered Wuterich a deal that did not rise to the level of a wrist-slap.

Sorting the chaos is a tedious task, made more difficult by the lack of information on critical issues and the Corps' resistance to provide clarification. Were the prosecutions doomed from the time Chessani decided not to investigate? Or was the false news release generated at the behest of Col. Sokoloski the root of the problems?

Was it Mattis's decisions about whom to charge that proved fatal?

Did the convening authority deliberately sabotage Chessani's possible conviction? Or did he think he was above the law?

Were the prosecutors incompetent, out-gunned and out-maneuvered, or just poorly led and not on the same level as the civilian attorneys?

Did the Corps deliberately delay the prosecutions to divert media public attention from what would have been the worst case of mass murder in the institution's history? Or were honest efforts to seek a resolution wrecked by circumstance?

Sadly, for a number of reasons, there are few answers. Puckett acknowledged during his January 2012 interview on San Diego radio that he suspected that the world would never know exactly what happened in Haditha because the Corps so badly botched the investigation and the prosecutions. Such a statement coming from a man intimately familiar with the case offers little hope for anyone outside the system to solve the puzzle. However, that does not preclude a search for clues as to why the Haditha proceedings have truly earned the crude designation FUBAR, the well-worn military acronym for Fucked Up Beyond All Recognition.

The Corps

The Corps is justifiably recognized as one of the world's premier fighting forces. Its reputation for performance on the battlefield is well earned and widespread. The Corps is a principal element in our country's martial history. Its mottos and slogans, such as "Send in the Marines," "Semper Fi," "Gung Ho," "First to Fight, "A Few Good Men," and "Second to None," are so well established in our idiom that they are almost clichés. I can say with pride that my father and uncle fought with the Corps in the Pacific in World War II, and I can add from my experience as a correspondent in Vietnam that nothing made me feel more secure than knowing that a Marine was at my back.

But the Corps has a dark side, too, one not often seen by the public. When removed from the war zones, some Marines assume a different persona. They may become cliquish, insular, obnoxiously boastful, and openly mistrustful of anyone who is not and never has been a Marine. As an institution, the Corps is infamous in some circles for its inscrutability, its detestation of the media, its arrogance, and its refusal to divulge information that it does not consider in its own best interest. These not-so-desirable traits were on full display during what I think of as "The Haditha Period." Starting in November 2005 and continuing today, the Corps has become captive of a self-imposed policy of non-revelation. Just as Chessani's "panel" treated reporter McGirk's questions about the incident with sarcasm, contempt, half- or no-truths, and dismissal, the Corps on a larger scale exhibited the same inclinations through its disdain of the public's right to know about the mismanaged legal proceedings. Its sole contribution to public discourse was the appearance of an officer who announced that charges had been preferred, then refused to answer questions and fled the stage.

The Corps' performance was spectacularly appalling during the proceedings when it became obsessed with protecting its self-interests and preserving its carefully cultivated reputation, which has no tolerance of fallibility. It declined to provide even minimal amounts of information; denied access to records; hid developments in closed meetings; repeatedly refused requests for comment; turned its back on queries about obscure points of military law, and routinely abused the Freedom of Information Act. The situation remains the same today. Lips are still zipped, records remain sealed, and personnel remain inaccessible.

Mattis—as any true Marine would be expected to do—fell on his sword when he flatly denied that he had received advice or direction from anyone in Corps headquarters, in the White House, in the Pentagon, on Capitol Hill, or from his peers. I, personally, do not believe that. Considering the political situation that existed in this country at the time and what I have learned about how Corps commanders operate, I find Mattis's remarks disingenuous or worse.

I said in my preface that I hoped that someday a more-skilled and better-connected writer than I might publish a book with deeper insight into what happened in Hadith and in Camp Pendleton offices and conferences in the years that followed the incident. Right now, that possibility seems as remote as the construction of an Earth colony on Mars. But it could happen; there is precedent. In 1990, a former Corps historian named Keith Fleming published a book giving the backstory of what occurred before, during and after the high-profile trial of a newly minted drill instructor court-martialed for his role in the drowning deaths of six recruits at Parris Island, the Corps' East Coast training facility.[1] That incident, like Haditha, was splashed across the front pages of newspapers around the world; the public was screaming for accountability. What could have been a disaster for the Corps was averted when a small group of the organization's wisest men jumped in to negotiate an agreement that saved the Corps' treasured boot camp program and prevented untold other calamities. The squad-sized group of forward-thinking Marines, speaking for the Corps, agreed to publicly accept responsibility for the incident and institute widespread reforms if Congress would not call hearings, which could only have inflamed the public. That story was not made public until 34 years after the developments took place—yet another testament to the Corps' obsession with keeping the public unaware.

In the wake of Haditha, though, there has been no Corps acceptance of responsibility and no announced intention of programmatic adjustments. In 1956, Marines acted quickly and purposefully to prevent an immediate catastrophe and what would have been an indelible black mark in the Corps' history. That attitude obviously was missing in decisions about Haditha. Evidently, a person or persons in power determined that the Corps would be better off with a strike against it for badly botched prosecutions than risk public knowledge about what courts-martial might have revealed. At least twice, Wuterich has publicly expressed regrets to the families of the Iraqis killed in the incident, but the Corps—as far as I know—has never even hinted that its representatives may have acted improperly in the worst incident of its kind in the Iraq War.

Realistically, there is little hope the Corps is going to change its ways; there is nothing to compel such a move. In effect, the Corps is a law unto itself. By statute, it is answerable only to the president, the secretary of defense, and the secretary of the Navy, public officials who seldom interject themselves into the organization's day-to-day operations or try to manage policy. A rare exception was Navy secretary Ray Mabus's order to kick Mendoza and Dela Cruz out of the Corps. Notably lacking is any mention of a Corps obligation to the public or a demand for accountability other than in its own conventions. Congress has only marginal influence in that it controls the Corps' budget. While Congress also has the power to hold hearings, that is of marginal benefit because hearings almost always are politically, not altruistically, motivated. It was no surprise that the chairs of both the House and Senate armed forces committees under President Bush donned blindfolds when it came to Haditha. Contrast that with the reaction by the current GOP-controlled House of Representatives, which cannot seem to curb urges to call hearings on Benghazi.

Hamdania and Fallujah

It is worth pointing out for comparative purposes that the Haditha proceedings were not the only Iraq-related legal activities taking place in the same time frame as the Haditha proceedings.

Naturally, there was Hamdania. Newswise, it was marginalized by Haditha, and that may have been one of the reasons the resulting prosecutions were so successful. Fifty-six-year-old Hashim Ibrahim Awad was murdered on April 26, 2006, five months after the Haditha killings.[2] Although seven Marines and a Navy corpsman from Battalion 3/5 claimed the retired policeman had been burying an IED when he was shot to death, the subterfuge quickly collapsed. There was no delay in an investigation, as there had been in Haditha, and no denials from ranking officers. The men were arrested and flown back to Camp Pendleton, where they were tossed in the brig. On June 21, less than two months after Awad's murder, they were charged with kidnapping, murder and various other crimes by the then–convening authority—Lt. Gen. John F. Sattler (Mattis did not assume command of the I MEF until mid–August, seven weeks later).[3] They remained incarcerated until their cases were called for trial. The first court-martial was held on October 6, 2006, three months after charges were preferred.[4] By the end of the year, four of the men had been tried: two pleaded guilty and two were convicted. The remaining four were tried in 2007, culminating in the court-martial of the unit leader, Sgt. Lawrence Hutchins III, who was convicted and sentenced to 15 years in prison.[5] The conviction rate by the same group of prosecutors from the Camp Pendleton Legal Services Support Section (LSSS) was 100 percent. The Corps has never tried to explain why the Haditha and Hamdania proceedings produced such different results.

Another Iraq-related legal development simmering in the background was a bizarre case involving three men who had been members of Battalion 3/1's Kilo Company during the Second Battle of Fallujah in November 2004.

On July 3, 2007, *North County Times* reporter Mark Walker published a story saying the NCIS was investigating a lead about the murders of four Iraqis in Fallujah on November 9, 2004, more than two and a half years previously.[6] A month and a half later, a policeman from Oceanside, California—Robert L. Nazario, Jr.—was charged in a civilian court with two counts of involuntary manslaughter in connection with the deaths of two Iraqi men.[7] Four days after that, Sgt. Jermaine A. Nelson was charged with murder and dereliction of duty[8] and almost seven months later a sergeant in the Reserves—Ryan Weemer—was recalled to active duty and accused of murder.[9]

Authorities said the charges resulted from an incident that allegedly occurred after Nazario, Weemer, and Nelson stormed a house on the opening day of the battle and captured four Iraqi men. An NCIS agent said the men killed the four unarmed Iraqis because they were ordered to rejoin the fighting and had no way of securing prisoners.[10] Nazario, then a sergeant, allegedly killed two of the men while Weemer and Nelson, both corporals, killed the other two.[11]

Weemer revealed the incident during a polygraph examination that was part of the screening process after he applied for a job with the Secret Service. The Secret Service reported it to the Justice Department, which told the Department of the Navy, which asked the NCIS to investigate.[12]

Nazario was acquitted by a civilian jury a year after he was charged.[13] Weemer was acquitted after court-martial on April 9, 2009,[14] and Nelson pleaded guilty to murder on September 29, 2009.[15] He was sentenced to a reduction in rank from sergeant to lance corporal.

Mattis's Influence

A man of average height, balding, and decorated with full-sleeve tattoos on both arms, the bachelor Mattis prides himself on two qualities: his ability to digest huge amounts of printed text (which earned him the nickname "Warrior Monk") and his combativeness on and off the battlefield (for which he is called "Mad Dog" or "Chaos," which became his radio call sign). However, being a successful battlefield commander does not always equate to competence in the political arena. Some feel Mattis got off to a bad start in the Haditha proceedings when he declined to follow Sattler's example of confining the

Haditha Marines pending trial. If Mattis had done so, Wuterich would not have been able to talk to Scott Pelley, and the 18-month delay caused by the outtakes fight with CBS would have been averted. Moreover, by not ordering their incarceration, Mattis seemed to be signaling that although the Haditha Marines had been accused, nothing serious was going to happen to them.

The decision to jail or not to jail, though, was of little consequence compared to the decisions Mattis made in other areas under his control. Because the Corps has refused to provide details, it is impossible to say who was giving Mattis advice on whom to charge, what the charges would be, when charges would be dropped, who would be given immunity, and who would be the investigating officers at the Article 32 hearings. If Mattis followed regulations, his legal advice came from Riggs, the MARCENT SJA. But the confusion over Ewers's involvement clouded the issue. Mattis could just as well have been receiving advice from the members of Team Charlie, who were never identified, or he could have ignored all the advice and acted on his own. There is nothing in the regulations saying he had to accept suggestions from anyone.

There has never been an explanation for why Dela Cruz, Sharratt, Tatum and Wuterich were accused in connection with the killings, while Salinas and Mendoza, who also were part of the assault team at houses One and Two, were not. Mendoza admitted on the stand that he killed two Iraqi men, one each in houses One and Two. Why were charges against McConnell, the Company K commander, dropped without an Article 32 hearing? Why was he given testimonial immunity when he—the superior officer for all four of the accused enlisted men—was never called as a witness? Had McConnell instructed men in the company to shoot first and ask questions later during violent confrontations, so that Wuterich was simply echoing what his commanding officer wanted? Had McConnell told them to clear houses "Fallujah style?" What action did he take in the immediate aftermath? Records indicate he did not question (debrief) the men about their roles. Why not? Did he recommend disciplinary action? If not, why not? What did the men tell him about what had occurred? Regarding Stone and Grayson, why were they charged with dereliction of duty when they obviously were out of the decision-making loop and had no authority to call for an investigation even if they wanted? Why did Team Charlie not properly vet Laughner and Watt before calling them as primary witnesses at Grayson's trial? Were these issues discussed at the long strategy meetings? The list goes on.

Who nominated Ware to be IO for all three enlisted men and why? Technically, he was appointed by Mattis, but who gave the commander his name? No single individual damaged the prosecution's cases against Wuterich, Sharratt and Tatum more than Ware, who imperiously declared the prosecution could not prove any of them guilty beyond a reasonable doubt, thereby assuming a judge's mantle when he was not authorized to do so. His sole duty as IO was to determine if there was enough evidence to bring the accused to trial, not to try to read the minds of future jurors and guess about how they would interpret the testimony or what would develop during a trial. The direction of a trial cannot be predicted by evidence presented beforehand. Mattis agreed with Ware's recommendation to dismiss charges against Sharratt, but he went a step farther by praising the former lance corporal in a release from Camp Pendleton's Public Affairs Office saying:

> With the dismissal of these charges, LCpl Sharratt may fairly conclude that he did his best to live up to the standards, followed by U.S. fighting men throughout our many wars, in the face of life or death decisions made in a matter of seconds in combat. With this dismissal of charges, [Sharratt] remains in the eyes of the law—and in my eyes—innocent."[16]

Sharratt may not have been convicted, as Ware predicted, but testimony at his court-martial would have added more details about the incident and led to a better understanding of what happened.

The largest question mark concerning Mattis's behavior, however, surrounded his decision to include—or not exclude—the tainted Ewers from the meetings in which Chessani's case was discussed. Even Judge Folsom, who heard all the testimony and had access to documents not available to the media, was unable to figure it out. Mattis bulled his way through his testimony without providing a satisfactory answer. Ewers—if not Mattis—should have known that his attendance at the meetings put the case against Chessani in grave danger. Mattis admitted on the stand that he had been sufficiently warned about Ewers's presence, but he tolerated it, even if he did not demand it. Ewers's weak excuse for attending he meetings was that his commanding officer had asked him to be there and he had been unwilling to say no. Before the Haditha proceedings were completed, Ewers was appointed to a judgeship and then promoted to deputy director of the Judge Advocate Division at Corps headquarters.[17] To me, that smacks of a lack of determination to demand accountability.

After Camp Pendleton

Mattis mysteriously disappeared from Camp Pendleton on September 9, 2007, three days after the conclusion of Wuterich's Article 32 hearing. It soon was learned that he had gone to Norfolk, Virginia, to become the designated Supreme Allied Commander [of] Transformation (SACT) in the U.S. Joint Services Command. It was a four-star billet, so Mattis's promotion still had to be ratified by the Senate, which it was three weeks later by an overwhelming vote.[18] According to newspaper reports, there was speculation that SACT would be Mattis's last command, since he had almost 36 years of service. The rumors appeared even more credible after he transferred command of SACT to a French general two years later and, a few months after that, it was learned that he had been passed over to be the next Corps commandant.

But then circumstances intervened. The commander of allied troops in Afghanistan—Gen. Stanley McChrystal—was forced to retire after a story in *Rolling Stone* magazine quoted members of his staff criticizing members of the Obama administration. Gen. David Petraeus, then the commander of the U.S. Central Command (CENTCOM), replaced McChrystal, leaving open the position as commander of CENTCOM. Unexpectedly, Mattis was selected to be Petraeus' replacement.

Ironically, Mattis ultimately suffered the same fate as had McChrystal and for much the same reason: he also was forced into early retirement because of conflicts with members of the Obama administration. Reportedly, Mattis clashed with National Security Advisor Tom Donilon over administration policy on Iran, so Mattis was given an early boot—a decision that did not sit well with the conservative groups that had been after Representative Murtha's scalp. Mattis's old admirer, author Thomas Ricks, writing in his blog on foreignpolicy.com, criticized Obama for "mishandling" the situation even though he conceded it was the president's prerogative to hire and fire. He wrote:

> The White House view, apparently, is that Mattis was too hawkish, which is not something I believe, having seen him in the field over the years. I'd call him a tough-minded realist, someone who'd rather have tea with you than shoot you, but is happy to end the conversation either way.[19]

There was talk on social media about starting a movement to nominate Mattis for president.[20] The general's retirement was noted in a flattering farewell from the Senate[21] and a friendly goodbye from Defense Secretary Chuck Hagel.[22]

The Future

Mattis's retirement may have signified more than the end of a career. It also may have been a precursor for drastic changes to the UCMJ. Once the consequences of the Haditha proceedings begin to sink in, there inevitably will be an examination of the court-martial process. When the UCMJ became law in 1951, and through subsequent revisions, it was never imagined that proceedings stemming from a single incident could drag on for six years and be conducted in such a secretive manner. Haditha raised new questions about the viability of the system that allows such a situation to develop. Courts-martial that continue for extended periods are counter-productive, they are expensive, and they solicit complicated legal issues, which, after Haditha, still remain unsettled. Should regulations regarding interlocutory appeals be revisited to limit the number of petitions or to refine the conditions under which they can be filed? Do ensuing procedural postponements interfere with an accused's right to a speedy trial? What about the government's right to a quick solution? What should be done when proceedings creep along so slowly that members of the military's legal system retire before the case is settled? Should military personnel and legislators begin examining ways of reducing the ample powers of the convening authority? It is this conundrum that appears destined to draw the most attention in the immediate future.

There is, for example, a movement endorsed by many influential members of Congress, including Senator Kirsten Gillibrand, a Democrat of New York, to remove the convening authority's power to prefer charges and refer charges to court-martial. It is interesting that the British already have traveled this road. In 1775, when American revolutionaries had to quickly create an army and navy to fight for freedom from King George III, they copied the British criminal justice system as a means of maintaining discipline in the new armed forces. The parallels between the two systems continued until the British began moving away from its traditional system early in this century. One of the first things to go was the office of convening officer, the equivalent of the U.S.' convening authority. This transferred control over courts-martial to civilians—which basically is the goal of the current movement in Washington. The British, however, did not stop there. The Parliament-approved Armed Forces Act of 2006 virtually turned the system inside out. Among other things, it abolished the separate courts maintained by the Royal Army, Navy, and Air Force and created a single court that sits permanently (as opposed to the U.S. system of *ad hoc* courts) and hears cases involving accused from all three of the British military branches. British judges—unlike those in the U.S. military justice system—are civilians. Moreover, British judges are appointed by a civilian rather than advancing to that position through the military process. By the same token, British prosecutors also are civilians, appointed by a civilian based on civilian courtroom experience. Would that have helped correct the imbalance observed in the Haditha proceedings, where they seemed little doubt that Camp Pendleton prosecutors were overwhelmed by more experienced defense lawyers? British defense attorneys, too, are almost always civilians whose fees may be paid by a special government fund. Almost the only remnants of the *military* still in evidence in the British system are the authority to conduct investigations of alleged violations of the military code by military police, and a commanding officer's right to conduct hearings in misdemeanor cases involving military personnel.

It is almost certain that there will be battles in Washington for months and perhaps years to come over reform in the military justice system. The ineptness in the way the Haditha proceedings were handled played no little role in cracking open this door. It can be said with utmost confidence that almost no one in either the military or civilian systems wants to see a repeat of the Haditha proceedings.

Appendix A: USMC Iraq Command, Mid-November 2005

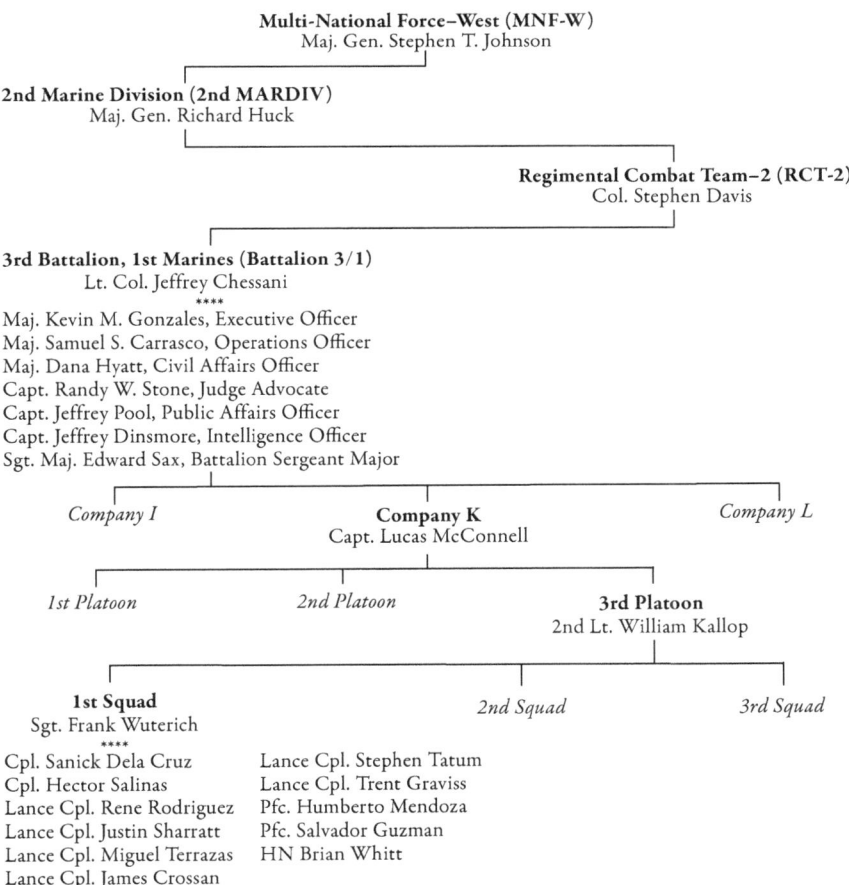

Appendix B: Abbreviations

AO	Area of Operations
Battalion 3/1	3rd Battalion, 1st Marine Regiment
BOI	Board of Inquiry
CA/CDA	Convening Authority/Consolidated Disposition Authority
CAAF	U.S. Court of Appeals for the Armed Forces
CERP	Commander's Emergency Response Program
CI	Counterintelligence
FB	Firm Base
GCM	General Court-Martial
HET	Human Exploitation Team
HUMINT	Human Intelligence
I MEF	I Marine Expeditionary Force
IED	Improvised Explosive Device
IO	Investigating Officer
JA	Judge Advocate
JEN	Journal Entry Note
KILO	The letter K in the military's phonetic alphabet
LWOP	Life (in prison) Without Parole
MARCENT	Marine Forces Central Command
MNF-I	Multi-National Force–Iraq (coalition command)
MNF-W	Multi-National Force–West (USMC command)
NCIS	Naval Criminal Investigative Service
NMCCA	Navy-Marine Court of Criminal Appeals
NJP	Non-Judicial Punishment
OIF	Operation Iraqi Freedom
PAO	Public Affairs Office/Officer
PID	Positive Identification
QRF	Quick Reaction Force
RCT	Regimental Combat Team
ROE	Rules of Engagement
SJA	Staff Judge Advocate
UCI	Unlawful Command Influence
UCMJ	Uniform Code of Military Justice

Appendix C: Marine Corps Personnel Abbreviations

Commissioned Officers

Second Lieutenant .... 2nd Lt.
First Lieutenant .... 1st Lt.
Captain .... Capt.
Major .... Maj.
Lieutenant Colonel .... Lt. Col.
Colonel .... Col.
Brigadier General .... Brig. Gen.
Major General .... Maj. Gen.
Lieutenant General .... Lt. Gen.
General .... Gen.

Enlisted

Private .... Pvt.
Private First Class .... Pfc.
Lance Corporal .... Lance Cpl.
Corporal .... Cpl.
Sergeant .... Sgt.
Staff Sergeant .... Staff Sgt.
Gunnery Sergeant .... Gunnery Sgt.
Master Sergeant .... Master Sgt.
First Sergeant .... 1st Sgt.
Master Gunnery Sergeant .... Master Gunnery Sgt.
Sergeant Major .... Sgt. Maj.
Sergeant Major of the Marine Corps .... Sgt. Maj. of the Marine Corps

Appendix D: Significant Dates

2005

Sept. 21	Battalion 3/1 arrives in Anbar Province.
Nov. 19	Haditha incident.
Nov. 19	Capt. Jeffrey Dinsmore builds story board giving official version of incident.
Nov. 20	2nd Marine Division issues news release saying civilians had died in IED blast or in firefight between Marines and terrorists.

2006

Jan. 19	Army Lt. Gen. Peter Chiarelli assumes command of Multi-National Force–Iraq.
Jan. 31	Maj. Gen. Richard Zilmer assumes command of all Marines in Iraq as head of Multi-National Force–West.
Feb. 12	In response to query from *Time* magazine, Chiarelli e-mails Zilmer asking if there has been an investigation of the Haditha incident.
Feb. 13	Zilmer tells Chiarelli there is nothing to investigate.
Feb. 14	Chiarelli sends Col. Gregory Watt to Haditha for a preliminary investigation called an AR 15-6 procedure.
Mar. 3	Watt finds Marines did not target civilians but recommends a more thorough investigation.
Mar. 9	Chiarelli sends Maj. Gen. Eldon Bargewell to Haditha to conduct a second, more methodical investigation of incident.
Mar. 12	Zilmer announces that he is asking the Naval Criminal Investigative Service (NCIS) to do an investigation for the Corps.
Mar. 19	*Time* publishes story questioning Corps version of Haditha incident.
Mar. 28	Battalion 3/1 returns to Camp Pendleton.
Apr. 7	Lt Col. Jeffrey Chessani and Capt. Lucas McConnell relieved of commands: Chessani of Battalion 3/1 and McConnell as commander of Company K.
May 17	Rep. John Murtha, Democrat of Pennsylvania, accuses Marines of killing civilians "in cold blood."

May 28	Sen. John Warner, Republican of Virginia and chairman of the Senate Armed Forces Committee, says he will hold hearings to find out what happened in Haditha. He later reneges.
June 6	Marine Corps Headquarters designates the Marine Corps Central Command (MARCENT) as the Consolidated Disposition Authority to handle legal issues resulting from the wars in Iraq and Afghanistan.
June 15	Bargewell completes report saying there was no evidence of a cover-up after Haditha, but he sharply criticizes Marines on several other fronts.
June 21	Seven Marines from the 3rd Battalion, 5th Marines and one Navy corpsman are charged with killing an elderly Iraqi and trying to stage the scene to make it appear he was planting an IED when he was shot.
Aug. 2	NCIS investigators say there is evidence supporting allegations that men of 1st Squad deliberately shot civilians at Haditha.
Aug. 2	Staff Sgt. Frank Wuterich files slander suit against Representative Murtha in a Washington federal court.
Aug. 13	Lt. Gen. James Mattis assumes command of the I Marine Expeditionary Force/Marine Forces Central Command.
Dec. 21	Corps announces that charges have been filed against eight Marines in connection with the Haditha incident; accused include Chessani, three other officers and four enlisted men from 1st Squad.

2007

February	Col. John Ewers named staff judge advocate for I MEF.
Mar. 18	Wuterich appears on *60 Minutes* to be interviewed by Scott Pelley; admits he shot the five men from the Opel because they were running away.
Apr. 2	Charges against Sgt. Sanick Dela Cruz dismissed.
Aug. 9	Charges against Capt. Randy Stone dismissed.
Aug. 12	Charges against Lance Cpl. Justin Sharratt dismissed.
Sept. 5	Navy secretary Donald C. Winter censures Maj. Gen. Richard Huck, former commander of 2nd Marine Division; his former chief of staff, Col. R. Gary Sokoloski; and former commander of RCT-2, Col. Stephen Davis.
Sept. 12	Mattis takes new job as chief of U.S. Joint Forces Command and NATO's Supreme Allied Commander Transportation in Norfolk, Virginia. Awarded fourth star.
Sept. 12	Charges against Capt. Lucas McConnell dismissed.
Oct. 19	Mattis orders charges against Lieutenant Colonel Chessani proceed to trial.
Dec. 28	New I MEF/MARCENT commander, Lt. Gen. Samuel Helland, orders charges against Lt. Andrew Grayson and Wuterich proceed to court-martial. Charges against Wuterich reduced; all murder charges dismissed.

2008

Jan. 16	Prosecutors subpoena CBS Broadcasting Co. demanding access to unaired portions (outtakes) of Wuterich/Pelley interview.
Feb. 22	At CBS's request, Wuterich's trial judge quashes subpoena, referring to it as a "fishing expedition."
Feb. 29	Wuterich trial postponed indefinitely pending appeals over government subpoena seeking outtakes from *60 Minutes* interview.
June 4	Grayson acquitted by a seven-officer jury.
June 17	Col. Steven Folsom dismisses charges against Chessani because of apparent unlawful command influence.
Mar. 28	Charges against Lance Cpl. Stephen Tatum dismissed.
Sept. 25	Former Lance Corporal Sharratt sues Representative Murtha for slander.
Nov. 21	Corps orders Wuterich's main military lawyer, Lt. Col. Colby Vokey, to retire.

2009

Apr. 14	Court of Appeals for the District of Columbia rules Representative Murtha cannot be sued for slander because he was speaking as a congressman.
May 5	Corps announces it will not pursue charges against Chessani.
Sept. 13	CBS delivers outtakes to Wuterich's prosecutors, ending a legal battle that delayed Wuterich's trial for more than 18 months.
Dec. 10	Board of inquiry finds Chessani's behavior "substandard" but allows him to retire at the rank of lieutenant colonel.

2010

Feb. 8	Representative Murtha dies at age 77.
March	Lt. Col. David Jones takes over as new judge in Wuterich case.
Mar. 26	Wuterich's defense team files first of a series of motions that will delay Wuterich's court-martial for another 15 months.
July 16	Chessani retires. His case consumed four and a half years.
Aug. 11	Mattis named new commander of U.S. Central Command.

2011

Jan.–Sept.	Wuterich trial delayed at least four times while lawyers fight in appeals courts over defense attempts to have charges against Wuterich dismissed.
Sept. 21	Court of Appeals for the Armed Forces, nation's highest military appeals court, denies request to review order from the Navy-Marine Court of Criminal Appeals, saying Wuterich must face trial.

2012

Jan. 9   Wuterich court-martial begins five years after charges were preferred; six years after the Haditha incident.

Jan. 23   Wuterich agrees to plead guilty to a misdemeanor charge of negligent dereliction of duty; agreement calls for no brig time and no fine, but his rank is reduced from staff sergeant to private.

Feb. 17   Wuterich separates from Corps with a General discharge under honorable conditions, one level below an honorable discharge.

Apr. 19   At the request of Navy secretary Ray Mabus, Corps begins discharge proceedings against Sergeant Dela Cruz and Sergeant Mendoza for lying to investigators during the Haditha investigations.

Appendix E: Military and Legal Terms and Expressions

AR 15-6 Investigation: A procedure conducted under the Army regulation with the same number designed to gather information about a particular subject and to determine if additional action is needed.

Accused: an individual against whom charges have been preferred. In the civilian system the term is "defendant."

Appeals courts: Two types of appeals courts are available to Marines. The first is the U.S. Navy–Marine Corps Court of Criminal Appeals (NMCCA), which hears cases involving Marines or sailors. The court membership occasionally fluctuates but as of 2013 it was composed of nine active duty judges, three from the Corps and six from the Navy. The court typically sits as a panel of three but occasionally meets as a full group, which is called an *en banc* hearing. There also are similar courts of criminal appeals for the Army, Air Force, and Coast Guard. Superior to the NMCCA is the Court of Appeals for the Armed Forces (CAAF), which is composed of five civilians, although they may be military retirees. The CAAF typically sits as a single panel for each case. Since 2008, the U.S. Supreme Court has had appellate jurisdiction over military cases in limited circumstances, such as when the CAAF has granted a petition for review. In practice, the Supreme Court rarely hears military cases. Staff Sergeant Wuterich asked the high court to hear his petition in connection with the outtakes dispute, but the court denied his request.

Article: A paragraph or section of law. The Uniform Code of Military Justice contains 145 articles, 88 of which deal with routine tasks (e.g., Article 7—Apprehension). These define the action and specify who is authorized to carry it out. The other 57—called punitive articles—are concerned with criminal violations. They define illegal activities (e.g., Article 128—Assault). Many of the crimes listed in the punitive articles are the same as would be found in civilian statutes. However, there are a number that apply only to the military (e.g., Article 89—Disrespect Toward a Superior Commissioned Officer, or Article 115—Malingering).

Article 32 investigation or hearing: A basic procedure in the military justice system, since it must be conducted before charges are referred to a General Court-

Martial. Similar to a civilian grand jury session or a pretrial hearing, an Article 32 hearing is designed to ascertain if there is sufficient evidence to proceed. Unlike a grand jury session, an Article 32 hearing is open to the public and the defense is allowed to call witnesses, challenge prosecutorial evidence, cross-examine prosecution witnesses, and introduce documentation it may consider exculpatory. During the proceeding, an accused has the option of making a sworn or unsworn statement. An unsworn statement is not subject to cross-examination. The presiding officer at an Article 32 hearing is called an investigating officer (IO), whose authority is limited to ruling on the introduction of evidence and questioning witnesses. An IO is not a judge and is not permitted to rule on legal issues. Although an IO usually is a judge advocate, having legal training is not a requirement. If the IO appointed by the convening authority is not a judge advocate, one is named as an adviser. The IO has 30 days after the conclusion of an Article 32 hearing to file recommendations with the Convening Authority (CA). The recommendations may vary from suggesting that the charges be dismissed to proposing a court-martial on the charges. The convening authority is not obligated to accept the IO's recommendations and may modify the proposal before referring charges to trial. The Convening Authority also may dismiss the charges.

Bargewell report: The 104-page document compiled by Army Maj. Gen. Eldon Bargewell following his AR 15-6 investigation of procedures conducted by the Marines in the wake of the Route Chestnut incident. The report was initially declared classified by Lt. Gen. James Mattis, but a declassified version was subsequently released. (See also *Watt report*.)

Board of inquiry (BOI): A non-judicial group convened to determine if an individual suspected of serious wrongdoing should be retained on active duty. Lieutenant Colonel Chessani was the only Haditha Marine to face a BOI. The board hears evidence from the prosecution and defense attorneys, and then makes a ruling based on a preponderance of the evidence. The burden of proof is lighter in a BOI than it would be at a trial, when guilt must be determined beyond reasonable doubt. The secretary of the Navy must approve the board's decision.

Collateral damage: Term commonly used to designate noncombatants killed or wounded during a military engagement.

Commander's Emergency Response Program (CERP): A program initiated in June 2003 designed to provide an avenue for local commanders to make condolence payments to Iraqis. The disbursements are not admissions of guilt or liability. The money comes from a fund established by Congress. (See also *Solatia payments*.)

Commissioned officer: A Marine holding the rank of 2nd Lieutenant or higher.

Consolidated Disposition Authority (CDA): A unit designated by the Corps commandant to adjudicate matters such as courts-martial resulting from alleged criminal violations occurring while deployed. For example, MARCENT was the designated CDA for issues involving Iraq and Afghanistan and the commander of I MEF/MARCENT was the Convening Authority.

Convening Authority (CA): a commanding officer authorized to convene a court-martial. A CA has broad powers including deciding what charges will be preferred, what charges will be referred to trial, and the type of court-martial. At the beginning of a trial, the CA nominates individuals for the military jury. The CA also appoints the investigating officers needed to preside at Article 32 hearings; grants immunity to witnesses; and negotiates plea agreements, if any, between prosecutors and an accused. Finally, the CA has the authority to dispense clemency or overturn a jury verdict. (See also *Consolidated Disposition Authority*.)

Corpsman: Unlike the Army, the Corps does not have battlefield medical specialists, or medics. Instead, combat troops rely on Navy enlisted personnel schooled in treating wounds and minor illnesses.

Court-martial (plural: courts-martial): A military trial authorized by the Uniform Code of Military Justice (UCMJ). There are three types of proceedings: Summary, Special and General. Only enlisted personnel may be tried at a Summary Court-Martial, and punishment may not exceed one month, plus fines. Either enlisted or commissioned personnel may be tried at a Special Court-Martial—a procedure often referred to as a misdemeanor court. Punishment may not exceed more than one year confinement, plus fines. A General Court-Martial (GCM) is a felony court and punishment could include death, or life in prison without parole. Either enlisted or commissioned personnel may be tried at a GCM. If the accused is an officer, only officers will sit on the jury, but an enlisted may request that the panel also include other enlisted personnel.

Detail (verb): A military term for "temporarily assigned." E.g., a HET unit commanded by Lt. Grayson was "detailed" to Company K, indicating it was not a permanent arrangement but existed only for the duration of the mission.

Detailed military defense counsel: a judge advocate detailed before charges are preferred to defend an accused at a General Court-Martial. Judge advocates do not specialize in prosecution or defense; in any given case they can be on either side. Prosecutors are selected by the commanding officer of the involved unit (see *Trial Counsel*). To prevent possible interference from within the chain of command, defense attorneys are selected by an independent unit called the Command Defense Counsel. Lieutenant Colby Vokey—the regional defense counsel for West Coast Marines—picked the defense attorneys in the Haditha and Hamdania cases. He also appointed himself as the lead military defense lawyer for Staff Sgt. Frank Wuterich. Both prosecutors and military defense lawyers commonly have assistants. In addition, an accused may hire civilian defenders, but the government does not pay the fee. Each accused in the Haditha cases was represented by at least one civilian lawyer.

Discharge (noun): Military law provides for five types of discharge: honorable, general, other than honorable, bad conduct, and dishonorable. Commissioned officers cannot be given bad conduct or dishonorable discharges. If a court-martial decides a punitive separation is in order, officers are "dismissed" from the service. However, the effect is that of a dishonorable discharge.

Enlisted: A Marine holding a rank between that of private and sergeant major.

Fallujah: A city in Iraq's Sunni-dominated Anbar Province west of Baghdad and southeast of Haditha. It was the scene of two battles between U.S. forces and insurgents seeking to establish a base from which to launch attacks. The first battle, called Operation Vigilant Resolve, took place April 5–9, 2004. The second battle—Operation Phantom Fury—was fought November 7–December 23, 2004.

Fallujah trials: In mid-2007 three men—two of them no longer in the service — were accused in connection with the alleged murder of four Iraqi detainees during the opening stage of the Second Battle of Fallujah on November 9, 2004. One of the men was tried and acquitted in a civilian court. Another was recalled to active duty and was tried and acquitted at a General Court-Martial. The third pleaded guilty to a lesser charge and was reduced in rank from sergeant to lance corporal.

Firm base: An installation used as a center of operations from which to conduct patrols and other missions. In Haditha, K Company established its headquarters in a school complex on the northeastern edge of the city and named it Firm Base Sparta. Company I was garrisoned at Haqlaniyah at Firm Base Raider, and Company L was at Barwanah in Firm Base Horno.

Haditha Dam: A five-and-a-half-mile-long, 18-story-tall structure spanning the Euphrates River just north of Haditha, it provides electricity and irrigation water to the fertile northeastern corner of Anbar Province and was considered a major insurgent target during the war. Lieutenant Colonel Chessani and his staff moved into offices in the interior of the dam and made it the headquarters of Battalion 3/1.

Hamdania trials: Procedures involving seven Marines and a Navy corpsman accused of kidnapping and then killing an elderly Iraqi in the village of Hamdania. All were convicted, but seven of the men were given relatively light sentences. The eighth man—Sgt. Lawrence Hutchins III—was sentenced to 15 years in prison after being convicted of murder. Hutchins's case would play a major role in attempts to delay or cancel Staff Sergeant Wuterich's court-martial.

Human Exploitation Team (HET): A small unit composed of a varying number of specialists in counterintelligence (CI) and human intelligence (HUMINT). The team's job is to identify insurgents and try to prevent attacks. Because of the small numbers in a team, HETs are detailed to larger units rather than being a permanent part of the organization. Lieutenant Grayson was the commander of the HET unit detailed to Company K.

Hutchins Motion: On April 22, 2010, the Navy-Marine Court of Criminal Appeals overturned the murder conviction of Sgt. Lawrence Hutchins III, who had been accused in connection with the death of an elderly Iraqi in Hamdania. The court said Hutchins had been denied his right to detailed military counsel because one of his defense lawyers was allowed to separate from active duty on the eve of Hutchins's trial. Staff Sergeant Wuterich's defense team seized on the ruling, filing what it called the "Hutchins Motion" to have charges dismissed against Wuterich. The motion contended that Wuterich, like Hutchins, had been denied his right to counsel because the Corps had ordered one of Wuterich's original lawyers to retire before Wuterich could be tried. The motion became irrelevant when the CAAF overturned the NMCCA ruling, which freed Hutchins. (See *Hamdania Trials*.)

Immunity: In the Haditha cases, the government granted "testimonial" or "use" immunity to 17 Marines to allow them to take the stand without fear of being prosecuted for their statements.

Interlocutory appeals: Pleas challenging a ruling or a point of law filed before a case is tried. In the Haditha proceedings, the pretrial requests went first to the NMCCA and subsequently to the CAAF. (See *Appeals Courts*).

Investigating officer (IO): An officer appointed by the Convening Authority to preside at an Article 32 hearing.

Journal entry note (JEN): An electronic message transmitted on a secure network providing information to officers up the chain of command.

Legal officers: A lawyer is called a judge advocate, but often is referred to as a JAG because military lawyers are part of the judge advocate general's command. JAs are responsible for activities that would be conducted within any large civilian organization, including administrative law, contracting law, and environmental law. They also advise Marines on wills, estate planning, and family law. However, unlike in a large corporation or civilian government entity, judge advocates also are responsible for elements of criminal law. They may serve either as prosecutors or defense attorneys in courts-martial and act as advisors to commanders who normally have no legal training. When detailed to serve as a prosecutor, a JA is referred to as a trial counsel, and when acting as a defense lawyer, a JA is referred to officially as a detailed military counsel.

Mandamus: An order issued by a court forcing a public official or a lower court to perform a specific duty. The conditions that have to be met before a court can issue a writ of mandamus are so demanding that pleas are not often successful. Requests for such writs are extremely rare in military courts, yet lawyers for two of the accused—Lt. Col. Chessani and Staff Sgt. Wuterich—requested them. Neither plea was granted.

Marine Forces Central Command (MARCENT): An administrative unit based at MacDill Air Force Base in Tampa, Florida. The three-star general who commands the I MEF also commands MARCENT. The unit played an important role in the Haditha proceedings because MARCENT, not the I MEF, was designated the Convening Authority/Consolidated Disposition Authority for all criminal cases stemming from criminal violations in Iraq and Afghanistan. (See also *Convening Authority* and *Consolidated Disposition Authority*.)

Members/jurors: A military juror is called a "member." A jury in a General Court-Martial—unlike one in a civilian felony trial—has no set number of members, but there must be at least five. The Convening Authority appoints potential members, and the final group is chosen through a winnowing process called *voir dire*, which is identical to that in civilian courts.

Noncombatant: A civilian or someone who does not take part in the fighting. One of the great difficulties in Iraq, as in Vietnam, was in distinguishing civilians from insurgents.

Non-commissioned officer (NCO): a Marine holding the rank of corporal, sergeant, staff sergeant, gunnery sergeant, master sergeant, first sergeant, or sergeant major. (See also *Enlisted*.)

Non-judicial punishment (NJP): A disciplinary procedure administered by a commanding officer as a penalty for a minor violation. The retribution depends upon the offender's rank and may include an admonition, a reduction in rank, confinement for up to 30 days, forfeiture of pay, or restrictions such as to base or to quarters for up to 60 days. In the Corps the procedure usually is called "captain's mast." In the Army, it is an "Article 15" and in the Air Force, "office hours." In the Haditha cases, Maj. McCann, the IO at Capt. Stone's Article 32 hearing, recommended that the criminal charges against Stone be dropped and the issue handled by Lt. Gen. Mattis at an NJP session.

Outtakes: Video sections removed from a larger file in the editing process.

Prefer: Charges are "preferred" rather than "filed."

Punitive articles: Articles 77–134 of the UCMJ. Called "punitive" because they deal with corporal punishment for criminal violations. Punishment upon conviction can include death (rarely), or life in prison without parole.

Refer: When charges are sent forward to court-martial by a Convening Authority they are "referred" to trial. Before charges can be referred a General Court-Martial, the accusations must have been examined at an Article 32 hearing. In the military system, it is the charges that are tried, not the accused.

Rules of Engagement (ROE): Frequently changing instructions determined by local commanders that define when, where, and against whom service members are allowed to engage in combat. They also regulate the extent of an engagement and define the end result of what that engagement is expected to produce. They differ from place to place and time to time, sometimes from hour to hour, or minute to minute. Other battlefield behavior determinants include the Law of Armed Conflict (LOAC)/The Law of War (LOW)—a body of agreements designed to protect civilians, POWs, the wounded and the sick; and the Law of Land Warfare (LOLW)—a document that includes a provision explicitly stating that obedience to an unlawful order is no defense against a charge of war crimes.

Solatia (solace) payments: Different from payments made under the Commander's Emergency Response Program (CERP) in that petitions are filed under the Foreign Claims Act and the money comes from local operational and maintenance funds, rather than a fund set aside by Congress. Solatia payments are compensation for death, injury, and damage to property resulting from injury or harm to noncombatants. Lieutenant Colonel Jeffrey Chessani authorized solatia payments of $10,000 to members of the family of the four brothers who were killed in House Four. This was in addition to the $38,000 paid to members of the families of those killed or wounded during the assaults on houses One and Two and the $3,000 given to the families for repairs to the houses. Those payments were made under CERP.

Staff judge advocate (SJA): A commander's chief legal adviser; also the chief of a group of judge advocates serving in the same command. There were two SJAs prominent in the Haditha proceedings: Col. John Ewers, SJA for the I MEF, and Lt. Col. G.W. Riggs, SJA for MARCENT.

"Team Charlie": The group responsible for managing the Haditha prosecutions.

Trial counsel: A prosecutor; a judge advocate detailed by a commanding officer; or an officer-in-charge before charges are preferred to prepare and try a GCM.

Uniform Code of Military Justice (UCMJ): A federal law (United States Code Title 10, Chapter 47) enacted by Congress on May 5, 1950, and signed into law shortly afterwards by President Truman. It replaced separate military justice systems governing the Army and the Navy in that it applies to all military service members irrespective of their branch.

Unlawful Command Influence (UCI): Sometimes called "the mortal enemy of military justice," UCI refers to instances in which a commander uses his position to punish or reward subordinates or project authority to accomplish a specific goal. When the issue is raised in a criminal case, it can be sufficient to end proceedings. It is regarded as such a threat to military justice that the offense itself does not have to be proved; even the *appearance* of UCI is enough to cause a case to be thrown out by the presiding officer.

Watt report: A document compiled by Army Col. Gregory A. Watt after an AR 15-6 investigation of the Haditha incident, which was ordered by Lt. Gen. Peter Chiarelli, commander of the Multi-National Force–Iraq. Watt's investigation was precursor to a similar, deeper, probe conducted by Army Maj. Gen. Eldon Bargewell. (See also *Bargewell report*.)

Chapter Notes

Preface

1. Tim McGirk, "Collateral Damage or Civilian Massacre in Haditha," *Time*, Mar. 19, 2006, http://content.time.com/time/world/article/0,8599,1174649,00.html
2. Josh White and Sonya Geis, "4 Marines Charged in Haditha Killings," *Washington Post*, Dec. 22, 2006, http://www.washingtonpost.com/wp-dyn/content/article/2006/12/21/AR2006122100124.html
3. Mark Walker, "Frank Wuterich No Longer in the Marine Corps," *San Diego Union-Tribune*, Feb. 20, 2012, web.
4. "Marine to Serve No Time in Haditha, Iraq Killings Case," Associated Press, Jan. 24, 2012, web.
5. *Wuterich v. U.S.A.*, NMCCA No. 200800183, "Review of Petition for Extraordinary Relief in the Nature of a Writ of Mandamus," Navy-Marine Court of Criminal Appeals, Aug. 25, 2011, 7. http://www.jag.navy.mil/courts/documents/archive/2011/WUTERICH,%20F.D.%20200800183.pdf
6. "Government's Notice of Appeal to the Navy-Marine Court of Criminal Appeals and Notice of Appeal to the Navy-Marine Court of Criminal Appeals," Appendices A and B, May 19, 2009.
7. "Government Notice of Appeal to the Navy-Marine Court of Criminal Appeals and Notice of Appeal to the Navy-Marine Court of Criminal Appeals," Appendices A and B, July 8, 2008.
8. Maj. Gen. Eldon Bargewell, report to Lt. Gen. Peter Chiarelli, June 15, 2006. http://warchronicle.com/DefendOurMarines/Documents/BargewellReport/000_MG_Bargewell_15-6_(Haditha_Report).BATES.pdf

Chapter 1

1. Thomas E. Ricks, *Fiasco: The American Military Adventure in Iraq* (New York: Penguin, 2006), 332.
2. Ibid., 343.
3. Ibid.
4. Jonathan Keiler, "Who Won the Battle of Fallujah," *Proceedings Magazine*, Jan. 2005, 58 http://pqasb.pqarchiver.com/proceedings/doc/205980306.html?FMT=ABS&FMTS=ABS:FT&type=current&date=Jan+2005&author=Keiler%2C+Jonathan+F&pub=United+States+Naval+Institute.+Proceedings&edition=&startpage=57-61&desc=WHO+WON+THE+BATTLE+OF+FALLUJAH%3F
5. "U.S. Marine Corps Operations in Iraq, 2003–2006," History Division, United States Marine Corps, 41. http://fas.org/irp/doddir/usmc/iraq03-06.pdf
6. Keiler, "Who Won the Battle of Fallujah," 59.
7. "U.S. Marine Corps Operations in Iraq, 2003–2006" 50.
8. Keiler, "Who Won the Battle of Fallujah," 59.
9. Battalions 2/1, 3/1, 1/5, and 3/5.
10. Battalions 3/4, 1/8, and 1/3.
11. Bing West, *No True Glory: A Frontline Account of the Battle for Fallujah* (New York: Bantam, 2005), 259.
12. Ibid.
13. "U.S. Marine Corps Operations in Iraq, 2003–2006," 59. http://fas.org/irp/doddir/usmc/iraq03-06.pdf
14. 1st Lt. John Jacobs, quoted by Dick Camp, *Operation Phantom Fury: The Assault and Capture of Fallujah, Iraq* (Minneapolis, Minn.: Zenith, 2009), 262.
15. "U.S. Marine Corps Operations in Iraq, 2003–2006," 61. http://fas.org/irp/doddir/usmc/iraq03-06.pdf
16. West, *No True Glory*, 303.
17. Camp, *Operation Phantom Fury*, 290.
18. Keiler, "Who Won the Battle of Fallujah," 62.
19. First Marine Division history page, http://www.1stmardiv.marines.mil/Units/1ST

MARINEREGT/3rdBattalion/History.aspx, n.d].
20. West, *No True Glory*, 325.
21. Ricks, *Fiasco*, 405.
22. Ibid., 401.

Chapter 2

1. Tony Perry, "Details Emerge of a Deadly Day in Haditha," *Los Angeles Times*, July 2, 2007.
2. "The Haditha Dam," Wikipedia, http://en.wikipedia.org/wiki/Haditha_Dam.
3. Ellen Knickmeyer, "14 Marines Die in Huge Explosion in Western Iraq," *Washington Post Foreign Service*, Aug. 4, 2005, http://www.washingtonpost.com/wp-dyn/content/article/2006/12/21/AR2006122100124.htm
4. Ibid.
5. Ibid.
6. Ibid.
7. Sgt. Frank Wuterich, statement at pre-trial hearing, Camp Pendleton, Calif., Sept. 6, 2007, *Defend Our Marines* http://warchronicle.com/TheyAreNotKillers/SSgtWuterich/Statement.htm
8. Ibid.
9. Ibid.
10. Justin Sharratt, statement at pre-trial hearing, Camp Pendleton, Calif., June 14, 2007, *Defend Our Marines* http://warchronicle.com/TheyAreNotKillers/LCplSharratt/Statement.htm
11. Ibid.
12. Ibid.
13. Perry, "Details Emerge of a Deadly Day in Haditha."
14. Ibid.
15. Stephen Tatum, statement to NCIS investigators on Mar. 19, 2 *Defend Our Marines* http://warchronicle.com/TheyAreNotKillers/LCplTatum/Article32-Testimony.htm
16. Wuterich, statement at pre-trial hearing. *Defend Our Marines* http://warchronicle.com/TheyAreNotKillers/SSgtWuterich/Statement.htm n.d.
17. Ibid.
18. Karl Vick, "Witness Describes Iraq Killings," *Washington Post*, Sept. 1, 2007, http://www.washingtonpost.com/wp-dyn/content/article/2007/08/31/AR2007083102043.html .
19. Staff Sgt. Frank Wuterich, Statement at Article 32 Hearing, Sept. 6, 2007, *Defend Our Marines* http://warchronicle.com/TheyAreNotKillers/SSgtWuterich/Statement.htm
20. Lt. Col. Paul J. Ware, "Investigating Officer's Report," section on Staff Sgt. Frank Wuterich, Oct. 2, 2007, 8, *Defend Our Marines* http://warchronicle.com/TheyAreNotKillers/SSgtWuterich/Art_32_Report_ICO_Wuterich.pdf
21. Thomas Watkins, "Haditha Squad Leader Headed to Court," Associated Press, Aug. 30, 2007, web.
22. Lt. Col. Paul J. Ware, "Investigating Officer's Report," section on Lance Cpl. Stephen B. Tatum, Aug. 23, 2007, 2, *Defend Our Marines*, Aug. 23, 2007, http://warchronicle.com/TheyAreNotKillers/LCplTatum/DefendOurMarines-IOReport.htm
23. Jesse Hamilton, "Deadly Questions—Far from the War," *Hartford Courant*, Aug. 31, 2007, web.
24. Ware, "Investigating Officer's Report," 1.
25. Ibid.
26. "Marine Testifies Against Accused Haditha Ringleader," Reuters, Aug. 30, 2007, web.
27. Ware, "Investigating Officer's Report," 2.
28. Ibid.
29. Perry, "Details Emerge of a Deadly Day in Haditha," web.

Chapter 3

1. Lance Cpl. Justin Sharratt, Article 32 hearing, June 14, 2007, *Defend Our Marines* June 14, 2007, http://warchronicle.com/TheyAreNotKillers/LCplSharratt/Statement.htm
2. Ibid.
3. Col. C.C. Conlin, "Executive Summary of Pretrial Investigative Report in the Case of Lieutenant Col. Jeffrey R. Chessani," July 10, 2007, 2, Response to FOIA request.
4. Ibid.
5. Ibid., 3.
6. Ibid.
7. Ibid.
8. "Sergeant Major Sax," *Defend Our Marines*, May 30, 2007.
9. Conlin, "Executive Summary," 3.
10. Ibid.
11. Ibid.
12. Paul von Zielbauer, "2 Marines Deny Suspecting Haditha War Crime," *New York Times*, May 31, 2007. http://www.nytimes.com/2007/05/31/world/middleeast/31haditha.html?page wanted=print
13. Thomas Watkins, "Marine Describes Scene Where 24 Iraqis Died," Associated Press, June 1, 2007, web.
14. Maj. Gen. Eldon Bargewell, "Report to Lt. Gen. Peter Chiarelli," June 15, 2006, 39, http://warchronicle.com/DefendOurMarines/Documents/BargewellReport/000_MG_Bargewell_15-6_(Haditha_Report).BATES.pdf
15. Ibid., 39–40.
16. Ibid., 40.
17. Ibid.
18. Ibid., 48.
19. Ibid., 49.
20. Ibid.

21. "Five Iraqis Shot at U.S. Checkpoint," BBC News, Nov. 21, 2005.
22. "German Woman 'Kidnapped in Iraq,'" BBC News, Nov. 29, 2005.
23. "Ten Marines Killed in IED Attack Near Fallujah," Fox News, Dec. 3, 2005.
24. Conlin, "Executive Summary," 4.
25. McGirk, "Collateral Damage or Civilian Massacre in Haditha," Mar. 19, 2006, http://content.time.com/time/world/article/0,8599,1174649,00.html
26. Conlin, "Executive Summary," 4.
27. Bargewell, "Report to Lt. Gen. Peter Chiarelli," 17.
28. Marine Corps Base Quantico, http://www.quantico.marines.mil/Tenants/4.
29. Mark Walker, "Intelligence Officer Says He Rejected Haditha Officials' Complaints," *North County Times*, May 12, 2007, web.
30. Josh White, "Marine Who Led Haditha Attack Was Recommended for a Medal," *Washington Post*, Aug. 30, 2006. http://www.washingtonpost.com/wp-dyn/content/article/2006/08/29/AR2006082901320.html
31. Ibid.
32. Bargewell, "Report to Lt. Gen. Peter Chiarelli," 4. http://warchronicle.com/DefendOurMarines/Documents/BargewellReport/000_MG_Bargewell_15-6_(Haditha_Report).BATES.pdf
33. Conlin, "Executive Summary," 4.
34. Rick Rogers, "8 Killed in Haditha Called Insurgents," *San Diego Union-Tribune*, May 13, 2007, web.
35. Bargewell, "Report to Lt. Gen. Peter Chiarelli," 8.
36. Ibid.
37. Conlin, "Executive Summary," 4.

Chapter 4

1. Maj. Gen. Eldon Bargewell, "Report to Lt. Gen. Peter Chiarelli," June 15, 2007, 57.
2. Rick Rogers, "Hearing Will Determine Whether a Captain Is Tried," *San Diego Union-Tribune*, May 10, 2007, web.
3. Bargewell, "Report to Lt. Gen. Peter Chiarelli," 59.
4. Lori Robertson, "A Matter of Time," *American Journalism Review*, Aug./Sept. 2006. http://www.ajr.org/article.asp?id=4158
5. Jeffrey Kluger, "How Haditha Came to Light," *Time*, June 4, 2006.
6. Ibid.
7. Robertson, "A Matter of Time."
8. Ibid.
9. Ibid.
10. Robert J. Muise, "Request for Witnesses," letter to Lt. Gen Samuel Helland, Feb. 27, 2008, 2.
11. Bargewell, "Report to Lt. Gen. Peter Chiarelli," 60. http://warchronicle.com/DefendOurMarines/Documents/BargewellReport/000_MG_Bargewell_15-6_(Haditha_Report).BATES.pdf
12. Robertson, "A Matter of Time."
13. Ibid.
14. John McChesney, "Marine Officers Strategized Their Haditha Responses," National Public Radio, June 12, 2007, http://www.npr.org/templates/story/story.php?storyId=10964980.
15. Ibid.
16. Ibid.
17. Ibid.
18. Ibid.
19. Ibid.
20. Ibid.
21. Ibid.
22. Ibid.
23. Ibid.
24. Ibid.
25. Ibid.
26. Bargewell, "Report to Lt. Gen. Peter Chiarelli," 60.
27. Ibid.
28. Ibid.
29. Ibid., 9.
30. Ibid.
31. Col. Gregory A. Watt, "Memorandum for Commander Multi National Corps-Iraq," Mar. 3, 2006, *Defend Our Marines* http://warchronicle.com/DefendOurMarines/Documents/WattReport/Investigation3-1Marines030306.pdf
32. Ibid., 4.
33. Ibid., 5.
34. Ibid., 3.
35. Ibid.
36. Ibid.
37. Ibid.
38. Ibid., 4.
39. Ibid., 6.
40. Ibid., 7.
41. Bargewell, "Report to Lt. Gen. Peter Chiarelli," 3.
42. Rodney Barker, *Dancing with the Devil: Sex, Espionage, and the Marines: The Clayton Lonetree Story* (New York: Simon and Schuster, 1996), 214.
43. Tim McGirk, "Collateral Damage or Civilian Massacre in Haditha?" *Time*, Mar. 19, 2006, http://content.time.com/time/world/article/0,8599,1174649,00.html
44. Ibid.
45. Ibid.
46. Thomas E. Ricks, "In Haditha Killings, Details Came Slowly," *Washington Post*, June 4, 2006, http://www.washingtonpost.com/wp-dyn/content/article/2006/06/03/AR2006060300710.html
47. Ibid.
48. "John Murtha," Wikipedia, http://en.wikipedia.org/wiki/John_Murtha.

49. "John Kline (politician)," Wikipedia, http://en.wikipedia.org/wiki/John_Kline_%28politician%29.
50. Ricks, "In Haditha Killings, Details Came Slowly."

Chapter 5

1. "Pessimism About Iraq War Growing," CNN, Mar. 16, 2006, web.
2. Thomas E. Ricks, "In Haditha Killings, Details Came Slowly," *Washington Post*, June 4, 2006, http://www.washingtonpost.com/wp-dyn/content/article/2006/06/03/AR2006060300710.html
3. Tony Perry, "Marines Held in the Slaying of Iraqi Man," *Los Angeles Times*, May 28, 2006, web.
4. Dana Milbank, "An Unlikely Lonesome Dove," *Washington Post*, Nov. 18, 2005, web.
5. Ibid.
6. Howard Kurtz, "Maligning Murtha," *Washington Post*, Nov. 22, 2005, web.
7. Charles Babington, "Freshman Republican Weathers Backlash," *Washington Post*, Nov. 23, 2005, http://www.washingtonpost.com/wp-dyn/content/article/2005/11/22/AR2005112201699.html
8. Jim Miklaszewski and Mike Viqueira, "Lawmaker: Marines Killed Iraqis 'In Cold Blood,'" NBC News, May 17, 2006, web.
9. Charles Gibson, *Good Morning America with Charles Gibson*, ABC News, May 30, 2006, http://thinkprogress.org/security/2006/05/30/5573/murtha-haditha/.
10. Paula Zahn, *Paula Zahn Now*, CNN, May 30, 2006, http://transcripts.cnn.com/TRANSCRIPTS/0605/30/pzn.01.html.
11. Soledad O'Brien, *CNN Morning with Soledad O'Brien*, May 30, 2006, http://transcripts.cnn.com/TRANSCRIPTS/0605/30/ltm.06.html.
12. "White House: Haditha Details to Be Public," Associated Press, May 31, 2006, web.
13. Tim Russert, *Meet the Press*, NBC, June 11, 2006, http://www.nbcnews.com/id/13296235/ns/meet_the_press/t/transcript-june/#.U00gnMe7mIgrussert.
14. "Response to Freedom of Information Act request," Mary M. Malone, FOIA Specialist, Sept. 19, 2012, Letter to author.
15. "Media Conservatives Attack Murtha over Haditha Comments," *Media Matters*, May 31, 2006, web.
16. Ibid.
17. Ibid.
18. Mike Rosen, *Mike Rosen Show*, Radio Station KOA, June 22, 2006, http://mediamatters.org/video/2006/06/22/coulter-if-murtha-did-get-fragged-hed-finally-d/136023.
19. Uncle Jimbo, "The National Committee to Horsewhip Murtha," *Black Five*, Feb. 21, 2007, http://www.blackfive.net/main/2007/02/the_national_co.html.
20. *Wuterich v. Murtha*, "Action for Libel; Invasion of Privacy/False Light; Republication by Third Parties," U.S. District Court for the District of Columbia, Aug. 2, 2006, 7.
21. Ibid., 22.
22. Ibid., 23.
23. Sally Donnelly, "The Haditha Massacre: A Congressman Apologizes," *Time*, Aug. 15, 2006, http://content.time.com/time/nation/article/0,8599,1227327,00.html.
24. Josh White, "Lawmaker Apologizes to Marines for Remarks," *Washington Post*, Aug. 15, 2006, http://www.washingtonpost.com/wp-dyn/content/article/2006/08/14/AR2006081401003.html
25. Ann Scott Tyson, "Death Toll Rises in Haditha Attack, GOP Leader Says," *Washington Post*, May 20, 2006, http://www.washingtonpost.com/wp-dyn/content/article/2006/05/19/AR2006051901732.html
26. Thom Shanker, Eric Schmitt, and Richard A. Oppel, Jr., "Military to Report Marines Killed Iraqi Civilians," New York Times News Service, May 26, 2006, http://www.nytimes.com/2006/05/26/world/middleeast/26haditha.html?pagewanted=all&module=Search&mabReward=relbias%3As%2C%7B%221%22%3A%22RI%3A5%22%7D&_r=0
27. Tony Perry and Julian E. Barnes, "Photos Indicate Civilians Slain Execution-Style," *Los Angeles Times*, May 27, 2006, web.
28. Ibid.
29. Ibid.
30. Liz Sidoti, "Senate Plans Hearings on Haditha Incident," Associated Press, June 7, 2006, web.
31. "Senate Plans Committee to Probe into Haditha Slayings by Marines," National Public Radio, May 29, 2006, http://www.pbs.org/newshour/bb/military-jan-june06-haditha_05-29/
32. Douglas Waller, "A Call for a Senate Hearing on Haditha," *Time*, June 6, 2006, web.
33. Margaret Warner, "Marine Corps Head Urges Patience in Haditha Investigations, National Public Radio, June 7, 2006, http://www.pbs.org/newshour/bb/military-jan-june06-iraq_06-07/
34. MilitaryBases.com, "Military Bases in California," http://militarybases.com/california/.
35. Josh White, "Marine Says Rules Were Followed," *Washington Post*, June 11, 2006, http://www.washingtonpost.com/wp-dyn/content/article/2006/06/10/AR2006061001129.html
36. Ibid.
37. Ibid.
38. Julian E. Barnes and Tony Perry, "Marines Missed 'Red Flags,' Study Finds," *Los Angeles Times*, June 21, 2006, web.

39. Eric Schmitt and David S. Cloud, "General Faults Marine Response to Iraq Killings," *New York Times*, July 8, 2006, web.
40. Sally Donnelly, "The Promotion After Haditha," *Time*, June 29, 2006, http://content.time.com/time/world/article/0,8599,1209345,00.html
41. *U.S. v Chessani*, "Review Pursuant to Article 62 (b)," U.S. Navy-Marine Corps Court of Criminal Appeals, Mar. 17, 2009, 2.
42. Each branch has a command that performs the same service as MARCENT. They are ARCENT, NAVCENT, AFCENT, and SOCCENT (Special Operations Central Command).
43. Mark Walker, "Mattis Assumes Command of the I Marine Expeditionary Force," *San Diego Union-Tribune*, Aug. 15, 2006.

Chapter 6

1. Clayton J. Lonetree, Wipipedia, http://en.wikipedia.org/wiki/Clayton_J._Lonetree. Lonetree was a Marine security guard posted to the U.S. Embassy in Moscow who fell under the spell of a female KGB agent and her collaborator and was duped into providing them with secret information. He was tried and convicted of espionage on Aug. 21, 1987. Although sentenced to thirty years, he was released after serving nine years in the military prison at Fort Leavenworth.
2. Josh White, "Marine Says Rules Were Followed," *Washington Post*, June 11, 2006, http://www.washingtonpost.com/wp-dyn/content/article/2006/06/10/AR2006061001129.html
3. Julian E. Barnes and Tony Perry, "Marines Missed 'Red Flags,' Study Finds," *Los Angeles Times*, June 21, 2006, web.
4. David S. Cloud, "Marines May Have Excised Evidence on 24 Iraqi Deaths," *New York Times*, Aug. 18, 2006, http://www.nytimes.com/2006/08/18/world/middleeast/18haditha.html?_r=1&oref=slogin
5. Thomas E. Ricks, "Officer Called Haditha Routine," *Washington Post*, Aug. 19, 2006, http://www.washingtonpost.com/wp-dyn/content/article/2006/08/18/AR2006081801366.html
6. Ibid.
7. Josh White, "Marine Called Haditha Shootings Appropriate," *Washington Post*, Aug. 24, 2006, http://www.washingtonpost.com/wp-dyn/content/article/2006/08/23/AR2006082301829.html
8. Ibid.
9. "Poll: Opposition to Iraq War at an All-Time High," CNN, Sept. 25, 2006, web.
10. Josh White and Sonya Geis, "4 Marines Charged in Haditha Killings," *Washington Post*, Dec. 22, 2006, http://www.washingtonpost.com/wp-dyn/content/article/2006/12/21/AR2006122100124.html
11. Press Statement, U.S. Marine Corps, http://www.marines.mil/unit/marforcent/Haditha%20Documents/2006/Haditha%20Press%20Statement%20061221.htm.
12. Ibid.
13. "John A. Bennet," Wikipedia, http://en.wikipedia.org/wiki/John_A._Bennett.
14. Manual for Courts-Martial United States (2005 Edition), II-125, http://www.monterey.army.mil/Legal/criminal_law/mcm.pdf
15. Ibid., IV-24.
16. Josh White, "Death in Haditha," *Washington Post*, Jan. 6, 2007, http://www.washingtonpost.com/wp-dyn/content/article/2007/01/05/AR2007010502248.html
17. Ibid.
18. Ibid.
19. Ibid.
20. Ibid.
21. Ibid.
22. Ibid.
23. Ibid..
24. Ibid.
25. Ibid.
26. William Finn Bennett, "Haditha Lawyers Protest Leak," *North County Times*, Jan. 16, 2007, web.

Chapter 7

1. Scott Pelley, *60 Minutes*, "The Killings in Haditha," CBS News, Mar. 18, 2007, updated Aug. 22, 2008, http://www.cbsnews.com/news/the-killings-in-haditha/.
2. Ibid.
3. Ibid.
4. Ibid.
5. Ibid.
6. Ibid.
7. Ibid.
8. It later was leaned that a woman named Hibbah—the daughter-in-law of the head of the household, Abdul-Hamid Hassan Ali—had escaped from House One with her two-month-old daughter during the assault. However, her body was not among those recovered from House Two.
9. Ibid.
10. Ibid.
11. Ibid.
12. Tony Perry, "8 U.S. Troops Charged in Iraqi's Death," *Los Angeles Times*, June 22, 2006, web.

Chapter 8

1. Ann Scott Tyson, "General Leading Haditha Probe Known for Integrity, Toughness," *Washington Post*, June 16, 2006, http://www.washington

post.com/wp-dyn/content/article/2006/06/15/AR2006061501887.html

2. Josh White, "Report on Haditha Condemns Marines," *Washington Post*, Apr. 21, 2007, http://www.washingtonpost.com/wp-dyn/content/article/2007/04/20/AR2007042002308.html

3. Maj. Gen. Eldon Bargewell, "Report to Lt. Gen. Peter Chiarelli," June 15, 2006, WarChronicle.com, http://warchronicle.com/DefendOurMarines/Documents/BargewellReport/000_MG_Bargewell_15-6_%28Haditha_Report%29.BATES.pdf.

4. Bargewell, "Report to Lt. Gen. Peter Chiarelli," 22.
5. Ibid., 18.
6. Ibid., 21.
7. Ibid., 12.
8. Ibid.
9. Ibid., 9.
10. Ibid.
11. Ibid., 29.
12. Ibid., 34.
13. Ibid., 51.
14. Ibid., 13.
15. Ibid., 48.
16. Ibid., 77.
17. Ibid., 13.
18. Ibid., 5.
19. Ibid.
20. Ibid., n33.
21. Ibid., 46.
22. Ibid., 48.
23. Ibid., 15.
24. Ibid.
25. Ibid.
26. Ibid., 60.
27. Ibid., 84.
28. Ibid.
29. Ibid., 17.
30. Ibid., 66.
31. Ibid., v.
32. Ibid., 13.
33. Ibid., iv.
34. Ibid., 14.
35. Ibid.
36. Ibid., 17.
37. Ibid., 40.
38. Ibid., v.
39. Ibid., 47.

Chapter 9

1. John McChesney, "Haditha Proceedings Begin with Marine Lawyer," National Public Radio, May 8, 2007 http: www.npr.org/templates/story/story.php?storyId=10069336

2. Paul von Zielbauer, "Propaganda Fear Cited in Account of Iraqi Killings," *New York Times*, May 6, 2007, http://www.nytimes.com/2007/05/06/world/middleeast/06haditha.html?scp=66&sq=Haditha&st=nyt

3. Ibid.

4. Mark Walker, "General's Aide Refuses to Testify in Haditha Hearings," *North County Times*, May 8, 2007, web.

5. "Marine Says Found Live Children Among Haditha Dead," Reuters, May 8, 2007.

6. Mark Walker, "Marine Lieutenant Testifies His Troops Did Nothing Wrong at Haditha," *North County Times*, May 9, 2007, web.

7. Ibid.

8. "Marine: Squad Leader Shot Unarmed Iraqis," Associated Press, May 9, 2007, web.

9. Ibid.

10. Ibid.

11. Mark Walker, "Marine: Some Civilian Slayings Were to Be Blamed on Iraqi Army," *North County Times*, May 10, 2007, web.

12. Mark Walker, "General Testifies Haditha Killings Appeared as Combat Deaths," *North County Times*, May 11, 2007, web.

13. Ibid.

14. Paul von Zielbauer, "Marine Says His Staff Misled Him on Killings," *New York Times*, May 11, 2007, http://www.nytimes.com/2007/05/11/world/middleeast/11haditha.html?ref=middleeast.

15. Mark Walker, "General: No Early Indications That Haditha Deaths Should Be Investigated," *North County Times*, May 10, 2007, web.

16. Rick Rogers, "General Says He Believed Marines," *San Diego Union Tribune*, May 11, 2007, web.

17. Ibid.

18. Steve Liewer, "Commanders Stay Resolute on Killings," *San Diego Union-Tribune*, May 12, 2007, web.

19. Paul von Zielbauer, "Lawyers on Haditha Panel Peer into Fog of War," *New York Times*, May 17, 2007, http://www.nytimes.com/2007/05/17/world/middleeast/17haditha.html?_r=1&oref=slogin

20. Ibid.

21. "Officer Says Did Not Mention Haditha Deaths in Homes," Reuters, May 12, 2007, web.

22. Mark Walker, "Intelligence Officer Says He Rejected Haditha Officials' Complaints," *North County Times*, May 12, 2007, web.

23. Von Zielbauer, "Lawyers on Haditha Panel Peer into Fog of War," http://www.nytimes.com/2007/05/17/world/middleeast/17haditha.html?_r=1&oref=slogin

24. Ibid.

25. Rick Rogers, "8 Killed in Haditha Called Insurgents," *San Diego Union-Tribune*, May 13, 2007, web.

26. Thomas Watkins, "Marines: Gory Civilian Deaths In Haditha Came During Combat, Didn't Need Investigation," Associated Press, May 12, 2007, web.

27. Mark Walker, "Legal Affairs Officer: Haditha Decision Not Criminal," North County Times, May 15, 2007, web.
28. Ibid.
29. Ibid.
30. Maj. Thomas G. McCann, "Investigating Officer's Report," June 8, 2007, 6.
31. Ibid.
32. Paul von Zielbauer, "Marine Refused Staff's Advice on Iraq Deaths, Major Testifies," New York Times, May 15, 2007, http://www.nytimes.com/2007/05/15/world/middleeast/15haditha.html
33. Ibid.
34. Ibid.
35. "Marine in Haditha Case Defends Actions," Associated Press, May 16, 2007.
36. Ibid.
37. McCann, "Investigating Officer's Report," 30.
38. Ibid., 31.
39. Ibid., 36.
40. Ibid., 37.
41. Ibid., 36.
42. Ibid., 37.
43. Ibid., 38.
44. Ibid., 39.
45. Ibid., 51.
46. Ibid., 52.
47. Ibid., 21.
48. Ibid., 29.
49. Ibid., 38.
50. Ibid.
51. Ibid., 39.
52. Ibid., 51–52.
53. Ibid.
54. Ibid., 54.
55. "Statement from Gen. Mattis on the Capt. Stone and LCpl. Sharratt Decisions," Camp Pendleton Public Affairs Office, Aug. 9, 2007.

Chapter 10

1. "Weather History," San Diego International Airport, May 30, 2007, http://www.wunderground.com/history/airport/KSAN/2007/5/30/DailyHistory.html?req_city=NA&req_state=NA&req_statename=NA
2. Mike Soraghan and Jon Aloysius Farrell, "Semper Finale?" Denver Post, June 5, 2007, web.
3. Thomas E. Ricks, Making the Corps (New York: Touchstone, 1997), 157.
4. Ibid., 206–07.
5. William Langewiesche, "Rules of Engagement," Vanity Fair, Nov. 2006, http://www.vanityfair.com/politics/features/2006/11/haditha200611
6. Soraghan and Farrell, "Semper Finale?"
7. Mark Walker, "Hearing Set for High-ranking Marine Charged in Haditha Case," North County Times, Mar. 7, 2007.
8. American Freedom Law Center, "Robert Muise Extends His Marine Corps Oath to Law Practice," National Catholic Register, July 5, 2012, http://www.americanfreedomlawcenter.org/leaders/3/robert-j-muise-esq.htm.
9. Combat Veterans for Congress, http://combatveteransforcongress.org/alumni/2814.
10. Paul von Zielbauer, "Lawyers in Haditha Case Say Gunshots, Not Grenades, Killed Many Victims," New York Times, June 1, 2007, http://www.nytimes.com/2007/06/01/world/middleeast/01haditha.html?ref=middleeast.
11. Rick Rogers, "Some Haditha Shootings Are Called Close-range," San Diego Union Tribune, June 1, 2007.
12. Von Zielbauer, "Lawyers in Haditha Case Say Gunshots."
13. Ibid.
14. Thomas Watkins, "Marine Describes Scene Where 24 Iraqis Killed," Associated Press, June 1, 2007, web.
15. Ibid.
16. Mark Walker, "Expert Says Haditha Killings Demanded Immediate Probe," North County Times, June 1, 2007, web.
17. Ibid.
18. Mark Walker, "General Says Chessani Should Have Told Him More," North County Times, June 1, 2007, web.
19. Paul von Zielbauer, "2 Marines Deny Suspecting Haditha War Crime," New York Times, May 31, 2007, http://www.nytimes.com/2007/05/31/world/middleeast/31haditha.html
20. "1st Lt. Adam Mathes," Defend Our Marines, June 4, 2007, web.
21. "Haditha Probe Called Political," Associated Press, June 6, 2007, web.
22. Rick Rogers, "Officers Response in Haditha Questioned," San Diego Union-Tribune, June 3, 2007, web.
23. Ibid.
24. Mark Walker, "Legal Officer Says No One Questioned Haditha Deaths," North County Times, June 6, 2007, web.
25. Alex Roth, "Marine Tells of Orders to Erase Photos," San Diego Union-Tribune, June 8, 2007, web.
26. Ibid.
27. "Sergeant Major Sax," Defend Our Marines, May 30, 2007. web.
28. Paul von Zielbauer, "At Haditha Hearing, Dueling Views of a Battalion Commander," New York Times, June 8, 2007, http://www.nytimes.com/2007/06/08/washington/08haditha.html?pagewanted=all
29. "The Accused Gave Unsworn Testimony in His Own Defense," Los Angeles Times, June 9, 2007, web.
30. Teri Figueroa, "Accused Officer Defends

Haditha Decisions," *North County Times*, June 10, 2007, web.
   31. Ibid.
   32. Ibid.
   33. Von Zielbauer, "At Haditha Hearing," http://www.nytimes.com/2007/06/08/washington/08haditha.html?pagewanted=
   34. Nathaniel R. Helms, "Whack-a-Mole!" *Defend Our Marines*, Aug. 8, 2007, web.
   35. Thomas More Law Center, "Government's Own Expert Exonerates Marine Officer in Haditha Case," June 5, 2007, http://www.thomasmore.org/news/governments-own-expert-exonerates-marine-officer-haditha-case-tmlc-goes-the-offensive-2/
   36. Ibid.
   37. Ibid.
   38. Col. C.C. Conlin, "Executive Summary of Pretrial Investigative Report in the Case of Lieutenant Col. Jeffrey R. Chessani," July 10, 2007, 6, Response to FOIA request.
   39. Ibid., 5.
   40. Ibid., 7.
   41. Ibid., 8.
   42. Ibid., 7.
   43. Ibid.
   44. Ibid.
   45. Ibid.
   46. Ibid., 5.
   47. Ibid., 6.
   48. Ibid.
   49. Ibid., 7.
   50. Ibid., 8.
   51. Ibid.
   52. Thomas More Law Center, "Objections to Investigating Officer's Report ICO U.S. v. Lieutenant Colonel Jeffrey R. Chessani, USMC," July 25, 2007, 1.
   53. Ibid.
   54. Ibid., 7.
   55. Ibid., 10.
   56. Ibid., 16.
   57. Ibid., 19.
   58. Ibid., 21.
   59. Ibid., 18.
   60. Ibid., 15.
   61. Ibid., 18.
   62. Col. C.C. Conlin, "Addendum to Executive Summary of Pretrial Investigative Report," Aug. 17, 2007, 1.
   63. Ibid., 2.
   64. Ibid.
   65. Ibid.
   66. Thomas More Law Center, "Objections to Investigating Officer's Addendum," Aug. 24, 2007, web.
   67. Ibid., 6.
   68. Ibid., 5.
   69. Chelsea J. Carter, "Courts-Martial for 2 in Haditha Deaths," Associated Press, Oct. 20, 2007, web.

Chapter 11

   1. Mark Walker, "Three Marine Officers Censured in Haditha Incident," *North County Times*, Sept. 6, 2007, web.
   2. Nathaniel R. Helms, "Letters of Censure Say Senior Officers Betrayed Trust of the Marine Corps," *Defend Our Marines*, Nov. 15, 2007, web.
   3. Gidget Fuentes, "3 Senior Officers Sanctioned on Haditha," *Marine Corps Times*, Sept. 7, 2007, web.
   4. Ibid.

Chapter 12

   1. Bing West, *No True Glory: A Frontline Account of the Battle for Fallujah* (New York: Bantam, 2005).
   2. "Hearing for Marine in Haditha Battle," Associated Press, June 11, 2007, web.
   3. Paul von Zielbauer, "Forensic Experts Testify That 4 Iraqis Killed by Marines Were Shot from a Few Feet Away," *New York Times*, June 15, 2007, http://www.nytimes.com/2007/06/15/world/middleeast/15haditha.html.
   4. Mark Walker, "Haditha Deaths Came in Day of Chaotic Battle," *North County Times*, June 14, 2007, web.
   5. Transcript of Graviss testimony, *Defend Our Marines*, June 13, 2007, web.
   6. Von Zielbauer, "Forensic Experts," http://www.nytimes.com/2007/06/15/world/middleeast/15haditha.html
   7. Mark Walker, "Accused Haditha Shooter Gets Day in Court," *North County Times*, June 12, 2007, web.
   8. Ibid.
   9. Steve Liewer, "Accounts Differ on Haditha Slayings," *San Diego Union-Tribune*, June 13, 2007, web.
   10. Mark Walker, "Accused Marine Says He Acted Properly in Haditha Shootings," *North County Times*, June 15, 2007, web.
   11. Ibid.
   12. Ibid.
   13. Mark Walker, "Hearing Officer Challenges Haditha Prosecution," *North County Times*, June 16, 2007, web.
   14. Ibid.
   15. Ibid.
   16. "Certificate of Release of Discharge from Active Duty" for Lt. Col. Paul John Ware (redacted), U.S. Marine Corps, n.d.
   17. Ibid.
   18. Ibid.
   19. Ibid.
   20. Ibid.
   21. Lt. Col. Paul J. Ware, "Investigating Officer's Report," July 6, 2007, 11.
   22. Ibid.

23. Ibid., 12.
24. Ibid., 14.
25. Ibid.
26. Ibid., 15.
27. Ibid.
28. Ibid., 16.
29. Ibid., 6.
30. Ibid., 3.
31. Ibid., 2.
32. Ibid., 3.
33. Ibid., 17.
34. Ibid.
35. Ibid., 18.
36. "U.S. Marine Adviser Steps Aside in Haditha Case After Criticizing Investigating Officer's Report," Associated Press, Aug. 15, 2007, web
37. Ibid.
38. Teri Figueroa, "General Drops Charges for Two Marines in Haditha Shootings," *North County Times*, Aug. 9, 2007, web.
39. Ibid.
40. Tony Perry, "Former Marine Justin Sharratt Sues Rep. John Murtha Over Haditha Killings," *Los Angeles Times*, Sept. 25, 2008, web.
41. "Marine Sues Rep. Murtha Over Haditha Comments," *North County Times*, Sept. 26, 2008, web.

Chapter 13

1. Sonya Geis, "Witness Testifies Marine Knowingly Shot Children in Haditha," *Washington Post*, July 18, 2007, http://www.washingtonpost.com/wp-dyn/content/article/2007/07/17/AR2007071701786.html
2. Ibid.
3. Ibid.
4. Ibid.
5. Ibid.
6. Ibid.
7. Ibid.
8. Sonya Geis, "Marine Knew Targets Were Families," *Washington Post*, July 19, 2007, http://www.washingtonpost.com/wp-dyn/content/article/2007/07/18/AR2007071802387.html.
9. Ibid.
10. Teri Figueroa, "Agent Says Pendleton Marine Knew He Shot Child," *North County Times*, July 19, 2007, web.
11. Ibid.
12. Allison Hoffman, "Marine Charged in Iraq Murders Wanted Leeway to Kill, Troop Says," Associated Press, July 17, 2007, web.
13. Ibid.
14. Sonya Geis, "Marine Knew Targets Were Families," http://www.washingtonpost.com/wp-dyn/content/article/2007/07/18/AR2007071802387.html
15. Teri Figueroa, "Forensics at Center of Haditha Hearing," *North County Times*, July 20, 2007, web.
16. "Naval Criminal Investigative Service Special Agent Tom Brady," *North County Times*, July 19, 2007, web.
17. Ibid.
18. Uncredited, "LCpl Tatum's Statement to the Investigating Officer (as Recalled by Legal Counsel)," *Defend Our Marines*, July 24, 2007, web.
19. Ibid.
20. Teri Figueroa, "'I Didn't Know There Was Women and Children," *North County Times*, July 25, 2007, web.
21. Lt. Col. Paul J. Ware, "Investigating Officer's Report," Aug. 23, 2007.
22. Ibid., 14.
23. Ibid., 15.
24. Ibid., 18.
25. Ibid., 20.
26. Ibid., 24.
27. Ibid., 27.
28. Ibid.
29. Ibid., 28.
30. Ibid., 29.
31. Ibid.
32. Chelsea J. Carter, "Courts-Martial for 2 in Haditha Deaths," Associated Press, Oct. 20, 2007.

Chapter 14

1. "SSgt Frank Wuterich's Statement to the Investigating Officer," *Defend Our Marines*, Sept. 6, 2007, http://warchronicle.com/TheyAreNotKillers/SSgtWuterich/Statement.htm.
2. Ibid.
3. Ibid.
4. Ibid.
5. Ibid.
6. Ibid.
7. "Exclusive! Family of Marine Named in Alleged Haditha Kills Speaks Out," Fox News, June 19, 2006, [URL].
8. *Wuterich v. Murtha*, "Complaint," U.S. District Court for the District of Columbia," Aug. 2, 2006, .
9. Sally B. Donnelly, "The Promotion After Haditha," *Time*, June 29, 2006, http://content.time.com/time/world/article/0,8599,1209345,00.html.
10. Sally Donnelly, "The Face of Haditha," *Time*, Sept. 17, 2006, web.
11. "The Killings in Haditha," CBS, Mar. 18, 2007, web.
12. Paul von Zielbauer, "At Marines' Hearing, Testament to Violence," *New York Times*, Sept. 1, 2007, http://www.nytimes.com/2007/09/01/world/middleeast/01haditha.html?pagewanted=print.
13. Mark Walker, "Marine Testifies Against

Accused Haditha Ringleader," *North County Times*, Aug. 30, 2007.
14. Mark Walker, "Prosecutor Says Marine Squad Leader Killed Women and Children," *North County Times*, Aug. 31, 2007, web.
15. Mark Walker, "Marine Testifies Against Accused Haditha Ringleader," *North County Times*, Aug. 30, 2007, web.
16. "Key Testimony and Arguments," *Defend Our Marines*, Sept. 7, 2007, http://warchronicle.com/TheyAreNotKillers/LCplTatum/Article32-Testimony.htm.
17. Von Zielbauer, "At Marines' Hearing," http://www.nytimes.com/2007/09/01/world/middleeast/01haditha.html?pagewanted=print
18. Tony Perry, "Witness Accuses Marine Squad Leader," *Los Angeles Times*, Sept. 1, 2007, web.
19. Mark Walker, "Witness Alleges Wuterich Wanted to 'Kill Everybody,'" *North County Times*, Sept. 1, 2007, web.
20. Von Zielbauer, "At Marines' Hearing," http://www.nytimes.com/2007/09/01/world/middleeast/01haditha.html?pagewanted=print.
21. Perry, "Witness Accuses Marine Squad Leader," web.
22. Walker, "Witness Alleges Wuterich Wanted to 'Kill Everybody.'"
23. Karl Vick, "Marine Says Leader Shot Haditha Civilians," *Washington Post*, Sept. 1, 2007, http://www.washingtonpost.com/wp-dyn/content/article/2007/09/01/AR2007090101178.html
24. Ibid.
25. Ibid.
26. Mark Walker, "Evidence Called Inconclusive in Wuterich Trial," *North County Times*, Sept. 6, 2007, web.
27. Rick Rogers, "Rules Unclear on Battlefield, Marine Testifies," *San Diego Union-Tribune*, Sept. 6, 2007, web.
28. Walker, "Evidence Called Inconclusive in Wuterich Trial," Sept. 6, 2007, web.
29. Lt. Col. Paul J. Ware, "Investigating Officer's Report," Aug. 23, 2007.
30. Paul von Zielbauer, "Marines' Defense team Ends Haditha Hearing Abruptly," *New York Times*, Sept. 7, 2007, http://query.nytimes.com/gst/fullpage.html?res=9C06E6DE133AF934A3575AC0A9619C8B63 .
31. Ware, "Investigating Officer's Report," Oct. 2, 2007, 14.
32. Ibid.
33. Ibid.
34. Ibid., 16.
35. Ibid.
36. Ibid.
37. Ibid.
38. Ibid., 17.
39. Ibid., 20.
40. Ibid., 23.
41. Ibid., 25.
42. Ibid.
43. Ibid., 26.
44. Ibid.
45. Ibid., 37.
46. Ibid., 37.
47. Ibid., 35.
48. Ibid.
49. Ibid.
50. Ibid.
51. Ibid.
52. Ibid.
53. Mark Walker, "Marines Ordered to Trial in Haditha Killings," *North County Times*, Oct. 20, 2007, web.
54. News release, U.S. Marine Corps, Dec. 31, 2007, http://www.usmc.mil/lapa/iraq-investigations.htm.

Chapter 15

1. Thomas Watkins, "Haditha Marine Rejects Plea Deal," Associated Press, Sept. 9, 2007, web.
2. Ibid.
3. Col. M.P. Stahlman, "Executive Summary of Investigating Officers' Report in the Case of First Lieutenant Andrew A. Grayson," Dec. 3, 2007, 3, Response to FOIA Request.
4. "Marine Told to Destroy Haditha Photos," Associated Press, June 8, 2007, web.
5. Mark Walker, "Final Haditha Hearing Set to Conclude," *North County Times*, Nov. 16, 2007, web.
6. Ibid.
7. Ibid.
8. Article 80, Attempts: "(a) An act, done with specific intent to commit an offense under this chapter, amounting to more than mere preparation and tending, even though failing, to effect its commission, is an attempt to commit that offense."
9. "1st lt. Andrew A. Grayson, Article 32 Summary," *Defend Our Marines*, Nov. 13, 2007, http://warchronicle.com/TheyAreNotKillers/LtAndrewGrayson/LtGraysonCourtMartial.htm.
10. Mark Walker, "Charges Against Haditha Defendant Questioned," *North County Times*, Nov. 17, 2007, web.
11. Mark Walker, "Charged Marine Praised by Fellow Officers," *North County Times*, Nov. 16, 2007, web.
12. Walker, "Charges Against Haditha Defendant Questioned," web.
13. Stahlman, "Executive Summary," 1.
14. Ibid., 2.
15. Ibid.
16. Mark Walker, "Marines Order Two More Haditha Trials," *North County Times*, Jan. 1, 2008, web.

Chapter 16

1. Gary D. Solis, *Son Thang: An American War Crime* (Annapolis, Md: Naval Institute Press, 1997).
2. *U.S. v. Wuterich and CBS Broadcasting, v. Navy-Marine Court of Criminal Appeals and Wuterich*, Court of Criminal Appeals for the Armed Forces, Nov. 17, 2008, 7.
3. Chelsea J. Carter, "Judge Denies Prosecutors Haditha Footage," Associated Press, Feb. 23, 2008, web.
4. "There Is No Substitute for Experience," White & Meeks, LLP, n.d, http://www.militarylawyers.com/Jeffrey-Meeks-Attorney.html.
5. Teri Figueroa, "Marine Found Guilty of Murder in Slaying," *North County Times*, Aug, 3, 2007, web.
6. Mark Walker, "Marines Balking at Orders to Testify Against Men They Served With, Prosecutor Says," *North County Times*, Feb. 21, 2008, web.
7. *U.S. v. Wuterich*, "Review Pursuant to Article 62, Uniform Code of Military Justice, 10 U.S.C § 862," Navy-Marine Court of Criminal Appeals, June 20, 2008, web.
8. Ibid., 6.
9. Ibid., 7.
10. Ibid., 8–9.
11. Ibid., 9.
12. Ibid., 11.
13. Ibid., 10.
14. *U.S. v. Wuterich and CBS Broadcasting Inc. v. Navy-Marine Court of Criminal Appeals and In re Frank D. Wuterich*, Court of Appeals for the Armed Forces, Nov. 17, 2008.
15. Ibid., 20.
16. Ibid., 34.
17. Ibid., 46.
18. Ibid., 48.
19. Ibid., 47.
20. *Wuterich v. U.S.A.*, "Petition for a Writ of Certiorari," U.S. Supreme Court, Mar. 10, 2009, http://www.supremecourt.gov/search.aspx?filename=/docketfiles/08-1133.htm
21. Dwight Sullivan, "Is the Military Cert Petition an Endangered Species?" CAAFLog, May 11, 2012, http://www.caaflog.com/2012/05/11/is-the-military-cert-petition-an-endangered-species-2/
22. *Wuterich v. U.S.A.*, "Petition for a Writ of Certiorari," 7.
23. Ibid., 8.
24. Ibid.
25. Mark Walker, "Judge Denies Marines Access to CBS Tapes," *North County Times*, Mar. 13, 2009, web.
26. Ibid.
27. Ibid.
28. *U.S. v. Wuterich*, "Review Pursuant to Article 62," Navy-Marine Court of Criminal Appeals, Aug. 31, 2009, web.
29. Ibid., 16.
30. "*Branzburg v. Hayes*, 408 U.S. 665 (1972)," Wikipedia, http://en.wikipedia.org/wiki/Branzburg_v._Hayes.
31. *U.S. v. Wuterich*, "Review Pursuant to Article 62," 11.
32. Ibid., 38.
33. Ibid., 12.
34. Ibid., 19.
35. Ibid., 20.

Chapter 17

1. Richard Thompson, "Barrage of Motions Unleashed in Defense of Marine LtCol Jeffrey Chessani—Hearings Begin Tomorrow," Thomas More Law Center, Feb. 19, 2008, http://www.thomasmore.org/news/barrage-motions-unleashed-defense-marine-ltcol-jeffrey-chessani-hearings-begin-tomorrow/
2. Mark Walker, "Judge Won't Dismiss Charges Against Haditha Commander," *North County Times*, Mar. 6, 2008, web.
3. Robert J. Muise and Brian J. Rooney, "Defense Motion to Dismiss (Selective Prosecution)," Western Judicial Circuit, Navy-Marine Corps Trial Judiciary, Apr. 1, 2008, 5.
4. Robert J. Muise and Brian J. Rooney, "Defense Motion to Dismiss (Unlawful Command Influence/Accuser Concept/Prosecutorial Misconduct)," Western Judicial Circuit, Navy-Marine Corps Trial Judiciary, Apr. 1, 2008, Response to FOIA Request.
5. *U.S. v. Thomas*, 222 M.J. 388 at 393, Court of Military Appeals, 1986. Unable to find any details on this case other than its mention in other trials.
6. *U.S. v. Simpson*, 58 MJ 368, Court of Appeals for the Armed Forces, 2003, http://www.armfor.uscourts.gov/newcaaf/opinions/2003Term/02-0001.htm.
7. Col. Steven Folsom, "Findings of Fact and Conclusions of Law," June 17, 2008, 12, http://warchronicle.com/TheyAreNotKillers/LtColJeffreyChessani/ChessaniUCIRuling.pdf
8. Ibid., 13.
9. Ibid., 16.
10. Muise and Rooney, "Defense Motion to Dismiss," 19.
11. Folsom, "Findings of Fact and Conclusions of Law," 11.
12. Ibid.
13. Ibid.
14. Ibid., 12.
15. Ibid.
16. Ibid., 15.
17. Ibid.
18. Ibid., 14.
19. "Government's Notice of Appeal to the Navy-Marine Court of Criminal Appeals and

Notice of Appeal to the Navy-Marine Court of Criminal Appeals," May 7, 2008, Appendices A and B.
20. Ibid., 50.
21. Ibid., 25.
22. Ibid.
23. Ibid., 26.
24. Ibid., 30.
25. Arun Rath, *Frontline*, "Rules of Engagement," Feb. 19, 2008, http://www.pbs.org/wgbh/pages/frontline/haditha/etc/script.html.
26. "Government's Notice of Appeal," Appendices A and B, 33.
27. Ibid., 40.
28. Ibid., 51.
29. Ibid., 52.
30. Mark Walker, "Undue Influence Cited in Chessani Case," *North County Times*, May 22, 2008, web.
31. Ibid.
32. Folsom, "Findings of Fact and Conclusions of Law," 22. *Defend Our Marines* http://warchronicle.com/TheyAreNotKillers/LtColJeffreyChessani/ChessaniUCIRuling.pdf

Chapter 18

1. Thomas Watkins, "Grayson Up for Medal," Associated Press, Apr. 26, 2007, web.
2. Thomas Watkins, "Lawyer: Haditha Marine Rejects Plea Deal," Associated Press, Sept. 11, 2007, web.
3. Nathaniel R. Helms, "Bittersweet Memorial Day," *Defend Our Marines*, May 19, 2008, http://warchronicle.com/DefendOurMarines Exclusive/LtGrayson-19May08.htm
4. Teri Figueroa, "Jury Selection Begins in First Haditha Court-Martial," *North County Times*, May 28, 2008, web.
5. Teri Figueroa, "Accused Marine 'Fall Guy' in Haditha Case," May 30, 2008, web.
6. Steve Liewer, "Analyst Says Marine Told Him to Get Rid of Haditha Photos," *San Diego Union-Tribune*, May 30, 2008, web.
7. Figueroa, "Accused Marine 'Fall Guy' in Haditha Case," web.
8. Ibid.
9. David Allender, "1st Lt. Andrew Grayson's Court-Martial," *Defend Our Marines*, June 4, 2008, http://warchronicle.com/TheyAreNotKillers/LtAndrewGrayson/LtGraysonCourtMartial.htm
10. Ibid.
11. Steve Liewer, "Army Investigator Testifies," May 30, 2008, web.
12. Allender, "1st Lt. Andrew Grayson's Court-Martial," http://warchronicle.com/TheyAreNotKillers/LtAndrewGrayson/LtGraysonCourtMartial.htm
13. Ibid.

14. Liewer, "Army Investigator Testifies," web
15. Teri Figueroa, "Judge Drops Obstruction Charge in Haditha Case Mid-trial," June 4, 2008, web.
16. Ibid.
17. Allender, "1st Lt. Andrew Grayson's Court-Martial," http://warchronicle.com/TheyAreNotKillers/LtAndrewGrayson/LtGraysonCourtMartial.htm
18. Teri Figueroa, "Haditha Marine Acquitted," June 5, 2008, web.
19. Ibid.
20. Ibid.
21. "Jury Acquits Grayson," Associated Press, June 4, 2008, web.
22. Chelsea J. Carter, "Jury Gets Case of Marine Accused of Iraq Cover-Up," Associated Press, June 4, 2008, web.

Chapter 19

1. Ann Scott Tyson, "Marine General Is Told to Speak More Carefully," *Washington Post*, Feb. 4, 2005, http://www.washingtonpost.com/wp-dyn/articles/A61672-2005Feb3.html.
2. "Record of Article 39(a) Session in the Case of Lt. Col. Jeffrey Chessani," June 2, 2008, 7, *Defend Our Marines* http://warchronicle.com/TheyAreNotKillers/LtColJeffreyChessani/ChessaniUCIRuling.pdf
3. Ibid., 9.
4. Ibid., 10.
5. Ibid., 12.
6. Ibid., 12–13.
7. Ibid., 20.
8. Ibid., 22.
9. Ibid., 27.
10. Ibid., 30.
11. Ibid., 52.
12. Ibid., 60.
13. A Broadway play by Aaron Sorkin made into a movie in 1992 starring Jack Nicholson, Tom Cruise, and Demi Moore.
14. "Record of Article 39(a) Session in the Case of Lt. Col. Jeffrey Chessani," June 2, 2008, 61.
15. Ibid., 63.
16. Ibid., 81.
17. Ibid., 89.
18. Ibid., 90.
19. Col. Steven Folsom, "Findings of Fact and Conclusions of Law," June 17, 2008, 3–4, *Defend Our Marines* http://warchronicle.com/TheyAreNotKillers/LtColJeffreyChessani/ChessaniUCIRuling.pdf
20. Ibid., 18.
21. Ibid., 26.
22. Ibid., 25.
23. Ibid., 19.
24. Ibid., 18.
25. Ibid., 26.

26. Ibid., 28.
27. Ibid.
28. *U.S. v. Chessani*, "Interlocutory Appeal by the United States, Case No. 200800299," Navy-Marine Court of Criminal Appeals, July 28, 2008.
29. Ibid., 29.
30. *U.S. v. Chessani*, "Review Pursuant to Article 62(b), Uniform Code of Military Justice, 10 U.S.C. § 862(b)," Navy-Marine Court of Criminal Appeals, Mar. 17, 2009, 8.
31. Ibid., 10.
32. Ibid., 11.
33. *U.S. v. Chessani*, "Order," Navy-Marine Court of Criminal Appeals, Apr. 29, 2009, web.
34. Mark Walker, "Commandant Deciding Fate of Chessani Case," *North County Times*, June 1, 2009, web.
35. Teri Figueroa, "Military: No Criminal Charges in Haditha Deaths for Marine Officer," *North County Times*, Aug. 28, 2009, web.
36. Ibid.
37. Ibid.
38. Ibid.
39. Walker, "Mixed Ruling for Marine in Civilian Slayings in Iraq," Dec. 11, 2009, web.
40. Tony Perry, "Top Marine Officer Charged in Haditha Killings Is Forced into Retirement," *Los Angeles Times*, July 19, 2010, web.
41. "A Sad Day for America and the Marine Corps—LtCol Chessani Retires," Thomas More Law Center, July 19, 2010, http://www.thomasmore.org/news/sad-day-america-and-the-marine-corps-ltcol-chessani-retires/
42. Nathaniel R. Helms, "Haditha Incident Commander Speaks Out for the First Time," *Defend Our Marines*, July 21, 2010, http://warchronicle.com/DefendOurMarinesExclusive/ChessaniSpeaks-21July10.htm
43. Ibid.
44. Ibid.
45. Ibid.
46. Ibid.

Chapter 20

1. Tony Perry, "Last Marine Charged in Haditha Killings Returns to Court at Camp Pendleton," *Los Angeles Times*, Mar. 21, 2010, web.
2. Mark Walker, "Jodka Sentenced to 10 Months for His Role in Hamdania Killing," *North County Times*, Nov. 16, 2006, web.
3. Teri Figueroa, "Jurors Not to Be Told Marine Faces Life in Prison in Hamdania Case," *North County Times*, May 11, 2007, web.
4. Tony Perry, "Marine Charged in Haditha Killings Wins Key Ruling from Judge," *Los Angeles Times* web, Mar. 23, 2010, .
5. Mark Walker, "Four-Star General Testifies on First Day of Hearing for Staff Sgt. Frank Wuterich," *North County Times*, Mar. 22, 2010, web.

6. Gloria Williams, "Col. John Ewers," Independent Panel Review of Judge Advocate Requirements of the Department of the Navy, Nov. 3, 2010, https://acf057f5-a-62cb3a1a-s-sites.googlegroups.com/site/506panel/documents/EwersBio.pdf?attachauth=ANoY7coe1juOVpTZWXBxi9RkKLQlE-UGK7x8N7UIQOti5HAdTaOk7Fnr5M4ln8yiBB_3srYJn6UmsCqDHXwxk0RADcZxK3zPLNw3OAPPKDOLiBn9-XgtR8Ie1uJ-hnAVSHcVpmus-63nqR5QAhjOUmvgqoXDUHSrBbD_6KL2sibu3Ifgx5pLBIxXVcRCvZHM4nzni-RA5LUgD8MoQCsR0RbP0gl9OHLMPQ%3D%3D&attredirects=0
7. Walker, "Four-Star General Testifies," web.
8. Tony Perry, "Ruling Could Lead Marine Corps to Drop Haditha Case," *Los Angeles Times*, Mar. 24, 2010, web.
9. Mark Walker, "Judge Rules Marine Must Stand Trial," *North County Times*, Mar. 26, 2010, web.
10. Ibid.
11. *U.S. v. Hutchins*, General Court-Martial, Navy-Marine Court of Criminal Appeals, Apr. 22, 2010, http://www.jag.navy.mil/courts/documents/archive/2010/HUTCHINS,%20L.G.pdf
12. Gary Warth, "General Gives Final 'Pendleton 8' Defendant 11 Years," *North County Times*, May 8, 2008, web.
13. *U.S. v. Hutchins*, General Court-Martial, 13.
14. *U.S. v. Wuterich*, General Court-Martial, "Defense Motion for Appropriate Relief to Dismiss All Charges and Specifications for Violation of Right to Detailed Counsel," Western Judicial Circuit, Navy-Marine Corps Trial Judiciary, Aug. 29, 2010, web.
15. Ibid., 1.
16. Ibid.
17. Ibid., 2.
18. Ibid., 3.
19. Ibid.
20. Ibid., 3–4.
21. Julie Watson, "Defense Lawyer Steps Down in Haditha Case," Associated Press, Sept. 14, 2010, web.
22. *U.S. v. Wuterich*, "Findings of Fact and Conclusions of Law; Motion to Dismiss for Violation of Right of Detailed Counsel," Western Judicial Circuit, Navy-Marine Corps Trial Judiciary, Oct. 26, 2010, web.
23. Ibid., 16.
24. Ibid., 18.
25. "Wuterich Trial Delayed," *North County Times*, Sept. 7, 2010, web.
26. Wuterich v. Jones, "Petition for Extraordinary Relief in the Nature of a Writ of Mandamus and Brief in Support," Navy-Marine Court of Criminal Appeals, Oct. 28, 2010, http://warchronicle.com/DefendOurMarinesExclusive/Petition%20for%20Extraordinary%20Relief%20

in%20the%20Nature%20of%20a%20Writ%20of%20Mandamus%20and%20Brief%20In%20support%20ICO%20US%20v.%20Wuterich%20with%20Appendix,%20Signed[1].pdf
27. *U.S. v. Hutchins*, Crim. App. No. 200800 393, Court of Appeals for the Armed Forces, Jan. 11, 2011.
28. *Wuterich v. Jones and U.S.A.*, "Review of Petition for Extraordinary Relief in the Nature of a Writ of Mandamus," Jan. 5, 2011, 5, http://www.armfor.uscourts.gov/newcaaf/opinions/2008SepTerm/08–6006.pdf
29. *Wuterich v. Jones and U.S.A.*, Court of Appeals for the Armed Forces, USCA Misc. Dkt. No. 111-8009/MC, Crim. App. Dkt. No. 2008 00183, Order, Apr. 8, 2011, http://www.armfor.uscourts.gov/newcaaf/journal/2011Jrnl/2011Apr.htm
30. U.S. Navy Judge Advocate General's Corp, http://www.jag.navy.mil/courts/documents/archive/audio/08_08_11.mp3.
31. *Wuterich v. U.S.A.*, "Review of Petition for Extraordinary Relief in the Nature of a Writ of Mandamus," Navy-Marine Court of Criminal Appeals, Aug. 25, 2011, http://www.jag.navy.mil/courts/documents/archive/2011/WUTERICH,%20F.D.%20200800183.pdf
32. Ibid., 4.
33. Ibid., 6.
34. Ibid., 7.
35. Appeals-Summary Dispositions, Miscellaneous Docket-Summary Dispositions, Misc. No. 12-8001/NA, *Wuterich v. Jones*, Court of Appeals for the Armed Forces, Sept. 21, 2011, http://www.armfor.uscourts.gov/newcaaf/journal/2011Jrnl/2011Sep.htm

Chapter 21

1. Mark Walker, "Jury Seated for Wuterich Trial," *North County Times*, Jan. 6, 2012, web.
2. Art Moore, "Lt. Col. West Fined $5,000, Avoids Court-Martial for Using Shock Tactics to Save lines," *WorldNetDaily*, Dec. 12, 2003, web.
3. Mark Walker, "Marine Alleges Haditha Defendant Told Him to Lie," *North County Times*, Jan. 11, 2012, web.
4. Mark Walker, "Former Lieutenant Defends Marines in Haditha Killings," *North County Times*, Jan. 13, 2012, web.
5. Mark Walker, "Wuterich Called a 'Great Marine,'" *North County Times*, Jan. 17, 2012, web.
6. Nathaniel Helms, "If I'm Receiving Fire, I've Got to Assume the House Is Hostile," *Defend Our Marines*, Jan. 17, 2012, http://warchronicle.com/DefendOurMarinesExclusive/Trial_of_SSgt_Wuterich/If_I'm_Receiving_Fire,_I've_Got_to_Assume_the_House_is_Hostile_3281.htm

Epilogue

1. Michael S. Schmidt, "Anger in Iraq After Plea Bargain Over 2005 Massacre," *New York Times*, Jan. 24, 2012, http://www.nytimes.com/2012/01/25/world/middleeast/anger-in-iraq-after-plea-bargain-over-haditha-killings.html
2. "Iraq Eyes Legal Action over Deadly Haditha Raid," CBS News, Jan. 26, 2012, web.
3. Graner was convicted of abusing prisoners at Abu Ghraib but was released after serving about two-thirds of his ten-year sentence.
4. Four Blackwater employees were accused of killing seventeen Iraqis in Baghdad's Nisour Square in September 2007. Their employer hustled them out of Iraq. They have never been tried in the United States, although manslaughter charges are pending.
5. "Editorial: Imperfect Justice," *North County Times* and *The Californian* Opinion Staff, Jan. 24, 2012, web.
6. Ibid.
7. Anna Mulrine, "Martine demoted to Private to End Haditha Trial," *Christian Science Monitor*, Jan. 24, 2012, http://www.csmonitor.com/USA/Military/2012/0124/Marine-demoted-to-private-to-end-Haditha-trial.-Did-military-justice-work
8. Arun Rath, "Marine to Serve No Time in Haditha War-Crimes Case," National Public Radio, Jan. 24, 2012.
9. "Stunning Denial by U.S. Marine at Haditha Massacre Court-Martial as Judge Rules He Will Serve ZERO Jail Time," Associated Press, *London Mail Online*, Jan. 25, 2012, web.
10. In response to an article by Con Coughlin, "World Last Updated," *London Telegraph*, Jan. 25, 2012, web.
11. Julie Watson, "Wuterich Receives General Discharge from the Corps," Associated Press, Feb. 21, 2012, web.
12. Mark Walker, "Wuterich Trying to Move on After Nightmare at Haditha," *North County Times*, Feb. 25, 2012, web.
13. Ibid
14. Ibid.
15. He was divorced from his wife, Marisol, the mother of his three girls, before his trial.
16. Jesse Buchanan, "Vets Welcome Wuterich Back to Meriden," (Meriden, Conn.) *Record-Journal*, Aug. 18, 2012, web.
17. Ibid.
18. Ibid.
19. "Truth of Haditha Case May Never Come Out: Wuterich Defense Attorney," *Midday Edition*, KPBS Radio, Jan. 30, 2012, http://www.kpbs.org/news/2012/jan/30/how-will-last-marine-trial-haditha-find-redemption/
20. Ibid.
21. Ibid.

22. "Navy Seeks Ouster of 2 Marines After Haditha Case," Associated Press, Apr. 19, 2012.
23. Ibid.
24. "Marines Involved in Haditha Killings Face Dismissal for Lying to Investigators," *Midday Edition*, KBPS Radio, Apr. 23, 2012.
25. Ibid.
26. Ibid.
27. Ibid.
28. Ibid.

Conclusions

1. Keith Fleming, *The U.S. Marine Corps in Crisis* (Columbia, S.C: University of South Carolina Press, 1990).
2. Josh White and Sonya Geis, "8 Troops Charged in Death of Iraqi," *Washington Post*, June 22, 2006, http://www.washingtonpost.com/wp-dyn/content/article/2006/06/21/AR2006062100887.html
3. Ibid.
4. Carolyn Marshall, "Corpsman Who Failed to Halt Killing of Iraqi Receives Prison Sentence," Associated Press, Oct. 7, 2006, web.
5. Teri Figueroa, "Marine Found Guilty of Murder in Slaying," *North County Times*, Aug. 3, 2007, web.
6. Mark Walker, "NCIS Confirms It's Investigating Slayings," July 3, 2007, web.
7. Mark Walker, "Manslaughter Charged in Fallujah Killings," *North County Times*, Aug. 17, 2007, web.
8. Mark Walker, "Sgt. Jerome A. Nelson Accused of Unpremeditated Murder in 2004 Incident," *North County Times*, Aug. 21, 2007, web.
9. Mark Walker, "Marine Charged in 2004 Insurgent Killings," *North County Times*, Mar. 19, 2008, web.
10. Ibid.
11. Ibid.
12. Ibid.
13. Mark Walker, "Marine Not Guilty in Fallujah Slayings," *North County Times*, Aug. 29, 2008, web.
14. Mark Walker, "Weemer Acquitted on All Counts," *North County Times*, Apr. 9, 2009, web.
15. Mark Walker, "Nelson Gets Reduction in Rank," *North County Times*, Sept. 30, 2009, web.
16. Statement from Lt. Gen. James Mattis, *Defend Our Marines*, Aug. 9, 2007, http://warchronicle.com/TheyAreNotKillers/GenMattis/DefendOurMarines-GenMattisStatements80907.htm
17. Judge Advocate Directory, Oct. 2010, 1, http://www.hqmc.marines.mil/sja/Leaders/tabid/9643/Article/167127/major-general-john-r-ewers.aspx
18. Donna Miles, "Senate Confirms Nominations to Four Defense Posts," American Forces Press Service, Sept. 28, 2007, http://www.globalsecurity.org/military/library/news/2007/09/mil-070928-afps04.htm
19. Thomas E. Ricks, "The Obama Administration's Inexplicable Mishandling of Marine Gen. James Mattis," Foreign Policy, Jan. 18, 2013, http://ricks.foreignpolicy.com/posts/2013/01/18/the_obama_administration_s_inexplicable_mishandling_of_marine_gen_james_mattis.
20. https://www.facebook.com/GeneralJamesMattisForPresident.
21. Congressional Record, SENATE S2453, Apr. 8, 2013, https://www.congress.gov/crec/2013/04/08/CREC-2013-04-08-pt1-PgS2453.pdf
22. Richard Sisk, "Hagel's Salty Farewell to Mattis," *DoD Buzz*, Mar. 22, 2013, http://www.dodbuzz.com/2013/03/22/hagels-salty-farewell-to-mattis/

Bibliography

Printed Matter

Alexander, Col. Joseph H., USMC (Ret.), with Don Horan and Norman C. Stahl. *A Fellowship of Valor*. New York: Harper Collins, 1997.
Allison, William Thomas. *Military Justice in Vietnam: The Rule of Law in an American War*. Lawrence: University Press of Kansas, 2007.
Ashe, David B. "The Law of War." *Marine Corps Gazette,* Feb. 2009, 33.
Barker, Rodney. *Dancing with the Devil: Sex, Espionage, and the U.S. Marines: The Clayton Lonetree Story*. New York: Simon and Schuster, 1996.
Belknap, Michael R. *The Vietnam War on Trial: The My Lai Massacre and the Court-Martial of Lieutenant Calley*. Lawrence: University Press of Kansas, 2002.
Berrigan, Frida. "The Fog of War Crimes." *In These Times*, Jan. 7, 2008, http://inthesetimes.com/article/3461/the_fog_of_war_crimes.
Berry, John Stevens. *Those Gallant Men on Trial in Vietnam*. Novato, Calif.: Presidio, 1984.
Bica, Camillo C., Ph.D. "Terrorism and Response: A Moral Inquiry into the Killing of Noncombatants." *Joint Services Conference on Professional Ethics (JSCOPE)*, 2004, http://isme.tamu.edu/JSCOPE04/Bica04.html
Biddle, Stephen. "Seeing Baghdad, Thinking Saigon." *Foreign Affairs*, Mar.–Apr. 2006, 2–14.
Boot, Max. "Fire the Incompetents, Find the Pattons." Leatherneck.com, May 31, 2007, http://www.leatherneck.com/forums/showthread.php?47488-Fire-the-incompetents-find-the-Pattons.
———. "The Corps Should Look to Its Small-Wars Past." *Armed Forces Journal*, Mar. 2006, 16.
———. "Win Baghdad and We'll Forgive Haditha." *Los Angeles Times*, June 7, 2006, http://historynewsnetwork.org/article/26425.
Boyne, Walter J., USAF (Ret.), and Clifton Ganyard, eds. *Alpha, Bravo, Delta Guide to the U.S. Marine Corps*. New York: Alpha, 2003.
Clark, Wesley, Reue Marc Gerecht, Gary Solis, and Philip Caputo. "Rules of Engagement." *Time*, June 4, 2006, http://content.time.com/time/magazine/article/0,9171,1200742,00.html
Cobbold, Richard. "Slaughter, Slaughter Everywhere, Nor Any Time to Think." *Royal United Services Institute Journal* 151, no. 3 (2006), web.
Coll, Steve. "The General's Dilemma." *New Yorker*, Sept. 8, 2008, 34.
Corn, Geoffrey S. "Haditha and the Laws of War." *Crimes of War Project,* June 14, 2006, web.
———. "Haditha and My Lai: Lessons from the Law of War." *Jurist*, Aug. 8, 2007, web.
Cowart, J.D. *Haditha Diary*. United States: Xulon, 2010.
Danyluk, Capt. Stephen B., USMC. "Preventing Atrocities." *Marine Corps Gazette*, June 2000, https://www.mca-marines.org/gazette/2000/06/preventing-atrocities.
Davidson, Michael J. *A Guide to Military Criminal Law*. Annapolis, Md.: Naval Institute Press, 1999.
Davis, Burke. *Marine! The Life of Chesty Puller*. New York: Bantam, 1962.
DiMona, Joseph. *Great Court Martial Cases*. New York: Grosset and Dunlap, 1972.

Duffy, Michael, Tim McGirk, and Aparism Ghosh. "The Ghosts of Haditha." *Time,* Jan. 4, 2006, http://content.time.com/time/magazine/article/0,9171,1200763,00.html#paid-wall.
Dworkin, Anthony. "The Crimes at Haditha: A Briefing." *Crimes of War Project,* June 9, 2006, web.
Eckhardt, William George. "Lawyering for Uncle Sam When He Draws His Sword." *Famous American Trials.* University of Missouri–Kansas City, n.d.
Falk, Richard, Irene Gendizer, and Robert Jay Lifton, eds. *Crimes of War: Iraq.* New York: Nation, 2006.
Fick, Nathaniel. *One Bullet Away: The Making of a Marine Officer.* New York: Houghton Mifflin, 2005.
Fleming, Keith. *The U.S. Marine Corps in Crisis: Ribbon Creek and Recruit Training.* Columbia: University of South Carolina Press, 1990.
French, Shannon E. *The Code of the Warrior: Exploring Warrior Values Past and Present.* Lanham, Md.: Rowman and Littlefield, 2003.
Gardner, Lloyd C., and Marilyn B. Young, eds. *Iraq and the Lessons of Vietnam, or, How Not to Learn from the Past.* New York: New Press, 2007.
Gordon, Michael R., and Gen. Bernard E. Trainor. *Cobra II: The Inside Story of the Invasion and Occupation of Iraq.* New York: Pantheon, 2006.
Greene, Wallace M. "UCMJ in Vietnam." *Marine Corps Gazette,* May 1990, https://www.mca-marines.org/gazette/1990/05/ucmj-vietnam.
Hammer, Richard. *The Court-Martial of Lt. Calley.* New York: Coward, McCann and Geoghegan, 1971.
Hansen, Victor. "The Haditha Double Standard." *Jurist,* Dec. 23, 2006, web.
Hersh, Seymour M. *Cover-up: The Army's Secret Investigation of the Massacre at My Lai.* New York: Random House, 1972.
Hillman, Elizabeth Lutes. *Defending America: Military Culture and the Cold War Court-Martial.* Princeton, N.J.: Princeton University Press, 2005.
Hoffman, Frank G. "Complex Irregular Warfare: The Next Revolution in Military Affairs." *Foreign Policy Research Institute,* Summer 2006, http://www.comw.org/qdr/fulltext/0605hoffman.pdf.
_____. "Changing Tires On the Fly: The Marines and Postconflict Stability Ops." *Foreign Policy Research Institute,* Sept. 2006, http://www.fpri.org/articles/2006/09/changing-tires-fly-marines-and-postconflict-stability-ops.
Hoppe, Ralf. "Marines on Trial for Haditha Murders." *Der Spiegel Online,* June 5, 2007, http://www.spiegel.de/international/world/marines-on-trial-for-haditha-murders-massacre-for-a-fallen-comrade-a-486182.html
Horton, Scott. "Bush Assails the JAG Corps." *Harper's,* Dec. 6, 2007, http://harpers.org/blog/2007/12/bush-assails-the-jag-corps/
_____. "Jim Haynes' Long Twilight Struggle." *Harper's,* Feb. 8, 2008, http://harpers.org/blog/2008/02/jim-hayness-long-twilight-struggle/
Immel, August. "My Tribe Is the Marine Corps." *Marine Corps Gazette,* July 2010, https://www.mca-marines.org/person/august-immel.
Kahl, Colin H. "How We Fight: War Crimes and Misdemeanors." *Foreign Affairs,* Nov./Dec. 2006, http://www.foreignaffairs.com/articles/62093/colin-h-kahl/how-we-fight
Kaplan, Fred. *Daydream Believers: How a Few Grand Ideas Wrecked American Power.* New York: John Wiley and Sons, 2008.
Kaplan, Robert D, "Five Days in Fallujah." *Atlantic Monthly,* July/Aug. 2004, 116–126.
Kennedy, David. *Of War and Law.* Princeton, N.J.: Princeton University Press, 2006.
Kluger, Jeffrey. "How Haditha Came to Light." *Time,* June 4, 2006, http://content.time.com/time/magazine/article/0,9171,1200780,00.html.
Krulak, Gen. Charles C. "The Strategic Corporal: Leadership in the Three Block War." *Marines,* Jan. 1999.
Krulak, Lt. Gen. Victor H., USMC (Ret.). *First to Fight: An Inside View of the U.S. Marine Corps.* Annapolis, Md.: Blackjacket Books, Naval Institute Press, 1999.
Langewiesche, William. "Rules of Engagement." *Vanity Fair,* Nov. 2006, 312.
Lichtblau, Eric. *Bush's Law: The Remaking of American Justice.* New York: Pantheon, 2008.
Maguire, Peter. *Law and War: An American Story.* New York: Columbia University Press, 2001.

Marlantes, Karl. *What It's Like to Go to War.* New York: Atlantic Monthly Press, 2011.
Mayer, Capt. Chris (USN). "Nonlethal Weapons and Noncombatant Immunity: Can We Ever Justify Attacking Noncombatants?" *Joint Services Conference on Professional Ethics (JSCOPE)*, 2004, web.
Millett, Allan R. *Semper Fidelis: The History of the United States Marine Corps.* New York: Free Press, 1980, 1991.
Morrison, C.H., Jr. "Command Influence and Military Justice." *Marine Corps Gazette*, Feb. 1976, https://www.mca-marines.org/gazette/1976/02/command-influence-and-military-justice.
Nagl, Lt. Col. Johan A., and Lt. Col. Paul Yingling. "New Rules for New Enemies." *Armed Forces Journal*, Oct. 2006, http://www.armedforcesjournal.com/new-rules-for-new-enemies/
O'Connell, Aaron B. *Underdogs: The Making of the Modern Marine Corp.* Cambridge, Mass.: Harvard University Press, 2012.
O'Donnell, James P. "The Corps' Struggle for Survival." *Marine Corps Gazette*, Aug. 2000, https://www.mca-marines.org/gazette/2000/08/corps-struggle-survival.
Ohman, Maj. Mynda G. "Integrating Title 18 War Crimes into Title 10: A Proposal to Amend the Uniform Code of Military Justice." *Air Force Law Review* 57 (Winter 2005): 1–112.
Pantano, Ilario, with Malcolm McConnell. *Warlord: No Better Friend, No Worse Enemy.* New York: Threshold Editions, 2006.
Parks, Maj. W. Hayes. "Crimes in Hostilities, Parts I and II." *Marine Corps Gazette*, Aug. 1976, https://www.mca-marines.org/magazine-archive-search?search_api_views_fulltext=Crimes+in+Hostilities.
Peterson, Matthew H. "Parallels Between Iraq and Vietnam." *Marine Corps Gazette*, Oct. 2006, https://www.mca-marines.org/gazette/2006/10/parallels-between-iraq-and-vietnam.
Pitluk, Adam. "The Lost Lamented Marine," *Time*, June 4, 2006, http://content.time.com/time/magazine/article/0,9171,1200766,00.html
Prugh, Maj. Gen. George S. "Law at War Vietnam, 1964–1973," Department of the Army, *Vietnam Studies*, n.d. http://www.history.army.mil/books/Vietnam/Law-War/law-fm.htm
Ricks, Thomas E. *Fiasco: The American Military Adventure in Iraq.* New York: Penguin, 2006.
_____. *The Gamble: General Petraeus and the American Military Adventure in Iraq.* London: Penguin, 2009, 2010.
_____. *Making the Corps.* New York: Simon and Schuster, 1997.
Sattler, John F. "Operation Al Fajr: The Battle of Fallujah–Part II." *Marine Corps Gazette*, July 2005, https://www.mca-marines.org/gazette/2005/07/operation-al-fajr-battle-fallujah-part-ii.
Savage, Charlie. *Takeover: The Return of the Imperial Presidency and Subversion of American Democracy.* New York: Back Bay/Little, Brown, 2007.
Scahill, Jeremy. *Blackwater: The Rise of the World's Most Powerful Mercenary Army.* New York: Nation, 2007.
Schmidle, Nicholas. "Three Trials for Murder." *New Yorker*, Nov. 14, 2011, http://www.newyorker.com/magazine/2011/11/14/three-trials-for-murder.
Shay, Jonathan. *Achilles in Vietnam: Combat Trauma and the Undoing of Character.* New York: Scribner, 1994.
Sheenhan, Neil. "Should We Have War Crime Trials?" *New York Times*, Mar. 26, 1971, http://query.nytimes.com/gst/abstract.html?res=9D04E6D8113BE73ABC4051DFB566838A669EDE#
Smith, Bryan. "Witness at Haditha," *Chicago*, July 2008, www.chicagomag.com/Chicago-Magazine/July-2008/Witness-at-Haditha/index.php?cparticle=1&siarticle=0#artanc.
Solis, Gary D. *Marines and Military Law in Vietnam: Trial by Fire.* Washington, D.C.: History and Museums Division, Headquarters, U.S. Marine Corps, 1989.
_____. *Son Thang: An American War Crime.* Annapolis, Md.: Naval Institute Press, 1997.
Stevens, John C., III. *Court-Martial at Parris Island: The Ribbon Creek Incident.* Annapolis, Md.: Naval Institute Press, 1999.
Stokes, Arch Y. "Speedy Trial: A Commander's Dilemma." *Marine Corps Gazette*, July 1973, https://www.mca-marines.org/gazette/1973/07/speedy-trial-commanders-dilemma.
Sturkey, Marion F. *Warrior Culture of the U.S. Marines.* 2nd Ed. Plum Branch, S.C.: Heritage Press International, 2002.

Swenk, James. "Military Justice and the Media: The Media Interview." *U.S. Air Force Academy Journal of Legal Studies* 12 (2002): web.
Swofford, Anthony. *Jarhead: A Marine's Chronicle of the Gulf War and Other Battles.* New York: Scribner, 2003.
Thomas, Evan, and Scoot Johnson. "Probing a Bloodbath." *Newsweek*, June 12, 2006, 20.
Trager, Dr. Frank N. "The National Security Act of 1947: Its Thirtieth Anniversary." *Air University Review* 29, no.1 (Nov./Dec. 1977): 2–15.
West, Bing, with Maj. Gen. Ray L. Smith. *The March Up: Taking Baghdad with the United States Marines.* New York: Bantam, 2003.
West, Bing. *No True Glory: A Frontline Account of the Battle for Fallujah.* New York: Bantam, 2005.
———. "The Road to Haditha." *Atlantic Monthly*, Oct. 2006, 95–100.
———. "Streetwise." *Atlantic Monthly*, Jan./Feb. 2007, 70–77.
West, Luther C. "A History of Command Influence on the Military Judicial System." *UCLA Law Review* 18, no. 1 (Nov. 1970): web.

Transcripts

"The Killings in Haditha: The *60 Minutes* SSgt. Frank Wuterich Interview." *CBS News.* Mar. 18, 2007.
"Last Haditha Trial Ends in a Plea, Was Justice Served?" *Midday Edition.* Radio Station KPBS. Jan. 30, 2012.
"Marines Involved in Haditha Killings Face Dismissal for Lying to Investigators." *Midday Edition.* Radio Station KPBS. Apr. 23, 2012.
Murtha, John. *Good Morning America with Charles Gibson.* ABC, May 30, 2006.
———. *CNN American Morning with Soledad O'Brien.* CNN, May 30, 2006.
———. *Paula Zahn Now.* CNN, May 30, 2006.
———. *Meet the Press with Tim Russert.* NBC, June 11, 2006.
"O'Reilly Interview with P.J. Crowley and Neal Puckett." *Fox News.* May 6, 2005.
"Rules of Engagement." National Public Radio. Feb. 21, 2008.

Index

Numbers in ***bold italics*** indicate pages with illustrations.

ABC (American Broadcasting Co.) 50; *see also* Gibson, Charles
Abizaid, Gen. John 8
Ali, Khamisa Tuema 22
Amir al-Kaysey 121
Amos, Gen. Jim 214
Anbar Province ***6***, 15, 18, 169; cities in 7, 48; City of Mosques 7; Sunni presence 7; U.S. Army in 8, 17–18; U.S. Marines in 8; Wahhabists 7
Armed Forces Act of 2006 (British) 224
Army investigation AR 15-6 43, 56, 76, 176–77
Associated Press 127, 149, 151, 174
"Attempts" 151; *see also* Grayson, 1st Lt. Andrew
Atterbury, Lt. Col. Paul 102, 104, 130, 178
Awad, Hashim Ibrahim 48, 157, 219; *see also* Hamdania

Bargewell, Maj. Gen. Eldon A. (Army) 4, 44–45, 60, 76, 96, 108, 151, 207; on Battalion 3/1 and RCT-2 81–82; on cities 7; and Ewers 168, 181, 183–84; on 1st Squad 78–79; on Kilo Company 79–82; report 56–57, 60–61, 65, 77–78, 82–84, 87, 181; on 2nd Division 82; on USMC Iraq Command 77; on Wuterich 61
Berlin, Seth D. 157
"Black Five" 52
Blunt, Rep. Roy 49
Board of Inquiry 114, 118, 188–89, ***191***
"BootMurtha" 52
Brady, Thomas 132, 140
Branzburg, Paul (*Branzburg*) 164–65; *see also* CBS
Bremer, L. Paul 8
Burke, Capt. Joseph (Navy) 151
Bush, Pres. George 33, 38, 40, 46, 55, 91; on Fallujah 8–9
Byrne, Col. Brennan 107

Camp Pendleton 8, ***85***, 99
Capers, Capt. Alonzo 140
Carrasco, Maj. Samuel S. 30, 32, 35, 81, 105, 107, 109; on investigation 39, 93–94
Casas, Joseph 149, 174–79; *see also* Grayson, 1st Lt. Andrew
Casey, Lt. Gen. George W. (Army) 42, 76, 81; *see also* Multi-National Force—Iraq
Cavanaugh, Maureen 212, 214
Cavuto, Neil 52
CBS 68, 72, 74, 75, 162, ***166***, 192, 195, 203, 221; appeal to Navy-Marine Court of Criminal Appeals (NMCCA) 158–59, 161, 163–64; appeal to U.S. Court of Appeals for the Armed Forces (CAAF) 160–61; *Branzburg* precedent 164–65; on reporter privilege 160; subpoena 156–59; Wuterich cross-appeal 158; Wuterich lack of standing 159; Wuterich petition to U.S. Supreme Court 161; Wuterich trial delay 158, 165; *see also* outtakes; *60 Minutes*
"Censure Murtha" 52
Chessani, Lt. Col. Jeffrey R. 4, 13, 18, 26–30, 32, 35, 37–40, 42–43, 45, 57, 59, 61–62, 64–65, 67, 77, 81, 83, 88, 91–92, 94–95, 99, 100–6, 107, 114, 116, 119, 129, 149, 150–51, 153, 155, ***156***, 167–72, 174–75, 179–80, 182–86, 183–86, 190, 192–94, 216–17, 222; at ambush site 31; amended charges 108; and Board of Inquiry 188–89; charges dismissed 188; original charges 62, ***63***; prosecution appeal to NMCCA 188; relieved of command 48; retired 189; timeline ***191***; *see also* Conlin, Col. Christopher C.; Muise, Robert; Rooney, Brian
Chiarelli, Lt. Gen. Peter W. 4, 42–45, 47, 56–57, 60, 76–77, 81, 90, 150–51, 176; *see also* Army investigation AR15-6
Christian Science Monitor 211
civil suits 52–53, 72, 128
Cloud, David S. 57, 61; *see also New York Times*; Schmitt, Eric

261

CNN 46–47, 62; *see also* O'Brien, Soledad; Zahn, Paula
"CNN Morning with Soledad O'Brien" 50–51
collateral damage 91, 95, 108
Commander's Emergency Response Program (CERP) 35, 38, 47
Conlin, Col. Christopher C. 99–102, 105, 107–14, 149, 167; *see also* Chessani, Lt. Col. Jeffrey; Muise, Robert; Rooney, Brian
Connelley, Maj. Carroll 88, 92, 94, 96, 106–7, 109
Conway, Lt. Gen. James 8, 117, 167, 188
Coulter, Ann 52
Court of Criminal Appeals for the Armed Forces (CAAF) 160–62, *166*, 188, 197–99
Crossan, Lance Cpl. James 17, 20, 71
Culp, Jim 122

Davis, Rep. Geoff 49
Davis, Col. Stephen 30, *36*–37, 57, 67, 87, 103, 108, 110, 112, 116–17, 189; *see also* Regimental Combat Team–2
Dela Cruz, Cpl. Sanick (later Sgt.) 17, 20–21, 27–28, *36*, 43, 63, 69, 78–79, 83, 88–89, 94, 116, 131–32, 136–43, 145–47, 153, 185, 206–7, 214–15, 219, 221; charges against *64*
Dinsmore, Capt. Jeffrey S. (later Major) 26–27, 31, 34, *36*–37, 44, 91–92, 94, 96–97, 105, 107, 151–52
Donilon, Tom 223
Donnelly, Sally 57
Dubrule, Capt. Michael (Navy) 151–52
Dunford, Lt. Gen. Joseph (commander I MEF/MARCENT) 162

Erickson, Maj. Daren 122, 126
Espinosa, 1st Sgt. Alberto 38, 93
Ewers, Col. John 93, 97, 168–71, 180–87, *191*–93, 221–22; and Chessani, 168; and Helland 169, 186, 192–93; and Mattis 169–70, 187, 192; tainted 168, 181, 183, 186, 193, 222; wounded in Iraq 169; *see also* Folsom, Col. Stephen; Mattis; RIAT

Fallujah 7, 18, 23, 33, 55, 70, 77–78, 80, 120–21, 157, 207, 219–21; Blackwater incident 8; and Chessani 101; Fallujah Brigade 9; Hell House 11–13, 17, 20, 118; Operation Phantom Fury 10–12; Operation Vigilant Resolve 8–9; *see also* Abizaid, Gen. John; Bremer, L. Paul; Conway, Lt. Gen. James; Mattis, Maj. Gen. James
Faraj, Lt. Col. Haytham 138, *165*, 195–96, 200, 202, 204, 205
Fields, Staff Sgt. Travis 141
Firm Base Sparta 15–16, 19, 21, 25–27, 30, *36*–37, 66, 107, 136
1st Squad 13, 15, 17, 19, 27–28, 30–32, 34–37, 44–45, 56, 62–63, 66–67, 69, 75, 78–79, 89, 91–92, 95, 103–5, 107, 113, 118, 136, 141, 153, 173, 201, 214

Flynn, Lt. Gen. George 188, *191*
Folsom, Col. Steven 167–68, 170–72, 182–88, *191*, 193–194, 222; appearance of Unlawful Command Influence 186; charges dismissed 186; *see also* Chessani, Lt. Col. Jeffrey; Ewers, Col. John; Mattis, Maj. Gen. James
Frank, 2nd Lt. Max 31, 103–4
Frontline 170, 211

Gannon, Capt. Nicholas 158, 165, 200, 203–7
Ghosh, Aparisim "Bobby" 39 *See also Time*
Gibson, Charles 50
Gillibrand, Sen. Kirsten 224
Gittins, Charles 87–88, 91–92
Gonzales, Maj. Kevin M. 31, 39, 40
Graviss, Lance Cpl. Trent 19, 120, 125
Grayson, 1st Lt. Andrew A. 27, 63, 65, 155, 185, 190, 205, 221; acquittal 178; amended charges 151; Article 32 hearing 148–53; and Laughner 27, 106, 148, 150–51; original charges *64*; rejects plea offer 149; trial 173–79; and Watt 83, 150, 175–77; *see also* Casas, Joseph; Human Exploitation Team (HET); Kasprzyk, Maj. Brian; Laughner, Staff Sgt. Justin; Stahlman, Col. Michael; Watt, Col. Gregory (Army)
Guzman, Pfc. Salvador 20–21, 71

Haditha (city) 1, 7, 13, 16, 18–19, 32, 39–40, 42, 43–48, 55–56, 59–60, 73, 80, 84, 90, 112, 115, 120–21, 125–26, 128, 130–31, 157, 169, 207; Bargewell in 56, 60, 76; City Council 35, 92, 105, 111, 189; Ewers in 168–69; hospital 18, 31; NCIS in 60
Haditha Dam: as battalion headquarters 26, 30, *36*, 94, 113, 120; battle for 18; as interrogation site 206; structure 18
Haditha incident 2, 45–47, 53, 58, 60–62, 73, 76–77, 101, 115, 117–19, 131, 140, 148–49, 167–68, 170, 202, 206–7, 210, 216
Haditha Marines 48, 53, 55, 66, 72–73, 83, 148, 153, 155, 158, 174, 190, 194
Haditha news release 32, 63, 82, 87, 90, 92, 95, 115–16, 128, 216
Haditha streets: Haditha Road 16–17, 19; River Road 16, 19, 26–27, 29; Route Chestnut 16, 20–21, 23, 26–28, 30–31, 39, 68, 77, 89, 113, 118, 142, 150, 206; Route Leopard 16–17, 19; Route Viper 19, 28; Watt in 150, 176
Hagee, Gen. Michael 14, 55
Hagel, Defense Secretary Chuck 223
Hamdania 55, 59, 73, 194; charges preferred 73; convening authority 59; incident 48, 73, 158, 185, 219; legal proceedings 127, 156–57, 185, 209; *see also* Hutchins, Sgt. Lawrence, III
Haqlaniyah (town) 18, 48
Hassan, Abdul-Hamid 22, 25
Hastert, House Speaker Dennis 48
Helland, Lt. Gen. Samuel 146–47, 152, 155, 162, 174, 192–94; chastised by Folsom 168–69, 171, 186

Helms, Nathaniel R. 190
House Four 29, *36*–37, 41, 44, 118–19, 122, 125, 136–37, 203
House One 22–23, 25, 35–*36*, 43–45, 66, 70, 89, 93–95, 103, 116, 129–30, 132–36, 138, 141, 143–44, 204–6, 212
House Three 28–29, 44, 119
House Two 22–23, *36*, 44, 66, 70, 94, 129–30, 132, 134–36, 138, 141, 143–46, 201, 204–5
Huck, Maj. Gen. Richard 35, 37, 43, 57, 67, 87, 90, 92, 104–5, 107–9, 112, 116–17, 176, 189
Human Exploitation Team (HET) 27, 61, 63–64, 106, 148–50, 173, 176, 205; *see also* Grayson, 1st Lt. Andrew; Laughner, Staff Sgt. Justin
Hunter, Rep. Duncan Lee 54–55
Hunter, Duncan Wayne 55
Hutchins, Sgt. Lawrence III 157, 194–95, 197–98, 219; *see also* Hamdania
"Hutchins Motion" 195–198
Hyatt, Maj. Dana 35, 92–94, 96, 153

ibn Abd, al-Wahhhab 2
immunity grants 94–97, 106, 115–16, 130, 134, 142, 153, 155, 175, 185, 190, 201, 203, 205, 213–14, 221
India (I) Company 18, 48

JEN: number 19-08 32; number 19–19 32; number 20-7 30, 32
Johnson, Maj. Gen. Stephen T. 57; *see also* MNF-W
Jones, Lt. Col. David 162, 165, 192, 194, 197–198, 201, 203, 207, 208; and Vokey 196; *see also* Wuterich, Sgt. Frank

K Company 16, 20, 27, 48, 57, 63, 173; in Fallujah, 11, 13; *see also* Kilo Company
Kallop, 2nd Lt. William 13, 21, 23, 25, 27–28, 34–*36*, 57, 63, 78, 80, 88–89, 92, 94, 116, 136, 141, 153, 206–7
Kasprzyk, Maj. Brian 174, 176–77, 179; *see also* Grayson, 1st Lt. Andrew
Kilo Company 15, 18, 25, 34, 39, 57, 61, 80, 90, 91, 100, 105, 115, 118, 120, 138, 140, 148, 153, 173, 220
Kimber, Capt. James S. 48
King, Capt. Jeffrey 102, 185
Kline, Rep. John 46, 53

Langewiesche, William 101; *see also Vanity Fair*
Laughner, Staff Sgt. Justin 43, 61–62, 221; at ambush site 27–28; at Chessani Article 32 hearing 106; at Grayson Article 32 hearing 148, 150–51, 153; at Grayson trial 175, 179; at Wuterich trial 205
Law of Armed Combat (LOAC) 38, 42, 43, 76, 105, 112–13, 169
Law of War (LAW) 2, 91, 95–97, 104, 108–10
Legal Support Services Section (LSSS) 102, 123, 156, 166, 219

Lima (L) Company 18
Los Angeles Times 48, 54–55, 60, 61

Mabus, Navy Secretary Ray 214
Making the Corps 100; *see also* Ricks, Thomas
Maloney, Michael S. 120, 141
Mannle, Nayda 121, 132
maps: ambush site, 24; Anbar Province 6
Marine Corps Forces Central Command (MARCENT) 58–59, 72–73, 102, 146, 159, 169, 171, 180–84, 186–87, 192–94, 221
Mathes, 1st Lt. Adam 40, 79, 91, 93, 105
Mattis, Maj. Gen. James (later Lt. Gen. and Gen.) 4, 73, 99–100, 111, 113–14, 116–117, 119, 122–23, 127, 128, 152, 155, *159*, 167, 169, *191*, 194, 220–23; and Chessani UCI 168, 180–88; as commander CENTCOM 223; as commander I MEF/MARCENT 60, 73, 83; as commander Marine Corps Combat Development Command 59; as convening authority 63, 67, 95–98, 115, 129, 133–35, 137, 146, 149, 163, 190, 216–19; and Ewers 169–71; in Fallujah 8; and Rooney 102; and Wuterich UCI 193
McCann, Maj. Thomas 91, 92, 95–97; *see also* Stone, Capt. Randy
McChrystal, Gen. Stanley (Army) 223
McConnell, Capt. Lucas M. 13, 25, 27, 29–31, 35, 37–38, 40, 56–57, 62–65, 67, 77, 79–80, 83, 93, 103, 105, 115–16, 153, 185, 221; *see also*, McDermott, Kevin
McDermott, Kevin 56, 116
McGirk, Tim 38–43, 45, 87–88, 90–91, 93–95, 103, 110–11, 217
Meeks, Lt. Col. Jeffrey 157–63, 165–*166*
Meet the Press 51
Mendoza, Pfc. Humberto (later Lance Corporal) 21–23, 63, 67, 116, 129–34, 138, 141, 143–44, 146, 153, 214- 215, 219, 221
Meyers, Gary 56
Muise, Robert 102, 105, 106, 108, 167, 170–71, 182–85, 189, 192; *see also* Thomas More Law Center
Multi-National Corps–Iraq (MNC-I) 42, 81; *see also* Chiarelli, Lt. Gen. Peter
Multi-National Force–Iraq (MNF-I) 37, 42, 81, 84, 111; *see also* Casey, Lt. Gen. George W.
Multi-National Force–West (MNF-W) 37, 39, 43, 45–46, 57, 76–78, 81–83, 86, 117; *see also* Johnson. Maj. Gen. Stephen T.; Zilmer, Maj. Gen. Richard
Murtha, Rep. John 46, 48–53, 72, 100, 128, 137, 167, 174, *191*, 223; *see also* civil suits
"MurthaMustGo" 52

National Public Radio (NPR) 40, 54
Naval Criminal Investigative Service (NCIS) 2, 4, 42, 45, 48, 59 62, 74, 77, 79, 83, 108, 120–21, 125–26, 129–32, 132, 140, 168, 175–76, 178, 181, 185, 190, 206, 212, 220; begins investigation 60; difference from Bargewell in-

vestigation 76, 78, *84*; report 65–67; *see also* Army investigation AR 15-6
Navarre, Col. Stewart 62, 63
Navin, Capt. Kathryn 138
Navy-Marine Court of Criminal Appeals (NMCCA) 3, 158–61, 163–64, *166*, 185, 187–88, *191*, 194–99
Nazario, Robert L. 220
Nelson, Sgt. Jermaine 220
New York Times 54–55, 57, 61, 108; *see also* Cloud, David S.; Schmitt, Eric
No True Glory 118; *see also* West, Bing
North County Times 151, 177, 210, 211, 220; *see also* Walker, Mark

O'Brien, Soledad 50
I Marine Expeditionary Force (I MEF) 7–8, 10, 13, 48, 58–60, 93, 127, 168–69, 171, 181–84, 187, 219
I MEF/MARCENT 58–59, 72–73, 102, 146, 162, 169, 180, 193–94
Opel/white sedan 1, 16, 20–21, 25, 28, *36*, 37, 43, 56, 63, 65, 68–69, 80, 89, 131, 136, 138–40, 142, 146–47, 150, 175, 201, 203–6
O'Reilly, Bill 52
Osterhoudt, Maj. Thomas 38
outtakes 75, 156–63, 165–*66*, 191–92, 195, 198, 203, 221; *see also* CBS; Court of Appeals for the Armed Forces (CAAF); Meeks, Lt. Col. Jeffrey; Navy-Marine Court of Criminal Appeals (NMCCA); *60 Minutes*

Pace, Gen. Peter 46, 54
Palm Groves 16, 23, 25–28, 30–32, *36*–37, 56, 80, 107, 110, 113, 116, 173, 190
Parks, William Hays 104, 109, 113
Pelley, Scott 68–72, 74–75, 89, 137, 156–57, 204, 221
Petraeus, Gen. David 223
Platt, Mark 121
Pool, Capt. Jeffrey 33, 37, 116
Positive Identification (PID) 69, 75, 133–34, 138, 143
Prentice, Lance Cpl. James 120, 125
Public Broadcasting System 170
Puckett, Neal 56, 60–61, 67, 72, 75, *163*, 195, 200, 202, 206, 212, 214–16; on judicial proceedings 213; on prosecutors 214; *see also* Faraj, Haytham; Wuterich Sgt. Frank

Radio Station KPBS 212, 214
Ramadi (city) 7, 9, 13, 32
Regimental Combat Team–1 (RCT-1) in Fallujah 10, 101; *see also* Chessani, Lt. Col. Jeffrey
Regimental Combat Team–2 (RCT-2) 30, 32, 34–37, 56–57, 63, 67, 87–88, 92, 96–97, 103, 106, 111, 189; in Bargewell report 76, 79, 81–82; *see also* Davis, Col. Stephen
Reportable Incident Assessment Team (RIAT) 169

Ricks, Thomas 9, 46, 61, 100, 223; *see also Making the Corps*; *Washington Post*
Riggs, Lt. Col. G.W. 127, 145, 169–70, 181, 183, 186–87, 193, 221; *see also* Marine Corps Forces Central Command (MARCENT)
Robertson, Lori 40
Rodriguez, Lance Cpl. Rene 20, 23, 28
Rooney, Brian 102, 106, 108, 167, 171, 185, 189, 192; *see also* Thomas More Law Center
Rouse, Lt. Col. Elizabeth A. (Air Force) 121, 132
Rove, Karl 51
Rules of Engagement (ROE) 34, 56, 61, 66, 69, 75, 77, 83–84, 89, 127, 133–34, 139, 141, 143, 206, 213
Rumsfeld, Secretary of Defense Donald 46, 54, 62
Russert, Tim 51–52

Salem, Safah Yunis 66
Salinas, Cpl. Hector (later Sgt.) 21–23, 28–29, 63, 116, 129, 130, 142, 153, 196, 206, 221
Salmoni, Barak 121, 124
San Diego Union-Tribune 59
Santmyer, Capt. William A. 175
Sattler, Lt. Gen. John F. 48, 59–60, 73, 194, 219–20
Sax, Sgt. Maj. Edward 30–31, 107, 207
ScanEagle 26, 29, 31, *36*, 116
Schmidt, Rep. Jean 49
Schmitt, Eric 57; *see also* Cloud, David S.
2nd Marine Division 32–33, 37–39, 42–43, 56, 76, 81–82, 104, 109
Sharratt, Lance Cpl. Justin L. 17, 20, 28, 56, 63, 83, 92, 116, 118–29, 132–33, 133, 137, 141, 145, 149, 163, 205, 221–22; charges against *64*; suit against Murtha 128; *see also* Culp Jim; Meyers, Gary; Ware, Lt. Col. Paul J.
Shelburne, Lt. Col. Jon 102, 185
Shumate, Lance Cpl. Jerry E. 157
Site X-380 30, 110
60 Minutes 68, 71–74, 89, 100, 137, 140, 156, *166*, 190, 195, 198, 200, 207, 208; *see also* CBS; outtakes; Wuterich, Sgt. Frank
Snow, Tony 51
Sokoloski, Col. R. Gary 33, 37, 39, 87–88, 90, 94, 103–4, 117, 216; *see also* Haditha news release
solatia payments 36, 124
Stahlman, Col. Michael 148–49, 150–52; *see also* Grayson, 1st Lt. Andrew
Stone, Capt. Randy W. 38, 63, 65, 83, 87–89, 91–98, 102–6, 119, 129, 138, 149, 153, 221; charges against *64*; *see also* Gittins, Charles W.
story board 34, 37–39, 43–44, 91, 111
Sullivan, Lt. Col. Sean 102–6, 108, 149, 174, 180–83, 185–86, 200, 203, 206

Tatum, Lance Cpl. Stephen B. 17, 20–21, 28, 63–64, 67, 78, 83, 116, 118, 123, 132, *135*, 137-

Index

38, 140, 144, 149, 153, 155, 158, 163, 203, 206, 221, 222; charges against *64*; in House One 22, 66, 129, 133; in House Two 23, 129–31, 134–35, 141; *see also* Ware, Lt. Col. Paul J.; Zimmerman, Jack
Team Charlie 65, 155, 171–72, 180, 185, 187–88, 192, 194, 207, 209, 213, 214, 221; *see also* Legal Services Support Section
Terrazas, Lance Cpl. Miguel 17, 20–21, 26, 34, 69, 71, 89, 131, 204
Thabet, Taher 38–39, 42
3rd Battalion, 1st Marine Regiment 7, 15, 115; *see also* Battalion 3/1
3rd Battalion 5th Marines 48, 73, 194
3rd Battalion 25th Marines 18
Thomas More Law Center (TMLC) 102, 109, 189; *see also* Muise, Robert; Rooney, Brian
Thompson, Richard 102, 109; *see also* Thomas More Law Center
Time magazine 1, 2, 38–40, 45, 47–51, 53–54, 57, 67–68, 82, 87, 90–91, 103, 110–11, 116–17, 122, 137
Towers, 1st Lt. Mark 107

Uniform Code of Military Justice (UCMJ) 3, 64, 83–*84*, 96, 98–99, 113, 160–61, 164, 174, 177, 178, 201–2, 208, 223–24; U.S. Central Command (CENTCOM) 8, 58–59, *159*, 223
U.S. Central Command (CENTCOM) 8, 58–59, *159*, 223
U.S. Supreme Court 161, *166*; *see also* CBS; Wuterich, Sgt. Frank
Unlawful Command Influence (UCI) 171–172, 180, *191*, 197; and Chessani 168–69, 186, 187; differences between Chessani and Wuterich 193; and Mattis 169; and Wuterich 192, 194

Vanity Fair 101
Vokey, Lt. Col. Colby 139, 195–96, *197*–98; *see also* Court of Appeals for the Armed Forces; Faraj, Haytham; Jones, Lt. Col. David; Navy-Marine Court of Criminal Appeals; Wuterich, Sgt. Frank

Waldhauser, Lt. Gen. Thomas 202, 208
Walker, Mark 211–12, 220
Ware, Lt. Col. Paul J. 119, 122–23, 129, 137, 139–40, 149, 165, 221–22; on Sharratt 124–27; on Tatum 133–35; 137; on Wuterich 139, 141–46
Warner, Sen. John 54, 55
Washington Post 46, 54–56, 60–61, 65, 77
Watt, Col. Gregory (Army) 47, 56, 83–*84*, 150–51, 174–79, 221; report 43–44; *see also* Grayson, 1st Lt. Andrew A.
weapons: carried by Marines 16; found in House Four 29
Weemer, Ryan 220
Weinberger, Sec. Caspar W. 45
West, Bing 11, 118; *see also No True Glory*
Western Judicial District 123, 157
White, Josh 56, 65–67; *see also Washington Post*
Whitt, HN Brian 17, 20
Winter, Navy Sec. Donald C. 116, 117, 167
Woodward, Lt. Col. Kevin 178
Wuterich, Frank, Sgt. (later Staff Sgt.) 13, 15–17, 20, 19–23, 27–30, 34, *36*, 43, 52–53, 56–57, 60–63, 65–67, 69–75, 77–79, 83, 89, 94, 100, 116, 119, 120, 123–24, 128–29, 131–32, 136–46, 148–49, 153, 155, 157–62, *163*, 165, *166*, 172, 179, 190–208, 210–16, 218, 221–22; in ambush 19–21; amended charges 146; charges against *64*; discharge 2, 211; Frank Wuterich Day 212; in House Four 28–29, 119, 122, 136; in House One 22, 70, 132, 141, 143; in House Three 119; in House Two 23, 71, 138, 141, 144; and Opel/white sedan 20–21, 63, 68, 131, 136, 138, 140, 142–43, 145; plea agreement 213; suit against Murtha 52–53

Zahn, Paula 50
Zaid, Mark S. 52, 53
Zielbauer, Paul von 108
Zilmer, Maj. Gen. Richard 2, 42–43, 45, 47, 78, 116–17
Zimmerman, Jack 67, 130–32

www.ingramcontent.com/pod-product-compliance
Ingram Content Group UK Ltd.
Pitfield, Milton Keynes, MK11 3LW, UK
UKHW041931140426
5217IPUK00014B/425